An Introduction to Regional Economics

Edgar M. Hoover
UNIVERSITY OF PITTSBURGH

Alfred A. Knopf NEW YORK

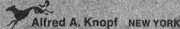

THIS IS A
BORZOI BOOK
PUBLISHED BY
ALFRED A. KNOPF, INC.

Copyright © 1971 by Alfred A. Knopf, Inc.
All rights reserved under International and Pan-American
Copyright Conventions. Published in the United States
by Alfred A. Knopf, Inc., New York, and simultaneously in
Canada by Random House of Canada Limited, Toronto.
Distributed by Random House, Inc., New York.

ISBN: 0-394-31040-3

Library of Congress Catalog Card Number: 77-136017

Manufactured in the United States. Composed by
Cherry Hill Composition, Pennsauken, N.J. Printed and
bound by H. Wolff Book Mfg. Co., Inc., New York, N.Y.

First Edition

987654321

Photographs on pp. 2, 8, 32, 58, 92, 118, and 250 courtesy of
Ewing Galloway; pp. 160 and 344 by Nobu Arakawa; p. 198
from Black Star (Werner Wolff); p. 296 from Rapho
Guillumette Pictures (Laurence Lowry); p. 322 from
Black Star (Lee Lockwood).

Cover and title page photograph by George W. Gardner.
Cover design by Hermann Strohbach.

∠

Preface

This book represents my third attempt, over a period of more than 30 years, to think through the application of economics to those social problems in which spatial relations play an important role.[1] The field of study now known as regional economics has developed extraordinarily fast in that interval, in terms of practical applications and general interest as well as in the advancement of theoretical insight. Specialists have probed deep into the intricacies of industrial location techniques, regional growth and development theory and policy, abstract models of spatial equilibrium and change, urbanization patterns, and problems of urban form, growth, and conflict. The flow of published output has long since outrun any one person's digestive capacity. Thus, it becomes more difficult yet perhaps also more necessary (lest we lose sight of the forest for the trees), that someone try from time to time to bring together in one integrated view the whole field of regional economics. Any such broad picture must inevitably sacrifice detail on particular topics.

I expect that this book will have its widest use as a college text for the student's first course in regional economics, at either the upper class undergraduate or the graduate level, and running for either one or two terms. It does not presuppose any previous exposure to regional economics as such, nor anything beyond a minimal background in basic economics, nor any mathematical expertise; it is, I think, comprehensible to the "intelligent layman." The wide range of topics covered is intended to serve the needs of the student who will not be going on to more advanced and specialized courses in the regional economics field; the minority who do use it as a stepping stone to such later work will find here some useful preview of questions (especially in regional growth analysis and policy and in urban economics) to which they will be addressing themselves more intensively later.

To keep this book from being either too long and expensive or too quickly dated, I have inserted very

---

[1] Results of the previous efforts are in *Location Theory and the Shoe and Leather Industries* (Cambridge, Mass.: Harvard University Press, 1937; reprinted 1968 by Johnson Reprint Corporation, New York and London) and *The Location of Economic Activity* (New York: McGraw-Hill, 1948).

v

little current descriptive material. Such facts as are provided are meant to illustrate relatively durable principles. The proper aim of education is not to inform but to stimulate—by posing relevant and provocative questions and by suggesting ways of thinking (that is, theories, hypotheses, and analytical tools) to enable the reader to tackle such questions. When the book is used as a text, the instructor will be able to mobilize concrete informational material that is more up to date and better suited to his purpose than anything that might have been included here.

I have made no attempt to include a comprehensive bibliography of the literature. At the end of each chapter, however, the reader will find some suggestions, arranged chronologically, for further enlightenment and stimulus on the subject-matter of that chapter. Certain far-ranging and fundamental works such as Harry W. Richardson's *Regional Economics* could not be done justice in a single reference and, accordingly, recur in several of the listings.

Those already acquainted with regional economics may notice two points on which there is more emphasis in this book than in other similar works.

One of these is the *generality* of the principles of the location of activities. Some location theories have been framed in terms of manufacturing industries alone, and others more broadly in terms of business activities in a competitive economy. I have tried to extend the coverage to such nonbusiness activities as nonprofit and public institutions and their services, as well as residence; and use the term "activity" rather than "industry" to signal these wide terms of reference. Similarly, I have adopted the broadest possible extension of the idea of transportation to embrace conveyance not only of goods but also of such intangibles as services, energy, and information. The broad term "transfer" signals this extension.

Secondly, I have tried to maintain some of the balance and symmetry between supply and demand that is so dear to the economist's heart. Various formulations of location theory, spatial competition, and regional economic growth have been subject to criticism on the grounds that they are too exclusively concerned with demand or with cost. I have tried consistently to see and show both sides of the picture, as will be evident particularly in some of the early location theory chapters and in the treatment of regional growth processes in Chapter 8.

This book gives some attention to the "microlocational" problem of location choice by the individual business firm or other unit, but is not designed to compete with the many excellent manuals providing advice on how to go about finding a good location. It is, I hope, somewhat more directly relevant to the concerns of planners and public policy makers. But it is really most explicitly addressed to that ultimate policy maker, the informed and responsible citizen.

I am indebted to many persons for ideas, assistance, and permission to quote; and have tried to acknowledge this at appropriate places. Apology is here made to those whom I may have inadvertently overlooked. Professors John Cumberland, William Miernyk, J. David Reed, and William Alonso supplied eminently helpful critiques of major parts of the manuscript. My colleagues David Bramhall, David Houston, Jack Ochs, and Roger Riefler, and many of my students also contributed reactions and valuable suggestions. Mrs. Regina B. Armstrong of the Regional Plan Association, Inc., New York, went to some pains to uncover pertinent unpublished data and references for me. The University of Pittsburgh has been generous in lightening my teaching schedule to provide me more time for writing.

Special appreciation goes to my wife for her unflagging patience and encouragement, and to my secretary Mrs. Esther Zavos for care and intelligence exercised far beyond the call of duty in the typing and editing of successive drafts of the manuscript.

Edgar M. Hoover

University of Pittsburgh
February, 1970

Contents

An Introduction to Regional Economics

WHAT IS REGIONAL ECONOMICS?

Regional or "spatial" economics can be summed up in the question *"What is where, and why—and so what?"* The first *what* refers to every type of economic activity: not only production establishments in the narrow sense of factories, farms, and mines but also other kinds of businesses, households, and public and private institutions. *Where* refers to location in relation to other economic activity; it involves questions of proximity, concentration, dispersion, and similarity or disparity of spatial patterns, and can be discussed either in broad terms, such as between regions, or microgeographically, in terms of zones, neighborhoods, and sites. The *why* and the *so what* refer to interpretations within the somewhat elastic limits of the economist's competence and daring.

Regional economics, one of the youngest branches of economics, is vigorous, relatively unregimented as yet, brash, and sometimes callow. Its late start exemplifies the regrettable tendency of formal professional disciplines to lose contact with one another and to neglect some important problem areas that require a mixture of approaches. Until fairly recently, traditional economists ignored the *where* question altogether, finding plenty of problems to occupy them without giving any spatial dimensions to their analysis. Traditional geographers, though directly concerned with *what is where,* lacked any real technique of explanation in terms of human behavior and institutions to supply the *why* and resorted to mere description and mapping. Traditional city planners, similarly deprived, remained preoccupied with the physical and esthetic aspects of idealized urban layouts.

This unfortunate situation has been corrected to a remarkable extent within the last few decades. Individuals who call themselves by various professional labels—economists, geographers, ecologists, city and regional planners, regional scientists, urbanists, even "ekisticians"—have joined to develop analytical tools and skills, and to apply them to some of the most pressing problems of the time.

The unflagging pioneer work and the intellectual and organizational leadership of Walter Isard since the 1940s played a key role in enlisting support from

1
Introduction

3

the various disciplines to create this new focus. His domain of "regional science" is extremely broad; this book will follow a less comprehensive approach, using the special interests and capabilities of the economist as the point of departure.

THE PLAN OF THIS BOOK

What, then, are the actual problems in which an understanding of regional economics can be helpful? They arise, as we shall see, on several different levels. Some are primarily "microeconomic," involving the spatial preferences, decisions, and experiences of such units as households or business firms. Others involve the behavior of large groups of people, whole industries, or such areas as cities or regions. To give some idea of the range of questions involved and also the approach that this book takes in developing a conceptual framework to handle them, I shall follow here a sequence corresponding to the successive later chapters.

The business firm is, of course, most directly interested in what regional economics may have to say about choosing a profitable location in relation to given markets, sources of materials, labor, services, and other relevant location factors. A nonbusiness unit such as a household, institution, or public facility faces an analogous problem of location choice, though the specific location factors to be considered may be rather different and less subject to evaluation in terms of price and profit. Our survey of regional economics begins in Chapter 2 by taking a "microlocational" viewpoint. That is, all locations, conditions, and activities other than the individual unit in question will be taken as given, and the individual unit's problem is to decide what location it prefers.

The importance of transport and communication services in determining locations will become evident in Chapter 2. Indeed, one of the cornerstones of regional economics is the fact that goods, services, information, and people are not freely mobile. The relation of distance to the cost of spatial transfer depends upon such factors as route layouts, scale economies in terminal and carriage operations, the length of the journey, the characteristics of the goods and services transferred, and the technical capabilities of the available transport and communication media. Chapter 3 will identify and explain such relations and will explore their effects upon the advantages of different locations.

In Chapter 4, location is considered in terms of the location *patterns* of whole *industries* (or analogous groupings of residential or other nonbusiness units). If an individual firm or other unit has any but the most myopic outlook, it will want to know something about shifts in such patterns. A firm producing oil drilling or refinery equipment should be interested in locational shifts in the oil industry; a business firm enjoying favorable access to a market wants to know whether it is likely that more competition will be coming its way; a banker or real estate speculator wants to know the kind of areas and sites to which industry will be attracted. Chapter 4 lays particular stress on the question of why certain kinds of businesses and other activities adopt highly decentralized patterns while others show a high degree of spatial concentration.

Chapter 5 introduces explicit recognition of the fact that activities require space. Space (or distance, which is simply space in one dimension) plays an interestingly dual role in the location of activities. On the one hand, distance represents cost and inconvenience when there is a need for access (for instance, in commuting to work or delivering a product to a market), and transport and communication represent more or less costly ways of surmounting the handicaps to human interaction imposed by space. But at the same time, every human activity requires space for itself. In intensively developed areas, sheer elbowroom as well as the amenities of privacy are scarce and valuable. In this context, space and distance appear as assets rather than as liabilities.

Chapter 5 treats competition for space as a factor helping to determine location patterns and individual choices. The focus here is still more "macro" than in Chapter 4; the location patterns of many industries or other activities are considered as constituents of the land use pattern of an area, like pieces in a jigsaw puzzle. Many of the real problems with which regional economics deals are in fact posed in terms of land use (how is this site or area best used?) rather than in terms of location per se (where is this firm, household, or industry best situated?). The insights developed in Chapter 5 are relevant, then, not only for individual locators but also for those owning land, operating transit or other utility services, or otherwise having a stake in what happens to a given piece of territory. The problems faced by city planners and community developers or redevelopers are involved here, and the basic land use analysis developed in Chapter 5 will provide groundwork for more specific attention to such problems in later chapters.

The kind of analysis introduced in Chapter 5 helps us to understand the spatial ordering of different types of land use around some special point of attraction—for example, zones of different kinds of agriculture around a market center or zones of different kinds of residential and other land use around the center of a city.

In Chapter 6, the focus is once more broadened in order to understand patterns of urbanization within a region: the spacing, sizes, and functions of cities, and particularly the relationship between size and function. Real world questions involving this so-called central-place analysis include, for example, trends in city-size distributions. Is the crossroads hamlet or the small town losing its functions and becoming obsolete, and if so, why? What size town or city is the best location for some specific kind of business or public facility? What services and facilities are available only in middle-sized and larger cities, or only in the largest metropolitan centers? In the planned development of an undeveloped region, what size distribution and location pattern of cities would be most appropriate? Any principles or insights that help to answer such questions are obviously useful to a wide range of businessmen, property owners, community planners and promoters, regional and transport planners, and politicians.

If the reader is undeterred by the theoretical abstractions of the first six chapters, his patience will be rewarded by encountering in the last six an increasing resemblance to the real world inhabited by real people. At the same time, he will find more attention paid to the usefulness and desirability of locational changes as distinct from mere rationalizations of observed behavior.

Chapter 7 deals specifically with people and their personal locational preferences, and is a necessary prelude to the consideration of regional and urban development and policy that follows. Migration is the central topic, since people most clearly express their locational likes and dislikes by moving. Some insight into the factors that determine who moves where, and when, is needed by anyone trying to foresee population changes (such as regional and community planners and developers, utility companies, and the like); and is even more important in connection with framing public policies aimed at relieving regional or local (for example, ghetto) poverty and unemployment.

Chapters 8 and 9, dealing with regional development and related policy issues, are concerned with the region as a whole plus a still higher level; namely, the national interest in the welfare and growth of the nation's constituent regions. Chapter 8 concentrates on the measurement, process, and explanation of regional growth. Viewing a region as a live organism, we develop a basic understanding of its anatomy and physiology. Chapter 9 proposes appropriate objectives for regional development (that is, defines regional economic "health"), analyzes the economic ills to which regions are subject (pathology), and ventures to assess the merits of various kinds of policy to help regions (therapy).

The last three chapters of the book treat the important special case of the urban "region" in a similar fashion. Chapter 10 dissects and explains the spatial structure of cities, making use of the framework of location principles developed in the first part of the book. Chapter 11 uncovers the reasons for and implications of changes in urban spatial structure. Chapter 12 discusses some major present-day urban problems and possible curative or palliative measures. The discussion centers around four areas of concern (downtown blight, ghettos, urban transport, and financing of urban public services) in which spatial economic relationships are particularly important and the relevance of our specialized approach is therefore strong.

SELECTED READINGS

August Lösch, *Die räumliche Ordnung der Wirtschaft* (Jena: Gustav Fischer, 1940; 2nd ed., 1944); W. H. Woglom (tr.), *The Economics of Location* (New Haven: Yale University Press, 1954).

Walter Isard, *Location and Space-Economy* (Cambridge, Mass.: The M.I.T. Press, 1956).

Walter Isard and others, *Methods of Regional Analysis* (New York: The Technology Press and Wiley, 1960).

John R. Meyer, "Regional Economics: A Survey," *American Economic Review,* 53, 1, Pt. I (March 1963), 19–54.

Walter Isard and Thomas A. Reiner, "Regional Science: Retrospect and Prospect," *Papers of the Regional Science Association,* 16 (1966), 1–16.

Edgar M. Hoover, "Spatial Economics: Partial Equilibrium Approach," in *Encyclopaedia of the Social Sciences* (New York: Macmillan, 1968).

Leon Moses, "Spatial Economics: General Equilibrium Approach," in *Encyclopaedia of the Social Sciences* (New York: Macmillan, 1968).

Hugh O. Nourse, *Regional Economics* (New York: McGraw-Hill, 1968).

Martin Beckmann, *Location Theory* (New York: Random House, 1968).

Horst Siebert, *Regional Economic Growth: Theory and Policy* (Scranton, Pa.: International Textbook Co., 1969).

Harry W. Richardson, *Regional Economics* (New York: Praeger, 1969).

LEVELS OF ANALYSIS AND LOCATION UNITS

Later in this book we shall come to grips with some major questions of locational and regional macro-economics; our concern will be with such large and complex entities as neighborhoods, occupational labor groups, cities, industries, and regions. We begin here, however, on a microeconomic level by examining the behavior of the individual components that make up those larger groups. These individual components will be referred to as "location units."

Just how microscopic a view we take is a matter of choice. Within the economic system, there are major production sectors, such as manufacturing; within the manufacturing sector are various industries. An industry includes many firms; a firm may operate many different plants, warehouses, and other establishments. Within a manufacturing establishment there may be several buildings located in some more or less rational relation to one another. Various departments may occupy locations within one building; within one department there is a location pattern of individual operations and pieces of equipment, such as punch presses, desks, or wastebaskets.

At each of the levels indicated, the spatial disposition of the units in question must be considered: industries, plants, buildings, departments, wastebaskets, or whatever. Although determinations of actual or desirable locations at different levels share some elements,[1] there are substantial differences in

2
Individual Location Decisions

---

[1] "A recurrent problem in industry is that of determining optimal locations for centers of economic activity. The problems of locating a machine or department in a factory, a warehouse to serve retailers or consumers, a supervisor's desk in an office, or an additional plant in a multi-plant firm are conceptually similar. Each facility is a center of activity into which inputs are gathered and from which outputs are sent to subsequent destinations. For each new facility one seeks, at least as a starting point if not the final location, the spot where the sum of the costs of transporting goods between existing source and destination points (such as the sources of raw materials, centers of market demand, other machines and departments, etc.) and the new location is a minimum." Roger C. Vergin and Jack D. Rogers, "An Algorithm and Computational Procedure for Locating Economic Facilities," *Management Science*, 13, 6 (February 1967), B-240. This article and the references appended give an up-to-date view of recently developed techniques for solving location problems, with special applicability to problems of layout at the intrafirm, intraplant, and even more micro levels.

the principles involved and the methods used. Thus, it is necessary to specify the level to which we are referring.

We shall start with a microscopic but not ultramicroscopic view, ignoring for the most part (despite their enticements in the way of immediacy, practicality, and amenability to some highly sophisticated new lines of spatial analysis) such issues as the disposition of departments or equipment within a business establishment or ski lifts on a mountainside or electric outlets in a house. Our smallest location units will be defined at the level of the individual dwelling unit, the farm, the factory, the store, or other business establishment, and so on. These units are of three broad types: residential, business, and public. Some location units can make independent choices and are their own "decision units"; others (such as branch offices or chainstore outlets) are located by external decision.

Many individual persons represent separate residential units by virtue of their status as self-supporting unmarried adults; but a considerably larger number do not. Roughly half the present population of the United States are married; another 30 percent or so are children under 14; and a substantial number of the remaining fifth are aged, invalid, or other dependent members of family households, or are locationally constrained as members of the armed forces, inmates of institutions, members of monastic orders, and so on. For these types of people, the residential location unit is a group of persons.

In the business world, the firm is the unit that makes locational *decisions* but the "establishment" (plant, store, bank branch, motel, theater, warehouse, and the like) is the unit that *is located*, and the great majority of such establishments are the only ones that their firms operate. In general, a business unit defined in this way has a specific site; but in some cases the actual operations of a business unit can cover a considerable and even fluctuating area. Thus, construction and service businesses have fixed headquarters but their workers range sometimes far afield in the course of their duties; and the "location" of a transportation company is a network of routes rather than a point.

Nonprofit, institutional, social, and public service units likewise have to be located. Though the *decision* may be made by a person or office in charge of units in many locations, the relevant locational unit for our purposes is the smallest one that can be considered by itself: for example, a church, a branch post office, a college campus, a police station, a municipal bus garage, or a fraternity house.

OBJECTIVES AND PROCEDURES
FOR LOCATION CHOICE

Let us now take a location unit—a single-establishment business firm, as a starting point—and inquire into its location preferences. First, what constitutes a "good" location? Subject to some important qualifications to be noted later, we can define "profits," in the sense of the rate of return on the owners' investment of their capital and effort, as the measure of desirability of alternative sites. We must recognize, however, that this does not mean just next week's profits but the expected return over a considerable future period, since a location choice represents a commitment to a site with costs and risks involved in every change of location. Thus, the prospective growth and dependability of returns are always relevant aspects of the evaluation.

Since it costs something to move or even to consider moving, business locations display a good deal of inertia—even if some other location promises a higher return, the apparent advantage may disappear as soon as the moving costs are considered. Actual decisions to adopt a new location, then, are likely to occur mainly at certain junctures in the life of the firm. One such juncture is, of course, birth—when the *initial* location must be determined. But at some later time, the growth of business may call for a major expansion of capacity, a new process or line of output may be introduced, or there may be a major shift in the location of customers or suppliers, or a major change in transport rates. The important point is that a change of location is rarely just that—it is normally associated with a change in scale of operations, production processes, composition of output, markets, or sources of supply, transport requirements, or perhaps a combination of many such changes.

It is quite clear that making even a reasonably adequate evaluation of the relative advantages of all possible alternative locations is a task beyond the resources of most small and medium-sized business firms. Such evaluation is undertaken, as a rule, only under severe pressure of circumstances (a strong presumption that something is wrong with the present location), and various short cuts and external aids are used. Perhaps the closest approach to a continuous scientific appraisal of site advantages is to be found in some of the large retail chains. Profit margins are thin and competition intense; the financial and research resources of the firm are very large relative to the size of the individual store, and the stores themselves are rather standardized, built on leased land, and easy to move. All these conditions favor a continuing close scrutiny of new site opportunities and the application of sophisticated techniques to evaluate locations.

Still more elaborate analysis is used as a basis for new location or relocation decisions by large corporations operating giant establishments, such as steel mills. These decisions, however, are few and far between, and involve in general a whole series of reallocations and adjustments of activities at other facilities of the same firm.

What has been said about the choice of location for a business establishment will also apply in essence to many kinds of public facilities. Thus, a municipal bus system will (or should) locate its bus garages on very much the same basis as would a private bus system. The objective in each case is efficiency, which implies the minimizing of costs of building and maintaining the garage, storing and servicing the buses, and getting them to and from their routes. In both cases the final product, transportation, is sold to individual users.

The correspondence is less close where the product is not marketed with an eye to profit, but is provided as a "public good" and paid for out of taxes or voluntary contributions, the objective being an improvement in social welfare. Thus, an evaluation of the desirability of alternative locations for a new police station or public health clinic would have to include a reckoning of costs, but on the returns side there will be some more elusive estimate of quality and adequacy of the service rendered to the community. The most readily available measuring rod might well be political rather than economic: Which location will find favor with the largest number of voters at the next election? This is in fact an essential feature of a democratic system of society.

Still more unlike the business firm example is that of the location of, say, the Second Presbyterian Church of Woodmere Hills or the Abner G. Murton Memorial Home for the Indigent. In neither case is success likely to be measured primarily in terms of numbers of people served or cost per person. Perhaps the judgment rests primarily on whether the facility is so located as to concentrate its beneficent effect on the particular neighborhood or group most needing or desiring it.

Finally, suppose we are considering the residence location of James H. Johnston and his family. Here again, cost is an important element in the relative desirability of locations. This cost will include acquiring or renting the house and lot, plus maintenance and utilities expenses, plus taxes, plus costs of access to work, shopping, school, social, and other trip destinations of members of the family. The returns may be partly measurable in money terms, if different sites imply different sets of job opportunities; but in any event there will be a large element of "amenity" reflecting the Johnstons' evaluation of houses, lots, and neighborhoods; and this factor will be difficult to measure in any way.

The Johnstons, like the business establishment, the municipal bus system, the church, and the settlement house, are likely to be ripe for a change in location only at certain junctures. There is ample and interesting evidence in Census reports that most moves are associated with entry into the labor force, marriage, arrival of first child, entry of first child into school, last child leaving the household, widowhood, and retirement—though for specific families or individuals a move can also be triggered by a raise in salary, a new job opportunity, or an urban redevelopment project or other sudden change in the characteristics of a neighborhood.

For all types of location units, locational choice normally represents a substantial long-range commitment, since there are costs and inconveniences associated with any shift. This commitment has to be made in the face of uncertainty about the actual advantages involved in a location, and especially about possible future changes in relative advantage. The home buyer cannot foresee with any certainty how the character of his chosen neighborhood (in terms of such factors as access, income level, racial mix, prestige, tax rates, or public services) will change—though he can be sure it will change. The business firm cannot be sure about how a location may be affected in the future by such things as shifting markets or sources of supply, transportation costs and services, congestion, changes in taxes and public services, or the location of competitors.

Such uncertainties, along with the monetary and psychic costs of relocation, introduce a strong element of inertia. They also enhance the preferences for relatively "safe" locations such as "established" residential neighborhoods or business centers. For business firms, the conservative tendency is reinforced by the fact that in a large corporate organization, decisions are made by managers whose earnings and promotion do not directly depend upon the rate of profit made by the corporation so much as upon maintenance of a "satisfactory" and stable earnings level and growth in output and sales. It is increasingly recognized that "profit maximization" may be an oversimplified conception of the motivating force behind business decisions, including those involving location.

The effect is in the direction of somewhat greater spatial concentration of activities and greater homogeneity within areas, in addition to more sluggish change than would be expected in the absence of costs and uncertainties of locational choice.[2]

LOCATION FACTORS

Despite the great variety of types of location units, they are all sensitive in some degree to certain fundamental "location factors." That is to say, we can categorize (for *any* type of unit) the advantages of locations into a standard set of a few elements.

Local Inputs and Outputs

One such element of relative advantage is the supply (availability, price, and quality) of "local" or "nontransferable"[3] inputs. Local inputs are materials, supplies, or services that are present *at* a location and could not

---

[2] See Harry W. Richardson, *Regional Economics* (New York: Praeger, 1969), pp. 90–100, on "alternatives to profit maximization as a locational objective."
[3] For convenience, we shall be using the very broad term "transfer" to cover both the transportation of goods and the transmission of such intangibles as energy, information, ideas, sound, light, or color. Modes of transfer service and some characteristics of the cost and price of such service are discussed in Chapter 3.

feasibly be brought in from elsewhere. The use of land is such an input, regardless of whether the land is needed just as standing room or whether it also contains minerals or other soil constituents actually used in the process, as in the "extractive" activities of agriculture or mining. Climate and quality of the local water and air fall into the same category, as do topography and physical soil structure insofar as they affect construction costs, amenity, and convenience. Locally provided public services such as police and fire protection are also local inputs. Labor is another, usually accounting for a major portion of total input costs. Finally, there is a complex of local amenity features, such as the esthetic or cultural level of the neighborhood or community, that plays an especially important role in residential location preferences. The common feature of all these local input factors is that what any given location offers depends upon conditions *at that location alone* and does not involve transfer from or to any other location.

In addition to requiring some local inputs, the unit choosing a location may be producing some outputs that by their nature have to be disposed of locally. These are called nontransferable outputs. Thus, the labor supply of a household is ordinarily used either at home or in the local labor market area, delimited by the feasible commuting range. Community or neighborhood service establishments (barber shops, churches, movie theaters, parking lots, and the like) depend almost exclusively on the immediately proximate market; and in varying degree, so do newspapers, retail stores, and schools.

One type of locally disposed output generated by almost every economic activity is waste. At present, only dangerously radioactive waste products are commonly transported any great distance for disposal; though the disposal problem is increasing so rapidly in many areas that we may see a good deal more long-distance transportation of refuse within our lifetimes. Other wastes are just dumped into the air or water or on the ground, with or without incineration or other conversion. In economic terms, a waste output is best regarded as a locally disposed product with *negative value.* The negative value is particularly large in areas where considerations of land scarcity, air and water pollution, and amenity make disposal costs high; this gives such locations an element of disadvantage for any waste-generating kind of unit.

It is not always possible to distinguish unequivocally between a local input and a local output factor. For example, along the Mahoning River in northeastern Ohio, the use of water by industries long ago so heated the river that it could no longer furnish a good year-round supply of water for the cooling required by steam electric-generating stations and iron and steel works. In this instance, excess heat is the waste product involved. The thermal pollution handicap to heavy-industry development could be assessed either as a relatively poor supply of a needed local input (cold water), or as a high cost for disposing of a local output (excess heat). This is just one example of numerous cases in which we can describe a single situation in alternative ways.

An often-neglected responsibility of government is to see that the full costs of environmental pollution are imposed upon the polluting activity. As President Richard Nixon put it in his State of the Union Message of January 22, 1970, ". . . to the extent possible, the price of goods should be made to include the costs of producing and disposing of them without damage to the environment."

Transferable Inputs and Outputs

A quite different group of location factors can be described in terms of the supply of transferable inputs—such as fuels, materials, services, or information—which can be moved to a given location from wherever they are produced. Here the advantage of a location depends essentially on its access to certain other locations, and is likely to vary at least roughly with distance from the sources of supply. Some kinds of activities (for example, automobile assembly plants) use an enormous variety of transferred inputs from different sources.

Analogously, where transferable outputs are produced, there is the location factor of access to places where such outputs are in demand. The seller can sell more easily or at a better net realized price when located closer to markets.

Classification of Location Factors

To sum up, the relative desirability of a location depends upon four types of location factors:

1. *Local input:* the supply of nontransferable inputs at the location in question
2. *Local demand:* the demand for nontransferable outputs at the location in question
3. *Transferred input:* the supply of transferable inputs brought from outside sources to the location in question, reflecting in part the transfer cost from those sources
4. *Outside demand:* the net receipts obtainable from sales of transferable outputs to outside markets, reflecting in part the transfer costs to those markets

It should be kept in mind that, throughout this chapter, "demand for output" means the demand for the output of the specific individual plant, factory, household, or other unit under consideration, and not the aggregate demand for all output of that kind. The demand for an individual unit's product at any given market is affected, of course, by the degree of competition; and other things being equal, each unit will generally prefer to locate away from competitors. The same holds true for supply of an input.

This and other interactions among competing units and the resulting patterns of location for types of activities are, however, the concern of Chapter 4.

MEASURING THE RELATIVE IMPORTANCE OF LOCATION FACTORS

The classification of location factors just suggested is based on the characteristics of *locations*. But in order to rate the relative merits of alternative locations for a specific kind of business establishment, household, or public facility, we need to know something about the characteristics of that kind of activity. Just how much weight should a pool hall or shoe factory or shipyard or city hall assign to the various relevant location factors of input supply and output demand?

There have been countless efforts to answer this question with respect to more or less specific classes of activities. Those concerned with location choice want to know the answer in order to pick a superior location. Those interested in community promotion seek the answer in order to make their community appear more desirable to industries, government administrators, and prospective residents.

Perhaps the commonest method of measurement is the most direct method: ask the people who are making the locational decision. In questionnaire surveys addressed to businessmen in connection with "industry studies," firms have been given a list of location factors, including such items as labor cost, taxes, water supply, access to markets, and power cost, and have been asked to rate them in relative importance, either by adjectives ("extremely important," "not very important," and so forth) or on some kind of simple point system.

This primitive approach, however, is unlikely to provide any insights that were not already available, and may sometimes be positively misleading. In the first place, it provides no real basis for a quantitative evaluation of advantages and disadvantages. If, for example, "taxes" are given an average importance rating of 4 by the respondents, and "labor costs" an average rating of 2, we still do not know whether a tax differential of 3 mills per dollar of assessed property valuation would offset a wage differential of 10¢ per man-hour. The respondent probably could have told us after a few minutes of figuring, but the question was not put to him in that way. A further shortcoming of the subjective-rating method is that the respondent is implicitly encouraged to overrate the importance of any location factors that may arouse his emotions or political slant, or if he feels that his response might have some favorable propaganda impact. It has been suggested, for example, that employers have often rated the tax factor more strongly in subjective-response surveys than would be supported by their actual locational choices.

A more quantitative approach is often applied to the estimation of the strength of various location factors involving transferred inputs and outputs. For example, one might seek to determine whether a blast furnace is more strongly attracted toward coal mines or toward iron ore mines by comparing the total amounts spent on coal and on iron ore by a representative blast furnace in the course of a year, and such a figure is easily obtained. Unfortunately, this method could not be relied on to give a useful answer where the amounts are of similar orders of magnitude. We might use it to predict that a blast furnace would be more strongly attracted to either coal mines or iron ore mines than it would be to, say, the sources of supply of the lubricating oil for its machinery; but it may be assumed that we know that much without any special investigation.

A little closer to the mark, perhaps, would be a comparison between the annual freight bills for bringing coal to blast furnaces[4] and for bringing iron ore to those furnaces. But this comparison is obviously influenced by the different average distances involved for the two materials as well as by the relative quantities transported, so again it tells us little.

We might instead simply compare tonnages and say that if it takes coke from 2 tons of coal to reduce 1 ton of iron ore, the choice of location for a blast furnace should weight nearness to coal mines twice as heavily as nearness to iron ore mines. Here we are getting closer to a really informative assessment (for these two location factors alone), although our answer would be biased if one of the two inputs travels at a higher transport cost per ton mile than the other (a consideration to be discussed in the next chapter).

It would appear that in order to assess the relative importance of various location factors for a specific kind of activity we need to know the relative *quantities of its various inputs and outputs.* If, for example, we want to know whether labor cost is a more potent location factor than the cost of electric power, we first need to know how many kilowatt-hours are required per man-hour. If this ratio is, say, 20, and if wages are 10¢ an hour higher in Greenville than in Brownsville, it would be worthwhile paying up to ½¢ more per kilowatt-hour for power in Brownsville (assuming of course that these two locations are equal with respect to all other factors and to labor quality as well).

This kind of answer is what the locator of a plant would need; but we should note that it is not necessarily indicative of the degree to which we should expect to find this kind of activity attracted to cheap power as against cheap labor locations. Perhaps differentials of ½¢ per kilowatt-hour or more are frequently encountered among alternative locations for this

---

[4] Blast furnaces use coke rather than coal, but as a rule the coke is made in ovens adjacent to the furnaces. Thus, for purposes of location analysis a set of coke ovens and the blast furnaces they serve may be considered as a single unit.

industry, whereas wage differentials of as much as 10¢ an hour are rather rare for the kind of labor it uses. In such a case, the power cost differentials would show up more prominently as decisive locational determinants than would labor wage differentials. Thus, we conclude that, for some purposes at least, we need to know something about the degree of *spatial variability of the input or output prices* corresponding to the location factors being weighed against one another.

When we consider a location factor such as taxes, we encounter a further complication: There is no appropriate way to measure the quantity of public services that a business establishment or household is buying with its taxes or to establish a "unit price" for these services. The only way in which we can get a measure of locational sensitivity to tax rates is to refer to the actual range of rates at some set of alternative locations and translate these into estimates of what the tax bill per year or per unit of output would amount to at each location. This procedure has been followed in a number of actual industry studies, such as the one carried out by Alan K. Campbell for the New York Metropolitan Region Study.[5] A major, relevant problem is how, if at all, to measure and allow for any differences in the *quality* of public services; this is related to tax burdens, although not in the close positive correspondence that one might be tempted to assume.

Insight into still another problem of assessing the relative strength of location factors comes from consideration of the implications of a differential in labor productivity. If wages are 10 percent higher in Harkinsville than in Parkston, but the workers in Harkinsville work 10 percent faster, the labor cost per unit of output will be the same in both places, and one might infer that neither place will have a net cost advantage over the other. In fact, however, the speedier Harkinsville workers will need roughly 10 percent less equipment, space, and the like than their slower counterparts in Parkston to turn out any given volume of output; so there will be quite a sizable saving in overhead costs at Harkinsville. This advantage, though resulting from a quality difference in production workers, will appear in cost accounts under the headings of investment amortization costs, plant heating and servicing, and perhaps also payroll of administrative personnel and other nonproduction workers.

A somewhat different kind of identification problem arises when there are substantial economies or diseconomies of scale. Suppose we are trying to compare two locations for the Ajax Foundry, with respect to supply of the scrap metal it uses as a principal input. The going price of scrap metal is lower in Burton City than in Evansville; but only relatively small

---

[5] E. M. Hoover and Raymond Vernon, *Anatomy of a Metropolis* (Cambridge, Mass.: Harvard University Press, 1959), pp. 55–60 and Appendix F, pp. 277–287. Campbell computed the state and local tax bills for a sample of 25 selected firms placed hypothetically at 64 alternative locations in the New York Metropolitan Region.

amounts are available at the lower price. If Ajax were to operate on a large scale in Burton City it would have to bid higher to attract scrap from a wider supply area, whereas in Evansville scrap is generated in much larger volume and supply would be very elastic: Ajax's entry as a buyer would not drive the price up appreciably. In this case, Ajax must decide whether the economies of larger volume would be sufficient to make Evansville the better location or so small that it would be better to operate on a reduced scale in Burton City. Similarly, some locations will offer a more elastic demand for the output than others, and here again the choice of location will depend in part on economies of scale.

The foregoing discussion has brought to light some of the less obvious complexities of the problem of measuring the relative importance of the various factors affecting the choice of location for a specific business establishment or other unit. It should now be clear that definite quantitative "weights" can be assigned to the various factors only in certain cases (to be discussed later in this chapter) involving transfer cost; and that the relative influence of the various factors upon location depends both on the amounts and kinds of inputs and outputs and on the geographical patterns of variation of the respective input supplies and output demands.

SPATIAL PATTERNS OF DIFFERENTIAL ADVANTAGE IN SPECIFIC LOCATION FACTORS

If we view the earth's surface from the vantage point of the moon, it looks completely smooth—after all, the highest mountain peaks rise above sea level by only about $\frac{1}{13}$ of 1 percent of the planet's radius, and the average orange is rougher than that. A closer view makes many parts of the earth's surface look very rough indeed. Again, if we look at a table top, it appears smooth, but a magnifying glass or a microscope will disclose mountainous irregularities.

The same principle applies to spatial differentials in a location factor: The interregional (macrogeographic) pattern is quite different from the local (microgeographic) pattern. For example, in considering the location factor of land cost, we should not expect land cost to be relevant in deciding whether to locate in Ohio or in Minnesota; but if the choice is narrowed down to alternative sites within the Cleveland metropolitan area, land cost will indeed be important, and large differences may appear even between one city block and the next.

Labor supply and climate, in contrast, are examples of location factors where there is little microgeographic variation (say, within a single county or metropolitan area), but wide differences prevail on a macrogeographic scale involving different regions.

Locational alternatives and choices are generally posed in terms of some specific level of spatial disaggregation. The choice is among sites in a neighborhood, among neighborhoods in an urban area, among urban areas, among regions, or among countries. No useful statements about location factors, preferences, or patterns can be made until we first specify the level of comparison or the "grain" of pattern we are concerned with.

This principle was in fact implicit in our earlier distinction between local and transferable inputs and ouptuts. After all, the only really non-transferable inputs are natural resources or land, including topography and climate. In a very fine-grained comparison of locational advantages (say, the selection of a site for a residence or a retail store within a neighborhood), we must recognize that all other inputs and all outputs are really transferred, though perhaps only for short distances. Water, power, trash, and sewage all require transfer to or from the specific site. Selling one's labor or acquiring schooling requires travel to work place or school; selling goods at a retail store requires travel by the customers.

Accordingly, our distinction between local and transferable inputs is a flexible one: It will vary according to how microgeographic or macrogeographic a view of location we are taking for the situation in hand. Thus, if we are concerned with choices of location among cities, "local" means not transferable between cities. Some inputs or outputs properly regarded as local in such a context are properly regarded as transferable between sites or neighborhoods *within* a city.

What, then, are the possible kinds of spatial differential patterns for a location factor as among various locations at any prescribed level of geographical detail?

The simplest pattern, of course, is uniformity: All the locations being compared rate equally with respect to the location factor in question. This is in fact a very common case. For example, utility services are provided at uniform rates over service areas far larger than neighborhoods, often encompassing whole cities or counties. Wage rates in an organized industry or occupation are generally uniform throughout the district of a particular union local, and in industries using national labor bargaining they may even be uniform all over the country. Tax rates are in general uniform over the whole jurisdiction of the governmental unity levying the tax (for example, city property taxes throughout a city, state taxes throughout a state, and national taxes nationwide). Many commodities are sold at a uniform delivered price over large areas or even over the whole country. Climate may be, for all practical purposes, the same over considerable areas.

The special term "ubiquity" is applied to inputs which are *available at the same price at all locations under consideration.* Air is a ubiquity, if we are indifferent about its quality. Federal tax stamps for tobacco or alcohol are a ubiquity over the entire country. If an input is ubiquitous, then its supply obviously cannot be a location factor—being equally available everywhere, it has no influence on location preferences.

The counterpart of a ubiquity on the output demand side is, of course, an output for which there is the same demand at all locations under consideration. There does not seem to be any special technical term for this, and it is in fact a much rarer case than that of the input ubiquity. We can envisage some type of business that distributes its product by letter mail, but with speedy delivery not being an important consideration. In such a case, proximity to the customers is inconsequential; output demand is in effect ubiquitous. The reason, in this special case, is that the postal service makes no extra charge for additional miles of transportation of letters.

A different pattern of advantage for a location factor can be illustrated by market access for a wheat grower. The demand for his wheat is perfectly elastic, and what he receives per bushel is the price set at a key market (such as Chicago) minus the handling and transportation charges. The price he receives, then, will vary geographically along a rather smooth gradient reflecting distance from Chicago. The locational effect of the output demand factor can be envisaged as a continuous economic pull in the direction of Chicago.

A third systematic pattern involves differentials of advantage according to size of city. This might apply to certain location factors involving the supply of or demand for inputs or outputs that are not transferable between cities. It would be surprising to find any kind of differential advantage that is precisely determined by size of place; but there are many location factors that in fact show roughly this kind of pattern. Some activities cater to local markets and cannot operate at a minimum efficient scale except in places of at least a certain minimum size. In selecting a location for such an activity, the first step in the selection process might well be to winnow down the alternatives to a limited set of sufficiently large places. Thus, one would not ordinarily expect to find patent lawyers, opera houses, investment bankers, or major league baseball teams in towns or small cities.

Finally, there are location factors for which the spatial pattern of advantage is not apparently systematic at all—that is, it cannot be described or predicted in any reasonably simple terms, although it is not necessarily accidental or random. Tax rates, local water supply, labor supply, and quality of public services seem to fall into this category. Some general statements can be made to explain the broad outlines of the pattern (such a statement is attempted for labor costs in Chapter 7); but in making comparisons for actual selection of locations there is no way of avoiding the necessity of collecting information about every individual location that we wish to consider.

Among the four kinds of patterns of differential advantage that location factors may assume, three merit further discussion: those determined by transfer costs, those determined by size of city or local market, and those involving labor cost. We turn here to the transfer cost case, reserving the other two for consideration in later chapters.

TRANSFER ORIENTATION

Until fairly recently, location theory laid an exaggerated emphasis on the role of transportation costs, for a number of reasons. Interest was particularly focused on interregional location of manufacturing industries, for which transportation costs are in fact relatively more important and obvious than for most other kinds of activities. Moreover, the effect of transfer costs on location is more amenable to quantitative analysis than the effects of other factors, so that the development of a systematic body of location theory naturally tended to use transfer factors as a starting point and core. A basic rationale for emphasis on transfer and related factors is given by Walter Isard:

> . . . only the transport factor and other transfer factors whose costs are functionally related to distance impart regularity to the spatial setting of activities.[6]

We can speak of a particular type of activity as "transfer oriented"[7] if its location preferences are dominated by differential advantages of sites with respect to supply of transferable inputs, demand for transferable outputs, or both; similarly we can call an activity "labor oriented" where the locational decisions are usually based on differentials in labor cost.

Let us look first at a simple model of transfer orientation. The unit in question is assumed not to be influenced by any location factors other than supply of transferable inputs and demand for transferable outputs (that is, all its other inputs and outputs are assumed ubiquitous). Costs of transfer are uniform per ton-mile, regardless of distance, direction, or the nature of the input or output transferred. Any specific kind of input is available from any of several sources, and any specific kind of output can be sold at any of several markets. Finally, it is assumed that the demand for each of the transferable outputs is perfectly elastic in each market and that the supply of each of the inputs is perfectly elastic at each source.

These assumptions constitute a drastic simplification of reality, and will be modified at later stages in order to approximate more closely the real world. For the present, they serve to highlight some of the basic principles of transfer orientation.

If the unit in question uses only one kind of transferable input (say, wood) and produces one kind of transferable output (say, baseball bats),

---

[6] *Location and Space-Economy* (Cambridge, Mass.: The M.I.T. Press, 1956), p. 140.

[7] "Orientation" is a word with an interesting origin. It seems that until a few centuries ago, maps were customarily presented with east at the top, rather than north as is now the convention. In reading a map, the first thing to do was to get it right side up; in other words, to place east (*oriens,* or rising sun) at the top. In location theory, then, orientation means specifying in which direction the activity is primarily attracted: toward cheap labor supplies, toward markets, toward sources of materials, and so on. Transferred-output (market) orientation and transferred-input (material) orientation are handily lumped together under the heading "transfer orientation."

Fig. 2-1. A Pair of Source and Market Locations

then the choice of the most profitable location is easy to describe. The first question to be settled is that of input orientation versus output orientation. Will it be preferable to make the bats at a wood source, or at a bat market, or at some point on the route between source and market? There are no other rational possibilities, since a detour would obviously be wasteful.

This question can be settled by considering any pair of source and market locations, as in Fig. 2-1. The possible locations are the points on the line *SM*. Input costs are reduced as the location is shifted toward *S,* but receipts per unit of output are increased as the location is shifted the other way, toward *M*. Which attraction will be the stronger? There is a close physical analogy here to a tug of war between two opposing pulls, but how are their relative strengths measured? In this case, simply by considering the relative weights of input and output. If it takes more than a ton of input to make a ton of output, then a shift of location in the direction of the input source will reduce costs by more than it reduces revenues, and the location of maximum profit will be at the input source: That is, the process will be input oriented.

In the case suggested (baseball bat manufacturing), that would seem to be the logical outcome, since there is a considerable sloughing off of weight in the process. This is an example of what is called a "weight-losing" activity, and we have now established the rule of thumb that *a weight-losing activity is prima facie likely to be input oriented.* Conversely, we can think of "weight-gaining" activities as those in which the transferable output weighs *more* than the transferable inputs required, because some local input also has been incorporated into the product. An example would be the dilution of a concentrate (such as soft-drink syrup, ammonia, or heroin) to produce a less concentrated output. Such weight-gaining activities, we may surmise, will be most profitably located at markets, in order to avoid transfer of the added weight.

It is, of course, theoretically possible for the weights of transferable input and transferable output to be exactly the same. The process, then, would be neither weight gaining nor weight losing, and orientation would be indeterminate: Every location along the line *SM* in Fig. 2-1 would be equally good. But such an exact balance of the two forces would be like tossing a coin and having it stand on edge. In fact, some further considerations to be introduced later make it even less likely than we might presently expect. Accordingly, we can say that in the single input, single output case the preferred location will be either at a source or at a market, depending on whether the weight of the transferred input exceeds or falls short of the weight of the transferred output.

This simple rule turns out to be useful in establishing a rough categorization of transfer-oriented activities into two classes, and points the way toward a more specific determination of location for particular activities. Suppose we have established that the unit we are considering is output oriented. Then the choice of possible locations is immediately narrowed down to the set of market locations, and all that remains is to select the most profitable of these.

For each market location, there will be one best input source, which can supply the transferred input to that market more cheaply than can any other source. Fig. 2-2 pictures this pairing of sources and markets. For each market, we have an input cost and a market demand. The profitability of each location at each market can thus be calculated, and a comparison of these profitabilities indicates where the activity should locate.

The situation shown in Fig. 2-2 has some other features to be noted. First, the *best* input source for a location at any given market is not necessarily the *nearest*. A more remote low-cost source may be able to deliver the input cheaper than a higher-cost source which is closer at hand. Second, any one input source may be the best source for more than one market location (but not conversely). Third, there may be some input sources that would not be used by any of the market locations. Finally, Fig. 2-2 could be used to picture the case of an *input*-oriented unit, by simply interchanging the S's and M's.

Next, let us complicate matters a little by considering an activity that uses more than one kind of transferable input (for example, a foundry that uses fuel and metal plus various less important inputs such as wood for patterns and forms and sand for molds). Initially, we shall assume that the various inputs are required in fixed proportions.

We now have three or more relative weights to compare. For each ton of output, there will be required, say, x tons of one transferable input plus y tons of another.

The question of orientation is now somewhat more complex. In Fig. 2-3, which pictures one market and one source of each of two kinds of input, the most profitable location might be at any one of those three points or at some intermediate point. We can see immediately, however, that the choice of intermediate locations is restricted to those inside or on the

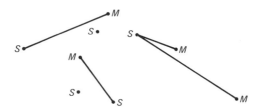

Fig. 2-2. Pairing of Sources and Markets

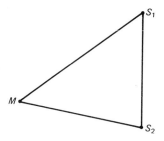

Fig. 2-3. A Locational Triangle: Sources of Two Inputs and a Market

boundaries of the triangle formed by joining the input sources and market points.

This constraint of the possible locations will always apply when there are just three points involved, as in Fig. 2-3. If there are more market or source points so that we have a "locational polygon" of more than three sides, the constraint will still apply if the polygon is "convex" (that is, if none of its corners points inward).

Looking at Fig. 2-3, we can envisage three forces influencing the activity location, each attracting it toward one of the corners of the triangle. Just as in the simpler case already considered, these forces are proportional to the relative weights of the transferred output and inputs. The most profitable location is where these three pulls balance, so that there would be a net loss from a shift in any direction. In fact, a simple analog computer can be built to determine optimum location under the simplified conditions we have assumed. Imagine Fig. 2-3 laid out to scale on a table top, with holes bored and small pulleys inserted at the corners of the figure. Three strings run over the three pulleys and are joined together within the figure. Underneath the table, each string has attached to it a weight proportional to the relative weight of the corresponding transferred input or output. The knot joining the three strings will then come to rest at the equilibrium point of the three forces, which is the maximum profit location.[8]

---

[8] This device is known as the Varignon Frame, after its inventor, and is far more frequently described than constructed or actually used. Its main service to location economics, in fact, is pedagogical: it helps in visualizing the economic interplay of location factors through a familiar physical analog. Alternatively and more precisely (though precision is scarcely relevant for this problem), the solution can be computed mathematically, as explained in H. W. Kuhn and R. F. Kuenne, "An Efficient Algorithm for the Numerical Solution of the Generalized Weber Problem in Spatial Economics," *Journal of Regional Science,* 4, 2 (1962), 21–23. A geometric method of solution for the case of a triangular figure was presented as early as 1909 by Georg Pick in the mathematical appendix to Alfred Weber, *Über den Standort der Industrien* (J. C. B. Mohr: Tübingen, 1909); C. J. Friedrich (tr.), *Alfred Weber's Theory of Location of Industries* (Chicago: University of Chicago Press, 1929). A Varignon Frame is pictured in Fig. 45 on p. 229 of the English edition.

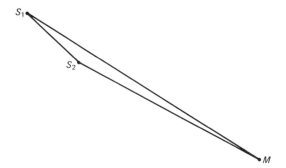

Fig. 2-4. A Locational Triangle Conducive to Minimum Transfer Cost Location at the Obtuse Corner

In the case of three or more factors of transfer orientation, we can no longer be positive about which force will win out. In fact, we can really be sure only if one of the weights involved is "predominant": that is, at least equal to the sum of all the other weights. In a many-sided tug of war, if one contestant is stronger than all the rest combined he can win even if they all pull together in one direction in opposition to him. Thus, for example, if we have a set of output and input weights such as 2, 4, 1, and 8, the optimum location will have to be at the source or market corresponding to the weight of 8.

It does not follow, however, that an intermediate location will be optimal in all cases where no one weight predominates. The outcome in such a case depends on the shape of the locational figure: that is, the configuration of the various source and market points in space. For example, in Fig. 2-4 the configuration is such that the activity would be input oriented to source S_2 even if the relative weights were 3 for S_1, 2 for S_2, and 4 for the market M.[9] With the same weights and a figure shaped like that in Fig. 2-3, an intermediate location within the triangle would be optimal, and we could not describe the activity as being either input oriented or output oriented.

We shall see in later chapters that under more realistic assumptions about transfer costs and other considerations, the likelihood of intermediate locations is still further reduced.

---

[9] In terms of the three-way tug-of-war analogy, a weaker puller can defeat two stronger ones if the latter two are pulling almost directly against one another, as S_1 and M are in this figure. For the specific numerical case in hand, it can be calculated that a force of 2 can prevail against combined forces of 3 and 4 if the latter two are pulling in directions at least 151.7° divergent. (The reader who has been exposed to elementary physics will recognize here a basic laboratory exercise involving the parallelogram of forces.) The geometric analysis and proofs for the case of the locational triangle will be found in the sources mentioned in footnote 8.

We find, then, that it is not as easy as it first appeared to characterize by a simple rule the orientation of any given type of economic activity. If the activity uses more than one kind of transferable input (and/or if it produces more than one kind of transferable output), we may well find that an optimum location can sometimes be at a market, sometimes at an input source, and sometimes at an intermediate point. The steel industry is a good example of this. Some steel centers have been located at or near iron ore mines, others near coal deposits, others at major market concentrations, and still others at points not possessing ore or coal deposits or major markets but simply a strategic transfer location between sources and markets. Intermediate and varying orientations are most likely to be found in activities for which there are several transferable inputs and outputs of roughly similar weight.

So far we have been assuming that for a particular economic activity the weights of transferred inputs and outputs were in fixed proportion, that is, the recipe could not be altered. In practice, this is often not true. For example, in the steel industry, steel scrap and blast furnace iron are both used as metallic inputs, but it is possible to step up the proportion of scrap at times when scrap is cheap and to design furnaces to use larger proportions of scrap at locations where it is expected to be relatively cheap. In almost any manufacturing process, in fact, there is at least some leeway for responding to differences in relative cost of inputs and relative demand for outputs. The same principle also applies more broadly to non-manufacturing activities, and includes substitution among nontransferable as well as transferable inputs and outputs. Thus, labor is likely to be more lavishly used where it is cheap, and to be replaced by labor-saving equipment where it is expensive.

How do these possibilities of substitution affect transfer orientation? The general answer is that they still further enlarge the possibilities for varying kinds of orientation at different times and places, broaden the range of location alternatives, and make transfer costs a less powerful determinant of location than they would otherwise be.[10]

SCALE ECONOMIES AND MULTIPLE MARKETS OR SOURCES

Another simplifying assumption that we adopted was that a unit disposes of all its output at one market and obtains all its supply of each input from one source. This accords with reality in many, but by no means all, cases. If a seller's economies of scale lead him to produce an output that is substantial in relation to the total demand for that output at a single

---

[10] For a full discussion of the locational implications of substitutability of inputs, see Leon N. Moses, "Location and the Theory of Production," *Quarterly Journal of Economics,* 72, 2 (May 1958), 259–272.

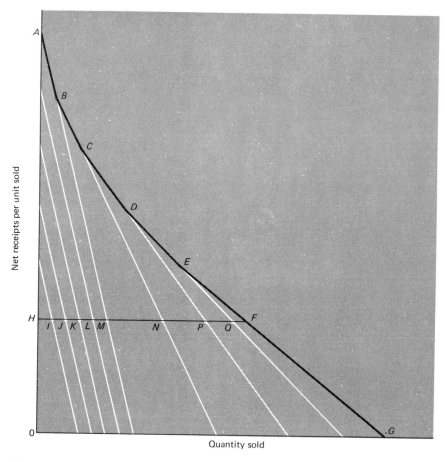

Fig. 2-5. Aggregation of Demand Schedules of Five Markets for the Product of a Single Seller

market, he will face a less than perfectly elastic demand in any one market and it may be profitable for him to sell in such additional markets as are accessible to him. In that event, the location factor of "access to market" will entail nearness not to just one point, but to a number of points or a "market area." Similarly, he may find he can get his supplies of any particular transferable input more cheaply by tapping more than one source if the supply at any one source is not perfectly elastic.

Fig. 2-5 shows how we might, in principle, analyze the market access advantages of a specific location in terms of possible sales to a number of different market points. In this illustration there are five markets in all, assumed to be located at progressively greater distances from the seller. If the demand curve at each of those markets is identical in terms of quantities bought at any given *delivered price,* then the demand curves as seen by the seller (that is, in terms of quantities bought at any given level of *net receipts* after transfer costs are deducted) will be progressively lower for the more distant markets. This is shown by the series of five steeply sloping lines in the left-hand part of the figure. If we now add up the sales that he can make in all markets combined, for each level of net receipts, we obtain the aggregate demand curve pictured by the broken line *ABCDEFG*. For example, at a net received price of *OH* (after covering transfer costs) he can sell *HI, HJ, HK, HL,* and *HM* in the five markets respectively. His total sales will be *HF*, which is the sum of *HM* plus *MN* (= *HL*) plus *NP* (= *HK*) plus *PQ* (= *HJ*) plus *QF* (= *HI*).

This aggregate demand schedule and the costs of operating at the location in question will determine what profits can be made there (by choosing the optimum price and output level). At possible alternative locations, both market and cost conditions will presumably be different, giving rise to spatial differentials in profit possibilities.

Though the foregoing may describe fairly well what determines the likelihood of success at a given location, it is hardly a realistic description of the kind of analysis that underlies most location *decisions*. Some cruder procedures for gauging access advantage of locations in the absence of comprehensive data are described in Appendix 2-1.

When a unit can serve many markets or draw from many input sources, the appraisal of alternative locations in terms of access is a complex matter. There is likely to be little opportunity to use the simple devices discussed earlier in this chapter, such as the balancing off of relative input and output weights, except perhaps as a means of initially narrowing down the range of locational alternatives. In such cases, the maps of costs and revenue prospects will show complex contours rather than simple ones as in the examples discussed earlier; and the evaluation of prospects at different locations will have to approach more nearly an explicit calculation of the expected costs, revenues, and profits at various possible levels of output at each of a large set of alternative locations.

For most types of locational decision units, an exhaustive point-by-point approach in which theory and analysis abdicate in favor of pure empiricism would be so expensive as to outweigh any gain from finally determining the ideal spot. So there will always be a vigorous demand for usable short cuts, ways of narrowing down the range of location choice, and better analytical techniques. The challenge to regional economists is to provide techniques better than hunch or inertia, and cheaper than exhaustive canvassing of locations.

SELECTED READINGS

Richard L. Nelson, *The Selection of Retail Locations* (New York: F. W. Dodge Corp., 1958).

Leon N. Moses, "Location and the Theory of Production," *Quarterly Journal of Economics,* 72, 2 (May 1958), 259–272.

L. C. Yaseen, *Plant Location* (New York: American Research Council, 1960).

James H. Thompson, *Methods of Plant Site Selection Available to Small Manufacturing Firms* (Morgantown: West Virginia University, 1961).

David L. Huff, "A Programmed Solution for Approximating an Optimum Retail Location," *Land Economics,* 42, 3 (August 1966), 293–303.

Edgar M. Hoover, "Some Programmed Models of Industry Location," *Land Economics,* 43, 3 (August 1967), 303–311.

Nina J. Gruen and Claude Gruen, "A Behavioral Approach to Determining Optimum Location for the Retail Firm," *Land Economics,* 43, 3 (August 1967), 320–327.

Benjamin H. Stevens and Carolyn A. Brackett, *Industrial Location: A Review and Annotated Bibliography of Theoretical, Empirical and Case Studies,* Bibliography Series No. 3 (Philadelphia: Regional Science Research Institute, 1967).

United Nations, Economic Commission for Europe, *Criteria for Location of Industrial Plants,* prepared by Antoni Kukliński (New York: United Nations, 1967).

Gerald J. Karaska and David F. Bramhall (eds.), *Locational Analysis for Manufacturing* (Cambridge, Mass.: The M.I.T. Press, 1969).

Harry W. Richardson, *Regional Economics* (New York: Praeger, 1969), 20–24 and Chs. 3–4.

APPENDIX 2-1

Evaluation of Access to Multiple Points: Some Short-Cut Approaches
(See page 29)

For simplicity's sake, let us consider just the question of evaluating access to multiple *markets.* If, for example, a producer seeks the best location from which to serve markets in 50 major cities in the United States, how might he proceed?

What he wants is some sort of "geographical center" of the set of 50 markets. Suppose that it were to be defined as a median point so located that half of the aggregate market lay to the north and half to the south, and likewise half to the east and half to the west.[11] Then (if it were to be assumed that transport occurs only on a rectilinear grid of routes) he would have the location from which the total ton-miles of transport entailed in serving all markets would be a minimum. This is an application of the "principle of median location."

Naturally, a number of objections might be made to this procedure. One of the most obvious is that it is irrational to assume that his sales pattern is independent of his location. It would be more reasonable to assume that he would have smaller sales (relative to the size of any given market) in

---

[11] This can be done by preparing a map showing the sales volume of each market noted at its proper location. Align a ruler north and south and push it across the map from one edge, keeping track of the total sales volume of markets passed as the ruler advances. Stopping when that total equals half of the aggregate sales volume for all markets, draw a vertical line. Repeating the process with the ruler held horizontally and moved gradually from top or bottom, get a horizontal line in similar fashion. The intersection of the two lines is the required minimum transport point.

markets more remote from his location, reflecting higher transport charges and competitive disadvantage.

A crude way to get around this difficulty would be to decide that he is really primarily interested in market possibilities within a radius of, say, 400 miles. He could then try drawing circles of that radius around various points on the map and select as his location the center of the circle with the largest market volume.

A somewhat more sophisticated procedure would be to apply a systematic "distance discount" in his evaluation of markets, by calculating what is called an index of market access *potential* for each of a number of alternative locations. Thus, to compute the potential index for Location X, he would divide the sales volume of Market 1 by the distance from X to 1, divide the sales volume of Market 2 by the distance from X to 2, and so on, and sum up all the resulting quotients. If a similar calculation for Location Y yielded a larger index, he would rate Y higher than X with respect to access to this set of markets.

Such potential measures are widely used, with the distance (or transport cost, if available) commonly raised to some power such as the square. If the square of the distance is used, the potential formula becomes

$$P_i = \sum_j \left(\frac{M_j}{D^2_{ij}} \right)$$

(where M is market size and D is distance); and any given market has the same effect on the index as a market four times as big but twice as far away.

The methods described here have all been widely used. They are, of course, equally applicable to assessment of the *input* access potential of locations, when the unit is drawing upon more than one source of the same kind of transferable input. They apply also to cases involving transfer of services rather than goods—for example, in measuring the job-access potential of different residence locations where a choice of job opportunities is advantageous, or in measuring the labor-supply access potential of alternative locations for an employer.

INTRODUCTION

The discussion of individual locations in the previous chapter assumed throughout an equivalence between distance and transfer cost. We disregarded the facts that in the real world different kinds of inputs and outputs are transferred at different costs, and that weight is often an inappropriate measure of input or output quantity. We ignored the fact that transfer generally has to follow a route between established terminal service points rather than going as the crow flies. We assumed that transfer costs along a route were proportional to distance and failed to distinguish between money costs, time costs, and still other kinds of cost entailed in transfer. We ignored the great differences in cost and service capabilities of different techniques or modes of transfer, as well as the distinction between costs to the transfer firm or agency and costs to the user of transfer service.

In this chapter we hasten to remedy those omissions in order to get a more realistic understanding of how transfer costs affect the location of activities.

SOME ECONOMIC CHARACTERISTICS OF TRANSFER OPERATIONS

It is much easier to develop an understanding of the complex variations of transfer services, costs, and rates if we first note some basic economic characteristics of transfer activities.

In transfer operations (except for a few primitive types) substantial components of the costs are *fixed* —that is, they reflect overall and long-run commitments such as the provision and maintenance of right of way and terminals. Partly for this reason, transfer operations are characteristically subject to important economies of scale. Costs per unit of service tend to be lower (and service more convenient and faster) on routes with larger volumes of traffic. Likewise, costs are generally lower when larger quantities are moved in single movement units (for example, ships, trains, or aircraft). There are additional savings in transfer cost when the single consignment (that is, what is moved at one time from one specific location unit to another) is larger. Some of these scale economies apply principally to costs

3
Transfer Costs

of actual movement between locations and others principally to costs of establishing and operating terminals and such operations as selling, accounting, and billing.

Because of these characteristics, firms or public agencies providing transfer services generally serve many pairs of points and many different classes of customers and operate with a substantial element of monopolistic control rather than in perfect competition. The rates for the various services rendered can be set so as to recoup disproportionate shares of the transfer operation's fixed costs from rates on those services for which demand is least elastic.

Finally, human ingenuity has continually devised new technologies or modes of transfer to serve various special purposes. Although each new mode may partly supplant an older one, it is rare for any mode to disappear completely. Somewhere in the world there is still in use nearly every transfer mode ever devised. Each mode has special advantages for a certain range of services, and is thus partly competitive and partly complementary to other modes.

As Table 3-1 shows, transfer operations can be classified according to

TABLE 3-1. Illustrations of Combinations of Transfer Modes and Objectives*

"The Medium"—type of transfer mode used	"The Message"—primary purpose of the transfer			
	Movement of people	Movement of things	Movement of energy	Movement of information
Passenger (walking, automobile, transit or other passenger vehicle, etc.)	Personal travel per se	Human carriers	Journey to (manual) work	Messengers, advisers, etc.
Freight (truck, train, ship, pipeline, etc.)	—	Freight transport per se	Transport of fuels	Transport of letters or other graphic matter, samples, etc.
Transmission cable or wire	—	—	Electric power transmission	Communication by wire or cable
Radio or other waves	—	—	—	Radio communication, etc.

* Illustrative examples are given in the table.

means or according to purpose. The purposes of transfer are to move people, goods, energy, or information from one place to another—information being broadly defined to include queries, esthetic and emotional effects, and in fact all messages via any of the senses.

The "hierarchical" ordering in Table 3-1 (as shown by the fact that the cells below the diagonal are blank) is interesting. It reflects the fact that the most primitive and versatile means of transfer is movement of people, which can accomplish any of the four purposes. Specialized modes of transfer for shipping goods other than on people's backs can at the same time serve to transfer energy and information. Still more specialized means of energy transmission can also transmit information; and finally we have specialized modes for information transmission (communication) which cannot move people, goods, or energy.

CHARACTERISTIC FEATURES OF
TRANSFER COSTS AND RATES

Route Systems and Service Points

Perhaps the most notable difference between reality and the "uniform transfer surface" assumed in the previous chapter is the channelizing of transfer services along definite routes, which only rarely represent the straight path of shortest distance between an origin and a destination point.

There are two distinct reasons for this channelization. One is the economies of traffic volume already referred to as a nearly universal characteristic of transfer. Even primitive societies where all transfer is pedestrian generally develop networks of established trails, which make it easier to move and harder to get lost. Each mode of transfer has its own set of route-volume economies. If these economies are substantial up to a large volume, the route network for that mode will tend to be coarse; if heavier traffic means only small savings, there can be a finer network of routes providing less circuitous connections between points.

The second reason for route channelization is that some areas are naturally harder to traverse than others. Thus, all modes of land transport have reason to favor level, well-drained land and temperate climate in laying out routes and to avoid unnecessary stream crossings. All routes crossing major mountain ranges funnel into a few selected passes or tunnels. Similarly, ocean shipping routes have to detour around land masses and also have to pay some attention to ocean currents, winds, shoals, iceberg zones, and, of course, the availability of harbors. As a result, there is a more or less recognized network of regular "shipping lanes." Even air transport is restricted in choice of routes between any two terminals by the system of navigational aids and safety regulations.

Any kind of communications system requiring either fixed line facilities (such as cables) or relay stations is likewise constrained to a limited set of routes. Transfer is really "as the crow flies" only within the range of direct wave transmission.

Scale economies apply not only to route facilities, such as trails, track, roads, pipelines, cable, or navigational aids, but also to "service points" where transfer by the mode in question can originate and terminate. Thus, there are certain minimum costs of establishing a railroad station or even a siding; the same applies to piggyback terminals, ports for ships and aircraft, transformer stations on long-distance electric transmission lines, or telephone exchanges and switchboards. There is an economic constraint on the spacing of bus stops along a route, since more stops slow the service. Anyone making a shopping trip will prefer to get all his errands done with a minimum number of separate stops (though this is apparently not always true if we change "his" to "her").

Consequently, the pattern of transfer services offered by any particular mode is always spotty, linking up a limited number of pairs of points by routes usually longer than the straight-line distance; and a transfer of a specific shipment, person, or item of information from initial origin to final destination frequently entails the use of more than one link or mode.

In addition to restricting the number of routes and service points, transfer scale economies in many instances have the effect of making costs and rates lower on more heavily used routes and to and from larger terminals. This works in several ways. In some cases, it is primarily a question of direct cost reduction associated with volume. Thus, a larger-diameter pipeline requires less material and less pumping energy per unit volume carried, and a four-lane highway can carry more than twice as much traffic as a two-lane highway, with less than twice as wide a right of way if the median divider is narrow.

Similarly, terminals and other transfer service points can often operate more efficiently if they handle large volumes of traffic. Examples are the huge specialized facilities for loading and unloading bulk cargoes such as grain, coal, and ores, and the more specialized equipment found at large communications terminals.

But apart from and in addition to such volume-of-traffic savings in cost to the *operator* of individual transfer services, there are likely to be important advantages for the *users* of the services in terms of quality of service. Your letters will probably be delivered sooner if you put them in a heavily used mailbox from which collections are made more frequently. If you are shipping goods to a variety of destinations it may pay to choose a location near a large transport terminal, not only because the departures are more frequent but also because there are direct connections to more points and a variety of special types of service.

Long-haul Economies

Virtually every kind of transfer entails some operation at the point of origin prior to actual movement, and also some further operation at the destination point. The cost of these "terminal" processes ordinarily does not depend on the distance to be traveled, whereas the costs of actual movement ordinarily do.

Because of these terminal costs, the relationship between route distance and the total costs of a shipment will generally behave as shown in Fig. 3-1. Transfer costs are characteristically less than proportional to distance, and the average transfer cost per mile decreases as the length of haul increases. This principle is a fundamental one and appears in every kind of transfer mode, even the simplest. When we leave our homes or work places on various missions, there is almost always some act of preparation that imposes a terminal cost in terms of time. Even if we go on foot, we may first have to make sure that we are acceptably clad against the strictures of convention or weather, turn off the television, put the dog out, and lock the door. If we drive, the car has to be activated. If we use public transit, we have to wait for it to appear.

In Fig. 3-1 the costs of movement per se (what is called the "line-haul" cost in transportation) appear to be nearly proportional to distance. This

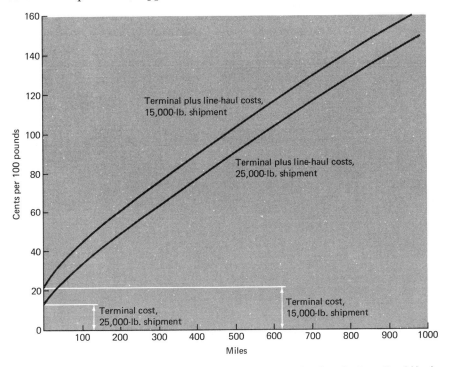

Fig. 3-1. Terminal and Line-haul Costs of Motor Common Carriers by Length of Haul and Size of Shipment, Central Region, 1963

SOURCE: Interstate Commerce Commission, Bureau of Accounts, *Cost of Transporting Freight by Class I and Class II Motor Carriers of General Commodities,* Statement No. 7-64 (Washington, D.C.: Government Printing Office, August 1964), pp. 30, 33. Costs of interchange of cargo at intermediate points are omitted.

implies that the marginal cost of transfer (the cost for each added unit of distance) is constant. We can think of a few circumstances in which movement costs per se might rise faster than in direct proportion to distance, such as in the case of a perishable commodity where it becomes increasingly difficult and expensive to prevent deterioration as time passes, or the case of journeys where after a certain point further travel becomes disproportionately more irksome. But these are rare exceptions. In general, we can expect movement costs to be either less than proportional or roughly proportional to distance.

When might they rise at a slower than linear rate? This can be expected in the case of transport of goods or people, since it takes some time to accelerate to "cruising speed" and to decelerate to a stop. An example is the case of transit vehicles with their frequent stops. A 1-mile journey between subway stations takes considerably less than twice as much time and power as two half-mile journeys, and accordingly costs less than twice as much. Somewhat more complicated instances are those of the intercity truck, intercity bus, or ship which have to thread their way slowly through congested areas at the first and last parts of their journeys, and the airplane which has to climb to cruising altitude and down again as well as to follow the prescribed takeoff and landing patterns. In all these cases, the overall speed of a trip increases with distance even if cruising speed is constant. Speed is not merely an aspect of quality of service but an important determinant of the costs of rendering the service, since such items as the wages of vehicle operators, interest on the capital invested in vehicles, insurance, and part of vehicle depreciation are proportionate to time rather than distance.

For long hauls such line-haul economies are, of course, relatively less significant: The difference in overall speed between an 800-mile and a 900-mile rail or truck haul is probably not great.[1] And in the case of telecommunication or electric power transmission, which do not entail moving any tangible objects over the route and in which transfer time is negligible, it is not obvious that average line costs per mile should systematically fall with greater distances. Line losses on transmission lines are proportional to distance, and booster or relay stations on cable or microwave communications routes are needed at more or less uniform distance intervals. For radio wave communication, however, the required transmitter power rises as the square of the range.

---

[1] In regard to trucking costs, "The ICC has consistently reported that *line-haul* costs decline with distance shipped. However, this is largely a spurious correlation, reflecting the fact that size of shipment and length of haul are correlated, and not attributable, as the ICC implies, to some operating characteristic that makes line-haul ton-mile costs substantially less on a two-hundred-mile than on a one-hundred-mile trip. Total unit costs do decline with distance, however, because of the distribution of *terminal* expense over a larger number of ton miles." John R. Meyer and others, *Competition in the Transportation Industries* (Cambridge, Mass.: Harvard University Press, 1959), p. 93.

Transfer Costs and Rates

As was noted earlier, many kinds of transfer service are performed by parties other than the user, and the usual presence of substantial fixed costs and limited competition gives a transfer agency a good deal of leeway in shaping tariffs so as to increase profits. Some classes of traffic may accordingly be charged barely enough to cover the out-of-pocket costs they occasion, while others will be charged far more than their pro rata share of the transfer agency's fixed costs. The general principle governing profit-maximizing price discrimination is to discriminate in favor of customers with more elastic demands and against those with less elastic demands.

Moreover, the rates charged by transfer agencies are themselves only part of the total time and money costs entailed in bridging distance. At longer distances, sales promotion and customer servicing are more costly or less satisfactory, and larger inventories need to be held against fluctuations in demand or supply.

TRAFFIC VOLUME. Taking these considerations into account, we can see that the advantages of location at or near larger transfer terminals can be even greater than was suggested earlier. At such concentrations of terminal activity, there is more likelihood of sharp competition among rival transfer agencies of the same or different modes. The bargaining power of transfer users is greater and their demand for the services of any one particular transfer agency is more elastic—consequently, they may get particularly favorable treatment in the establishment of rates or especially good service, over and above the cost and service advantages inherent in the scale economies of the terminal operations themselves.

RELATION OF RATES TO LENGTH OF HAUL. In the relation between short-haul and long-haul rates, matters cannot be quite so simply stated. First, a transfer agency with a monopoly would generally be impelled to set rates discriminating against short-haul traffic. With reference to Fig. 3-1, the line showing *rates* in relation to distance would then have a flatter slope than the line showing the relation of *costs* to distance.

The rationale for such discrimination is that for longer hauls the transfer charge is a larger part of the total price of the goods at their destination than it is for a shorter haul of the same goods. Consequently, the elasticity of demand for transfer service is likely to be greater for longer hauls, and the rational monopolist will discriminate in favor of such hauls. (See Appendix 3-1 for a simple mathematical statement of this point.)

In practice, however, a single transfer agency is unlikely to hold a monopoly over a very wide range of lengths of haul. The greater the distance, the more likely it is that there will be alternative providers of the same mode of service. Even more to the point is the probability of effective intermodal competition.

Each technique or mode of transfer has its own cost and service characteristics and is more efficient than other modes for some classes of service and less efficient for other classes (were it not so, we should not have the variety of modes that exists for very long). Thus, jet aircraft excel in providing fast long-distance transport; waterways and pipelines are generally the cheapest ways of moving bulk materials in large quantities; the motor vehicle has special advantages of flexibility and convenience in local and short-distance movement; and so on. Clearly, if we are considering a wide range of lengths of haul for some commodity, the lowest-cost mode for short hauls need not be the same as the lowest-cost mode for long hauls. The cost gradients might be expected to intersect as in Fig. 3-2, which has often been used to represent truck, rail, and water transport costs, but would also be applicable to a variety of other intermodal comparisons.

In a situation similar to that in Fig. 3-2, the operators of each mode will find that the demand for their service is particularly elastic in those distance ranges where some alternative mode can effectively compete for the traffic; consequently, there is likely to be competitive rate cutting on those classes of traffic. The final rate pattern might look something like the black line in Fig. 3-2: For each distance range, the lowest-cost mode determines the general level of rates, and the progression of rates is rounded off in the most competitive distance ranges where two or more different modes share the traffic.

We should expect this outcome regardless of whether the rates in question are for goods transport, people transport, or communication, since

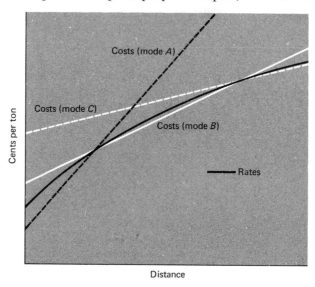

Fig. 3-2. Transfer Rates and Transfer Cost Gradients for Three Competing Modes

the essence of the situation is that different modes have comparative advantages for different distances. The effect, as graphically shown in Fig. 3-2, is to make the gradient of transfer rates with respect to distance much more curved than the single-mode transfer cost gradients shown earlier in Fig. 3-1. In other words, the tendency to a falling *marginal* cost of transfer (to the user) with increased distance is accentuated. We shall see later the locational implications of this and the other characteristics of transfer cost and rate gradients being noted here.

COMPETITIVE AND NONCOMPETITIVE ROUTES. Still another way in which comparative rates differ from comparative transfer costs is with respect to different routes. Between some pairs of points there is effective competition among two or more alternative transfer agencies or modes, while between other pairs of points one agency or mode has such a cost advantage as to constitute for practical purposes a monopoly. The margin between rates and out-of-pocket costs will be small where there is effective competition and large where there is more monopoly power.

The effects of this kind of discrimination upon transfer rate structures are discussed in considerable detail in every textbook on the economics of transportation, usually in reference to the structure of railroad and truck freight rates as affected by competition among the rail, highway, and waterway modes and among alternative railroad routes. Regulatory agencies have developed elaborate rules to limit the scope of discrimination in rate making in the interest of some rather elusive objectives of maintaining competition and preserving equities of particular areas and transport agencies.

DISCRIMINATION AMONG SERVICES AND COMMODITIES. Some transfer services are by their nature costlier to provide than others, and we should expect to see such differences reflected in rates. A ton of pingpong balls or automobile bodies is much bulkier than a ton of steel plates. Since extra bulk adds to transport cost in every mode of transport except possibly the use of pack animals or human carriers, we are not surprised to see systematically higher freight rates per ton on bulky goods. This is one basis for the official commodity classifications governing regulated tariffs. Similarly, we should expect to pay more for shipping a perishable, fragile, or dangerous commodity (like meat, glassware, or sulfuric acid). Extra-fast service and the carrying of small shipments are more expensive. In passenger transport it costs more to provide extra space and comfort. In addition, the marginal costs of added service at slack times are far less than at times of peak capacity use of the facilities, so that we are not surprised to be charged more for a long-distance phone call during business hours, for using a parking lot on the afternoon of a football game, or for crossing the Atlantic in summer.

None of the above differentials in rates necessarily involves any discrimination on the part of the transfer agency, since in every case there is an underlying difference in costs which is passed on to the user.

But there are still further systematic transfer rate differentials that reflect discriminatory rate-making policy rather than costs. In particular, we find that rates are high relative to costs for the transfer of things of high value, and low relative to costs for things of low value.

The rationale is essentially the same as that already adduced in the case of long versus short hauls; namely, that a seller's profits are enhanced by discriminating against buyers with relatively inelastic demands and in favor of buyers with relatively elastic demands.

When a commodity like cigarettes or scientific instruments, with a high value per pound, is shipped any given distance, transport costs will be a smaller part of the delivered price than will be the case when a low-value commodity like coal or gravel is shipped the same distance. Consequently, the demand for transport of cigarettes will be much less sensitive to the freight rate than will the demand for transport of coal, and any rational profit-seeking transport agency will charge a higher margin over out-of-pocket costs on cigarettes than on coal. Such discrimination, by the way, is not merely in the interest of the carrier but under some conditions may serve the public interest as well, through promoting a more efficient allocation and use of resources. It may enable a greater amount of transfer service to be provided with any given amount of investment in transfer facilities.

Consequently, we find that freight tariff classifications and special commodity rates rather systematically reflect the relative prices per ton of the various commodities, in addition to such other factors as have already been mentioned. This means that finished goods as a rule pay much higher freight rates than intermediate goods or raw materials, since production processes normally involve getting rid of waste components and adding value.

For the transfer of people and for communication, the measure of unit value corresponding to the price per pound of a transported commodity is not so easy to assign or visualize. The basic rule of transfer rate discrimination according to value still applies but is generally obscured by the fact that in the transport of people and information a "higher-value" consignment is given a qualitatively different transfer service.

When it is a question of passenger travel, people set their own valuations simply in terms of how much they are willing to pay for a trip rather than forego it. Transfer agencies do not attempt to "charge what the traffic will bear" on a person-by-person and trip-by-trip basis, but often provide special services (higher speed, greater comfort, and the like) to those willing to pay more. Similarly in the case of communications, it is generally impossible for the seller of the service to judge how valuable a particular transmission is to the communicator and charge accordingly; but a choice of different speeds or other qualities of service can be set up, and rates for these adjusted in such a way as to reflect the estimated relative elasticities of demand as well as the relative costs.

DIFFERENTIATION OF RATES ACCORDING TO DIRECTION. Most modes of transportation use vehicles that must be returned to the point of origin if the trip is to be repeated. Only by coincidence will the demand for transport in both directions balance; ordinarily one direction or the other will have excess vehicle capacity that could accommodate more goods or people at an extremely low out-of-pocket cost. A rational rate-making policy will then quote lower "back-haul" rates in the underutilized direction.

That direction can sometimes change rather often—for example, in intraurban travel there is a morning inbound and an afternoon outbound rush hour, and in some instances lesser reversals around the noon hour and in the evening. On weekends there is a reverse pattern of recreational travel from and to the main urban area. In this particular case, highway and bridge tolls and transit fares do not embrace the back-haul pricing principle, but they easily could and it might be persuasively argued that they should.

Differentiation of charges on passenger travel according to direction is likewise not applied to intercity or other interregional travel within a country. We may wonder why not, in view of the frequency of the practice in commodity transport. The essential difference between people and goods in this context is that people want to return home eventually and goods do not. Accordingly, "people flows" have a natural tendency to balance out over any substantial time interval. On certain international travel routes, however, the seasonal imbalance of travel demand is enough to induce airlines and shipping firms to vary their rates seasonally according to direction.

Interestingly enough, there are a few kinds of goods transport that use no durable vehicles and for which there is consequently no question of back-haul rates. Some rivers are one-way routes for the transport of logs or for primitive goods-carrying rafts which are broken up at the downstream end, and pipelines normally operate in similar one-way fashion.

Telecommunications media and power transmission lines likewise have no back-haul problem. Nothing is moved, so nothing needs to be brought back.

SIMPLIFICATION OF RATE STRUCTURES. The foregoing discussion gives some idea of the many "dimensions" in which transfer rates can logically be differentiated: according to mode, direction, specific origin and destination, quality of service, size of consignment, and nature of the commodity or service transferred. Clearly, there is some point at which

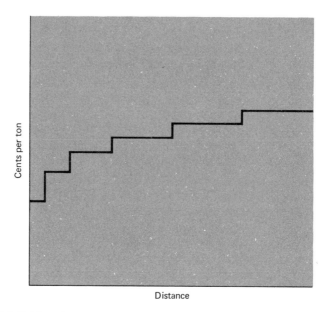

Fig. 3-3. Typical Stepwise Progression of Transfer Rates by Distance Zones

detailed proliferation of individual rates produces a tariff schedule of impractical complexity, and various simplifications and groupings commend themselves.

The variety of rates charged for transport of different commodities, for example, is held within bounds by assigning most commodities to one of a limited number of classes and letting a single schedule of rates apply to that class as a whole. The determination of individual rates for each and every pair of points served by a transfer system is analogously simplified by grouping most of these points into zones or rate "blocks." For example, rail freight rates between Pittsburgh and other parts of the country are applied not just to Pittsburgh proper but to a much larger area embracing the major part of six contiguous counties. An illustration of the application of the rate block principle to rates graded by route distance is shown in Fig. 3-3, which gives us a still more realistic picture of rate patterns than we had in Figs. 3-1 and 3-2.

Time Costs in Transfer

We have already indicated one way in which the time consumed in transfer is felt in costs: Both the labor and the capital used in the transfer operation are hired on a time basis, so the labor cost and the capital cost of a trip will be less if the trip is faster. It is the high speed of aircraft, particularly jets, that enables them to transport passengers and certain kinds of freight at costs per mile comparable to those of ground transport:

The capital and labor costs per hour are spread over at least ten times as many miles.

Quite apart from this, speed means cheaper transfer for the user because he bears "inventory costs" associated with the length of time that the trip takes.[2] In goods shipments, there is the money cost of interest on the value of the goods and insurance on them and the risk of delay. Moreover, many kinds of goods deteriorate so rapidly with the passage of time that it is well worth paying more for their fast delivery. There are the obvious physical perishables like fresh meat, fish, fruit, or vegetables, and also a further class of perishables like fashion clothing, magazines, and newspapers, which lose value as they become out of date. In the transmission of information, the very word "news" suggests quick perishability, and the more quickly perishable forms of information provide a rapidly rising demand for a variety of telecommunication services.

Finally, in the transfer of human beings, the time of the user of the service is even more highly valued than are the rather high costs of transporting this delicate type of freight. The basis for the high valuation placed on travel time is primarily that of opportunity cost: People begrudge the time spent in traveling because they could be using that time pleasantly or profitably in some other way.

The value each of us imputes to the time he spends on travel can vary greatly according to circumstances, length and purpose of the trip, and the characteristics of the person. Recreational travel is supposed to be a pleasure in itself. For such obligatory journeys as commuting to work, it is sometimes suggested that the commuter's hourly earnings rate while working should be applied to the travel time also. However, such a basis may be somewhat too high.[3] In order to suggest the magnitude of time costs of human travel, let us consider the case of the moderately well-off man who values his travel time at $5 an hour. If he travels, say, at 30

---

[2] Illustrative of the indirect "inventory economics" of faster transport, United Air Lines in 1961 suggested that "UAL Air Freight can be profitable when the added cost of shipping by air freight is less than 9½% of the cost value of the goods involved." This is based on the estimate that air freight shipment can, on the average, reduce warehousing requirements by about 40% and inventory requirements by about 20%. For the average product shipped, warehousing charges run about 12% of cost value and inventory charges about 25%; thus, the total saving by air freight amounts to a little more than 9½% of the cost value of the goods. It is easy to see that the appeal of air freight is likely to be higher for goods with a high value per pound.

[3] For a review of the considerable recent literature on the private and social valuation of travel time, see Colin Clark, *Population and Land Use* (London: Macmillan, and New York: St. Martin's Press, 1969), 377–379. The consensus, if any, seems to be that people generally rate the disutility of travel at about half of their earnings rate, but that there are additional costs of longer commuting time (increased absenteeism or tardiness and lowered productivity through fatigue) that tend to be borne by the employer and are perhaps of about the same order of magnitude as the costs borne by the commuter himself.

miles an hour, his time costs are nearly 17¢ a mile, or about the same as the money costs of driving an expensive car.

LOCATIONAL SIGNIFICANCE OF CHARACTERISTICS OF TRANSFER RATES

We have seen that, in practice, the structure of transfer rates departs markedly in a number of ways from the straightforward proportionality to distance which was assumed in our discussion of individual locations in Chapter 2. What does this mean in terms of modified conclusions or new insights?

Effects of Rate Differentials among Goods and Services upon Orientation

The basic principles of transfer orientation were illustrated in Chapter 2 by examples in which the relative strength of the various transfer factors of location (access to input sources and access to markets) could be measured simply by the relative weights of inputs and outputs. One of the conclusions was that a weight-losing activity using one input and producing one output would be input oriented; that is, the most profitable location would always be at some source of the input.

In the real world, sheer physical weight is often not a good measure of the difficulty of transporting an object, and, of course, in the case of transfer by power line or telecommunication there is no weight moved at all. The more sophisticated concept of "ideal weight" must then be substituted for sheer physical weight.

The simplest way to do this in the case of transported goods is to multiply the relative physical weights by the relative transport rates per ton-mile. Thus, in the example given in Table 3-2, there is a physical weight loss of 90 percent between transported inputs and output. But the product travels at such a relatively high freight rate that the incentive to locate near market is greater than the incentive to locate near input sources. The ideal weight of the product being predominant, this process is unequivocally market oriented.

By looking at Table 3-2 in a slightly different way we can see how ideal

TABLE 3-2. Illustrative Calculation of Ideal Weights

	Output	Input A	Input B
(1) Actual weights (tons per day)	250	2,000	500
(2) Transport rates (cents per ton-mile)	32	2	4
(3) Ideal weights—(1) × (2) (transport cost per day per mile of distance from source or market in question)	$80	$40	$20
(4) Ideal weights scaled down to smaller numbers for convenience	4	2	1

weights may be estimated for inputs or outputs with no physical weight. Row 3 of the table tells us that if we could shift the location 1 mile closer to market, without changing anything else, we could get $80 per day more net revenue on the same amount of output. If we could move 1 mile closer to the source of Input A without changing anything else, we could save $40 a day on costs. Similarly, going 1 mile closer to the source of Input B would save $20 a day. These three figures 80, 40, and 20 (or, if we prefer, 4, 2, and 1, as shown in Row 4) represent the relative effects upon profits of moving the location a unit distance closer to each of the three points in turn.

Consequently, if we have an input not measured in terms of physical weight (such as electric energy or telegraphic messages), we can evaluate it as a factor of transfer orientation by estimating how much it costs (per unit of output or per day) to be located 1 mile farther away from the source of that input. There can be an ideal weight even where physical weight is zero or irrelevant.

Using the more sophisticated concept of ideal rather than physical weight, we can distinguish a number of different classes of output-oriented and input-oriented activities, as in Table 3-3. Weight, bulk, perishability,

TABLE 3-3. Types of Input-oriented and Output-oriented Activities

Process characteristic	Orientation	Examples*
Physical weight loss	Input	Smelters; ore beneficiation; dehydration
Physical weight gain	Output	Soft-drink bottling; manufacture of cement blocks
Bulk loss	Input	Compressing cotton into high-density bales
Bulk gain	Output	Assembling automobiles; manufacturing containers; sheet-metal work
Perishability loss	Input	Canning and preserving food
Perishability gain	Output	Newspaper and job printing; baking bread and pastry
Fragility loss	Input	Packing goods for shipment
Fragility gain	Output	Coking of coal
Hazard loss	Input	Deodorizing captured skunks; encoding secret intelligence; microfilming records
Hazard gain	Output	Manufacturing explosives or other dangerous compounds; distilling moonshine whiskey

* In some of these cases, the actual orientation reflects a combination of two or more of the listed process characteristics. Thus, some kinds of canning and preserving involve important weight and bulk loss as well as reduction of perishability. A further reason for the usual output orientation of modern by-product coke ovens is that the bulkiest output, gas, is in demand at the steel works where the coking is done. Coke produced by the earlier "beehive" process was generally made at coal mines, since weight loss more than offset fragility gain.

fragility, and hazard are recognized there as characteristics determining relative transfer costs of inputs and outputs. Cases of "value loss" and "value gain" could perhaps have been formulated as well.

Effects of Limited Route Systems and Service Points

In our initial discussion of transfer orientation, the economic advantages of proximity to markets and input sources were envisaged as conflicting forces, and the most profitable location appeared as the point on a two-dimensional surface where those forces just balanced.

Some route networks are so dense that transfer can be effected in an almost straight path between any two points. A relatively close approximation to a uniform transfer surface is a city street system; although even here the shortest possible route and the fastest possible route may both be substantially longer than the crow-flight distance. On a coarse route network, the locational pulls toward input sources and markets are exerted in a one-dimensional way, along the routes. Does this significantly affect orientations of specific units of activity?

The best way to visualize the effect is to consider a route system connecting three points *A, B,* and *C,* which we might identify as the market and the sources for two transferable inputs for a unit of some type of economic activity. Fig. 3-4 shows four different configurations that this route system might take.[4]

Let us now assign ideal weights to *A, B,* and *C.* It is easy to see that if any of these ideal weights is predominant (exceeds the sum of the other two), there is no contest: that point is the optimum location so far as transfer costs are concerned, regardless of route layout. But what if the ideal weights are more evenly balanced, with none predominant— say, 2, 3, and 4 for *A, B,* and *C* respectively? These are the weights shown in parentheses at the *A, B,* and *C* points on System 1 on the left side of Fig. 3-4.

In System 1, we shall see that the optimum location now turns out to be *B.* For all possible locations between *A* and *B,* there would be a net gain in moving toward *B,* since in that direction we have a pull corresponding to the combined ideal weights of *B* and *C,* or 3 + 4 = 7, whereas there is a counterpull toward *A* of only 2. The strengths and directions of these pulls are shown by the small circled numerals with arrows at-

---

[4] The "forks" mentioned in Fig. 3-4 are defined as three-branch (Y) junctions. The reader may wish to amuse himself by constructing the four additional kinds of networks that are possible with no more than three ends and no more than three forks: no ends, two forks; one end, three forks; two ends, two forks; and three ends, three forks. The sum of the number of forks and ends is always even.

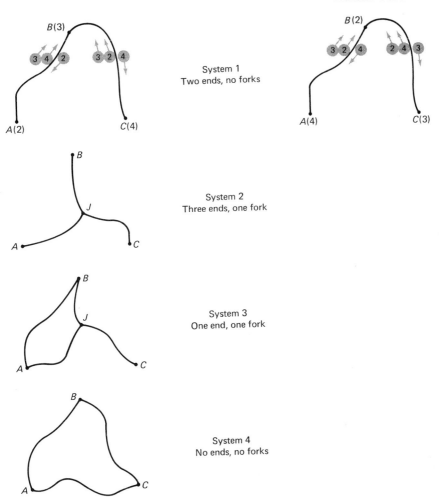

Fig. 3-4. Some Possible Route Systems Connecting Three Points

tached. If the ideal weights represent, say, cents per mile per unit of output, then there will be a net transfer cost saving of 5¢ per ton of output in moving 1 mile closer to B from any alternative location to the left of B. Similarly, we find that for any location between B and C, there is a net gain of 1¢ per ton of output (3 + 2 − 4) from shifting the location 1 mile nearer B. Once at B, there is no incentive to shift further; the optimum location has been found.

This device of totaling the forces in each direction and thus finding the favorable direction of location shift along each route segment is a handy technique for analyzing network location in simple cases, and is the conceptual basis of the linear programming approach for determining the optimum point.[5]

Let us now apply it again to System 1 of Fig. 3-4, changing the ideal weights from 2, 3, 4 to 4, 2, 3 as shown in the map at top right in the figure. Again, we come out with the intermediate point *B* as the optimum location, despite the fact that it has the smallest ideal weight of the three! We begin to suspect that there is some special advantage in being in the middle; and this is, in fact, the "principle of median location," mentioned in Appendix 2-1. If we have three points arranged along a route as shown, and if none of their ideal weights is predominant, then the transfer orientation is always to the middle point.[6]

Applying the same technique to System 2 of Fig. 3-4, we find the optimum point is the junction *J*. In System 3 it is *A, J,* or *B,* depending on the relative lengths of the route segments *AB, BJ, AJ* and the ideal weights of *A, B,* and *C.* And in System 4 it could be *A, B,* or *C.* We note, then, that in every one of the four systems the optimum location is always at an intermediate point (one from which routes lead in at least two directions) and never at an end point.

This holds true regardless of the ideal weights *so long as none is predominant,* and regardless of the length of the dead-end route segments (*AB* and *BC* in System 1; *AJ, BJ,* and *CJ* in System 2; *CJ* in System 3). Finally, it is quite immaterial which of the points are markets and which are input sources. In these illustrations, I deliberately avoided such identification.

It is clear that when none of the ideal weights predominates, we cannot predict the orientation of a locational unit simply on the basis of its inputs and outputs; we can say, however, that it will not locate at dead ends but at points reachable from at least two directions—whether these be input sources, markets, or junctions.

General Locational Effect of Transfer Rates Rising Less than Proportionally with Distance

The ideal weight, or force of attraction of a transfer cost factor of location, is really an expression of the extra cost imposed per unit of added distance: in other words, the marginal cost of transfer with respect

---

[5] See Robert Dorfman, "Mathematical or 'Linear' Programming: A Nonmathematical Exposition," *American Economic Review,* 43 (December 1953), 797–825.

[6] This conclusion throws some additional light on the significance of the shape of the locational polygon where the route constraint is ignored (see Figs. 2-3 and 2-4 in the previous chapter). In Fig. 2-4, the locational triangle was compressed so that the obtuse corner was the optimum transfer location. As the triangle is squeezed, it obviously approaches closer and closer to the configuration of a single line, with the obtuse-corner point becoming the intermediate point on the line, like point *B* in System 1 of Fig. 3-4.

to distance. Our initial image of the relation of transfer cost to distance (Fig. 3-1) showed this marginal cost as almost uniform, corresponding to a constant ideal weight regardless of distance.

The more realistic transfer rate gradient in Fig. 3-3, flattening off at longer distances, implies that ideal weights and the locational pulls of transfer cost factors are not constant but systematically weaker at long range and stronger at short range. If we seek a physical analogy, then, it should not be that of a weight on a string as in the Varignon Frame, nor a spring, but a force something like gravitation or magnetism.

This feature of transfer rates tends to enhance the advantages of location at input sources and markets and to reduce the likelihood of location at intermediate points. Each input source and market point, in fact, becomes a "local optimum" location, in the sense that it is better than any location in the immediately adjacent area. The search for the most profitable location for a unit, then, is a little like the search for the highest altitude in a landscape studded with hillocks and minor and major peaks. In such a landscape we could not rely on getting to the highest point by simply continuing to walk uphill, but would have to make some direct comparisons of the heights of various peaks. Similarly, a program for determining the ideal location of a transfer-oriented activity unit generally cannot rely entirely on gradients of transfer cost or measurements of ideal weights but at some stage must incorporate direct comparison of specific source and market locations.

This principle is illustrated graphically in Figs. 3-5 and 3-6. In Fig. 3-5, we have the transfer charges per unit of output as they would be at various points along a route running through the input source and the market point. The two black lines show how the input transfer and output transfer charges per unit of output vary with location of the facility. The white line at the top of the figure shows total transfer charges on a unit of output plus the amount of input required to produce it.

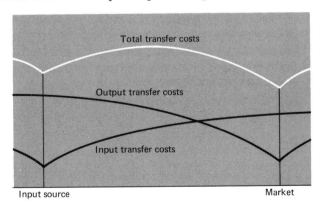

Fig. 3-5. Gradients of Transfer Cost on Input and Output, per Unit of Output

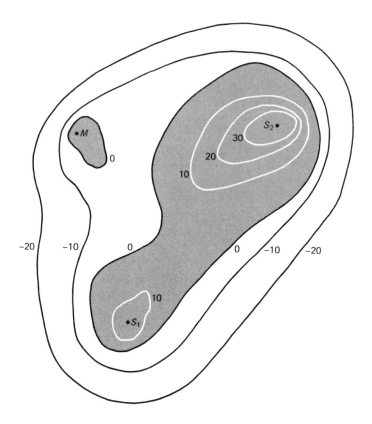

Fig. 3-6. Isoprofit Lines for a Transfer-oriented Activity (Profits are positive for locations within the shaded areas)

It will be observed that there are local minima of total transfer charges at the input source and at the market. In this case, the total costs for a location at the market would be slightly lower than for a location at the source, but both are much lower than those at surrounding locations.

Fig. 3-6 shows a two-dimensional pattern of profits with three transfer points involved: They could be, say, two input sources and a market. Here the profits per unit of output[7] are shown by contour (isoprofit) lines connecting points of equal advantage. A local peak appears at each of the three points with that at S_2 the highest.

---

[7] We are assuming that all inputs and outputs other than those specifically mentioned are ubiquitous, so that processing costs would be the same at all locations. The activity is assumed to be wholly transfer oriented.

Modal Interchange Locations

It has been suggested above that the long-haul discount characteristic of transfer costs and rates lessens the transfer advantages of locations which are neither sources nor markets for transferable inputs and outputs. Some kinds of intermediate points, however, are relatively attractive in terms of transfer costs.

Most transfers involve one or more changes of mode or other terminal type of operation en route rather than proceeding right through from initial origin to final destination. This situation becomes more frequent as the variety of available transport modes increases, each with its special advantages for longer or shorter hauls, larger or smaller shipments, high speed or low money cost, and so on.

Textbooks generally tell us that points of transshipment or modal interchange, such as ports, are particularly strategic locations because location of a processing facility at such a point "eliminates transshipment costs." Such a statement is, however, quite misleading. Let us take a simple example: a flour mill. Grain is collected at an inland point connected by rail to a port, from which there is shipping service to a market for flour. We want to choose among three possible locations for the mill: the grain-collection point, the port, and the market. Let us denote the elements of cost as follows, per barrel of flour:

M Milling cost
L Cost of each loading of grain or flour
U Cost of each unloading of grain or flour
R Cost of shipping grain or flour from the collection point to the port
W Cost of shipping grain or flour from the port to the market

The costs involved, for each of the three mill locations, are, then, as follows:

Mill at the grain-collection point		Mill at the port		Mill at the market	
M					
L		L		L	
R	flour	R	grain	W	grain
U		U		U	
		M			
L		L		L	
W	flour	W	flour	R	grain
U		U		U	
				M	

In each case, the total cost is the same: $M+R+W+2(L+U)$. Though the transshipment point location is apparently just as good as either of the others, it has no special advantage. In fact, we might suspect that more realistically it would be under some handicap. With either of the other two locations, it might be possible to transfer the grain or flour from rail to ship (the U and L operations at the port) at less cost than is involved in the two separate port transfers (grain from rail to mill, and flour from mill to ship) which are involved if the mill is located at the port.

If we modify the above case by assuming that flour is more costly to ship, unload, or load than is grain, then the most economical location is at the market; location at the grain-collection point would be less advantageous, and location at the port would be intermediate in terms of cost.

Clearly, then, we must explain the observed concentrations of activity at ports and other modal interchange locations on the basis of other factors. Some (the transport advantages of junction points with converging or diverging routes) have already been mentioned. A modal interchange point is likely to have such nodal characteristics, if only because different transfer modes have route networks of different degrees of fineness, so that where they come in contact, there is likely to be more than one route of the mode with the finer network.

The focusing of transfer routes upon points of modal interchange reflects scale economies in transfer and terminal operations, and sometimes also the lay of the land. Thus, along a coastline suitable natural harbors are limited in any event, and scale economies tend to restrict the development of major ports to an even smaller selection of points. The same applies to crossings of a mountain range or a large river.

A further characteristic advantage of modal interchange points is that they are likely to be better provided than most other points with specialized facilities for goods handling and storage.

Finally, additional attraction to modal interchange points arises because many modes of transfer serve only a limited set of points along their routes. In Fig. 3-7, we examine the case of a stretch of territory between an input source S and a market M. There is air freight service between the airports at A_1, A_2, and A_3, and transfer of input and output between source, airports, and market is performed by truck. Processing costs and the costs of local inputs are assumed to be the same at all locations, so that the choice of location for the processing facility is simply a matter of minimizing total transfer cost.

Trucking charges on input from any point follow a continuous gradient like $S'F$, with SS' representing the minimum local trucking charge that is incurred even if the facility is located at an airport. Such gradients are erected upon S, B, and C to indicate transfer costs involving truck hauls from the source, A_2, and A_3 respectively.

Similarly, trucking charges on output follow a gradient like $M'P$. Such gradients are erected upon M, D, and E to indicate output transfer costs involving truck hauls to the market, A_2, and A_1 respectively.

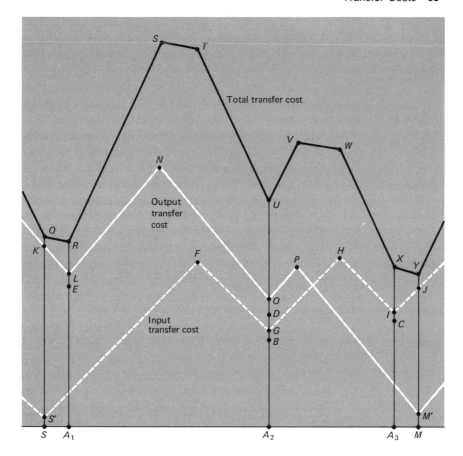

Fig. 3-7. Hypothetical Gradients of Transfer Cost Involving Two Transfer Modes (Costs are per unit of output)

Truck charges on input from S to A_1, plus air freight charges from A_1, are A_2B to A_2 and A_3C to A_3. Truck charges on output from A_3 to M, plus air freight charges to A_3, are A_2D from A_2 and A_1E from A_1.

In transferring the input, the cheapest combination of truck and air will presumably be used, so the gradient $S'FGHIJ$ represents costs of transporting the input from the source to any given location. Similarly, the gradient $KLNOPM'$ represents costs of transferring output from any given location to the market.

Summing these two gradients gives the gradient of total transfer costs, $QRSTUVWXY$. In this case, the gradient has a minimum (MY) at the market, which is therefore the most economical location for the facility. There are local minima $(A_1R$ and $A_2U)$ at two of the airport locations, which illustrate the strategic advantages of modal interchange points.

SELECTED READINGS

John R. Meyer, M. J. Peck, J. Stenason, and C. Zwick, *The Economics of Competition in the Transportation Industries* (Cambridge, Mass.: Harvard University Press, 1959).

Benjamin Chinitz, *Freight and the Metropolis*, a report of the New York Metropolitan Region Study (Cambridge, Mass.: Harvard University Press for the Regional Plan Association, 1960).

Benjamin Chinitz, "The Effect of Transportation Forms on Regional Economic Growth," *Traffic Quarterly*, 14 (1960), 129–142. Reprinted in Gerald J. Karaska and David F. Bramhall, *Locational Analysis for Manufacturing* (Cambridge, Mass.: The M.I.T. Press, 1969), 83–96.

Gunnar Olsson, *Distance and Human Interaction: A Review and Bibliography* (Philadelphia: Regional Science Research Institute, 1965).

R. E. Quandt and W. J. Baumol, "The Demand for Abstract Transport Modes: Theory and Measurement," *Journal of Regional Science*, 6 (1966), 13–23.

APPENDIX 3-1

Rate Discrimination by a Transfer Monopolist
(See page 39)

Assume that a good is to be shipped to various markets from a single point of origin. At each market the quantity sold (and consequently the quantity shipped to that market) will be

$$q = a - b(p + r)$$

where p is the price at the point of origin (the same for all markets) and r is the transfer charge.

The transfer agency's cost of carrying the good to a market x miles away from the point of origin is $(g + tx)$ per ton, where g is terminal cost and t is line-haul cost per mile.

On shipments to a market at a distance x, therefore, the transport agency will make a net return of

$$Z = (a - bp - br)(r - g - tx)$$

Differentiating,

$$dZ/dr = a - bp - 2br + bg + btx$$

and the most profitable rate to charge (r^*) is calculated as follows:

$$a - bp - 2br^* + bg + btx = 0$$

$$r^* = \frac{a - bp + bg}{2b} + \frac{1}{2}tx$$

The ideal tariff will be a flat charge equal to

$$\frac{1}{2}\left(\frac{a}{b}+g-p\right)$$

plus half the line-haul cost for each mile of haul.

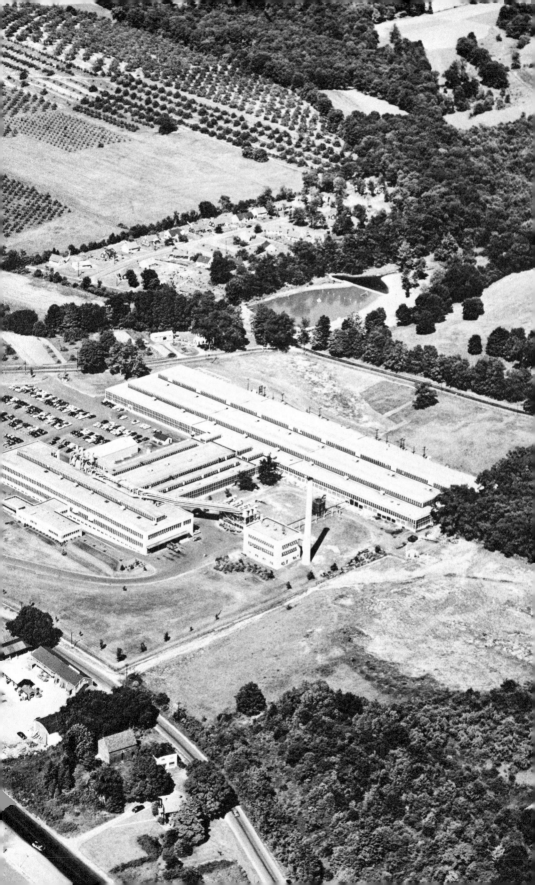

INTRODUCTION

Unit Locations and the Pattern of an Activity

So far, we have considered only the location preferences and decisions of the individual unit. We now move to a different level of inquiry in which attention is focused on the patterns in which similar units array themselves.

We shall refer to an "activity" as a category of closely similar location units.[1] In manufacturing, this corresponds to an "industry" such as flour milling or job printing. In trade or services, we speak of a "line" of business in the same sense. We shall extend the term "activities" to cover analogous groupings such as residential units of a particular class, types of public facilities with a particular function, and so on. Thus, the postal system is an activity, with a spatial pattern comprising the locations of many post offices.

Location patterns can take various forms, as we see when we set out to map the locations of different activities. The pattern of the copper smelting industry could be shown as a small number of dots, each representing one smelter. Fashion garment factories are found mainly in tight clusters (such as in midtown Manhattan), each of which contains many firms. Automobile dealers in urban areas tend to be concentrated in linear clusters. Particular crops, or types of farming, are often found in continuous zones which they preempt to the exclusion of any other major activity.

Sometimes the location pattern of an activity is a planned configuration because there is just a single decision unit involved. In a nonsocialized economy, however, this situation is confined essentially to certain types of public facilities (such as schools within a city school system) and to the few lines of private businesses that are controlled by total monopolies. More characteristically, the location pattern of an activity is the unplanned outgrowth of the behavior of the many location decision units making up the activity.

4
Location Patterns

---

[1] Martin Beckmann, in his *Location Theory* (New York: Random House, 1968), adopts a different terminology in which "activity" corresponds to what I have been calling "locational unit" and "industry" to what I call "activity."

The evolution of location patterns cannot be explained simply in terms of the factors governing individual unit locations which were examined in Chapter 2. In going to the more macro level of analysis corresponding to the activity, we need to recognize two further considerations: *competitive survival* and *interdependence*.

Competitive Survival

Individuals and business firms (particularly new and small firms) must make location decisions in the face of great uncertainty, and are strongly influenced by personal preferences and constraints not closely related to any calculus of money cost, revenue, or profit. Tables 4-1 and 4-2[2] illustrate typical findings of surveys of management attitudes on location.

TABLE 4-1. Reasons Given for Location of Manufacturing Establishments in New England

Principal reason for locating in New England	All firms	New firms	Branch plants	Plant relocations
Personal reasons	37	29	2	6
Market advantages	28	7	11	10
Production relationships	19	1	18	—
Material availability	11	2	6	3
Management relationships	8	1	6	1
Labor considerations	6	2	2	2
Other considerations	9	—	8	1
Total	118	42	53	23

SOURCE: George Ellis, "Why New Manufacturing Establishments Located in New England: August 1945 to June 1948," *Monthly Review of the Federal Reserve Bank of Boston,* 31 (April 1949), 6.

"Personal reasons" are prominent among the location factors identified, and this is especially true of small and new firms.

Establishment of new locations is, however, only one of the ways in which the locational pattern of an activity is altered. The mortality among new and small firms is high, and establishments are continually being abandoned or converted to other uses. Business locations, whether based on wisdom, profound study, personal whim, or guesswork, have to meet the test of survival.

> A good analogy is the scattering of certain types of seeds by the wind. These seeds may be carried for miles before finally coming to rest and nothing makes them select spots particularly favorable for germination. Some fall in good

[2] Both tables were reproduced in Charles M. Tiebout, "Location Theory, Empirical Evidence, and Economic Evolution," *Papers and Proceedings of the Regional Science Association,* 3 (1957), 81.

TABLE 4-2. Reasons Given for Location of Manufacturing Establishments in Michigan*

Reasons for location in Michigan	Number of workers in plant		
	100 or more	Less than 100	All plants
Personal reasons	46% †	75%	51%
To be near markets	39	10	33
Enabling factors	12	10	12
To be near materials	10	2	8
Available manpower or skills	5	9	6
Assistance or encouragement by local groups	2	1	2
Other miscellaneous reasons	6	5	5

* The sample intentionally excluded automobile manufacturing firms.

† Totals add up to more than 100 percent because many respondents gave more than one answer.

SOURCE: Julia Kessler (ed.), *Industrial Mobility in Michigan* (Survey Research Center, Institute for Social Research, University of Michigan, December 1950), 40.

places and get a quick and vigorous start; others fall in sterile or overcrowded spots and die. Because of the survival of those which happen to be well located, the resulting distribution of such plants from generation to generation follows closely the distribution of favorable growing conditions. So in the location of economic activities it is not strictly necessary to have both competition and wise business planning in order to have a somewhat rational location pattern emerge: either alone will work in that direction.[3]

The role of the invisible hand of competition in promoting efficient location patterns should not be overstressed. The "survival test" may weed out multitudes of small mistakes in location, though at a substantial cost in wasted resources. *Big* mistakes in oligopolistic activities—for example, in the location of a steel mill or a major transport terminal—are considerably more durable. Not only is the fixed investment greater and the competitive pressure less threatening, but in addition such a facility

---

[3] E. M. Hoover, *The Location of Economic Activity* (New York: McGraw-Hill, 1948), p. 10. This point has been further developed by Armen A. Alchian, "Uncertainty, Evolution, and Economic Theory," *Journal of Political Economy*, 58 (June 1950), 211–221, and by Tiebout, *op. cit.* Tiebout (p. 85) cites the case of brewing, in which "in the evolutionary struggle to survive, Milwaukee gained the dominant position," and that of the automobile industry in which Detroit emerged as chief victor in the struggle. In both instances, personal or other "fortuitous" factors played a large part in the initial locations.

Another interesting case is that of the Hershey Chocolate Co., an early giant in its industry. The founder chose the location for the works and for the planned town of Hershey because he had grown up in that part of Pennsylvania and wanted to live there. The locational decision was based on personal preference. But at the same time it happened to be an excellent choice in terms of access to milk and imported cocoa beans, nearness to the largest market centers, and labor supply. Without those economic advantages, Hershey's success would certainly not have been so great, and he might even have failed or moved elsewhere.

radically changes its environment. It may attract a variety of complementary activities, and, in any event, will build up a larger local market, thus partly "justifying itself." The need for informed planning of locations in order to forestall misallocation of resources is obviously greater where large-scale units or complexes are involved.

Such major decisions are in fact based on more objective criteria and fuller information than is the typical small-unit location. In Tables 4-1 and 4-2, we see that the influence of "personal reasons" is far less for larger plants, for relocations, and for branch plants of multiunit firms than it is for small initial locations.

Interdependence

Competition among business firms is merely one of the countless ways in which locations depend upon one another—a fact that we conveniently ignored in Chapter 2 when considering just one unit at a time. Whether they be factories, stores, public facilities, offices, or homes, individual location units are never indifferent to locations of other units of the same kind, but can be either repelled or attracted by them. Proximity can be an advantage or a disadvantage, or sometimes both at the same time. We shall first look at activity patterns shaped by *mutual repulsion* among the units, or "dispersive" forces, and then consider the contrasting kinds of patterns in which *mutual attraction,* or "agglomerative" forces, dominate.

PATTERNS DOMINATED BY DISPERSIVE FORCES

Business firms often go to some pains to select locations where there is no nearby competition; and householders likewise shy away from too much proximity with other households, whether from a desire to avoid high rents or congestion, a desire for privacy, or a dislike for some particular category of neighbors. These are instances of locational repulsion among units of the same specific or general type. But several different basic reasons for a dispersed pattern can be identified.

One reason is competition for scarce local inputs, such as land, privacy, quiet, or clean air or water. A high concentration of occupancy makes these local inputs scarcer and more expensive, and discourages further concentration. The importance of this effect is so great that we shall devote the entire next chapter to it.

Another reason for an activity to have a dispersed pattern is that the activity is output oriented and its markets are dispersed. Thus, an effective demand for generally used consumer goods exists wherever there are people with income; and a closely market-oriented activity like grocery stores will have a pattern closely resembling that of population. The individual stores prefer locations apart from one another, because they are selling basically the same items and the customers will tend to patronize the nearest store. The demand for the goods of any one store will be greater where there is little or no nearby competition. As a result of this mutual repulsion, the stores are widely distributed. The degree of dispersion (the closeness of fit to the market pattern) is limited only by the high costs of operating a small store, and the pattern thus represents an economic compromise between the factors of market access and scale economy.

Where scale economies call for a still further restriction on the number of separate units that can survive, we find individual units selecting not just neighborhoods but cities or regions on a similar basis of avoidance of proximity: They try to find a relatively undersupplied area where the competition is least intense. In both the intracity and the intercity situation, the individual unit has a "market area" within which it has the advantage of better access to the market than its competitors.

Similarly there are activities, oriented to the supply of transferable *inputs,* that tend to have a dispersed pattern because the pattern of input sources is itself dispersed. Crop-processing activities in agricultural areas are an example. Individual cheese factories, beet sugar refineries, and the like repel one another in the sense that each can get its inputs more cheaply or easily if it has a "supply area" to itself and is to that extent insulated from competition.

We shall now examine more closely these types of activity patterns involving market areas or supply areas. For brevity's sake, the discussion will refer basically to market areas, but it should be kept in mind throughout that the same principles apply to supply areas as well.

Market Areas

First, we may note that the importance of keeping a distance from one's rivals, and the feasibility of carving out a market area, depend on the degree of interchangeability of one's products with those of the competitors. If the products are not closely standardized, the buyers cannot be relied on to prefer the cheapest nor to patronize the nearest seller. But if the products are standardized, there are likely to be considerable scale economies in producing them, since there is relatively great scope for mechanization and even automation of processes and the organization and management problems are simpler.

Some economies of large scale refer to the size of the individual establishment or *location unit,* while others depend primarily on how large the *firm* is. The economically justifiable size of the individual location unit is constrained by the fact that larger size requires a larger market area and increased transfer costs; but the size of the firm is not under that constraint, and may be associated with such substantial savings in costs of management, purchasing, research, advertising, and finance that it is profitable for one firm to operate a number of separate location units. Branch plants are increasingly common in manufacturing and utilities, as are chain stores in retailing. Within the past few decades, multiunit firms have assumed a notably larger role in such activities as hotels and motels, automobile rental, restaurants, theaters, and university education. This trend probably reflects, at least in part, the improvement of communications and data processing and management techniques which have widened the scope of economies of large-scale management more than they have affected the scale of individual establishments.

Consequently, one of the important types of market area patterns is that involving the sales or service areas of *different branch units of a single firm*—here the relationship among units is obviously different from what it is when the units belong to rival firms.

The simplest case of market area patterns to consider is that involving a completely standardized output, equal operating costs for all sellers, and transfer costs increasing linearly with distance.

Between any two sellers' locations under these conditions, the "natural" market area boundary will be a straight line that bisects at right angles a line drawn between the two locations. For all markets on one side of the line, the seller on that side has the advantage of lower output-transfer cost; on the other side of the boundary, the other seller has the advantage. In any direction where there is no competition, a seller's market area

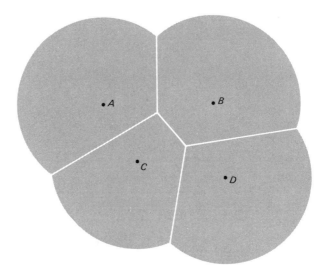

Fig. 4-1. Market Areas of Four Locations with Equal Production Costs and Equal Transfer Costs per Mile

will extend outward to some limiting distance beyond which there will be no sales at a price that would cover costs including transfer: That part of the market area boundary, then, will be a circular arc. This situation is shown in Fig. 4-1 for a set of four competing sellers.

The case just described is, of course, too simplified to represent any real situation; but it serves as a convenient point of departure for discovering the effects of various more realistic conditions upon market areas. First, the costs at the two selling locations are unlikely in practice to be exactly equal. If they are unequal, the market area boundaries look more like the one in Fig. 4-2, bending away from the lower-cost seller's

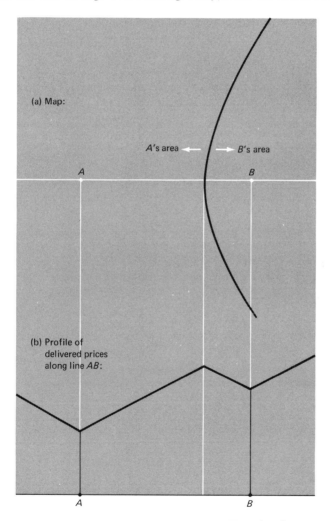

Fig. 4-2. Market Areas of Two Sellers with Equal Transfer Costs per Mile but Different Levels of Production Cost

location. The boundary, in this case, comprises all markets at which the sellers' cost differential at their respective locations is exactly offset by the extra transfer cost from the lower-cost seller.[4] Under our assumption of transfer costs rising linearly with distance, the boundary can never be a closed curve—that is, the lower-cost seller can never have a market area entirely surrounding that of the higher-cost seller.

Another possibility is that the two sellers incur different costs of transfer per ton per added mile. The result is shown in Fig. 4-3 for a set of three

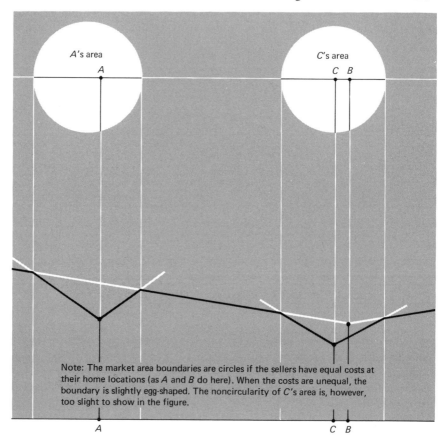

Note: The market area boundaries are circles if the sellers have equal costs at their home locations (as A and B do here). When the costs are unequal, the boundary is slightly egg-shaped. The noncircularity of C's area is, however, too slight to show in the figure.

Fig. 4-3. Market Areas with Both Production Costs and Transfer Costs Unequal

---

[4] If transfer costs rise linearly with distance, and if seller A's costs are $1 a ton lower than seller B's, the distance of any point on the boundary from A will exceed the distance of that point from B by a fixed amount—the distance for which the line-haul cost of transfer is $1 a ton. The shape of the market area boundary will be a hyperbola, since a hyperbola can be defined as the locus of all points whose distances to two fixed points differ by a fixed amount.

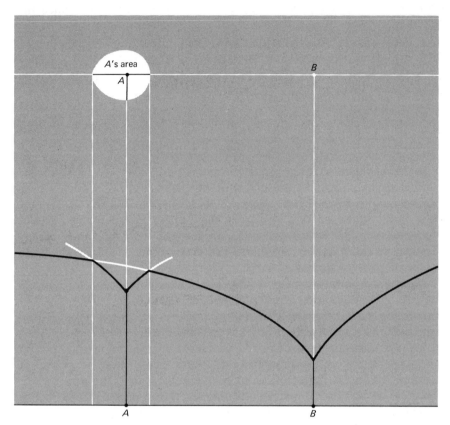

Fig. 4-4. Surrounded Market Area Resulting from Characteristic Long-haul Economies of Transfer

sellers, with *B*'s transfer costs lower than those of *A* or *C*. This might reflect the situation if, for instance, *B* is shipping his product in a more easily transportable form, is conducting his own transport operation with superior efficiency, or has been able somehow to make more advantageous arrangements with transport contractors than have his competitors. The market area boundary is now a closed curve: *B*'s market area completely surrounds those of *A* and *C* (the white areas). In this particular situation, we have the additional curious result that *B* cannot sell at his home location but only elsewhere!

Fig. 4-4 demonstrates that market surrounding can occur even if both sellers are subject to the *same* transfer tariff—simply by virtue of the characteristic long-haul discounts.

Market area surrounding of this type, resulting from the normally convex shape of transfer rate gradients, is extremely common in practice. Consider, for example, the circulation area of a major metropolitan newspaper in relation to the circulation areas of suburban and small-town newspapers in the same region, or the market areas of "national" brands of beer vis-à-vis those of local brands. The counterpart in terms of *supply* areas appears in the milksheds of small cities, completely surrounded by the larger milksheds of larger cities. The geographic price pattern for the product, in this case, is like that of a land surface rising to a mountain peak but punctuated with various hillocks and mounds on the slopes.

Market-Area Overlap and Pricing Policies

So far in this discussion of market and supply areas, we have concentrated on the "natural" areas for a fully standardized product—each seller's natural market area comprises those markets that he can supply at a lower delivered cost (costs at the seller's location plus transfer charges) than the sellers at any other locations. Under these circumstances, we might expect cleanly defined areas, similar to those shown in the accompanying figures.

In practice, however, market and supply area boundaries are blurred, and the areas somewhat overlap. This can result from "absorption" of part of the added transfer costs of distance by any of the three parties involved: the transfer agency, the buyers, or the sellers.

Reference was made in Chapter 3 to the practice of simplifying transfer rate schedules by setting a uniform rate over a whole "mileage block," or range of distances. When this is done, there are likely to be zones where the areas of two or more sellers overlap, as shown schematically in Fig. 4-5. Such overlap would be still more common if the time cost of transfer did not increase with distance (except in the case of telecommunications or electric power transmission) even when the rate charged may not.

The *buyers* can be regarded as absorbing some of the extra transfer costs of distance whenever they do not rigorously observe the principle of

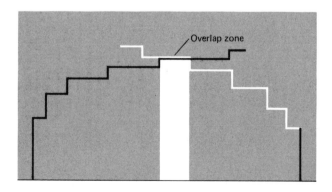

Fig. 4-5. Overlap of Market Areas Resulting from Bracketing of Transfer Rates

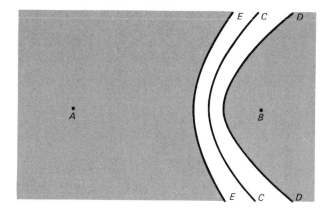

Fig. 4-6. Overlap of Market Areas Resulting from Diversity of Buyer Preferences

buying the cheapest good or service of a given type (or, if they are doing the transferring themselves, as in the case of retail shopping, patronizing the most easily accessible seller). In the real world, the buyer does not often show this perfectly neutral attitude toward competing sellers, but for one reason or another has a preference even if the prices are equal. Such preference is least likely to be an important consideration in business purchases of such standardized goods as wheat or cement, and most likely to occur for retail purchases of such highly differentiated or even "personalized" items as medical or educational services, high fashion clothing, and recreation. It is important to note that the buyer-preference factor will produce market area overlap, but only to the extent that buyers have *diverse* preferences. Thus, in Fig. 4-6 (where it is assumed that A produces more cheaply than B), the line CC might be the market area boundary for buyers who are neutral to A's goods as compared to B's, and would simply choose whichever is cheaper at their location. For those who believe that A's product is really worth 5¢ a pound more than B's, the boundary will be DD, which runs through points where the delivered cost from A is 5¢ greater than from B. For those who believe that B's is worth 5¢ a pound more than A's, the boundary will be EE. Assuming that at every location there are buyers representing the whole intermediate gamut of preferences, the "boundary" or zone of overlap will comprise the belt between DD and EE. Both A and B will make sales throughout this overlap zone, though each will predominate in the part that is closer to him.

Finally, it may be *sellers* who are absorbing some of the added costs of distance. The one case where this is unlikely to happen is the special case mentioned earlier, in which the sellers are branch units of a single firm, public agency, or other multilocation decision unit. It is ordinarily in the interest of a firm or agency to distribute the product from its various facility locations in such a way as to minimize the total cost of supplying any given pattern of demand. This will ordinarily rule out "crosshauling" or overlap of the market areas of those facility locations (except to the extent that it might reflect transfer cost absorption on the part of buyers or transfer agencies, as already considered). Accordingly, specific sales territories are allotted to the various branches. These market areas tend to be larger for branches with lower cost or higher capacity, and larger where demand is sparse than where it is dense.

Such definitive demarcation of areas is even more prevalent in public and administrative agencies. The Federal Reserve System divides the United States into twelve districts, and within some districts there are subdistricts such as the Pittsburgh branch of the Cleveland Federal Reserve Bank. Similarly, every federal government agency with field activities has its set of districts exclusively allocated to their respective branch offices.

In other activities, however (including most lines of business), the market rivalry between selling locations mainly involves rival firms rather than different branches of the same firm. This situation introduces considerable possibilities for transfer cost absorption and consequently market area overlap, depending on the pricing policies that the firms find advantageous.

What might seem at first to be the logical or "normal" pricing policy is to let the buyers pay the transfer charges. The seller charges a uniform f.o.b. price (that is, price at his own location, before transfer) to all buyers, and more remote buyers pay that price plus all the expenses associated with transfer. In fact, in some instances, such as most kinds of retail trade, the buyer gets the product at the seller's location and transfers it himself. Under this policy of uniform f.o.b. pricing, there is no transfer cost absorption by the sellers, and the market areas are formed subject to the various conditions already described.

Such a pricing system is, however, not necessarily a norm in the sense of being more rational, more usual, or more conducive to the public interest than any other system. If at any one location there is just a single seller or a small enough number to cooperate with one another, there are inviting opportunities to extend that location's market area by "absorbing freight"—that is, discriminating in favor of more distant buyers. The extreme situation involves *complete* freight absorption, with the seller paying all transfer charges (and presumably setting a price that covers *average* delivery costs plus his other costs). In that case, each seller sells at a uniform *delivered* price to buyers in various locations but receives a smaller net revenue per unit on his sales to the more distant buyers. Each seller then can afford to serve only those markets within a maximum distance determined by how much transfer cost he can afford to pay and still cover his out-of-pocket costs. Market areas (if transfer rates are the same in all directions) will thus be circular, and will overlap if the sellers are sufficiently close together. In zones of overlap, all the participating sellers share equally in sales. It is still to the interest of each seller (insofar as he is market oriented) to locate close to concentrations of demand and far from competitors.

More sophisticated pricing policies entail a *partial and selective* absorption of transfer costs by the seller: Neither the f.o.b. price nor the delivered price is uniform on sales to different markets. The resulting patterns of price and market areas will depend largely on the extent to which competitive pricing is based on short-term or long-term advantage.

The various sellers may take a long-term view of the possibilities and decide that they will all be better off the more closely they can collectively approximate the behavior of a single profit-maximizing monopolist. Such a monopolist, if he likewise took a long-term view, might well set his prices somewhat below levels that would yield the maximum immediate profit, in order to avoid encouraging the entry of new firms.

If the sellers do pursue such a policy of complete collusion, cooperation, or foresight (whichever may be more appropriate for the case in hand), they will behave like branch units of a monopolistic firm or agency, which means that in general they will observe clean-cut market area boundaries and avoid unnecessary transfer costs, such as might be involved in cross-hauling. There could still be some market area overlap, but only to the extent that the transfer agency or the buyers absorb transfer costs in the ways discussed earlier (involving mileage-block rates and qualitative preferences respectively).

How much of the transfer charges will be absorbed by the sellers, assuming they are not under any external prohibition against spatial price discrimination? Presumably, the answer will be the same regardless of whether we consider an actual monopoly with separate branch locations or a set of sellers at different locations who find it in their mutual interest to price as would a single monopoly.

It turns out that (if we assume linear demand schedules at the markets) the sellers will maximize their profits by systematically discriminating against the nearer markets, absorbing exactly half of the transfer expenses.[5]

---

[5] This conclusion can be reached mathematically as follows: Assume that at any market the sales are $a - bp$, where p is the delivered price, and that variable costs per unit of sales are c. Net receipts from sales to any market, over and above transfer expenses and variable costs, are then $(a - bp)(p - c - t)$, where t is the unit transfer expense to that market. By differentiating this expression with respect to p and setting the derivative to zero, we find that the net receipts are maximized if p, the delivered price, is equal to $(c + a/b)/2 + t/2$. The first term in this expression is the price that buyers are to be charged at the seller's location, where transfer costs are zero. It is the average between c (variable costs) and a/b (the price at which no sales would be made, that is, the vertical intercept of the demand curve). For sales to all other markets, the ideal delivered price increases with distance just half as fast as the transfer cost does. (Compare Appendix 3-1.)

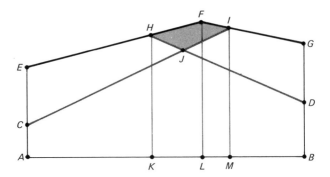

Fig. 4-7. Market Area Invasion with Freight Absorption

If the sellers' locations and the market locations are given, the market area boundaries will be in the same places regardless of whether the sellers follow this ideal discriminatory pricing policy or a nondiscriminatory policy under which delivered prices include the full transfer costs. Indeed, the areas will still be unchanged if the monopoly firm or the monopoly-simulating set of sellers chooses to absorb all of the transfer charges and sell at a flat delivered price, while at the same time choosing to avoid crosshauling. This situation will, of course, require that the market area boundaries as well as the uniform delivered price be agreed to and specified.

If the individual sellers are not so far-seeing or cooperative as we have here assumed, they will try to invade each other's market areas by cutting prices. Consider the situation diagrammed in Fig. 4-7, where sellers at *A* and *B* are competing for markets along the line between them, *AB*. The out-of-pocket costs of the two sellers at their own locations are *AC* and *BD*. Each, initially, is selling on the basis of an ideal system of price discrimination in favor of remoter buyers and absorbing half the transfer costs, thus, *A*'s delivered prices follow the gradient *EF* and *B*'s follow the gradient *GF*. The lines *CI* and *DH* represent out-of-pocket costs plus full transfer costs from *A* and from *B* respectively. It should be noted that the ideal discriminatory delivered prices *EF* and *GF* rise at exactly half the slope of *CI* and *DH*, since the sellers are systematically absorbing half of the transfer costs. The market area boundary is at *L*, where the delivered prices are both equal to *FL*.

In this situation, *A* may see a short-run gain in undercutting *B*'s delivered prices to points as far as *M*, thus stealing the market territory *LM* away from *B*. The possible invasion cannot go any farther, however, because when *A* sells to point *M* at a delivered price *MI* he is barely covering his out-of-pocket costs including transfer charges. *B* can logically be expected to retaliate by cutting his delivered prices along the whole stretch

KM, thus staging a counterinvasion of *A's* market area. Carried to its logical conclusion, this game will produce a delivered price schedule *EHJIG.* Between *K* and *M, A* and *B* will be sharing the market. What has happened is that the market area boundary is now a zone rather than a line; the sellers are both making less profit; and the pattern of locational advantage for the buyers has changed, with locations in the competitive zone *KM* now more economical than they were before. The shaded area in the figure shows the maximum extent of price cutting.

The various cases discussed do not by any means exhaust either the theoretical possibilities or the variety of spatial pricing systems actually used by firms. Notably, there is the "basing-point" system, which has at various times been used in selling steel and other products. It is most often used in situations where the sellers are few and their market orientation is strongly constrained by access to transferable inputs, large-scale economies, and large fixed investments, and where the amount and location of demand fluctuate widely. In a basing-point system, there is an agreed pattern of delivered prices observed by all the sellers: The price at any market is the lowest sum of the fixed f.o.b. price at a basing point plus the actual transport charges from that basing point to the market. Basing points can be established at one, some, or each of the sellers' locations. In such a system, all sales entail some freight absorption except those by a seller at a basing point to markets within the area governed by his basing point; there is likewise a considerable amount of market area overlap and crosshauling. For further discussion of this and still other variants, the curious reader will have to look elsewhere.[6]

Choice of Locations and the Pattern of an
Output-oriented Activity

The preceding discussion of market areas and spatial pricing policies has described the behavior of sellers at *given* locations. What does this tell us about where they will *prefer* to locate?

Regardless of the price strategy involved, an output-oriented seller will still try to find the most rewarding location in terms of access to markets. He will not simply be comparing individual markets nor, as a rule, access to all markets wherever situated. Rather, he will have to evaluate the advantage of any location on the basis of how much demand there will be within the market area that he could expect to command from that location. Each location that he might choose entails a market area and a

---

[6] Handy references on the varieties of spatial competition and pricing systems include Martin Beckmann, *Location Theory* (New York: Random House, 1968), 30–50; M. L. Greenhut, *Microeconomics and the Space Economy* (Chicago: Scott Foresman and Co., 1963); and Fritz Machlup, *The Basing-Point System* (Philadelphia: Blakiston, 1949).

sales potential determined by where the buyers are and where the competition is.[7]

The best location from this viewpoint is one where demand for his kind of output is large relative to the nearby supply. This suggests that he will look for a "deficit area" into which the output in question is flowing in preference to a "surplus area" out of which it is flowing. The direction of flow is "uphill" in the sense of increasing price of the output; thus he will be attracted toward peaks in the pattern of prices rather than toward low points. In other words, he will try to find the largest *gap in the pattern* of already-established units of his activity as the most promising location for himself. If demand for the outputs of his activity were distributed evenly, he would simply look for the location farthest from any competition: that is, the center of the largest hole in the pattern. Since any new unit will aim to fill gaps in this way, the tendency will be toward an equal spacing of units of the activity, with market areas of approximately equal size and shape.

If the market areas had to be literally identical and symmetrical, there are only three possible market area shapes that would completely fill up the space: equilateral triangles, squares, or hexagons. Any other uniform shape (for example, circles) would leave gaps. This geometrical constraint has intrigued theorists but is scarcely relevant to the real world, where demand is not spread evenly, competitors and sites are not identical, and transfer costs do not simply rise linearly with distance in all directions.

Output Orientation and Patterns of Nonbusiness Activities

As was noted earlier, market areas and supply areas are not peculiar to profit-motivated business activities. Public agencies, and a variety of private and semipublic institutions whose outputs and inputs are mainly services given rather than sold, are likewise subject to the factors of transfer cost and scale economy that give rise to market area or supply area patterns. In some cases, the boundaries of such service areas are administratively defined and perfectly clean cut, for example, police or electoral precincts, dioceses, tax collection districts, areas of citizens' associations, or chapter areas of a fraternal lodge or professional association. In others, there is a considerable market area overlap. Thus, church worshippers or

---

[7] In an activity characterized by blurred market area boundaries for any of the reasons discussed earlier, evaluation of the market potentialities of any location is somewhat more complicated; the locator must estimate what his market share will be in the penumbra of his market area where it overlaps with that of one or more competitors. See also the discussion in Appendix 2-1.

communicants need not choose the nearest church of their denomination; and colleges, welfare agencies, and social clubs likewise compete spatially, though generally they have a limited area of market dominance. There are always added transfer costs in operating at a greater distance, but these can be absorbed by the provider, the transfer agency, or the recipient.

The principle of mutual repulsion between units of the same transfer-oriented activity likewise holds good in many nonbusiness activities. Thus, a philanthropic agency, group, or individual setting up neighborhood recreation centers or nursery schools in an urban ghetto will be able to give better service if the units are spaced so that they are more accessible from different parts of the "market," and each will have its "market area."

Still further extension of the concept of attractive and repulsive forces is involved when we recognize such factors as the individual's desire for privacy. Human beings and other animals have strong preferences for maintaining certain critical distances from their fellows, when interacting socially or even when simply minding their own business, and social anthropologists have uncovered some interesting ethnic and intercultural differences as to what is regarded as the optimum degree of proximity. The study of these preferences and their physical and psychological bases has obviously much to contribute to our understanding of the stresses induced by crowding and to the proper design of facilities for urban living —here as elsewhere, the economist becomes keenly aware of the limitations of a narrow disciplinary approach in dealing with complex human problems.[8]

PATTERNS DOMINATED BY COHESION

In sharp contrast to the market area or supply area patterns of activities in which there is strong spatial repulsion among the individual units, other activities show highly clustered patterns.

Cluster is, of course, the logical pattern for units of an output-oriented activity whose markets are concentrated at one or a few locations and correspondingly for units of an activity oriented to inputs whose source locations are few. There is a high concentration of producers and suppliers of theatrical inputs such as actors, stage designers, and theatrical makeup specialists in Los Angeles and New York because so much moviemaking and theater activity is concentrated there. The making of vintage wines is confined to relatively few areas where the right kinds of grapes will flourish.

---

[8] A fascinating popular treatment of such space relations as the anthropologist sees them is Edward T. Hall's *The Hidden Dimension* (New York: Anchor Books, 1966).

Output Variety and Market Attraction

There are other situations, however, where the basis for clustering is the mutual attraction among the competing units of a particular activity, and this attraction outweighs any repulsion that might arise from their rivalry. Thus, it is frequently alleged that a chainstore firm makes a practice of locating branch stores as close as possible to the stores of its leading competitors. A tendency toward agglomeration is unmistakable in the juxta-position of car salesrooms along "automobile rows" and in the formation of financial districts, nightlife districts, civic centers, produce markets, and high-class shopping areas in cities. The larger the city, the more specialized and numerous are such neighborhood agglomerations. In New York, large advertising agencies are so clustered along a section of Madison Avenue that the street has given its name to the industry. Similarly, a section of Seventh Avenue is preempted by the garment trades, part of 46th Street by diamond merchants, and so on for many other specialties. The common feature of all such clusterings is that each unit finds the location good *because of the presence of the others:* There is a positive *mutual attraction* rather than a repulsion. The explanation of such mutual-attraction clusters lies in special characteristics of the activity itself, its markets, or its suppliers.

In some activities, the basic reason for the agglomerative tendency is that the outputs of individual units are not standardized; they are not perfect substitutes for one another, and, moreover, they differ in such manifold and changing ways that they cannot be satisfactorily compared by the buyer without actual inspection. The locational significance of this characteristic can best be seen by a pair of contrasting examples.

A manufacturer buying sheet steel simply decides on his specifications and then finds out which steel producer will give him the best price and the fastest delivery. It would not occur to him to visit warehouses or rolling mills to look over the sheets and make his selection, because the specifications themselves (plus conceivably a sample sent to him for testing in his own plant or laboratory) fully identify what he is getting. Consequently, the transfer costs involved are those of shipping the steel from producer to user, and there is nothing in the situation that would make it desirable or convenient for the rival sheet steel producers to be concentrated in one place.

Contrast this with a man buying a car, his wife buying a new hat, a department store selecting its line of fall fashions, or a fashion designer searching for something simply devastating in the way of novelty buttons. In any of these cases, the buyer does not know exactly what he is going to buy. He will be selecting one item (in the case of the car) or maybe more (in the case of the hat) or a very large number (in the case of the department store's fall line). The items cannot be adequately described in a catalog, and it would be much too expensive and time consuming for the producers to supply each prospective buyer with a full set of samples. Under these circumstances, the "demand" is not so much demand for specific items as it is demand for a *varied display of products;* and the wider the variety presented at a particular location, the more demand that location will attract.

Therefore, the buyer makes a shopping trip, preferring the largest display center accessible to him. The more he is prepared to spend, the farther he will be prepared to go in the interest of variety. Thus, most of us would be willing to journey farther out of our way to select a camera than a necktie; still farther to select a new car; and still farther to select a job with career possibilities or a child for adoption.

It is clear that the activity that is presenting the displays will tend to adopt a clustered pattern, with its units positively attracting one another. A newcomer to the cluster may even be welcomed, because he enriches the variety and draws still more demand to the location.

It should be noted that the significant transfer costs in this kind of situation are borne by the buyer, and their major element is personal travel time. The transfer of the goods bought may be handled by the buyer himself (he may drive his new car home or carry his other purchases). In any event, however, the transfer cost is not enough to counteract the advantage (to both buyers and sellers) of having the selling units agglomerated.

When the purchases are transferred separately, it is, of course, feasible to separate production from display. Thus, new car dealers sometimes have to order from the nearest assembly plant after the buyer has made his choice; and in recent years more and more garment producers have moved their factories out of the city in order to reduce production costs, and maintain in the city only the functions of display and associated entertainment for the out-of-town buyers.

These examples illustrate one important kind of external economy of agglomeration of an activity: "external" to the individual unit involved, because the advantages depend on how many other units of its type are joining it to make a cluster that attracts demand.

External Economies and Scale

Some closely analogous external economies of agglomeration involve supply of inputs, and these tend to affect many of the same activities. If products are complexly differentiated and changeable from one day or week to the next, the chances are that at least some of the inputs also share those characteristics. Thus, a fashion garment shop will have a constantly changing need for different fabrics, thread, buttons, zippers, and the like. With the nature of the output continually changing, manpower needs can vary unpredictably and suddenly; with speedy delivery at a premium and production scheduling intricate, equipment repairs and parts must be quickly available. Since perhaps the most important task of the manager is to estimate what the buyers will want and what his rivals will offer, a crucial input is fresh information, gathered largely by mixing with the right people and keeping the eyes and ears open.

Every one of these input requirements, plus others, is best satisfied in a tight cluster. The basic reason can be made clear by the following example. Suppose we have a small plant that manufactures ladies' coats. A long sequence of separate operations is involved, including such operations as cutting and binding the buttonholes. Specialized equipment exists for making buttonholes rapidly and cheaply in large quantities, but it represents a sizable investment. The individual coat manufacturer would not find it worthwhile to invest in such a machine since he could not keep it busy all the time; he has to resort to making his buttonholes in a slower way, involving greater labor cost. However, if he is located in a cluster with enough other clothing manufacturers, their combined need for buttonholes may suffice to keep at least one of the specialized buttonhole machines reasonably busy. In that event, a separate firm specializing in buttonhole making joins the cluster. The clothing manufacturers contract that operation out to him, to the advantage of all concerned, including the customer who gets the coat cheaper.

This example can be extended to embrace dozens of other individual operations which likewise can be delegated to specialized firms when there is a cluster, enabling a sufficient number of firms using the specialized service to enjoy convenient access to the specialist.

Three highly significant facts emerge here. First, we have explained an *external* economy for the clothing manufacturers in terms of the *internal* economies entailed in the specialized operations (the buttonhole-making establishment and other such auxiliary suppliers must have at least a certain minimum amount of business or they cannot cover their fixed costs). Second, the result of the mutually beneficial symbiosis of the garment makers and the buttonhole maker is that the former are now also more specialized: They are confining themselves to a narrower range of operations, and for any given level of output of coats they will have smaller plants and fewer employees. This in itself is an advantage: The principal constraint on the size of their plants is the complexity of management decision making in an industry where the products are continually changing (in response to or in anticipation of a volatile demand), orders are small, and the production cycle is extremely short in time. A further constraint, in many cases, is supply of capital for the individual entrepreneur.

Third, in such an industry there is little or no rationale for the development of multiplant firms. As we have just noted, the economic size of the individual plant is effectively limited by the problems faced by management. There is no point in the firm's establishing branch plants since all the activity is at one location and the management must constantly give close attention to what is going on inside the plant. This situation contrasts sharply with that of a business like food retailing, where the constraint upon the size of an individual store is the maximum size of its market area (reflecting transfer costs). The multistore firm enjoys great advantages in mass purchasing, advertising, research, financing, and management; the optimum firm size far exceeds the optimum size for a single store unit.

We can thus distinguish three levels at which economies of size appear. There are, in respect to any particular activity, (1) economies associated with size of the individual *location unit* (plant, store, or the like); (2) economies associated with the size of the individual *firm;* and (3) economies associated with the size of the agglomeration of that activity at a *location*. We can refer to these, for brevity's sake, as "unit," "firm," and "cluster"[9] economies, and the size at which each of these economies peaks can be thought of as the optimum *unit* size, the optimum *firm* size, and the optimum *cluster* size.[10]

These optima are determined by the characteristics of the activity, including its locational sensitivity to transfer costs and other locational factors. When firm optimum is larger than unit optimum, there are multiunit firms with operating branches, ordinarily in different locations, as in retail chains and some kinds of manufacturing. Otherwise, the single-unit firm is the norm. When cluster optimum exceeds the optimum for units or firms, there are multiunit and/or multifirm clusters of the activity; otherwise, separate locations are the norm, as is illustrated by primary processing plants for farm or forest products.

Lichtenberg's Study of "External-Economy Industries"

The classic analysis of the clustering of certain manufacturing industries on the basis of agglomeration economies external to the individual location unit and firm was made in the late 1950s by Robert M. Lichtenberg

---

[9] What are identified here as "cluster" economies are sometimes referred to as economies of localization. Alfred Marshall's succinct characterization of the "economies of localized industries" is often quoted from his *Principles of Economics*, 8th ed. (London: Macmillan, 1925), Book IV, Ch. X. F. S. Hall's Census monograph, "The Localization of Industries" (U.S. Census of 1900, *Manufactures,* Part I, pp. cxc–ccxiv), reported on the development of highly clustered patterns of individual manufacturing industries toward the end of the nineteenth century. Unfortunately, however, the term "localization" has also been used synonymously with "location" and even in the sense of dispersion, so it is best avoided.

[10] A thorough and original discussion of business organization and location in terms of these several optima is in E. A. G. Robinson, *The Structure of Competitive Industry,* rev. ed. (Chicago: University of Chicago Press, 1958).

TABLE 4-3. Manufacturing Industries Relatively Concentrated in New York City by External Economies

Industry	New York Metropolitan Region's share of total U.S. employment (percent)
Hatters' fur	99.9*
Lapidary work	99.5*
Artists' materials	91.9*
Fur goods	90.4
Dolls	87.4*
Schiffli-machine embroideries	86.5
Hat and cap materials	85.7
Suspenders and garters	84.7*
Women's neckwear and scarves	84.7
Hairwork	82.7*
Embroideries, except Schiffli	80.0
Tucking, pleating, and stitching	76.8
Handbags and purses	75.6
Tobacco pipes	75.3
Millinery	64.7
Children's coats	61.6
Belts	60.9*
Artificial flowers	60.6
Women's suits, coats, and skirts	58.8
Dresses, unit price	58.7
Furs, dressed and dyed	56.9*
Umbrellas, parasols, and canes	54.5*
Robes and dressing gowns	54.3
Small leather goods	53.1
Miscellaneous bookbinding work	53.0*
Handkerchiefs	49.8*
Buttons	49.5
Trimmings and art goods	49.0
Men's and boys' neckwear	48.3
Watchcases	48.1*
Phonograph records	48.0*
Books, publishing and printing	46.8
Periodicals	46.5
Lamp shades	46.0
Corsets and allied garments	45.9
Children's outerwear, n.e.c.†	43.2
Knit outerwear mills	42.3
Blouses	41.7
Finishing wool textiles	41.5
Bookbinding	41.1
Jewelry	40.5
Suit and coat findings	39.6
Costume jewelry	39.5
Children's dresses	39.3
Men's and boys' cloth hats	38.0
Waterproof outer garments	37.6

Industry	New York Metropolitan Region's share of total U.S. employment (percent)
Printing ink	34.7
Coated fabrics, except rubberized	34.5*
Women's and children's underwear	34.4
Luggage	34.3
Apparel, n.e.c.	34.0
Needles, pins, and fasteners	33.8
Jewelry and instrument cases	33.7
Engraving and plate printing	33.6
Miscellaneous publishing	33.3
Curtains and draperies	32.9
Typesetting	32.9
Straw hats	32.8*
Women's outerwear, n.e.c.	32.7
Jewelers' findings	32.6*
Games and toys, n.e.c.	32.1
Engraving on metal	30.4
Leather and sheep-lined clothing	30.4
Textile products, n.e.c.	30.4
China decorating for the trade	29.0
Housefurnishings	28.9
Photoengraving	28.2
Book printing	25.5
Electrotyping and stereotyping	25.5
Fabric dress gloves	25.3
Greeting cards	25.2
Galvanizing	24.4*
Candles	23.5
Mirror and picture frames	22.7
Men's and boys' suits and coats	22.3
Knitting mills, n.e.c.	21.2
Finishing textiles, except wool	20.6
Signs and advertising displays	20.4
Plating and polishing	18.7
Knit fabric mills	18.3
Lithographing	17.9
Enameling and lacquering	16.7
Statuary and art goods	16.6
Commercial printing	16.5
Felt goods, n.e.c.	16.0*
Narrow fabric mills	15.4
Dresses, dozen-price	12.9

* Approximate figure estimated by Lichtenberg: exact figures unavailable because of Census disclosure rules.

† n.e.c.: not elsewhere classified.

SOURCE: Robert M. Lichtenberg, *One-Tenth of a Nation* (Cambridge, Mass.: Harvard University Press for the Regional Plan Association, 1960), 265–268; based on data from U.S. Census of Manufactures, 1954.

for the New York Metropolitan Region Study. Table 4-3 lists 87 industries which he identified as dominated by external-economy factors of location and which are relatively concentrated in the New York Metropolitan Region.

"Relatively concentrated" means that the Region's share of national employment in the industry exceeded 10.4 percent (which was the Region's share of total national employment, and which accounts for the title of Lichtenberg's book.[11]

Lichtenberg's study provides documentation and illustration on some of the points we developed earlier. Table 4-4 sums up some salient characteristics of those manufacturing industries that he rated as least affected by transport orientation. It covers, in his words, "all industries for which the dominant locational factor is inertia, labor, or external economies, and those for which no dominant locational factor could be assigned." It is clear from this tabulation that prevalence of single-unit firms (which we previously noted as a characteristic of industries clustered because of external economies) is associated with small size of plants, high labor intensity (as suggested by small energy use per worker), and (for consumer goods industries) small inventories implying fast turnover.

Table 4-5 examines the relation between degree of concentration in New York and proportion of single-plant firms, in the same set of industries as in the preceding table. Industries most heavily clustered in the New York Metropolitan Region are consistently characterized by a prevalence of single-plant firms. In other words, New York as the chief metropolis of the nation appears to have strong special attractions for industries of the single-plant type; which, as Table 4-4 showed, are characterized by small units and high labor intensity.

Table 4-6 compares average plant sizes (number of employees per establishment) in the New York Metropolitan Region and the United States as a whole, for different classes of industries. In transport-sensitive industries selling to national markets (the first row of figures in the table), the situation is roughly as follows: New York plants are *larger* than plants

---

[11] Robert M. Lichtenberg, *One-Tenth of a Nation* (Cambridge, Mass.: Harvard University Press for the Regional Plan Association, 1960). Lichtenberg's list of "external-economies industries" includes five more, in which the Region's share was less than 10.4 percent: industrial patterns and molds, separate trousers, men's dress shirts and nightwear, woolen and worsted fabrics, and special dies, tools, and metalworking machinery attachments. He does not explicitly categorize any nonmanufacturing activities as external-economy oriented, though he does discuss the heavy concentration of central offices of large industrial corporations in the New York Metropolitan Region. Among the 500 largest such corporations as listed by *Fortune* magazine in 1959, 155 (31 percent) maintained their headquarters in the Region. The Region's share was greater still for the largest corporations, rising to 44.2 percent of those with $750 million or more in assets (*op. cit.*, Ch. 5 and specifically Table 37, p. 155).

TABLE 4-4. Characteristics of Industries Other than Transport-sensitive,* Classified by Domination of Single-plant Firms, United States, 1954

Industries grouped by percentage of plants operated by single-plant firms	Average number of employees per establishment	Horsepower per employee	Inventory of materials, supplies, and fuels as percentage of sales	
			Consumer goods industries	Intermediate goods industries
Very high (95% and over)	25	1.5	5.1%	6.8%
High (90–95%)	47	2.1	6.6	7.2
Low (80–90%)	81	3.5	6.3	6.7
Very low (under 80%)	308	8.4	7.7	6.5

* This table covers 261 "4-digit" manufacturing industries—all except those in the transport-sensitive category. In other words, it includes all industries for which the dominant locational factor is inertia, labor, or external economies, and those for which no dominant locational factor could be assigned. They are all considered to be national-market industries.

SOURCE: Robert M. Lichtenberg, *One-Tenth of a Nation* (Cambridge, Mass.: Harvard University Press, 1960), Table 8, p. 57; based on data from U.S. Census of Manufactures, 1954.

TABLE 4-5. Industries Other than Transport-sensitive,* Classified by Domination by Single-plant Firms† and by Concentration in New York Metropolitan Region, 1954

Industries grouped by percentage of plants operated by single-plant firms	Number of industries in which Region's share‡ of national employment is:			
	30% or more	20–30%	10–20%	Under 10%
Very high (95% and over)	47	8	7	4
High (90–95%)	16	12	7	10
Low (80–90%)	16	9	20	22
Very low (under 80%)	10	9	18	46

* Like Table 4-4, this table covers all 4-digit industries not classified as transport-sensitive. All 261 industries are considered to be national-market industries.

† Based on data for the United States, not Region.

‡ In some industries, the Region's share had to be estimated by Lichtenberg because the Bureau of the Census, following its "disclosure rule," furnished the Region's employment only within a range. In these cases, he took the midpoint of the range.

SOURCE: Robert M. Lichtenberg, *One-Tenth of a Nation* (Cambridge, Mass.: Harvard University Press, 1960), Table 9, p. 62; based on data from U.S. Census of Manufactures, 1954.

elsewhere in industries that show a definite tendency to concentrate in New York (that is, the Region has more than 20 percent of national employment), and in other industries they are *smaller*. In a market-oriented industry, we should expect that the main centers of the industry would have the largest plants, since they are the locations with best access to markets, and the economic size of plants in such industries is constrained primarily by the added transport costs involved in serving a wider market area. In addition, at least four of the transport-sensitive national-market industries[12] most heavily concentrated in New York (chewing gum, rattan and willow ware, copper refining, and cork products) use imported materials, and New York's status as a major port of entry helps to explain its advantage.

The external-economy industries, which are nearly all rather highly concentrated in the New York Region, show a significantly contrasting size relationship. Despite the great prominence of New York as a location for such industries, the plants there are *smaller* than those elsewhere. This

TABLE 4-6. Average Number of Employees per Establishment in the New York Metropolitan Region and the United States, 1954, by Locational Category and Degree of New York Concentration of Industries

| | New York Region's share of total U.S. employment | | | | | | | | | |
| | 30% and over | | 20–30% | | 10–20% | | 5–10% | | Under 5% | |
	Reg.	U.S.	Reg.	U.S.	Reg.	U.S.	Reg.	U.S.	Reg.	U.S.
Transport-sensitive	n.a.*	n.a.	n.a.	n.a.	n.a.	n.a.	n.a.	n.a.	n.a.	n.a.
National market	276	139	232	187	106	86	89	157	86	214
Sectional and										
local market	n.a.	n.a.	n.a.	n.a.	n.a.	n.a.	n.a.	n.a.	n.a.	n.a.
Not transport-										
sensitive†	52	47	132	122	219	236	70	97	30	170
External-economy	27	31	29	34 ⎫	‡		‡		‡	
Other	117	87	162	148 ⎭						

* n.a.: Not shown by Lichtenberg.

† Includes all industries for which the dominant factor is inertia, labor, or external economies, and those for which no dominant locational factor could be assigned (that is, the same set of industries as are covered in the two preceding tables).

‡ External-economy industries were not separately distinguished in the classes of industries where the Region's employment is less than 20% of the United States total, since they were a very small proportion of the total of non-transport-sensitive industries in those classes.

SOURCE: Robert M. Lichtenberg, *One-Tenth of a Nation* (Cambridge, Mass.: Harvard University Press, 1960), Table 5, p. 46, and Table 10, p. 64.

should be expected according to the considerations already discussed. A plant of an external-economy industry located in New York is in a position to contract out more operations to specialists, like our buttonhole maker. Within any Census industry classification, those firms and plants which to the greatest degree share the special characteristics of clustered external-

---

[12] Lichtenberg provides a full listing of industries by locational category in his Appendix B, *op. cit.*

economy activities (such as variable demand and product, rapid production cycle, and low degree of mechanization) will be the ones most likely to find the New York location attractive; and those characteristics are, as we have seen, strongly associated with small plant size. Plants in the same Census industry located elsewhere are more likely to be turning out a less variable kind of product, and their optimum plant size is somewhat larger.

Thus, industries of the clustered type as a class have the peculiar characteristic of operating in smaller units (in terms of both plants and firms) in locations of major concentration than they do elsewhere.

Single-activity Clusters and Urbanization

The advantages of a clustered location pattern for certain types of activities are now apparent. But what does such a cluster contain besides the major beneficiary of those advantages?

There are certainly some types of cluster that need contain nothing else —for example, "automobile rows." Here the mere juxtaposition of a number of salesrooms makes the area attractive to prospective buyers, and that is the basis of the agglomeration tendency. The same is true for many other types of "single-activity" neighborhood cluster in cities, such as art shops, antique stores, second-hand bookstores, wholesale and retail produce markets, and the like.

But in each of those cases, what really draws the buyers is variety: There would be no advantage in agglomeration (so far as buyers are concerned) if the wares of the different sellers were identical. Accordingly, still other product lines or activities may contribute to the advantage of the cluster, provided they offer something that the same buyers might want to pick up on the same trip. In this way, the attractions of a cluster of high fashion dress shops may well be enhanced by the addition of a shop specializing in high fashion shoes or jewelry, or even a travel agency catering to high-income travelers. At a more plebeian level, the familiar suburban shopping center includes a wide assortment of retail trade and service activities. The developers of the center usually plan rather closely in advance the kinds of businesses to be included and take pains to pin down at least some of the key tenants (such as a department store branch, a bank, or a movie theater) even before ground is broken. Other relatively broad and diverse clusters based on attraction of a common demand are recreation centers and cultural centers.

A cluster in which availability of common inputs plays an important role (such as in the external-economy industries analyzed by Lichtenberg) is also more likely to be a complex of closely related activities than just a clump of units of one activity. Thus, an essential part of a cluster that is advantageous to garment manufacturers is a variety of related activities such as machine rental and repair; designing; provision of special components such as buttonholes, fasteners, and ornaments; trucking services; and so on. Indeed, the Lichtenberg list includes such ancillary activities indiscriminately along with the producers of garments and other final products; this is quite fitting since the tightly knit complex of activities really yields the external economies that help motivate the cluster.

But where does this stop? Some of the contributing activities (like buttonhole making) may be so specialized that they help just one line of activity; but others (such as trucking or forwarding services, entertainment facilities for visiting buyers, and a variety of business services) are not so restricted. They are essentially elements of a large urban agglomeration. Their presence, and the quality and variety of the services they offer, depends more on the size of the *city* than on the size of the local concentration of any one of the activities they serve.

There is a continuous gradation, then, between external economies reflecting *concentration of a single activity* and external economies reflecting *urban size* ("urbanization economies"). The latter are basic to the whole question of city formation, function, and structure, which will be discussed in Chapters 6, 10, and 11. Some of the advantages that a particular activity gets by concentrating in New York could not be duplicated by simply having an equal amount of that activity clustered in, say, Columbus, Ohio —though, of course, it is possible that Columbus might offer some compensating attractions of a different nature.

There have been, and still are, some noteworthy multifirm clusters of single activities in relatively small places (historic examples are glove making in Gloversville, New York; hat making in Danbury, Connecticut, and furniture making in Grand Rapids, Michigan).[13] But it is apparent that this type of single-activity cluster (in which the bulk of an activity is found in a few "one-industry towns") has rather gone out of style since Hall proclaimed its heyday in 1900. Such concentrations depended heavily on the external economies of a pool of specialized labor skilled in operations peculiar to one industry, and often predominantly of one nationality group;[14] on a reservoir and tradition of entrepreneurship similarly specialized; and on the inertial factor of acquired reputation. Technological changes and enhancement of the mobility of labor and entrepreneurship explain why such local specialization has become increasingly rare. On the other hand, external economies on the broader basis of urban size have remained a powerful locational force.

---

[13] F. S. Hall's 1900 Census monograph, previously cited, gives numerous further examples.

[14] Economic historians have often noted the important role of the influx of Germans to the United States in the mid-nineteenth century in establishing concentrations of certain industries in which they had special skills, such as optical and other scientific instruments in Rochester, brewing in Milwaukee and St. Louis, and tanning and shoemaking in these and other midwestern cities.

MIXED SITUATIONS

In order to bring out certain controlling factors, we have been considering sharply contrasting types of activity location patterns. We have distinguished patterns dominated by mutual *repulsion* from those dominated by mutual *attraction*. We have also distinguished patterns involving *market* areas from patterns involving *supply* areas.

It is now time to recognize that in the real world there are various intermediate stages between the extreme cases described. In one and the same activity, it is not uncommon to find (1) dispersive forces dominant at one level and agglomerative forces at another level of spatial detail, or (2) coexistence of market area and supply area patterns. Let us take a brief look at each of these types of "mixed" situations.

Attraction Plus Repulsion

In any given activity, the forces of repulsion and attraction among units are both usually present in some degree, even though one generally predominates. Thus, in an activity characterized by a mosaic of market areas, some of the locations will have more than one plant, store, or other such unit. Though we think of retail grocery stores or gasoline stations as primarily mutually-repulsive, it is not uncommon to find groupings of two or more adjacent competitors showing some degree of mutual attraction. Being at essentially the same location, these rival units are likely to share the same market area, though one might have a somewhat wider reach than another. If we think of them as simply sharing "the market area of that location," the statements made earlier about market area determination and pricing policies are still largely valid, except that spatial pricing systems involving systematic transfer cost absorption become less feasible when the seller is not alone at his location.[15]

Similarly, an activity that we think of as basically clustered, like the making of fashion garments, often has several widely separated clusters. Among the external-economy industries of New York enumerated in Table 4-3, it will be noticed that only a few come close to being *exclusively* concentrated in the New York Region. The rest are also found in substantial, lesser clusters in other large cities. One reason for replication of clusters is, of course, that over long distances transfer costs (in time if not in money) become a significant constraint on concentration relative to far-flung markets or input sources. Thus, when we look at the country as a whole, we see a pattern of market or supply areas showing some force

---

[15] If there are many sellers at one location so that they are in nearly perfect competition, any seller could dispose of his entire output while confining his sales to that part of the market providing the largest profit margin: Consequently, any attempt to establish a discriminatory pricing system would break down.

of mutual repulsion among competing centers. If such an activity is concentrated primarily in, say, New York, Los Angeles, and Chicago, there will be three roughly demarcated market areas or supply areas, each shared by all the members of the corresponding cluster. In this connection, it is much more likely that market areas rather than supply areas will be involved, since most external-economy activities produce transferable outputs that need fast delivery to rather widespread markets, and their transferable inputs come from fewer sources and are of a more staple character.

Coexistence of Market Areas and Supply Areas, when Both Sellers and Buyers Are Dispersed

Somewhat different from the case just discussed is a not uncommon situation in which there are many selling locations and many markets, and not necessarily any significant clustering tendencies at all. Sales from one producing district are distributed over many market points, and at the same time any one market district buys from many supplying points. The situation does not lend itself to analysis purely in terms of a set of supply areas or a set of market areas. How, then, can we most effectively analyze such a pattern?

Except in the unlikely situation in which the patterns of supply and demand coincide (which would mean that no transfer is required and that each point is self-sufficient in this particular product), there will be surplus areas, where local demand exceeds local supply. The product will be transferred from surplus areas to deficit areas; and in order to motivate the flow, there must be a price differential corresponding to the costs of transfer along the paths of flow.

The relationship between price patterns and transfer can be demonstrated as follows. Suppose we were to map the spatial variations in the price of the good, depicting a "price surface" by plotting a set of contour lines, each connecting points at which the price is at some particular level. The isoprice lines ("isotims") corresponding to the highest prices would occur in the principal deficit areas, and those corresponding to the lowest prices would occur in the principal surplus areas. The price gradient along any path would be determined by the frequency with which we cross successive isoprice contours as we traverse that path. Shipments of the commodity would be most likely to occur along the paths with the steepest price gradients, and such paths would cross the isoprice lines at right angles. Actual shipments would occur wherever there is a price gradient at least as steep as the gradient of transfer costs; and in an equilibrium situation, we should expect that these shipments would result in no price gradient being substantially steeper than the transfer cost gradient.

Such a graphic analysis does not, however, explicitly recognize the relation between supply and demand patterns that creates the price differentials giving rise to shipments. William Warntz has suggested an empirically feasible short-cut method of measuring this supply-demand relation, which utilizes the device of the "access potential index" described in Appendix 2-1.[16]

For any given point *i,* we can construct an index of local and nearby supply, or "access to supply," by the following formula:

$$S_i = \Sigma \left(\frac{s_j}{t^x_{ij}} \right)$$

where s_j is the output at any supply location *j,* t_{ij} is the transfer cost from that supply location *j* to the given point *i,* and *x* is an exponent empirically chosen to provide the best fit to the observed statistics. For the same point *i,* we can also construct an index of local and nearby demand, or access to market by the analogous formula:

$$D_i = \Sigma \left(\frac{d_j}{t^x_{ij}} \right)$$

With both indices derived for each location, we can identify surplus areas as those where the supply index is greater than the demand index and deficit areas as those for which the demand index is greater than the supply index. We should expect that spatial variations of the price of the good should be positively correlated with the demand index and negatively correlated with the supply index; this expectation was borne out in some of Warntz' studies of the price patterns of agricultural commodities.

SELECTED READINGS

P. Sargant Florence, *Investment, Location, and Size of Plant* (Cambridge, Eng.: University Press, 1948); also the sequel, *Post-War Investment, Location and Size of Plant* (Cambridge, Eng.: University Press, 1962).

C. D. Hyson and W. P. Hyson, "The Economic Law of Market Areas," *Quarterly Journal of Economics,* 64 (1950), 319–327.

Charles M. Tiebout, "Location Theory, Empirical Evidence, and Economic Evolution," *Papers and Proceedings of the Regional Science Association,* 3 (1957), 74–86.

E. A. G. Robinson, *The Structure of Competitive Industry,* rev. ed. (Chicago: University of Chicago Press, 1958).

Robert M. Lichtenberg, *One-Tenth of a Nation* (Cambridge, Mass.: Harvard University Press for the Regional Plan Association, 1960).

[16] William Warntz, *Toward a Geography of Price* (Philadelphia: University of Pennsylvania Press, 1959).

Melvin L. Greenhut, *Microeconomics and the Space Economy* (Chicago: Scott Foresman & Co., 1963).

Brian J. L. Berry, *Geography of Market Centers and Retail Distribution* (Englewood Cliffs, N. J.: Prentice-Hall, 1967).

Benjamin H. Stevens and Carolyn A. Brackett, *Industrial Location: A Review and Annotated Bibliography of Theoretical, Empirical and Case Studies* (Philadelphia: Regional Science Research Institute, 1967).

Robert G. Spiegelman, *A Study of Industry Location Using Multiple Regression Techniques,* U.S. Department of Agriculture, Economic Research Service, Agricultural Economic Report No. 140 (Washington, D.C.: U.S. Department of Agriculture, August 1968).

Harry W. Richardson, *Regional Economics* (New York: Praeger, 1969), Chs. 2, 4.

5
Land Use

In the previous chapter, competition for scarce local inputs was identified as one of the factors limiting spatial concentration and favoring the dispersal of activities. We are now ready to see how this works.

The present chapter deals with the dispersive effects of competition for "land" which first and foremost denotes *space*. Every human activity requires some space as standing room or elbowroom. The qualities of land include, in addition, such attributes as the topographic, structural, agricultural, and mineral properties of the site, the climate, the availability of clean air and water, and finally, a host of immediate environment characteristics such as quiet, privacy, esthetic appearance, and so on. All these things, plus the availability of such local inputs as labor supply and community services, the availability of transferable inputs, and the accessibility of markets, enter into the judgment of what a particular site is worth for any specific use.

Labor as a local input will be discussed in Chapter 7. The present chapter will focus almost entirely on space per se as the prototype of scarce local input. But it will be appropriate to keep in mind that in an increasingly populous and urban economy, more and more of what were initially the free gifts of nature (such as water, clean air, and privacy) are assuming the character of scarce local resources, and this scarcity constrains the concentration of activities in somewhat the same way as does the inherent scarcity of space itself. Competition for space in an urban area is highly complex because of the many ways in which an activity affects its close neighbors. Such "neighborhood effects" and "local externalities" have been touched upon in Chapter 4 and will be further explored in Chapters 10–12 as basic features of the urban environment.

COMPETITION FOR THE USE OF LAND

Most land can be utilized by any of several activities. Even an uninhabitable and impassible swamp may have to be allocated between the competing claims of those who want to drain or fill it and those who want to preserve it as a wetland wildlife sanctuary. The normal multiplicity of possible uses means that in considering spatial patterns of land use we can no longer think in terms of the individual location unit (as in Chapter 2) or of one specific activity (as in Chapter 4), but must move up to another level of analysis: that of the multiactivity area or region.

Competition for land plays an especially important locational role in areas where activities tend to concentrate for any reason. Locations having good soil, climate, and access to other areas, and areas suitable for agglomeration under the influence of local external economies, as discussed in Chapter 4, are in demand. The price of land, which is our best measure of the intensity of demand and competition for land, varies with quality and access and rises abruptly to high peaks in the urban areas. Anything we can discover about the locational role of land-use competition, then, has particular relevance to the urban and intraurban problems that have become so important in recent years.

On the other hand, there are activities that need large expanses of land in relation to value of output and are, at the same time, sensitive to transfer cost considerations—agriculture being the most important, though the same considerations apply to forestry and some types of outdoor recreation as well. These activities require so much space that although they do not effectively compete for urban land, their location patterns are strongly affected by competitive uses. Such activities are a second important area of application for land-use analysis.

In societies where land use is governed through a price system, the price of land is identified as "rent,"[1] and in principle each parcel of land goes to the highest bidder. Whoever owns the land will, if he wants to maximize his own economic welfare, see to it that the land goes to that activity and specific "occupant" (firm, household, public agency, and the like) that will pay a higher rent than any other. At the same time, each occupant will ideally compare different sites on the basis of how much rent he could afford to pay for each if he utilized it in the most efficient way available to him, and will look for the site where the rent he could afford to pay exceeds what is charged by the largest possible margin.

Needless to say, land markets are not in fact so perfect in their allocation, nor are owners or users possessed of omniscience or exclusive devotion to the profit motive.

---

[1] Through most of this discussion we shall use the convenient term "rent" to indicate the price for the use of a piece of land. If a new user buys the land instead of renting it from an owner, the price he will have to pay represents a capitalization of the expected rents, at the appropriate going rate of interest. Thus, if each of them could get a 6 percent interest return on capital invested in other ways, the buyer and the seller should agree on $20,000 as a fair price for a piece of land which will be yielding a net rent (after all costs including property taxes) of $1,200 a year for the foreseeable future. At that price, the returns will be 6 percent of the investment.

It is almost equally obvious that allocation of the land based purely on individual profit maximization, even if competition worked more efficiently than it does, could not produce a socially optimum pattern of land use (not even in the sense of maximizing the gross national product, to say nothing of more comprehensive criteria of welfare). Here, as in every other area of economics, some social intervention is required to take account of a wide range of costs and benefits that the existing price system ignores. Just because a paper mill can outbid any other user for a riverside site, it does not follow that it is socially or economically desirable that it should pre-empt the river from other users who would refrain from befouling it. Direct controls upon land use (including zoning ordinances, urban renewal subsidies, and condemnation or reservation of land for public use) are vital elements of rational public policy even where free competition is most enthusiastically espoused.

Socialist countries initially nationalized all land, and attempted to assign it without using any system of market or imputed prices. A retreat from this doctrinaire position has been in evidence in recent years in some of these countries (notably Yugoslavia), with competitive market forces being given an increasing role in land-use allocation, though severe constraints prevail as to the amount of land any one individual may own.

In 1966, four Soviet legal experts pointed out the economic waste involved in allocating land without explicit regard to its productivity in alternative uses. In a striking reversal of orthodox Socialist doctrine, they proposed "that we speed the introduction of a land registry, which would incorporate the registering of land use, a record of the quantity and quality of land, and an appraisal of its economic value." They proposed, further, that the price of land be included in cost estimates of construction projects. "Only thus will a true picture of economies in construction become apparent. Let the economists work out the form, but it seems to us that the attitude that land costs nothing must be decisively rejected."[2]

Despite the fact that Soviet planners had even earlier adopted the practice of including an interest charge on plant and equipment in evaluating projects, the guardians of Marxist orthodoxy have apparently thus far balked at setting any kind of valuation on land. In the most recent statement of land-allocation policy in the U.S.S.R. available at the time of this writing,[3] proposals for pricing the use of land were explicitly rejected: "Use of the land free of charge is one of the greatest achievements of the Great

---

[2] The statement appeared in *Pravda,* May 30, 1966, and was reported in *The New York Times* of that date, p. 12.

[3] A set of draft principles of land legislation submitted in a report by Deputy F. A. Surganov, Chairman of Council of the U.S.S.R. Agricultural Committee. The report was published in *Pravda* and *Izvestia,* December 14, 1968, and in a condensed translation in *The Current Digest of the Soviet Press,* 21, 1 (January 22, 1969), 12–20. I am indebted to my colleague Professor Janet Chapman for this reference.

October Socialist Revolution." Agricultural land use is given priority, with strong restrictions on its expropriation for nonagricultural purposes. Perhaps some glimmerings of a pricing system appear in the provisions for compensation when land is taken over for state or public needs and when agricultural land is reallocated for nonagricultural use. The principal concern appears to be deterrence of such uses where highly productive farm land is involved.

Still another situation applies in many less-developed countries: A few large landowners still own the bulk of the land and have been able to stave off or subvert any efforts to achieve land reform. The adverse effects of this concentration of ownership would be far less if the owners were primarily concerned with maximizing returns from use of the land. They have generally been either inert in the face of such economic opportunities or convinced that their long-term interests are better served by blocking the industrial and political changes that might follow a breakup of the static feudal order in which they attained their positions.

In order to understand the way in which land is allocated to various activities, we shall first ask what determines how strong a bid any particular activity can make for the use of land—that is, what is the maximum rent per acre that that activity could pay for land in various locations. In a society that uses prices, costs, and profits as a principal mechanism for allocating resources, this line of inquiry will help explain actual location patterns. It will also provide a rough guide as to which location patterns represent an efficient allocation of resources from the standpoint of the economy as a whole. Later (particularly in Chapter 12), we shall give more explicit attention to the important problem of divergences between individual interests and the general public interest.

AN ACTIVITY'S DEMAND FOR LAND:
RENT GRADIENTS AND
RENT SURFACES

There are countless reasons why an individual, firm, or institution will pay more for one site than for another. A site may be highly desirable because of its mineral resources, soil quality, water supply, climate, topography, agreeable surroundings, good "input-output access" (that is, from input sources and to markets), supply of labor, supply of public services, prestige, and so on. In fact, the number of possible reasons for offering more for one site than for another is equal to the number of relevant location factors, less one (the price of the site).

For any particular activity, or kind of land use, there is a geographical pattern of site preference, represented by the amounts that practitioners of that activity would pay for the use of each of the various sites. If we picture such a pattern with the activity's "bid rent" (or "rent bid") represented by height, we have a "rent surface" with various hollows at the least useful sites and peaks at the most useful sites. The rent surface for some different land use will have a different conformation, and we shall see later how space can be allocated among alternative uses on the basis of their bids.

First, however, it will be useful to see a bit more clearly how an individual user's pattern of rent bids arises. For this purpose, we shall consider a particularly simple kind of situation, in which site desirability reflects just the one location factor of *market access to a single given market*. We ignore, for the time being, all other distinguishing features of sites. The sites being compared are all within the supply area of a single market center: For example, they might be dairy farm sites comprising an urban milkshed. For still greater simplification, we shall assume that there are so many individual producers in this supply area that each can take the market price as given in deciding about his own output and location preference.

Rent Gradients and Surfaces with Output Orientation

Fig. 5-1 shows a plausible relationship between the various possible amounts of a particular kind of output on an acre of land and the cost of the inputs (other than the land itself) required to produce that output. There are some fixed costs (F), and some variable costs, which rise more and more rapidly as the intensity of use approaches its feasible maximum. Total costs are as shown by TC, and in symbolic terms,

$$TC = F + aQ^b$$

where b is some number larger than 1. The average unit cost curve AC is of the familiar **U** shape. Fig. 5-1 is drawn with F=100, a=1, and b=3.

In Fig. 5-2 we can see how the user of this site will determine the degree of intensity of use (input and output per acre) that will maximize his rent-paying ability. The three diagonal lines show receipts at three possible net prices for the output at this site. They rise proportionately to output since we are assuming that the demand for the output of this producer is perfectly elastic (this is generally the case in agricultural or other activities involving many relatively small sellers).

At the highest of the three prices, which might reflect a location rather close to the market, the receipts curve is OL and the largest surplus of receipts over nonland costs is BC, with an output of OA. Accordingly, BC represents the maximum amount of rent that this activity could afford to pay for the use of this acre. It will be noted that at point C the total cost curve TC has the *same slope* as the total receipts curve at that level of output. In other words, at that optimum level of output, marginal costs are equal to marginal receipts or price.

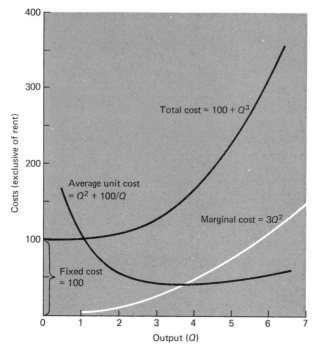

Fig. 5-1. Hypothetical Cost Curve (Exclusive of Rent) for Production on One Acre of Land

At a location more remote from markets, the receipts curve will be *OM,* reflecting a lower net price because of higher transfer costs. In that situation, the best level of output is again the one for which the receipts and cost curves have the same slope; but here, the maximum rent-paying potential of the acre (the *bid rent* of this activity) is zero. At any level of output smaller or larger than *OE,* the land user could not cover costs even on rent-free land, and this acre will consequently be worth precisely zero to him.

At a less advantageous location where the net price is still lower (receipts curve *ON*) there is no level of output that would cover costs, to say nothing of providing anything for rent. The minimum subsidy or negative rent required to make it worthwhile for this activity to use the land would be *HJ,* at an output level *OG.* Once again, this is the output at which the receipts and cost curves are parallel.

Let us assume, then, that our land user acts rationally and so adjusts the intensity of his land use and the output per acre as to maximize the excess of receipts per acre over costs exclusive of rent, and that this excess represents the most he would bid as a rent payment for the acre.

Now let us compare the situation at sites located at different distances from a market, as in Fig. 5-3. At each site, the net price received per unit

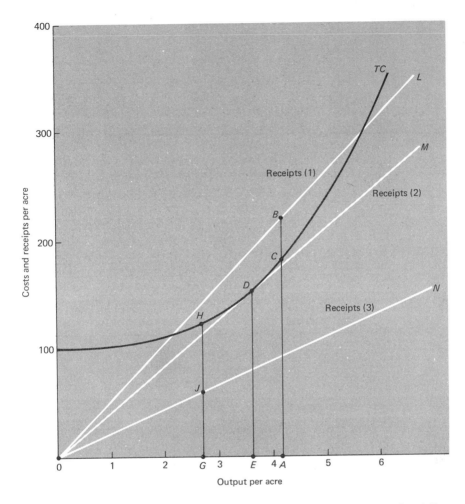

Fig. 5-2. Effect of Change in Output Demand upon Optimum Intensity of Land Use

of output is reduced by the costs of transfer to market. It will be observed that the curve showing rent in relation to net price, in the upper panel of the figure, is concave upward—in other words, the rent falls more rapidly near the market and more gradually farther out. This characteristic feature of rent gradients reflects the fact that we have allowed for some flexibility in the intensity of land use in this activity. Output per acre is larger at locations close to the market: This means that the revenue per acre, and therefore the rent that can be earned, is more sensitive to transport cost at such nearby locations than at more remote locations where a smaller amount of output is shipped from each acre. Of course, if there were complete flexibility in intensity (that is, immunity from diminishing

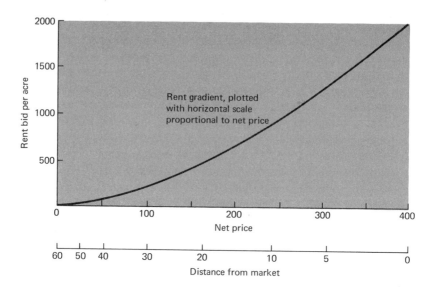

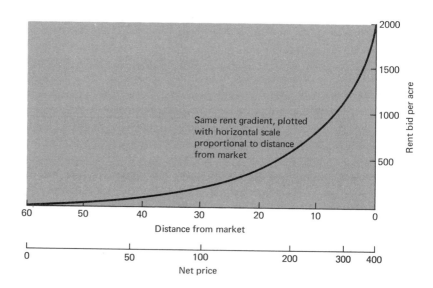

Fig. 5-3. Effect of Long-haul Transfer Economies on Shape of Rent Gradient

returns), all of the activity could best be concentrated in a single sky-scraper at the market. The rent gradient would be almost vertical.

The lower panel of Fig. 5-3 shows the same rent gradient, but this time charted in relation to *distance from the market*. Because of the character-istic economies of long-haul transfer discussed in Chapter 3, the net price of the product will fall more and more slowly with increasing distance: Each extra dollar per ton buys more and more extra miles of transfer as we go farther from the market. Consequently, we can expect rent as a function of distance to have the accentuated concavity shown in the figure.

Over a geographic area, we have a *rent surface* whose basic shape is a cone with its peak at the location of highest possible rent; in the cases discussed here, the peak is at the market.

But for a number of reasons real rent gradients and surfaces are never so smooth and regular as our diagrams suggest. In the first place, we have been assuming throughout that all the land is of equal quality for this particular kind of use, in all respects save access to market. A location or zone of locations with some superior advantages (for instance, higher soil fertility or cheaper labor) would be marked by a hump on the rent surface and a place with higher costs by a dent (or even a complete gap in the surface, if for some reason that activity could not be practiced there at all). The rather common stepwise variation of transfer rates produces a corresponding terracing of rent surfaces. Rent gradients will be flatter along routes of cheaper or better transfer; so if we think of a rent surface around a market as a mountain, it will fall away in sloping ridges along such routes and more abruptly elsewhere. Finally, there is usually more than just one market; thus, the rent surface of an activity over any sizable area will rise to a number of separate peaks.

Rent Gradients and Surfaces
with Input Orientation

One may well ask at this point why the theory of land use places so much stress upon access to markets. Why not access to the sources of transferable inputs? In such a case, of course, we should have rent gradients and surfaces peaking at such sources, rather than at markets.

Such patterns do occur. Residents (particularly in resort areas but to some extent elsewhere too) have a tendency to cluster around certain foci of consumer attraction, such as beaches. The activity here is residence, which requires space for which it is willing to bid rent. The input is enjoyment of the beach, which is more easily available the shorter the distance. The intensity of land use is measured by the degree of crowding of residents (persons per acre). In addition, we observe characteristic gradients of intensity and rent. If there are no considerations of desirability except access to the beach, and if the residents represent a "homogeneous" activity (that is, they are not too unlike in income and tastes), then the land values will be lower and the lot sizes larger the greater the distance from the beach. If the beach is a long one, equally attractive throughout its length, the rent surface will rise not to a peak but to a ridge or cliff along the shore, falling away to landward.

We should expect to find an analogous situation in an urban external-economy activity if the principal attraction to a cluster lies in better access to production inputs, such as supplies and services. A location in the center of such a cluster is more valuable than one on the periphery.

By and large, however, rent gradients are much more often. focused around markets than around input sources. The great space-using activities are agriculture, forestry, and livestock grazing. They produce bulky transported outputs but require relatively insignificant amounts of transported inputs; consequently, their transfer orientation is overwhelmingly toward markets. The basic reason for this is that their main inputs are *nontransferable* ones: solar energy, water, and organic properties of the soil. They have a large stake in being close to markets, but a very small stake in being close to sources of any transferable input, such as fertilizer or pesticide factories.

On the urban scene, the greatest land-using activity is residence, and the transfer orientation of residences is mainly toward markets for labor services; that is, toward employment locations. Only a household consisting wholly of consumers, without any members employed outside, is free to orient itself completely to amenity "inputs" as in a resort community. Even in cities known as retirement havens, it seems that the great majority of households contain at least one worker.[4] Though within urban areas we do see neighborhood rent gradients rising toward parks or other amenity locations, the overall pattern of rents and land values appears to be shaped to a greater extent by access to jobs. High densities of urban population occur almost exclusively in areas close to major job concentrations.[5]

The various business and government activities of an urban area, insofar as they serve the local market, are strongly market oriented because their transferable outputs are so much more perishable and valuable than their transferable inputs. Consequently, they have a large stake in access to the distribution of residences, jobs, or both. Once again, we have rent gradients rising in the direction of markets: in this case, generally toward the center of the urban concentration.

---

[4] For example, the 1960 Census showed that in the Miami, Florida, Standard Metropolitan Statistical Area the ratio of the number of employed persons to the number of households was a little *larger* than the corresponding ratio for the United States as a whole.

[5] Unfortunately, this does not mean that the inhabitants of the highest density areas in our cities (the slums) necessarily enjoy adequate access to jobs, despite being located near the center. One of the most serious aspects of present-day black urban slums (ghettos) is that many of the jobs that the inhabitants can fill have tended to move to suburbs, and that the inhabitants of the ghettos have poor access to those jobs because both adequate transport and suburban housing are unavailable to them. This question will be taken up in Chapter 12.

For an interesting attempt to separate statistically the access and amenity components of land value differentials, see R. N. S. Harris, G. S. Tolley, and C. Harrell, "The Residence Site Choice," *Review of Economics and Statistics,* 50, 2 (May 1968), 241–247.

Finally, manufacturing industries oriented toward sources of transferable inputs are mainly those engaged in the first-stage processing of rural products (crops, including timber, and minerals). They are input oriented, as noted in Chapter 3, because their processes characteristically reduce weight and sometimes (as in the case of canning and preserving) perishability as well. But these processing activities themselves are not extensive land users in a rural context. In fact, they are highly concentrated relative to their suppliers, and have supply areas rather than being part of market areas. Consequently their locations are not significantly affected by land costs, but each of the units of such a primary processing activity may represent a peak in the rent surface of the activity supplying it with inputs.

The foregoing discussion has justified the application of the rent gradient and rent surface concepts primarily to output-oriented activities, with the gradients and surfaces rising as we approach the market for the activity's transferable output.

INTERACTIVITY COMPETITION FOR SPACE

Although we have explained why any one activity can afford to pay a higher price for land in some locations (primarily, closer to market), and why that activity's intensity of land use shows a similar spatial pattern of variation, nothing has been said yet about land requirements as a factor influencing the *relative locations of different activities*.

If we consider a number of different activities, all locationally oriented toward a common market point, a comparison of their respective rent gradients or surfaces will indicate which activity will win out in the competition for each location.

The Basic Sequence of Land Uses

The foundations for a systematic understanding of the principles of land use were laid almost a century and a half ago by a scientifically minded North German estate owner named Johann Heinrich von Thünen.[6] He set himself the problem of how to determine the most efficient spatial layout of the various crops and other land uses on his estate, and in the process developed a more general model or theory of how rural land uses

---

[6] See reference at the end of this chapter. A thumbnail summary of the main ideas of von Thünen's pioneer theory of land uses is in Martin Beckmann, *Location Theory* (New York: Random House, 1968), Ch. 5.

Von Thünen indulged in a convenient simplifying assumption to the effect that any given activity (such as wheat growing) requires land *in a fixed ratio to the other inputs and the output*. In other words, the intensity of land use and yield per acre are fixed regardless of the relative prices of the land, the other inputs, and the output. Although this assumption has generally been retained by later theorists, we are here trying for a little more realism by allowing variation in intensity.

should be arranged around a market town. The basic principle was that each piece of land should be devoted to the use in which it would yield the highest rent.

In von Thünen's schematic model he assumed that the land was a uniform flat plain (not too unrealistic for the part of the world where he farmed), equally traversable in all directions. Consequently, the various land uses could be expected to occupy a series of concentric ring-shaped zones surrounding the market town, and the essential question was the most economical ordering of the zones.

A set of rent gradients for three different land uses, extending in both directions from a market, is shown in the upper part of Fig. 5-4, and in the lower part of the figure this is translated into a map of the resulting pattern of concentric land use zones. Each land use (activity) occupies the zone in which it can earn a higher rent than any of the other activities. In the case shown, it appears that the land nearest the market town should be devoted to forestry, the next zone outward to wheat, and the outermost zone to grazing. The land beyond the pasturage zone would not have any value at all in agricultural uses to supply this market town.[7]

The gradient of actual land rents and land values in Fig. 5-4 is the solid line following the uppermost individual-crop gradient in each zone. Such a composite gradient will necessarily be strongly concave upward, since the land uses with the steeper gradients get the inner locations and the gradients are flatter and flatter for land uses located successively farther out.

Finally, we may note that this solution of the crop location problem can be applied regardless of whether (1) one individual owns and farms all the land, seeking maximum returns; (2) one individual owns all the land but rents it out to tenant farmers, charging the highest rents he can get; or (3) there are many independent land owners and farmers, each seeking his own advantage. In a perfectly competitive situation, the rent going to land owners and the value of land would be maximized, and rents would be set at the maximum that any user could afford to pay; as a result, land owners and tenants would all be indifferent as to which zone they occupied, since the rate of return on capital and labor would be the same in all of the zones that are used.

Activity Characteristics
Determining Location

In von Thünen's basic model (which assumes that each crop has a fixed intensity of land use regardless of location or rent), the rule for determin-

---

[7] Von Thünen did indeed assign forestry to a nearby zone as this illustration shows, which seems bizarre to us today. The explanation is that in his time the woods supplied not only construction timber but also firewood, a quite bulky necessity for the townspeople.

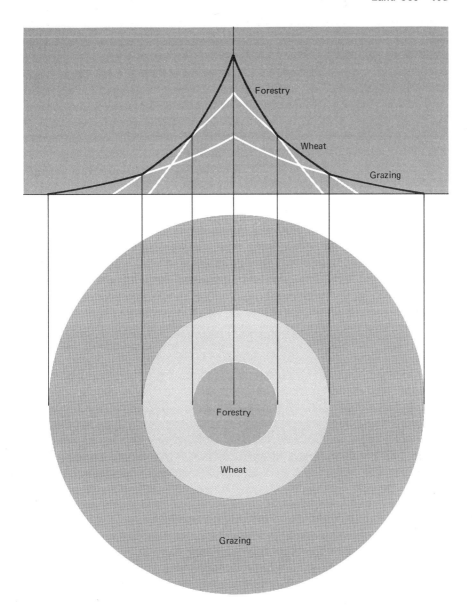

Fig. 5-4. Hypothetical Rent Gradients and Land Use Zones

ing which land use comes where in the sequence is a simple one. The activity with the largest *amount of output per acre* has the steepest rent gradient and is located closest to the market, and the other activities follow according to their rank in per-acre output.

The situation is not quite so simple, however, when we recognize that land use intensity and output per acre can vary for any given activity; that the outputs of the different activities are transferred at different rates of transfer cost per ton-mile; and that the rent gradients themselves are characteristically curved rather than straight so that conceivably any two of them might intersect twice rather than just once. Accordingly, we need to look more closely into what characteristics of the various activities determine their location sequence in relation to the market.

The question can be posed as follows: If the rent gradients for two different activities intersect (that is, they have the same rent level at some given distance from market) and if we know something about the characteristics of these two activities, what can we say about which is likely to have the *steeper gradient at the point of intersection* and, consequently, the inner land use zone?

We have suggested earlier that a reasonable form of cost function for any one of the activities is

$$TC = F + aQ^b$$

where TC is the cost of nonland inputs on an acre, F the fixed cost per acre, and Q the output of the acre; a and b are coefficients characterizing the technology of the activity. A large value for a means that at any given level of output per acre the variable costs are relatively high; a large b value means that variable costs rise rapidly with increased intensity.

According to this formulation of the relationship between output per acre and nonland costs per acre, the rent gradient for the activity is, as shown in Appendix 5-1,

$$R = a(b-1)\left(\frac{P-tx}{ab}\right)^{\frac{b}{b-1}} - F$$

where R is the maximum rent payable per acre, P is the unit price of the activity's output at the market, t is the transfer charge per unit of output per mile, and x is the distance to the market in miles.

Each of the various identifying characteristics of an activity (a, b, F, and t) affects the shape and slope of the rent gradient in some way; and from that effect we can surmise how each of those characteristics affects the likelihood of the activity's being a prime candidate for the occupancy of the land near the market.

The effects are shown in Fig. 5-5 in a series of four diagrams (see Appendix 5-1 for explanation of the underlying calculations and a proof of the general validity of the relationship shown). In the first panel (upper

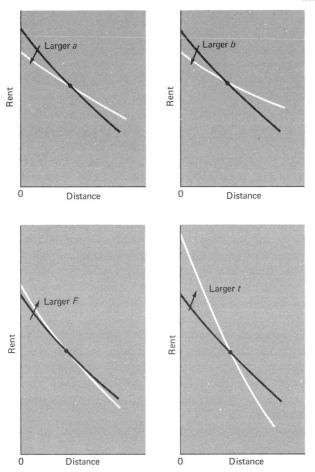

Fig. 5-5. Effect of Production and Transfer Cost Characteristics on Rent Gradient Slopes (See Appendix 5-1 for details)

left), we have intersecting rent gradients for two activities that differ only with respect to the value of *a* in their production functions. The steeper gradient (implying location in the inner zone) is that of the activity with the *smaller a*—that is, the activity in which a given amount of input per acre yields a larger tonnage of output. This makes sense since such an activity could be expected to have a larger stake in proximity to markets than an activity producing small amounts of transported outputs per acre.

The upper-right panel in Fig. 5-5 shows, in like fashion, the locational effect of the *b* coefficient, which measures the strength of "diminishing returns" to the more intensive use of land. The steeper gradient is that of the activity with the *smaller b* (in other words, the activity with the greater flexibility in intensity, permitting higher intensities nearer the market). Again this is the expected result. Activities that can use high-rise buildings can bid more for central city land than can activities that must have a one-story layout.

The lower-left panel indicates that *higher fixed costs per acre* are associated with steeper gradients and close-in locations. When a large proportion of costs are fixed regardless of output per acre, the rise in unit variable costs with higher intensity has less effect on rent-earning ability.[8]

The locational effect of differences in transfer rates is shown in the last panel of Fig. 5-5. As expected, an activity whose product is bulky, perishable, valuable, or for any other reason *expensive to transfer* has an especially strong market orientation and can pay a high premium for locations near its market.

The provision of downtown off-street parking for cars provides an interesting example of the relevance of the characteristics we have identified. Parking services are oriented toward the destination of the car user after he leaves his car, since he will be making the rest of the journey on foot. In a parking lot, the fixed nonrent costs are mainly the wages of an attendant, and the capacity of the lot has a definite limit. Here, then, we have an activity with a high t, a low F, and an extremely high b. A multilevel parking *garage* has the same t but a fairly high F, since there is now an investment in a structure, and a low b reflecting the fact that the building can vary in height. Consequently, the parking garage will have an even steeper rent gradient than the parking lot and will be the predominant form of facility in areas where the demand for parking and the demand for space in general are greatest.

Equilibrium of Land Uses and Rents

We now have some explanation of the sequence in which we could expect a series of different activities to arrange themselves around a common focal point, such as a market. Such a sequence was illustrated in Fig. 5-4. But what determines how wide a zone each activity will occupy or, indeed, whether it will be present at all?

Since we are still assuming that the land is of equal quality everywhere, any given activity will appear if there is enough demand for its output at the market, and will have a larger zone the greater the demand. In a stable pattern of land uses around the focal point, not only are the uses in the right sequence, but the market prices of the various outputs are such as to balance the demand for each output with the supply forthcoming from each activity's zone.

---

[8] It may be noted here that the von Thünen assumption of an unchangeable intensity of land use in any given activity is most closely approached in our model if we have a very high b coefficient. The total-cost curve (see Fig. 5-1) then looks almost ⌐-shaped.

Suppose, for example, that in the case shown in Fig. 5-4 there is a decline in the demand for wood at the market (perhaps because coal or oil has become available to the townspeople). The price of wood will fall and the rent gradient for forestry will likewise fall.[9] Its point of intersection with the next gradient (wheat) will shift nearer to the town, and we can envisage farmers in the zone of transition felling the trees, digging up the stumps, and planting wheat. But this additional wheat supply will depress the market price of wheat (if we assume no change in its demand), so that the wheat gradient will fall slightly. At the outer edge of the wheat belt, then, some wheat lands will be converted to pasture; and finally, some land at the outer fringe of the grazing zone will be abandoned. Thus, the initial change in demand for one of the products produces a new equilibrium pattern through a series of marginal shifts in the use of land.

In the same fashion, a large enough rise in the demand and price for some new land use in the Fig. 5-4 situation could introduce an additional zone. The new land use would elbow its way into the sequence, and its neighbors would have to move over to accommodate it in its appropriate place.

This kind of adjustment goes on all the time in the real world. In transition neighborhoods in cities, we see old dwellings and small stores being demolished to make way for office buildings and parking garages; old mansions being subdivided into apartments, replaced by apartment buildings or converted to funeral homes; and in the suburbs, farm lands and golf courses yielding themselves up to the subdivider.

Rent Gradients and Multiple Access

It is now time to recognize explicitly one of the drastic simplifying assumptions underlying the foregoing exposition of rent gradients. We have been assuming heretofore that a land user's willingness to pay rent for the use of a site depends solely upon that site's access to some single point, typically a market for his output. Locational advantage of market access will be at a peak at that unique focal point, and so will the amount of rent he can afford to pay. The pure "supply areas" case identified in Chapter 4 fits these specifications: Each market is served by many scattered sellers, and each seller disposes of his entire output in just one market. Rural land uses, and particularly agriculture, are the classical

---

[9] Somewhat more accurately, the gradient will shift *sidewise*, toward the market. A price fall at the market, equivalent to the cost of transporting wood 5 miles, means that the new price of wood at any given woodlot location will be the same as the old price was at a location 5 miles farther out. Thus, the new bid rent for wood production at each location will be the same as the former bid rent 5 miles farther away. The gradient shift will thus be strictly parallel sidewise, if transfer costs rise linearly with distance.

example. The multiplicity of sellers sharing the same market, moreover, implies relatively pure competition. Any one seller's output is small compared to the total purchases of any one market; thus he has a perfectly elastic demand for his output and can sell as much as he chooses to produce without affecting the price. Appropriately, then, in our simplified analysis the price at the market was assumed fixed.

As has already been suggested in Chapters 2 and 4, however, real life situations are often more complex. Specifically, the access advantages of a location may depend upon nearness to more than one other point. Even small producers, particularly if their outputs are not completely standardized, may sell to more than one market. In addition, with respect to other kinds of access also—for example, supply of transported inputs or labor or the serving of customers who are themselves mobile, like retail shoppers —the true access advantage of a location is often a composite reflecting transfer costs to a number of points. In such a situation, the rent surface may well have a number of peaks, hollows, and ridges, and may peak at points of maximum access potential which are intermediate between actual market centers.

URBAN LAND USES

The general principles of land use competition and the location of space-using activities that we have developed thus far are relevant to the highly extensive rural land uses to which this theory was originally addressed and also to the relatively microscale land use patterns within urban areas. But the urban context does present some important additional relationships that we need to understand as a basis for our direct confrontation with some of the critical problems of urban economics in later chapters.

Scale and Agglomeration Economies and Land Use

In considering broad continuous zones of extensive activities, as exemplified by major crop zones in agriculture or residential areas in cities, it was not really necessary to consider the size of the individual unit in terms of output or occupied land area since such zones contain a large number of adjacent units. Accordingly, we have looked for explanations of rent-paying ability and location in terms of inputs, costs, outputs, and rents on a per-acre basis. We could appropriately consider costs as affected by intensity of land use rather than by the size of the producing unit, the firm, or the cluster.

Let us now consider an activity, such as university education, which, on the basis of its production characteristics, can best be located, say, 5 miles from the center of the metropolitan area supplying the bulk of the students. A more central location would mean excessive land costs, while a less central one would mean poor access to the homes of the commuting students and perhaps also to various other urban activities with which contact is desired. If we brashly apply the basic von Thünen model, we get the answer that a university should occupy a ring-shaped zone with a 5-mile radius. If the amount of space needed were, say, 300 acres, the ring-shaped campus would be about 80 feet wide and more than 31 miles long. Since such a layout would preclude both having a sizable stadium and getting to classes on time, it is clearly unacceptable. In the interests of its own internal logistics, the university would prefer a blob to a doughnut. Two different institutions in the same city might find some external-economy advantage in being close to one another in a single "university district," but if they are intensely competing for commuter students, they might prefer to locate on opposite sides of town.

The point here is that a university is a locational unit subject to considerable *economies of scale,* so that there will be only a few unit locations, perhaps only one, in any given urban area; while at the same time it is sufficiently space-using to need an off-center or even suburban location. The same principle applies to any activity with these characteristics. As a result, the concentric ring pattern appears within urban areas only with respect to certain broad classes of activities such as residence. For other noncentral uses, the pattern can range from scattered fragments of a ring to a single off-center concentration. As we shall see in Chapter 10, still further complication is introduced by the fact that each such concentration can become a focal point for a neighborhood constellation of associated land uses. Any sizable urban area contains a number of such subcenters in addition to the principal downtown center.

Multiple Access and
Location in Cities

Another aspect of location that comes to the fore when we look inside cities is that an activity unit is likely to be oriented to a whole series of market points rather than to just one market point, as is generally the case with extractive industries. A wholesaler serves many separate retail merchants; a retailer serves perhaps thousands of customers living in different places; and a household wants access to a variety of different points for work, job, school, shopping, recreational, and social purposes.

As a result, it is inaccurate to assume that the transfer costs for an urban activity are measured simply by distance to the central point or downtown. For any individual retailer or householder, nearness to downtown will be of little significance if most of his contacts are with nondowntown points.

However, if we are concerned not with an individual unit but with the location pattern of an urban activity as a whole, the center and certain other points do emerge as foci of attraction. Thus, for office and service workers the density of job opportunities does rise toward a central peak, so that the job-access factor affects residence location for such occupations in the same directions (though not quite as strongly) as it would if all the jobs really were at one central point. Similarly, a department store or public service facility catering to the urban population as a whole is drawn toward the center; not because that is where the clients are, but because it is the point where clients from all parts of the city can converge with the least total transfer cost in money and time. As we noted in Chapter 2, the location with best access to a market area as a whole is a central point within that area, and the attraction toward the center is increased if the density of market is not uniform but rises as we approach the center.

Some urban activities have a major part of their markets, input sources, or both outside the urban area altogether. In such a case, the best place within the area from the standpoint of transfer cost is likely to be at or near service points for intercity transfer services: rail, truck or piggyback terminals, docks, airports, or even the central post office, depending on the nature of the outputs or inputs to be transferred. The locations of such terminals do not necessarily, or even usually, coincide with the location of best access to that particular urban area as a whole, which is in general the central business district. For export- or import-oriented urban activities, then, there is a somewhat different principal focus of transfer advantage.

"Neighborhood Effects" and Land Use Constraints

In urban areas, the intensity of land use and the proximity of various activities make the value of a particular site highly dependent on what is going on around it. The householder is as much concerned with the appearance and demeanor of his neighborhood as with the size and quality of his own property and its access advantages. Most other urban activities are in some degree sensitive to their immediate environments, and this affects the rent they are prepared to bid for various locations. Some neighborhood effects are favorable and others unfavorable, depending on the nature of the activities involved and on who is affecting whom. The external economies of agglomeration of shopping-goods retailers, discussed in Chapter 4, are an example of a mutually favorable neighborhood effect, while the juxtaposition of a sewage treatment plant and a gourmet restaurant can only be to the disadvantage of the latter.

RENT, LAND VALUE, AND LAND TAXATION

Our discussion of rents and competition for land has placed almost exclusive emphasis on the *location* of a site (relative to markets and sources of inputs) as an index of its value. Location determines how much rent any particular activity could afford to pay for the use of a site; the purchase price was explained as simply the capitalized value of the expected stream of future rents. At this point we need to recognize some significant complications that have been ignored till now.

Speculative Value of Land

First, the expected future returns on a parcel of land may sometimes be quite different from current returns, particularly in locations where radical changes of use are taking place or expected. This is generally true around the fringes of urban areas, where the change involves conversion from farm to urban uses. The price that anyone will pay for the current use of the land may be quite low in relation to the speculative value based on a capitalization of expected returns in a new use.

This point is illustrated in the results of a study of agricultural land near the city of Louisville, Kentucky, more than half a century ago (see Table 5-1). It will be observed that in the zones farther than 8 or 9 miles

TABLE 5-1. Acreage, Rent per Acre, and Value per Acre of Farms, by Distance from Louisville, Kentucky

	Distance from Louisville (miles)			
	8 or less	9 to 11	12 to 14	15 or more
(1) Average acres per farm	102	221	256	257
(2) Land rent per acre ($ per annum)	11.85	5.59	5.37	4.66
(3) Land value per acre ($)	312	110	106	95
(4) Capitalization rate (%) (2)/(3)	3.8	5.1	5.1	4.9
(5) Rent per farm per annum ($) (1)×(2)	1,210	1,235	1,430	1,295

SOURCE: J. H. Arnold and Frank Montgomery, *Influence of a City on Farming,* Bulletin 678 (Washington, D.C.: U.S. Department of Agriculture, 1918).

from the city, the current annual rent was consistently about 5 percent of the average value of the land. In other words, the value was approximately 20 years' rent at the current rate. Closer to the city, the land was worth, on the average, more than 26 times the current annual rent; the capitalization rate was only 3.8 percent. This obviously reflected the expectation that returns on the nearby land would rise as the urbanized area spread.

Incidentally, the same table (Rows 1, 5) shows that the size of the farm unit increased consistently with greater distance from the city in terms of acreage but remained roughly constant in terms of total land rent. This is consistent with the idea that the scale of the individual farm unit is constrained by firm-size considerations of management capability and financial resources. The same study showed systematically greater inputs of labor and fertilizer per acre and per farm nearer to the city.

Improvements on Land

A further complication that needs to be recognized here is that land is ordinarily priced, sold, and taxed in combination with whatever buildings and other "improvements" have been erected on it, since such structures are usually durable and difficult (if not impossible) to move. On urban land, improvements may account for a major part of the value of the parcel of real estate; and in all cases it is probably difficult to estimate just how much of the price does represent pure space or "site value." Sometimes the improvements have a negative value: In other words, the land would be more desirable if it were cleared of its obsolete structures.

Such structural obsolescence is an important aspect of some of the most serious urban problems that confront us today, which we shall discuss in the final chapters of this book. Moreover, the distinction between site value and total real property value is crucial to an evaluation of the role of the real property tax, which is the fiscal mainstay of local governments. As we shall see in Chapter 12, certain injurious effects upon land use patterns and urban development might be avoided by tax reforms involving a more explicit recognition of site value per se.

SELECTED READINGS

Johann Heinrich von Thünen, *Der isolirte Staat in Beziehung auf Nationalökonomie und Landwirtschaft* (Stuttgart: Gustav Fischer, 1966; reprint of 1826 edition); Carla M. Wartenberg (tr.), *von Thünen's Isolated State* (London: Pergamon Press, 1966).

Richard M. Hurd, *Principles of City Land Values* (Washington, D.C.: Homer Hoyt Associates, 1967; reprint of 1924 edition).

August Lösch, *Die räumliche Ordnung der Wirtschaft* (Jena: Gustav Fischer, 1940; 2nd ed., 1944); W. H. Woglom (tr.), *The Economics of Location* (New Haven: Yale University Press, 1954), 36–67.

Edgar S. Dunn, *The Location of Agricultural Production* (Gainesville: University of Florida Press, 1954).

Raleigh Barlowe, *Land Resource Economics: The Political Economy of Rural and Urban Land Resources Use* (Englewood Cliffs, N.J.: Prentice-Hall, 1958).

Michael Chisholm, *Rural Settlement and Land Use* (New York: Wiley, 1962).

William Alonso, *Location and Land Use* (Cambridge, Mass.: Harvard University Press, 1964).

Eugene F. Brigham, "The Determinants of Residential Land Values," *Land Economics,* 41, 4 (November 1965), 325–334.

Homer Hoyt, *According to Hoyt* (Washington, D.C.: Homer Hoyt Associates, 1968).

A collection of his writings, 1916–1966, mainly on urban land economics.
Edwin von Böventer, "Land Values and Spatial Structure: Agricultural, Urban, and
   Tourist Location Theories," *Papers of the Regional Science Association*, 18 (1966),
   231–242.

APPENDIX 5-1

Derivation of Formulas for Rent Gradients and Their Slopes
   (See page 106)

Let the total cost of production per acre (exclusive of rent) be

(1) $$C=F+aQ^b$$

where F is fixed cost per acre, Q is output per acre, and $b>1$.

The bid rent, or maximum rent per acre that could be paid, is

(2) $$R= (P-tx)\ Q-aQ^b-F$$

where P is the unit price of the output at the market, t is the unit transfer
cost per mile, and x is the distance to market. Let

(3) $$dR/dQ=P-tx-abQ^{b-1}$$

(4) $$d^2R/dQ^2= (1-b)\ abQ^{b-2}<0$$

Since the second derivative is negative because $b>1$, setting the first derivative to zero will give the output which maximizes R.

(5) $$P-tx-abQ^{b-1}=0$$

(6) $$Q=\left(\frac{P-tx}{ab}\right)^{\frac{1}{b-1}}$$

Substituting in (2), and simplifying,

(7) $$R=a(b-1)\left(\frac{P-tx}{ab}\right)^{\frac{b}{b-1}}-F$$

This is the rent gradient with respect to distance from the market.

(8) $$dR/dx=-t\left(\frac{P-tx}{ab}\right)^{\frac{1}{b-1}}<0$$

∴ The rent gradient always slopes downward from the market.

$$(9) \qquad d^2R/dx^2 = \frac{t^2}{ab(b-1)}\left(\frac{P-tx}{ab}\right)^{\frac{2-b}{b-1}} > 0$$

$\therefore$ The rent gradient is always concave upward.

The procedure followed in deriving the rent gradients shown in Fig. 5-5, which indicate the effect of each of the parameters on the slope, was as follows:

Since the question of which one of two activities takes the zone closer to market is determined by the relative slopes of the two gradients *at their point of intersection*, it is necessary to set the market prices at a level, P^*, such that the gradients representing activities with different a, b, F, or t values would intersect. Let the coordinates (rent and distance respectively) of the point of intersection be R^* and x^* (which were set at 1,000 and 50 respectively in calculating the gradients plotted in Fig. 5-5).

Then

$$R^* = a(b-1)\left(\frac{P^*-tx^*}{ab}\right)^{\frac{b}{b-1}} - F$$

and from this,

$$\frac{P^*-tx^*}{ab} = \left(\frac{R^*+F}{a(b-1)}\right)^{\frac{b-1}{b}}$$

Substituting in (8) gives the slope (S^*) at the intersection point:

$$S^* = -t\left(\frac{R^*+F}{a(b-1)}\right)^{\frac{1}{b}}$$

From this it is clear that

$$\partial S^*/\partial a > 0$$
$$\partial S^*/\partial b > 0$$
$$\partial S^*/\partial F < 0$$
$$\partial S^*/\partial t < 0$$

In other words, if two activities have intersecting rent gradients and are alike with respect to all but one of the four parameters a, b, F, t, the activity with the steeper (more strongly negative) slope at their intersection will be the activity with the lower a, or the lower b, or the higher F, or the higher t.

In calculating the illustrative gradients shown in Fig. 5-5 the following parameters were used:

	a	b	F	t
"Standard case" for comparison, which appears in each of the four panels of Fig. 5-5	10	2	100	1
"Larger a"	20	2	100	1
"Larger b"	10	4	100	1
"Larger F"	10	2	500	1
"Larger t"	10	2	100	2

INTRODUCTION

6

Towns, Cities, and Regions

Thus far, we have taken for granted the existence of cities and towns. Some intimations of why they arise, however, have already emerged in the course of our inquiries into locational principles. In Chapter 3, reference was made to the special transfer advantages of large junctions and terminals, including intermodal transshipment points. In Chapter 4, we found that some types of activities favor a highly clustered pattern in which certain external economies of agglomeration can be secured.

Thus, if we define an urban place (town or city) as a spatial concentration involving a variety of activities, we can already see some good economic reasons for the existence of such concentrations. The present chapter is addressed to questions of size, spacing, and functional types of urban places.[1] Here we shall be treating each such place as a single location, reserving further discussion of the internal spatial form of cities for Chapter 10.

There are two different (and basically complementary) approaches to an understanding of the location of cities. The first is historical: It asks why specific cities arose where they did, and why certain cities grew and others did not in a particular historical context.[2] From this kind of study we learn much about the diverse origins of individual cities. We find that for some the decisive initial advantage of the site was its security against armed attack; for others, a good natural harbor convenient to a productive hinterland; for others, an easy place to cross a wide river or a mountain range; for still others, a pleasant climate or other amenities. However, we also find that in many cases the original reason is no

---

[1] For convenience, we shall often use the word "city" to refer to any urban place, regardless of size and inclusive of suburbs.

[2] The word "historical" is not meant to imply any lack of relevance to the future. The characteristic of the approach described here is that it considers changes (past and prospective) in *specific* cities. A pioneer American study along these lines was Adna F. Weber's *The Growth of Cities in the Nineteenth Century,* Columbia University Studies in History, Economics, and Public Law, 11 (London: published for Columbia University by the Macmillan Co.; P. S. King and Son, 1899; revised edition, Ithaca, N.Y.: Cornell University Press, 1963.) There are also countless histories of the origin and development of individual cities.

longer the principal basis of continued growth, and that once a city reaches substantial size it develops important economies of agglomeration that encourage still further growth.[3] As Wilbur R. Thompson puts it in his exposition of "the urban size ratchet,"

> . . . if the growth of an urban area persists long enough to raise the area to some critical size (a quarter of a million population?) structural characteristics, such as industrial diversification, political power, huge fixed investments, a rich local market, and a steady supply of industrial leadership may almost ensure its continued growth and fully ensure against absolute decline—may, in fact, effect irreversible aggregate growth.[4]

The complementary approach seeks to explain not individual cities and their peculiarities, but spatial distributions of cities as related to size and function. In developing a theory of "systems of cities," we first assume away all the special advantages of particular sites and imagine a uniform landscape, with all inputs equally available everywhere, demand for outputs evenly distributed, and transfer costs uniform in all directions. On such a *tabula rasa,* would economic forces give rise to some orderly pattern of urban concentrations? If so, what would it look like? The basic principles of urbanization patterns, disclosed by this kind of highly simplified analysis, can then be appropriately developed and modified to provide some useful insights about the real world. This is the approach pioneered by Christaller and Lösch and subsequently developed by many economists and geographers, notably Brian Berry.[5] It is often called "central-place theory."

REGIONS AND CENTERS

We are concerned now not simply with the location of individual units or activities, as in previous chapters, but with *regional* economics in terms of

---

[3] The self-reinforcing nature of urban growth, in a particular historical context, is especially well brought out in Allen R. Pred's *The Spatial Dynamics of U.S. Urban-Industrial Growth, 1800–1914* (Cambridge, Mass.: M.I.T. Press, 1966).

[4] *A Preface to Urban Economics* (Baltimore: Johns Hopkins Press, 1965), p. 24.

[5] Walter Christaller, *Die zentralen Orte in Süddeutschland* (Jena: Gustav Fischer, 1933); C. W. Baskin (tr.), *Central Places in Southern Germany* (Englewood Cliffs, N.J.: Prentice-Hall, 1966). An abstract of the theoretical parts of Christaller's work appears in Brian J. L. Berry and Allen R. Pred, *Central Place Studies: A Bibliography of Theory and Applications* (Philadelphia: Regional Science Research Institute, 1961), which is also the most comprehensive guide to the vast literature on central-place theory. See also August Lösch's work, *Die räumliche Ordnung der Wirtschaft* (Jena: Gustav Fischer, 1940); W. H. Woglom with the assistance of W. F. Stolper (trs.), *The Economics of Location* (New Haven: Yale University Press, 1954). Berry's definitive article, "Cities as Systems within Systems of Cities" (which deals also with intracity location patterns) first appeared in *Papers of the Regional Science Association,* 13 (1964), 147–163. Still more recent material is in several chapters of P. M. Hauser and L. F. Schnore (eds.), *The Study of Urbanization* (New York: Wiley, 1965) and also in Martin Beckmann, "City Hierarchies and the Distribution of City Size," *Economic Development and Cultural Change,* 6 (1968), 243–248.

Fig. 6-1. Regions of the United States as Demarcated by Regional Economics Division, U.S. Department of Commerce (Far West region includes Alaska and Hawaii)

SOURCE: Charles F. Schwartz and Robert E. Graham, Jr., *Personal Income by States Since 1929*, Supplement to *Survey of Current Business* (Washington, D.C.: Government Printing Office, 1956).

the location and functions of diversified *complexes of activities*. First, we need a more definite idea of what a "region" is.

A substantial, possibly redundant, literature has been devoted to this question, and the resulting definitions are legion. It has been suggested, in fact, that a region means an area that a regional economist gets a research grant to study. Be that as it may, it is clear that the most appropriate and useful definition depends on the particular purpose to be served.

Common to all definitions is the idea of a geographical area constituting an entity, so that significant statements can be made about the area *as a whole*. Aggregation into regions is useful in connection with *description*, because it means that fewer separate numbers or other facts must be collected and handled. Thus, for many purposes, totals and averages for a Census tract or a county are just as informative and much easier to handle and present than stacks of Census returns would be, even if one had access to them. Similarly, aggregation is obviously economical in connection with *analysis* of data; and it is particularly important if there is a good deal of interdependence of units or activities within the area so that the whole really is different from the sum of its parts. Finally, and for similar reasons, aggregation is necessary for the formulation and implementation of *public policies*. From this standpoint at least, the most useful regional groupings are those that follow the boundaries of governmental jurisdictions.

Basic to the idea of a region is a high degree of correlation of behavior among its various parts. Since this correlation can reflect either of two quite distinct features of internal structure, we distinguish two different types of regions, the homogeneous and the nodal.

A homogeneous region is demarcated on the basis of internal *uniformity*. The winter wheat belt in the central part of the United States is a homogeneous agricultural region because all its parts grow the same main crop in the same way. Some external change, such as a new farm price support or loan program, a series of drought years, or a change in the world demand for wheat, will affect all of the region in a similar way; what is true of one part of the region is true of other parts, and the various parts resemble each other more than they resemble areas outside the region. The distinctive land use zones of the von Thünen model, discussed in the previous chapter, can be recognized as homogeneous regions. America's Appalachia and Italy's Mezzogiorno are regions defined on the basis of a common set of problems of poverty, arrested economic development, and limited human opportunity.

The set of nonmetropolitan State Economic Areas established by the U.S. Bureau of the Census for tabulation of various kinds of data, such as migration, forms another example. Those State Economic Areas that do not simply coincide with Standard Metropolitan Statistical Areas are made up by grouping contiguous counties within a state. The grouping is system-

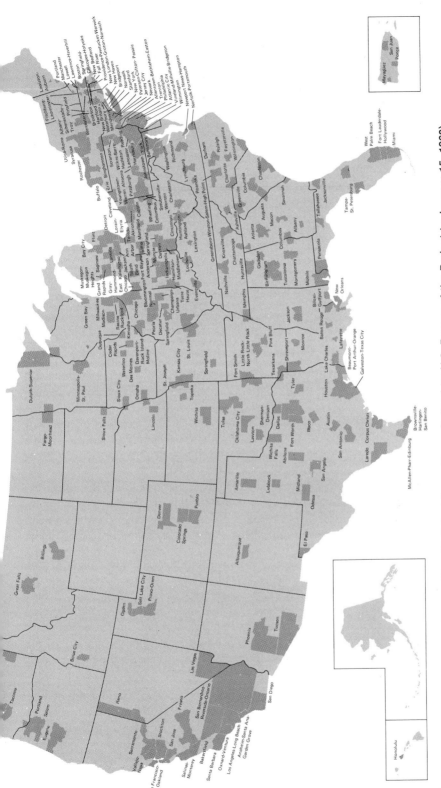

Fig. 6-2. Standard Metropolitan Statistical Areas (Areas Defined by U.S. Bureau of the Budget to January 15, 1968)

123

atically worked out by computer so that (with respect to a large number of characteristics such as income level, racial mix, and principal economic activity) the counties within any one State Economic Area are highly similar but the different State Economic Areas are highly dissimilar. The Regional Economics Division of the U.S. Department of Commerce has similarly developed a breakdown of the whole United States into 8 relatively homogeneous groups of contiguous states (see Fig. 6-1).

The alternative principle of regionalization gives us nodal regions. Here the structure is like that of a living cell or an atom: There is a nucleus and a complementary peripheral area. *Functional integration,* rather than homogeneity, is the basis of the correlation or community of interest within such a region.

A city and its surrounding commuting and trading area make a nodal region. The parts with the main concentration of business and employment are in sharp contrast to the residential areas and "bedroom suburbs" but are tightly linked to them by flows of labor, goods, and services. Thus, the region is usefully considered a unit in its reaction to changed conditions affecting economic growth or well-being. Neither core nor periphery can flourish without the other. Standard Metropolitan Statistical Areas (see Fig. 6-2) are demarcated on a nodal basis, using such criteria as commutation flows, circulation areas of metropolitan newspapers, and frequency of telephone calls. Under present rules, each such area must have a "central city" (or pair of "twin cities") with a population of at least 50,000.

Individual administrative agencies, such as the Federal Reserve System or the U.S. Department of Labor, have their own sets of nodal regions, each region being served from a field office. Each agency is subject to different efficiency considerations and political pressures in setting up its net of centers and areas, but problems of coordination can become serious if the nets are all different, as they tend to be in the absence of any special effort at uniformity. In 1969, the President announced the establishment of a common set of regions and regional centers for the Department of Health, Education and Welfare, the Department of Housing and Urban Development, the Department of Labor, the Office of Economic Opportunity, and the Small Business Administration, as shown in Fig. 6-3.

Though both homogeneous and nodal regions make sense as useful groupings, they play different roles in the spatial organization of society. This is particularly evident in regard to the flow of trade. The usual basis for a homogeneous region is a common exportable output: The whole region is a surplus supply area for such an output, and consequently its various parts have little or no reason to trade extensively with one another. By contrast, in the nodal region, internal exchange of goods and services is the very *raison d'être* of the region. Typically, there is a single main nucleus (the principal city of the region), perhaps some subordinate cen-

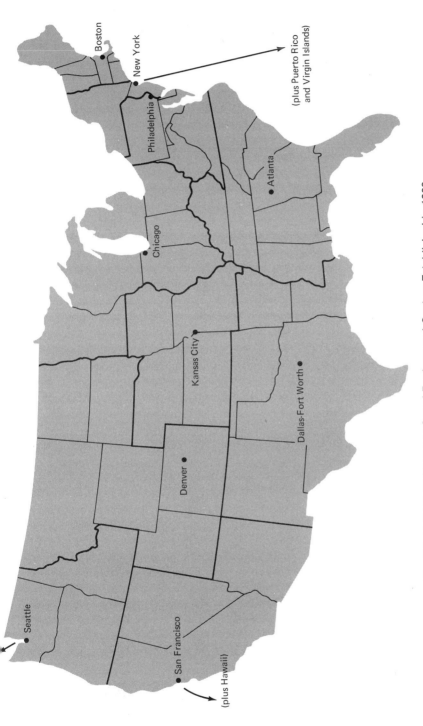

Fig. 6-3. Uniform Multiagency Set of Regions and Centers Established in 1969

Boston

New York

(plus Puerto Rico
and Virgin Islands)

Philadelphia

Atlanta

Chicago

Kansas City

Dallas-Fort Worth

Denver

Seattle

San Francisco

(plus Hawaii)

ters, and the rural remainder of the territory. These two or three specialized parts of the organism complement one another and are linked by internal transfer media.

Our main concern in this chapter is with the formation and spatial structure of nodal regions and, in particular, their centers and subcenters. Chapters 8 and 9 will more fully explore the economics of regional structure, growth, and policy, and Chapters 10–12 will be devoted to what goes on inside the nuclei of regions; that is, in urban agglomerations.

THE FORMATION OF A SYSTEM OF CITIES

Some Simplifying Assumptions

In order to highlight the basic factors that give rise to spatial patterns of cities and nodal regions, we shall start with the highly simplified central-place model conceived by Christaller and Lösch. There are only two activities in this model: one rural and one urban. The rural activity is an extensive land user like agriculture, having no significant economies of agglomeration. The urban activity is subject to substantial agglomeration economies (internal, external, or both), but can use land intensively and requires a relatively insignificant amount of space. People engaged in each of the two activities require the output of the *other* activity.[6] All land is of uniform quality and transfer costs are proportional to straight-line distance in any direction. The extensive rural activity, and consequently the demand for the output of the urban activity, is uniformly distributed.

It will be noted that in this rudimentary economic system, there are only two location factors: transfer costs and agglomeration economies.

Shapes of Trading Areas

A single seller, located somewhere in a limitless plain uniformly seeded with customers, would serve a circular market area, its radius being determined by *transfer costs, scale economies,* and *density of the market.*[7] But if we now envisage the urban activity being taken up in more and more different locations, the market areas of the various urban centers will touch. As long as there are opportunities for profitable establishment of more production centers, these areas will become more numerous. Eventually, the areas will be compressed to the point where profits are barely sufficient to keep the existing firms in business.

---

[6] In Lösch's exposition, *op. cit.,* pp. 105 ff., the two activities were exemplified as agriculture and commercial brewing respectively. The brewers need grain and other farm products and the farmers need beer.

[7] See Appendix 6-2.

What will this "equilibrium" pattern of centers and trade areas look like? If all parts of the market are served from one center or another, and if all the centers have equal locational advantages, the areas must be identical polygons bounded by straight lines, as was stated in Chapter 4. Only three uniform shapes of market area will fill the surface under these conditions: squares, hexagons, and triangles. Of these, the hexagon is the "most efficient" in the sense that it gives the smallest average distance between sellers and buyers.[8]

A honeycomb is a good example of how initially circular areas (cells) become hexagonal when pressure squeezes them into a shape that will utilize all the available space. But in many cases the transport grid is basically *rectilinear*—as in most modern urban street patterns and over a major part of the rural area of the United States, where the land surveys were made in terms of a checkerboard of square townships and sections and where most local roads have followed section and township boundaries. Under such conditions, market area boundaries and the trading areas of towns tend to be not hexagonal or triangular but square.

A Hierarchy of Trading Areas

Next, we shall take a more realistic approach by recognizing more than just a single urban-type activity. I have already suggested that the size of the trade area for a specific product depends on three basic factors: *transfer costs* (per ton-mile), *market density* (per square mile), and the extent of *scale or other agglomeration economies*. Obviously, each of these conditions varies from one activity to another. Accordingly, we might expect that each additional product we introduce will have a different appropriate size of market area and spacing of supply centers. The appropriate area will be small, and the appropriate number of centers large, for products for which there is little economy in large-scale production, or for which the density of market demand is high. Where the contrary conditions hold (important scale economies or sparse demand), we should expect production to be concentrated in a few widely spaced centers each serving a large area.[9]

But should we really expect to find as many different and independent systems of market areas and production centers as there are different products—an almost infinite variety? We might expect this were it not for the economic advantages of channelizing transfer along a limited num-

---

[8] Martin Beckmann, *Location Theory* (New York: Random House, 1968), 46–47.

[9] It might appear obvious as well that products with *lower transfer costs* (per unit quantity and distance) would be produced in fewer centers, and distributed over larger market areas, than products with higher transfer costs. For reasons that will be shown later in this chapter, however, no such simple, general statement about the relation of transfer costs to area size can be made.

ber of efficient routes and the advantages of clustering different activities in the same place so as to get the external economies of agglomeration discussed in Chapter 4. Recalling those considerations, we can see why two or more activities for which the "ideal" pattern of centers may be only slightly different are, in fact, likely to settle for a common "compromise" set of production locations. And if two activities do have very different ideal sizes of areas, the tendency is for the activity with the larger-sized areas to locate at some of the centers of the other activity— say every other one, or every third, fourth, or tenth one. In this way, each activity can have a pattern of centers more or less appropriately spaced to fit its conditions, while at the same time *the total number of centers is kept down.* This is an advantage because bigger centers provide more economies of agglomeration and because more of the total flow of goods and services can travel on efficient high-volume transfer routes.

The pressure for reduction of the number of size classes of areas is so basic that we might even embellish the vocabulary of regional economics by referring here to a "Procrustean Law" of market areas. Procrustes was a mythical innkeeper who provided only one bed for all his guests and achieved a perfect fit by stretching or cropping each guest as required.

What all this implies is a *hierarchy* of central places, a stylized example of which is shown in Fig. 6-4. In this particular hierarchical pattern, it is assumed that the areas are square. Four "orders" or size classes of centers are represented by different sizes of dots, and their respective areas are bounded by black and gray lines.

There are many possible variations on this scheme; they have been analyzed in detail for both the square and the hexagonal systems and need not detain us here. However, one particular feature is important for an understanding of urban and regional structure. In the system of cities shown in Fig. 6-4a, each of the largest cities is a center not only for its area but also for an area of each of the smaller sizes. The implication is, in fact, that *each order of centers carries on the activities of all lower orders of centers plus some further activities not found in such places.*

It can be shown that the hierarchical system in Fig. 6-4a is a more likely and efficient one than the possible alternative system in Fig. 6-4b. In both cases, the size of the market area of the smallest class of centers is the same, but system *a* has some important economic advantages.

First, there are four sizes of centers (shown at the right of the figure) rather than three, thus making possible a closer fit to the different ideal area sizes of specific activities. The Procrustean constraint is less restrictive. In system *a,* each area is twice as large as the next smaller one, while in system *b,* each area is four times as large. Second, the total number of centers is smaller in the system *a;* thus economies of agglomeration can be more fully realized. Finally, system *a* lends itself to the fully hier-

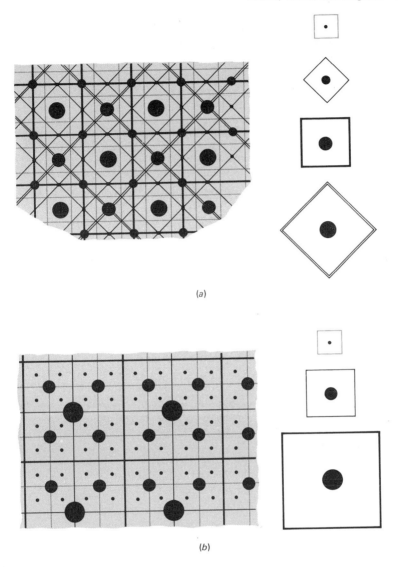

(a)

(b)

Fig. 6-4. Two Possible Central-Place Patterns with Square Areas

archical organization of production already referred to; namely, that each order of centers carries on the activities of all lower orders plus some other activities not found in smaller places. System *b* makes sense only if we assume that each order of centers serves only centers of the next lower order, with only the lowest order directly serving the dispersed rural market.

As we shall see from some empirical evidence to be introduced later, the actual mix of activities in urban places of various sizes does in fact conform rather closely to what we should expect under a fully hierarchical organization: Larger centers do have most if not all of the kinds of urban activities found in smaller centers.

Some Practical Limitations

The highly simplified central-place model presented so far provides a rationale for patterns of cities like the one shown in Fig. 6-4a. There are many size classes of cities; each larger size has a more comprehensive array of urban activities and includes a smaller number of cities spaced farther apart. We should expect the various extensive rural activities (for example, distinctive types of agriculture) to be arranged in concentric zones around the centers, in the manner shown in Fig. 5-6 in the previous chapter. Any given city above the lowest order will have more than one rural market area (for its various outputs) and more than one rural supply area (for its various rurally produced inputs); there is no reason to expect any of its market areas to coincide with any of its supply areas. In addition, all cities except those in the largest class may be getting urban products from cities of larger size.

This is obviously not an adequate picture of cities, areas, and trade flows in the real world. We begin now to consider some of the additional factors involved.

First, the simple model assumed a uniform transfer cost per mile on a fine and regular grid of routes, and also assumed that the rural market was distributed with uniform density. Recognition of a less regular transfer network with some routes cheaper or better than others, and recognition of variations in the density of demand, would lead us to expect a substantial deformation of the areas and city patterns. Still further deformation arises because the costs of inputs and the resulting costs of production are not really the same in different cities, even among those of the same size class. The considerable number of activities that are sensitive to location factors other than agglomeration economies and access to markets were ignored in the simple model; superimposing their locations on the basic central-place scheme further complicates the pattern, creating additional cities (and/or larger cities) by adding both more urban activity and more demand. Finally, the whole pattern of locations is constantly shifting in delayed response to changes in such conditions as population, regional income levels, transfer costs, and technology, so that no picture of an equilibrium situation can be realistic.

These practical considerations are ample to explain why the distribution of cities by size is not stepwise by discrete hierarchical classes but is continuous;[10] and also why there are only loose relations between the population of a city and the size of its trading area, and between city size and the range of activities represented in a city.

Generalized Areas of Urban Influence

Although the central-place model described implies that any city above the smallest class has a variety of different-sized market and supply areas, people frequently refer to "the" trading area (or tributary area, or area of dominance) of a city, as if there were only one. The identification of appropriate and useful nodal regions, as discussed earlier in this chapter, leans heavily on the notion that (for a considerable range of purposes, though perhaps not for all purposes) we can mark out some single area as particularly related to a given center.

For example, in one of the early studies of spatial trading patterns by marketing specialist William J. Reilly,[11] an attempt was made to induce an empirical formula to explain retail trading areas of cities in terms of their size. "Reilly's Law of Retail Gravitation" says that "two cities attract retail trade from any intermediate city or town in the vicinity of the breaking point [between their spheres of dominance], approximately in direct proportion to the populations of the two cities and in inverse proportion to the squares of the distance from these two cities to the intermediate town."

Some overlap of market areas is recognized, but according to this law, the market area boundary in the sense of the "breaking point" (where trade is equally distributed between the two supplying cities) runs through points where

$$D_A^2/D_B^2 = P_A/P_B$$

---

[10] The size distribution of cities within a large and relatively self-contained area has been found empirically to resemble a particular form described by the "Rank-Size Rule." In its simplest formulation, this rule states that the size of a city is inversely proportional to its rank. Thus, the second biggest city would be half the size of the biggest, the third biggest would be one-third the size of the biggest, the 500th biggest 1/500 the size of the biggest, and so on. This rule, originally wholly empirical, has been extensively tested, modified, and given some theoretical rationalization by Berry and others. See Brian J. L. Berry, "Research Frontiers in Urban Geography," and Harold M. Mayer, "A Survey of Urban Geography," both in Hauser and Schnore (eds.), *op. cit.*

[11] W. J. Reilly, "Methods for the Study of Retail Relationships," *University of Texas Bulletin* 2944 (Austin, Texas, 1929), and *The Law of Retail Gravitation* (New York: Knickerbocker Press, 1931). The term "gravitation" reflects rough analogy to the Newtonian law of gravitation (bodies attract one another in proportion to their masses and inversely in proportion to the square of their distance). Subsequent to Reilly's work, John Q. Stewart and others introduced gravity-type relationships in application to a wide variety of economic and social distributions. See also Appendix 2-1 above

if P_A and P_B are the respective populations of the two cities A and B, and D_A and D_B are their respective distances from the boundary. This means that if A and B are of equal size, the market area boundary is a straight line midway between them; but if, for example, A is twice as large as B, each point on the market area boundary is 1.4 times as far from A as from B. Fig. 6-5 shows a hypothetical set of four centers and their areas.[12]

Reilly's Law works reasonably well when tested against actual situations (which might be expected since it was derived empirically rather than theoretically), and has proved more durable than many other "laws." Let us see how it might be rationalized in terms of the simple central-place model by making the situation a little more realistic.

Consider a rural family living midway between a small town and a somewhat larger town. If they want to buy gasoline and a loaf of bread, there will be no particular reason to prefer one town to the other, and shopping trips wholly devoted to such "convenience purchases" would tend to be about equally divided. If the trip is to include going to a movie and buying a suit of clothes, however, the preference would be for the larger town, since its clothing stores have a wider selection and it may have two movie theaters compared to one in the smaller town. Trips of this sort, then, will be directed predominantly to the larger shopping center. Finally, there are some things (perhaps binoculars, or parts for the washing machine) that cannot be purchased at all in the smaller town but are available in the larger one. Any shopping trip including such an errand will have to be directed to the larger town.

For obvious reasons of economy of time and money, people try to consolidate their errands and perform multipurpose trips. It is clear, then, that the majority of trips for this family located at the half-way point will be in the direction of the larger town[13] because of the greater range of its activities. To find a family that splits its trips evenly between the two towns (that is, to locate the trading area boundary) we would have to go some distance down the road toward the smaller town.

---

[12] If there are two cities w miles apart, one of which has a population m times that of the other, it can be shown that the market area boundary according to Reilly's Law is a *circle* of radius $w\sqrt{m}/(m-1)$ with its center $w/(m-1)$ miles from the smaller city, in the direction away from the larger city. The larger city's market area completely surrounds that of the smaller city. See Appendix 6-1 for derivation of these formulas, which were used in constructing Fig. 6-5. The centers of the circles are marked by small crosses in the figure.

[13] An ingenious and workable method of determining the predominant direction of trips from a rural residence involves simply driving past and observing which way the heavier tracks turn from the driveway.

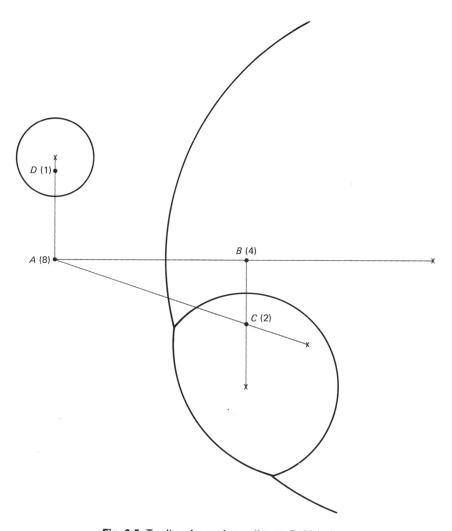

Fig. 6-5. Trading Areas According to Reilly's Law
The relative populations of the four towns A, B, C, and D are as indicated in parentheses. A's trading area includes all territory outside the circles. All boundaries consist of circular arcs.

TRADE CENTERS IN AN AMERICAN REGION—THE UPPER MIDWEST STUDY

The applicability and relevance of the central-place approach is brought out in a recent study of urban places in the Upper Midwest, a region defined for purposes of the study as coterminous with the Ninth Federal

Reserve District. This study was part of a much larger project analyzing economic activity and trends in the area.[14]

The purpose of this investigation was to provide some guidance to planning and development activities involving cities and towns in the Upper Midwest region. No attempt was made to predict growth or recommend development policies for any specific urban place. But as a basis for any subsequent efforts with such local application, the study developed some interesting and useful findings regarding the characteristics and growth trends of *categories* of places, corresponding conceptually to the "orders" of the theoretical central-place hierarchy.

The first step was a listing of retail and wholesale activities, arranged according to the smallest size of community in which they are consistently represented. Fig. 6-6 shows this grouping and the way in which it was applied in classifying the individual trade centers. Thus, in order to rank as a "minimum convenience" center, a place had to have all of the last six activities shown, and at least two of the next four (garage, auto, implement dealer; variety store; meat, fish, fruit; general merchandise). To qualify for the highest rank,[15] a trade center had to have every one of the activities listed. The category of "hamlets" was added as the lowest order of trading center: In general, they contained a gasoline station and an eating place but no consistent set of further trade activities.

In all, more than 2,200 centers were thus classified (see map, Fig. 6-7). Table 6-1 shows the numbers and sizes by hierarchy level. It will be observed that the higher orders of center are progressively fewer and larger; but there is much overlapping of size ranges, reflecting the fact that a center's trading activity is not the sole determinant of its employment or population.

The study explicitly recognized that each type of center higher than a hamlet has *more than one size of trade area*.[16] The method used to determine the trade areas of the highest orders of centers (primary and secondary wholesale-retail) was based on relative frequency of telephone calls. From shopping and convenience centers within its area, a "whole-

---

[14] See James M. Henderson and Anne O. Krueger, *National Growth and Economic Changes in the Upper Midwest* (Minneapolis: University of Minnesota Press, 1965), for the final general report on "the economic development phase of the Upper Midwest Economic Study (UMES) research program" and a listing of earlier reports. The results of the UMES Urban Research Program were published in a series of eight Urban Reports by John R. Borchert and others, listed *op. cit.,* p. 228. The material quoted in this chapter is taken from John R. Borchert and Russell B. Adams, *Trade Centers and Trade Areas of the Upper Midwest,* Upper Midwest Economic Study, Urban Report No. 3 (Minneapolis: September 1963).

[15] Minneapolis and St. Paul were considered separately in view of their unique role as the primary center for the entire region.

[16] "Large centers have multiple trade areas because they function at more than one level. For example, Fargo-Moorhead has successively larger trade areas at the complete shopping, secondary, and primary wholesale-retail levels." Borchert and Adams, *op. cit.,* p. 5.

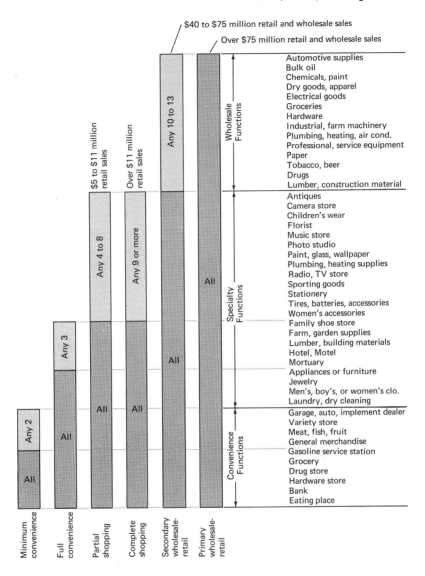

Fig. 6-6. Specifications of Six Orders of Trade Centers in the Upper Midwest Study

SOURCE: John R. Borchert and Russell B. Adams, *Trade Centers and Trade Areas of the Upper Midwest,* Upper Midwest Economic Study, Urban Report No. 3 (Minneapolis: September 1963), p. 4.

sale-retail center" received more calls than any other center at its own level, and at least half as many calls as any "metropolitan center."[17]

[17] The only metropolitan center within the Upper Midwest is Minneapolis-St. Paul, but such outside cities as Chicago, Portland, Seattle, Milwaukee, Des Moines, Omaha, and Denver received substantial proportions of the calls from nearby parts of the Upper Midwest. (See Fig. 6-9.)

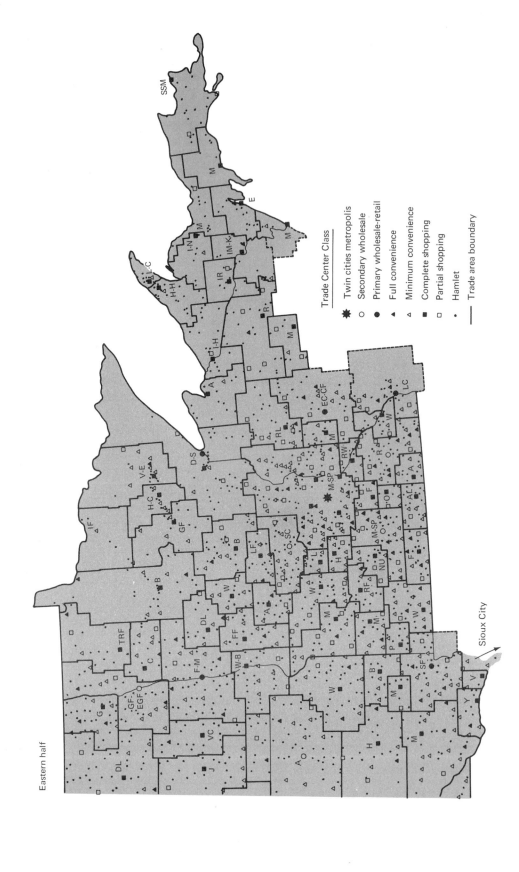

Eastern half

Trade Center Class

✴ Twin cities metropolis
○ Secondary wholesale
● Primary wholesale-retail
◄ Full convenience
◁ Minimum convenience
■ Complete shopping
□ Partial shopping
· Hamlet
— Trade area boundary

SSM

Sioux City

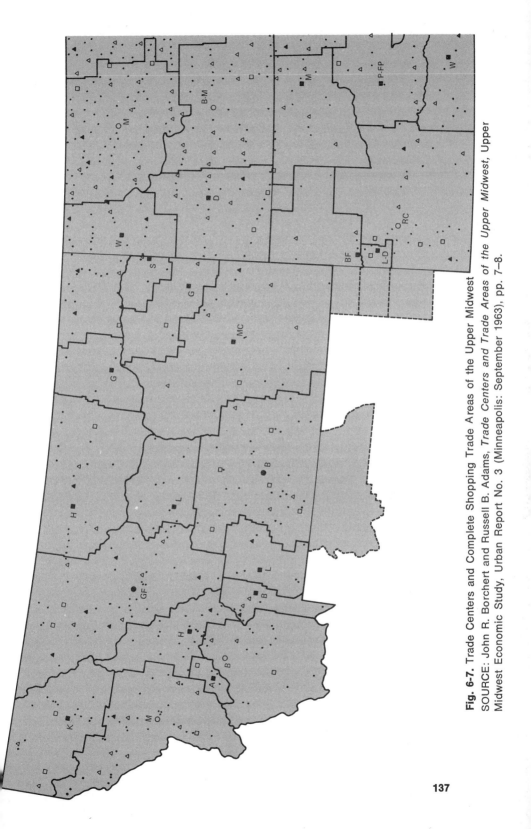

Fig. 6-7. Trade Centers and Complete Shopping Trade Areas of the Upper Midwest

SOURCE: John R. Borchert and Russell B. Adams, *Trade Centers and Trade Areas of the Upper Midwest*, Upper Midwest Economic Study, Urban Report No. 3 (Minneapolis: September 1963), pp. 7–8.

137

TABLE 6-1. Population and Number of Retail Functions in Upper Midwest Trade Centers

Type of center	Number of centers	Mean number of retail functions	Median population	Population range
Wholesale-retail	17	45.6	42,400	23,100–155,800
Complete shopping	79	35.8	9,500	3,700–27,900
Partial shopping	127	27.1	2,500	1,200–8,700
Full convenience	111	21.7	1,600	800–3,600
Minimum convenience	378	14.4	800	300–3,700
Hamlet	1,820	6.0	160	30–1,800

SOURCE: John R. Borchert and Russell B. Adams, *Trade Centers and Trade Areas of the Upper Midwest,* Upper Midwest Economic Study, Urban Report No. 3 (Minneapolis: September 1963), Table 1, p. 2.

Trade areas at the "complete shopping" level were "defined by lines drawn at highway half-distances between complete shopping centers, then adjusted for barriers, such as mountain ranges, and differences in sizes of competing centers."[18] It is interesting to note in Fig. 6-7 that these areas are larger (that is, the complete shopping centers are spaced farther apart) in the western and northeastern parts of the Upper Midwest, where the density of population and income per square mile is less. This is in accord with the theoretical expectation indicated earlier: Trade area size is inversely related to market density.

Fig. 6-8 shows the much larger trade areas at the *secondary wholesale-retail* level. Here again, the areas are more extensive where population is sparser, and there is an observable tendency for the areas to be asymmetrical, extending farther in the direction away from metropolitan centers. This same asymmetry was noted as a theoretical expectation in Fig. 6-5, but there is an additional reason for it. A large part of the goods distributed from the wholesaling centers are bought from manufacturers or large distributors in the metropolitan centers and other places outside the region, and transfer costs make their prices higher as we go farther from those sources. Consequently, a trade center in the Upper Midwest can compete more effectively with other centers of its own rank located farther from the sources of the goods than it can with competing centers located closer to the sources.

Trade and service areas of metropolitan centers serving the Upper Midwest are shown in Fig. 6-9. This demarcation of areas was based on relative frequencies of telephone calls received from wholesale-retail

[18] Borchert and Adams, *op. cit.,* p. 9. ·

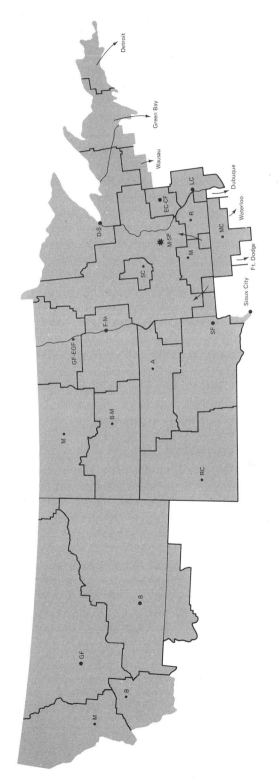

* Metropolitan center • Primary wholesale-retail center • Secondary wholesale-retail center —— Trade area boundary

Fig. 6-8. Trade Areas at the Secondary Wholesale-Retail Level

SOURCE: John R. Borchert and Russell B. Adams, *Trade Centers and Trade Areas of the Upper Midwest*, Upper Midwest Economic Study, Urban Report No. 3 (Minneapolis: September 1963), p. 29.

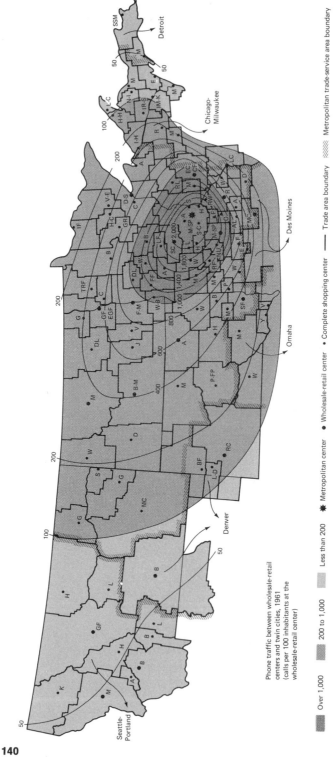

Fig. 6-9. Metropolitan Trade and Service Areas

SOURCE: John R. Borchert and Russell B. Adams, *Trade Centers and Trade Areas of the Upper Midwest*, Upper Midwest Economic Study, Urban Report No. 3 (Minneapolis: September 1963), p. 25.

Phone traffic between wholesale-retail centers and twin cities, 1961 (calls per 100 inhabitants at the wholesale-retail center)

✳ Metropolitan center   ● Wholesale-retail center   • Complete shopping center   —— Trade area boundary   ///// Metropolitan trade-service area boundary

■ Over 1,000   ■ 200 to 1,000   ■ Less than 200

centers, and the progression of frequencies is mapped for Minneapolis-St. Paul. It will be observed that the number of calls (per 100 inhabitants at the wholesale-retail centers where the calls originate) first falls off very rapidly and then more and more gradually with increasing distance from the metropolitan center.

ACTIVITIES EXTRANEOUS TO THE CENTRAL-PLACE HIERARCHY

Let us now consider more explicitly some of the limitations of the simple central-place model. So far in this chapter, our assumption has been that both markets and sources of transferable inputs for urban activities are *ubiquitous*. The resultant theoretical patterns of market areas and central places simply reflected the locational effects of the economies of agglomeration available to various kinds of urban activities. We have as yet no rationale for any flows of goods or services (other than primary rural products) either "up" the steps of the urban hierarchy or horizontally among cities of equal status. Yet in reality, enormous flows of these types occur. Clevelanders buy cigarettes from Durham, North Carolina, automobile tires from Akron, frozen orange juice made in small towns in Florida, and government services from Washington and Columbus. How does all this relate, if at all, to the hierarchical scheme of urban places, activities, and market areas?

The clue is that neither markets nor transferable inputs are really ubiquitous. Although for most kinds of consumer goods and services there is a market wherever people live, there are some consumer goods and services that are used mainly or exclusively by people in certain regions, by people in larger cities, or by rural and small-town people. For inputs, the lack of ubiquity is even more pervasive. Labor supply, of a sort, exists wherever people live; but other inputs such as specific crops, minerals, or manufactured goods or services are found only in certain places and with a wide variety of costs and qualities.

Let us consider the locational implications. We can usefully distinguish three classes of activities, according to whether their locations are (1) predominantly in larger cities, (2) predominantly in small cities or towns, (3) not associated with any particular size of city. (Certain manufacturing industries are cited as examples in Appendix 6-3.)

Those activities dependent on the external economies of urban concentration are predominantly located in large cities. This class of activities has already been discussed in Chapter 4. Their outputs are disposed of in the cities where produced, in other cities of all sizes, and in rural areas as well: In other words, the flow is mainly downward in the hierarchy, but it is also horizontal at the highest levels. Activities of this type fit reasonably well into the hierarchical central-place scheme.

There are several reasons why an activity might be found mainly in small centers. First, this is the normal location pattern for processing operations strongly oriented to rural inputs or to other inputs derived from extensive land uses; these are likely to be crowded out from highly urbanized regions by more intensive claimants for land. Forestry and grazing are such land uses: Sawmills and meat-packing plants are most often not located in large cities, because they must be close to types of land use which are usually associated with sparse settlement. Meat packing would be even more a small-town industry were it not for the practice of shipping cattle from range lands to fattening areas prior to slaughter.[19] The processing of perishable crops is so strongly input oriented that individual plants have quite small supply areas; and simply on a probability basis, very few of those areas will contain a large city.[20]

Small-town locations are more characteristic for activities associated with extensive outdoor recreation. These activities need plenty of space, and in some cases (such as ski resorts) topographical or climatic conditions not typical of large cities.

Finally, small cities and towns usually provide lower living costs and wage levels; thus, activities strongly oriented to cheap labor as such, and footloose with regard to other locational considerations, are likely to prefer the smallest size place that will provide enough workers for a plant of efficient scale. Most American textile mills, and a wide variety of industries making fairly standardized apparel items (such as shoes), are now found in rather small cities and towns, the principal explanation being labor-cost economies (Chapter 7 will give further attention to the origins and effects of labor-cost differentials).

There are even some basically clerical activities for which a small-town location is appropriate for serving a nationwide market, since labor and space are cheap and the inputs and outputs move by mail. For example,

[19] The meat-packing industry in the United States is an interesting example of major locational shift. Initially highly dispersed in the days when transport was costly and slow, and refrigeration in transit impracticable, the industry developed massive concentration in the later nineteenth century at the larger Midwestern cities on the basis of rail transport of both livestock and meat products and the economical utilization of by-products. But the ideal weights of transported input and output were never very different, and in the mid-twentieth century a trend toward decentralization set in. The giant stockyards and packing plants of Chicago, Omaha, Kansas City, St. Paul, and other old-time meat-packing centers were in the process of dismantlement in the 1950s and 1960s. Two major factors causing this location shift were apparently (1) the shift of consumer markets toward the West Coast and the Gulf Coast and (2) the greater use of refrigerated transport of meat products by truck and air freight, without any corresponding improvement in the transportability of live animals. Facilitating the transfer of output tends, of course, to move an activity closer to its sources of inputs, and truck shipment permits more decentralization out of major terminal locations.

[20] Flour milling and some other processing activities involving little if any loss of perishability or bulk and subject to considerable economies of scale are more often found in middle-sized or even large cities (such as Buffalo and Minneapolis).

the U.S. Bureau of the Census maintains its central office for the searching of Census files to establish birth records for individuals at Pittsburg, Kansas. One of the larger life insurance companies maintains its central office at the very small city of Montpelier, Vermont. Most other firms in this field, however, are in larger cities. For activities located in small cities, the flow of outputs is mainly *up* the urban hierarchy to markets in larger cities; but it is also partly horizontal, since only some but not all small places have the activity in question.

There is a large variety of activities for which size of city seems essentially irrelevant: they occur indiscriminately in small, middle-sized, and large cities. Some of these are primarily oriented to a localized natural advantage such as water (for processing or for transport) or a mineral resource, and their agglomeration economies are internal, involving merely the scale of the individual unit. Thus, salt mining and processing works are found both in isolated locations and within the city of Detroit; steel works are found both in large cities like Chicago and in quite small cities like Butler, Pennsylvania, or Provo, Utah; and automobile parts, electrical equipment, furniture, whiskey, candy, and many other manufactured goods are made in locations seemingly selected without any systematic concern for city size. There is no discernible relationship here to the hierarchical scheme of central places in terms of market areas, industry distribution patterns, or the flow of inputs or outputs.

In view of such kinds of activity that do not seem to fit the hierarchical central-place scheme at all, we can readily understand why the relation of range of retail and wholesale functions to size of trade area and to city size is less than exact. In fact, it may be surprising that there is as much evidence of hierarchical regularity as does appear. Let us take another look at the principles involved.

The relationship between trade area size (that is, spacing of cities) and urban functions principally involves retail and wholesale trade, which were in fact the basis of the hierarchical ranking in the Upper Midwest investigation. Some kinds of manufacturing also play a similar role. Bakeries, soft drink bottling plants, sheet-metal shops, ice cream plants, job printing and newspaper plants, breweries, and many other industries can be arranged in a reasonable sequence according to the minimum size of market required, in the same way that different kinds of retail lines of retailing or wholesaling can; and it is possible to identify roughly the "threshold size" of place above which each is likely to be found. Many kinds of services (shoe repairing, movies, bowling alleys, doctors, lawyers, hospitals, realtors, morticians, broadcasting stations, and so on) can likewise be more or less appropriately fitted into the central-place order. Moreover, something very like the trade center hierarchy appears in the public services provided in the hierarchy of unincorporated settlements, villages, towns, county seats, and state capitals.

But many urban places, at all size levels, also contain what we can call "noncentral-place" activities. Consider, for example, a small town whose retail trading area extends only a dozen miles, but which now acquires a shoe factory, serving a wide regional or even national market. That town now has a large employment and population compared to either the size or the population of its rural trading area: in this respect, it has been put out of line with the hierarchical scheme. But we must recognize that its trading area includes itself: The town needs grocery stores and drug stores and the like to serve the shoe factory employees as well as the rural customers and the people employed in central-place activities. Both the *amount and the variety of its central-place business* will become greater than they were before the shoe factory came. Thus, the town will occupy a higher *rank in the hierarchy.* Finally, by virtue of the wider range of available goods, we can expect the town to draw rural customers from a larger *area* than before, at the expense of rival towns not blessed by new factories. (Some of those towns may as a result lose previous retail functions and sink in the hierarchy.) The ultimate equilibrium situation may turn out to be reasonably close, after all, to what the central-place formulas would suggest in terms of the relation between town sizes, range of central-place activities, and size of trade area.

This example shows that there may be a good deal more relevance in the theoretical central-place relationships than one might infer in view of the fact that so many activities (like the shoe factory in this example) are located extraneously. It is no longer quite so surprising that we find the degree of hierarchical regularity that does appear in the real world. We can also see how individual towns and cities can break out of their positions in the hierarchy and either rise or fall: The system, even in theory, has internal mobility. The causes and processes of urban and regional growth will be discussed more fully in later chapters.

TRENDS IN URBAN PATTERNS

In later chapters we shall be considering some of the reasons why certain cities and regions grow faster than others and what some of the major observable trends of change are. We now consider briefly how the central-place model can throw some light on changes in the relative importance of cities of different orders of size.

The Upper Midwest study and others have brought to light a tendency for the smaller trade centers to grow more slowly than the middle-sized and large ones in recent decades, and it is clear that a great many hamlets and villages have actually disappeared. Table 6-2 provides some evidence of this trend.

> . . . there is some tendency for population growth of a place to be directly related to its size, and hence to its previous growth. This is to be expected

TABLE 6-2. Proportion of Upper Midwest Trade Centers in 1930–1960 Population Growth Rate Classes

	Total	Fast or very fast (46 percent or more)	Moderate (17 to 45 percent)	Slow (zero to 16 percent)	Decline
Wholesale-retail centers					
Metropolitan*	100	100	0	0	0
Primary	100	72	14	14	0
Secondary	100	80	10	0	10
Shopping centers					
Complete	100	62	26	4	8
Partial	100	54	26	9	11
Convenience centers					
Full	100	43	36	15	6
Minimum	100	28	30	23	19
Hamlets†	100	12	11	41	37

* Minneapolis-St. Paul is the only "metropolitan wholesale-retail center."

† Percentages do not add exactly to 100 because of rounding off.

SOURCE: John R. Borchert, *The Urbanization of the Upper Midwest: 1930–1960,* Upper Midwest Economic Study, Urban Report No. 2 (Minneapolis: February 1963), Table 3, p. 19.

throughout the main agricultural regions of the Upper Midwest since the chief functions of most communities are trade, service, and agricultural processing. The past thirty years' change in these areas has been characterized by adjustment to modern transport and modern agricultural methods. Although farm population in the trade areas of these cities has declined, the value of agricultural production has been sustained or increased. The changes that have taken place have involved mainly consolidation and centralization of many business functions and, hence, employment opportunities. In general, the larger a place was at the beginning of the automotive era, the better have been its chances to retain old functions and acquire new ones.[21]

This trend is the result of two kinds of change, and considerable further investigation would be needed to measure the two influences separately. First, there may be a tendency for many specific central-place activities to assume a more concentrated urban pattern (abandoning smaller places for larger places) because of changes in the basic conditions determining their efficient scale and dispersion. These conditions we have identified as (1) the density of demand for their outputs, (2) the degree to which they are subject to scale or other agglomeration economies, and (3) the level of transfer costs on their outputs.

Increased density of demand makes it possible for the activity to sustain itself with smaller trade areas. In many agricultural areas in the Upper

[21] John R. Borchert, *The Urbanization of the Upper Midwest: 1930–1960,* Upper Midwest Economic Study, Urban Report No. 2 (Minneapolis: February 1963), p. 19.

Midwest and elsewhere, the farm population has notably thinned out in recent decades because of the trend toward larger and more mechanized farms employing fewer people on any given area. The American farm population shrank steadily after 1935, and not until the end of the 1960s did stabilization appear imminent. In many areas, of course, per capita farm income rose more than enough to compensate; but it is reasonable to surmise that a smaller number of farmers, even with the same aggregate income, represents a reduced demand for the kinds of goods and services available in the smallest settlements. At the same time, there has been a tendency for more farmers to live in town and commute to their farms, or to move to town in the winter. Consequently, farm population trends of recent decades appear to provide some of the explanation for the slow growth or decline of the smallest trade centers.

Increased economies of scale for an activity have the effect of enlarging trade areas and concentrating the activity in fewer and larger urban centers. Scale economies have not been as conspicuously enhanced in trade activities as in industrial activities; but the modern supermarket and shopping center have developed mainly within the past generation and constitute a major change. We must also reckon with the fact that higher living standards make consumers more sensitive to the appeals of variety in "shopping goods" and hence add to the competitive advantages of larger trading centers that can provide such a variety. Recognition of scale economies has been evidenced also in the trend toward consolidation and concentration of many public activities, such as schools and health services. Thus, we have here another plausible reason for the observed trend of faster growth of middle-sized and larger trade centers at the expense of smaller ones.

The advent of good rural roads and the automobile has, of course, enabled rural and small-town people to make longer shopping, crop-delivery, and other trips, and this factor also should be recognized as part of the explanation for the observed trends of urban growth. But the effect of changes in the level of transfer costs on trade area size and the spacing of trading centers is (as suggested earlier in this chapter) less straightforward than it might appear.

If transfer were assumed to be altogether costless, then activities could be concentrated at the points of lowest operating cost, and economies of agglomeration would tend to concentrate all of an activity in one spot. At the other extreme, if transfer were infinitely costly (that is, impossible), each location would have to be self-sufficient. From this contrast of extremes, we might infer that cheaper transfer always enlarges trade areas and leads to fewer, larger, and more widely spaced central places. A similar inference could be drawn by regarding transfer services and the services of factors of production as complementary inputs, with possibilities of substituting a cheaper input for a more expensive one. Then if transfer services became cheaper we should expect that more transfer would be used in relation to output: that is, distances between seller and buyer would increase and trading areas would be larger. This is what we may call the "substitution effect" of a change in transfer cost.

This simple formulation, however, overlooks some side effects of changes in the level of transfer cost. First, there is what might be called the "income effect" of such changes. If transfer becomes cheaper, buyers at any distance from the trade center will get the goods cheaper and will normally buy more. With greater sales per buyer, a smaller trade area will suffice to provide the scale economies needed to sustain a center. More centers can survive. The *income* effect of a reduction in transfer costs is, then, a *reduction* in trade area size, and is similar to the effect of an increase in demand density (that is, population density, per capita income, or both).[22]

There is another way, too, in which cheaper transport may tend to reduce the size of trading areas and lead to a more dispersed pattern of centers. The degree to which activity is concentrated in locations of low operating cost depends on (1) transfer costs and (2) the magnitude of the differentials in operating cost. If transfer becomes cheaper while the operating cost differentials remain the same, activity will become less transfer oriented and will tend to cluster more in efficient operating locations. But, at the same time, reduced transfer costs are likely to narrow the operating cost differentials (since they enhance labor mobility and tend to equalize the costs of various transferable inputs). Thus, here again, a change in the level of transfer cost cuts both ways in regard to agglomeration versus dispersion, and the net effect could be in either direction.[23]

The urban pattern is also affected by changes in the mix of activities. It has been mentioned already that, as a result of higher levels of income

---

[22] Where travel by retail buyers is involved, the benefit to the buyers is mainly a saving in time rather than money. To this extent, the transfer cost reduction in itself does not increase effective market density and shrink trade areas as the income effect implies; the substitution effect dominates, and buyers respond to easier transfer by using more transfer (that is, traveling greater distances in search of cheaper or better goods and services).

The reader with some training in economics will recognize this conflict between substitution effect and income effect as something that quite generally occurs whenever an activity calls for two or more complementary inputs that are to some extent mutually substitutable. For example, if machinery becomes cheaper, there is an incentive to add machines and reduce employment; but, at the same time, the cheaper machinery leads to a cheaper product and greater sales, which increases the demand for labor. The net effect on labor demand depends upon the terms of substitution between the two inputs and upon the elasticity of demand for the product.

[23] For further discussion of transfer cost effects in the framework of simplified central-place models, see Walter Isard, *Location and Space-Economy* (Cambridge, Mass.: The M.I.T. Press, 1956), 86–87; Hugh O. Nourse, *Regional Economics* (New York: McGraw-Hill, 1968), 215–216; and Edgar M. Hoover, "Transport Costs and the Spacing of Central Places," *Papers of the Regional Science Association,* 24 (1970), 255–274.

and leisure, consumer demand tends to shift from staple necessities to a wider range of shopping goods and luxuries, with variety becoming a more important dimension of competitive advantage for producers. This clearly favors the larger trade center. Moreover, as the economy develops, a greater proportion of productive activities involves later stages of processing and handling and a smaller proportion uses rural products directly as inputs. Fewer and fewer activities (like canneries or sawmills) need to be oriented closely to inputs from rural extractive activity; in contrast there is the widening range of activities (like the production of electrical equipment, pharmaceuticals, or books) that are technologically remote from any extractive process. Accordingly, there is less and less reason for many activities to be located in small settlements for the sake of easy access to agricultural, forest, or mineral products. Finally, the increasing variety and complexity of goods, services, and productive operations calls for more close interfirm and interactivity contact and tends to increase the locational importance of urban external economies of agglomeration.

These trends in noncentral-place activity orientation constitute still more reason for the observed trend toward relatively slow growth, or even decline, in the smaller centers. In particular areas and activities, there are some offsetting tendencies that will be noted in later chapters.

THE ROLE OF CITIES IN REGIONAL DEVELOPMENT

In the process of regional growth (which will be the subject of Chapter 8), cities play a unique role. The existence of sizable urban centers seems to be a necessary (though not always sufficient) condition for the transition from a basically agrarian economy to an advanced economy of high productivity and a wide range of productive activities. Why is this so?

The internal and external economies of agglomeration discussed in Chapter 4, and the transfer advantages of location at major multimodal transfer nodes discussed in Chapter 3, help to explain why there is so much urban concentration of those activities that are not bound to dispersed markets or input sources and do not need large amounts of cheap space. But this does not make it clear why cities are so important in a *dynamic* way. Let us investigate not why cities exist, but why they lead the way in regional and national development. Certain further characteristics of the urban scene need to be recognized, specifically in the context of a changing world.

First, there is the relatively cosmopolitan aspect of cities. They are a region's eyes and ears perceiving the outside world. "Foreign" ideas, goods, and procedures have much to contribute to the development of even the most advanced region, and cities, as *entrepôts* for interregional transfer, are the main points where these vital inputs gain admittance. This aspect of cities is most abundantly evident in the less-developed countries, where the principal cities impressively resemble their counterparts in advanced countries, even though a few miles away we can step back centuries in time.

Quite apart from their interregional contact function, cities serve an important role in the development process simply by being places in which people from other parts of the same region or country are brought together in densities and living conditions sharply contrasting with those of the rural areas. Conservative traditions and outlooks that persist in the hinterland tend to dissolve rather quickly in the urban melting pot; the results are always conducive to more rapid social and economic change, though they often are painful and destructive in terms of personal satisfaction and orderly social and political adjustment. Social effects of urbanization that can be of major importance in overpopulated countries are the mutually reinforcing tendencies toward smaller families and toward greater labor force participation of women. For the working population as a whole, urbanization represents exposure to a way of life in which work is more scheduled and organized, monetized transactions and impersonal relationships play a larger part, literacy and adaptability to change are more valuable personal assets, and the choice of occupations and lines of individual development is widened.

Such considerations as these go far to explain why cities (especially large ones with far-reaching external contacts) have always been the main seedbeds of innovation; in economic terms, this involves the genesis of new techniques, new products, and new firms. Such places provide the exposure to a wide range of ideas and problems from which solutions emerge. They represent large concentrations of individuals whose propensities to innovate and adapt to change have been reinforced by selectivity of migration (see Chapter 7). They provide the largest concentrations of customers and suppliers most receptive to new products and requirements. They provide the diversified supply of skills and supporting services that enable a producer to start small and concentrate upon a narrowly specialized function (see the discussion of external economies in Chapter 4). They provide a social and business climate in which impediments of tradition and personal inertia are minimized, and initiative and innovation carry prestige; and in which the innovator can learn much from his day-to-day contacts with competitors and can most easily tap the stock of accumulated know-how, exploiting inventions arising not only in his own city but elsewhere.[24]

---

[24] For a penetrating and well-documented analysis of the interaction between *industrial* innovation and urban concentration in the United States, see Allen R. Pred, *The Spatial Dynamics of U.S. Urban-Industrial Growth, 1800–1914* (Cambridge, Mass.: The M.I.T. Press, 1966), Chapter 3.

Pred's analysis covered the period up to 1914, and as he suggested, the nature and strength of some of the cumulative forces of urban-industrial agglomeration

But there is another side to the issue. Major cities are the locations at which the newest types of activities can most easily get a foothold within any region or country, and the advent of industrialization in an undeveloped country is generally accompanied by explosive growth of the largest centers and a heightening of economic and social contrasts between those centers and the rural backwaters. But as development proceeds, two things happen. Some of the sensitive infant industries of yesterday attain maturity: Their techniques become less experimental and their products more familiar to a wider market. As a result, these activities are no longer so dependent upon the special advantages that large cities provide. The fledglings are ready to leave the nest. At the same time, the positive incentives to decentralize out of the initial large-city concentration tend to increase. With a larger and wider market for the product, a location pattern involving a number of regional production centers offers economies in distribution costs, without undue sacrifice of the economies of scale. The external economies of cluster become less important with the increase in financial and technical resources of firms and the greater standardization of process and product. Costs of labor and other local inputs in the initial large-city location now appear unnecessarily high in relation to what these inputs cost in smaller places. And in the original centers where the industry developed, maturity may well have meant some development of rigidities and loss of initiative because of the aging of both business leaders and the labor force and the growth of defensive practices to protect seniority rights, painfully acquired but obsolescent skills, positions of power, and other accumulated perquisites. Thus, the city that hatched the industry and saw it through its infancy may lose it altogether when it grows up.

The evolutionary process sketched here in terms of locational change accompanying the birth, infancy, and maturing of an activity is a strikingly

---

have subsequently changed. His study is noteworthy in its stress upon the interaction between concentration and innovation: that is, technological advance and innovation flourish in the large urban-industrial center, and give rise to new industries that are established in those same centers and stimulate their further growth. There are many examples of this process in the nineteenth century: the inception of the electrical equipment manufacturing industry in New York, Boston, and Pittsburgh, the making of scientific instruments and optical equipment in Rochester, N.Y., and so on. But (as Pred points out) under more recent conditions innovation at one location can as easily give rise to new industry in *other* locations. This is true because technical knowledge is much more diffused and transferable now, and also because large multi-plant and multi-industry corporations now play a commanding role in the research and development that gives rise to new processes and industries. Such a corporation is perfectly free to choose locations for the new industry quite remote from the headquarters or research-center city.

This and other changes help to explain why specific manufacturing industries are no longer as strongly or persistently concentrated in their "parent cities" as they used to be; and perhaps also, why the fastest growing metropolitan areas today are not the very largest but those of intermediate size.

familiar one. Wilbur Thompson has referred to it in terms of "a filter-down theory of industrial location" and "the urban-regional growth loop."[25] As he points out, "New York has lost nearly every industry it has ever had—flour mills, foundries, meat-packing plants, textile mills and tanneries." Pittsburgh pioneered and then lost preeminence in a long series of major industries including oil refining, aluminum, and electrical machinery.

It appears, then, that large cities characteristically have a disproportionate component of new and small "growth industries" in their mix of activities, but generally fail to maintain their shares of activities that are past the early stages. Smaller cities and towns, and less advanced regions, are more likely to show competitive gains in the sense of increasing their shares of the national total of employment in the activities represented there, but their overall growth is held down by the fact that their mix of activities is heavily weighted with slow-growth and low-wage activities.[26] The relative rates of growth of major cities versus smaller places, then, can depend to an important extent on how rapidly the filter-down or dispersion of maturing urban activities proceeds compared to the initiation of new urban activities. In Thompson's words, faster development of the smaller, less-developed urban area "would seem to require that it receive each successive industry a little earlier in its life cycle, to acquire the industry at a point in time when it still has both substantial job-forming potential and high-skill work."[27]

Further implications will be explored in later chapters, in connection with explanations of overall regional growth (Chapter 8), growth promotion policies and the focusing of development promotion efforts upon urban growth centers (Chapter 9), and some structural problems arising from urban growth (Chapters 11 and 12).

SELECTED READINGS[28]

August Lösch, *Die räumliche Ordnung der Wirtschaft* (Jena: Gustav Fischer, 1940; 2nd ed., 1944); W. H. Woglom (tr.), *The Economics of Location* (New Haven: Yale University Press, 1954).

Otis Dudley Duncan and others, *Metropolis and Region* (Baltimore: Johns Hopkins Press, 1960), Chs. 2, 3.

Hal H. Winsborough, "Occupational Composition and the Urban Hierarchy," *American Sociological Review*, 25, 6 (December 1960), 894–897.

---

[25] Wilbur R. Thompson, "The Economic Base of Urban Problems," in Neil W. Chamberlain (ed.), *Contemporary Economic Issues* (Homewood, Ill.: Irwin, 1969), 6–9.

[26] See Appendix 9-1 for some discussion of measures of regional economic growth in terms of components reflecting activity-mix and competitive gain or loss.

[27] *Op. cit.*, p. 9.

[28] See also references cited in footnotes on pages 120 and 131.

Gerald Hodge, "Prediction of Trade Center Viability in the Great Plains," *Papers of the Regional Science Association,* 15 (1965), 87–118.

Allen R. Pred, *The Spatial Dynamics of U.S. Urban-Industrial Growth, 1800–1914* (Cambridge, Mass.: M.I.T. Press, 1966).

David Thorpe, "The Main Shopping Centres of Great Britain in 1961: Their Locational and Structural Characteristics," *Urban Studies,* 5, 2 (June 1968), 165–206.

Martin Beckmann, *Location Theory* (New York: Random House, 1968), Ch. 5.

Eric E. Lampard, "The Evolving System of Cities in the United States: Urbanization and Economic Development," in Harvey S. Perloff and Lowdon Wingo, Jr. (eds.), *Issues in Urban Economics* (Baltimore: Johns Hopkins Press, 1968), 81–139. A list of further references appears on his page 139.

Hugh O. Nourse, *Regional Economics* (New York: McGraw-Hill, 1968), Ch. 3.

Charles G. Field and Charles Reiss, "An Introduction to Central Place Theory," *Reviews in Urban Economics,* 1, 1 (Winter 1968), 47–68.

Wilbur R. Thompson, "The Economic Base of Urban Problems," in Neil W. Chamberlain (ed.), *Contemporary Economic Issues* (Homewood, Ill.: Irwin, 1969), 1–47.

Colin Clark, *Population Growth and Land Use* (London: Macmillan, and New York: St. Martin's Press, 1969), Ch. VIII.

Harry W. Richardson, *Regional Economics* (New York: Praeger, 1969), Ch. 7.

Peter Scott, *Geography and Retailing* (Chicago: Aldine, 1970).

Edgar M. Hoover, "Transport Costs and the Spacing of Central Places," *Papers of the Regional Science Association,* 25 (1970), 255–274.

APPENDIX 6-1

Trading Area Boundaries under Reilly's Law
(See page 131)

Assume two centers A and B located w miles apart, with center A having m times the population of center B. According to Reilly's Law, the square of the distance from A to any point on the trading area boundary will be m times the square of the distance from B to that point.

In the diagram below, the locations are plotted with A at the origin and B on the horizontal axis at a distance w. A point X on the boundary is shown with coordinates x and y.

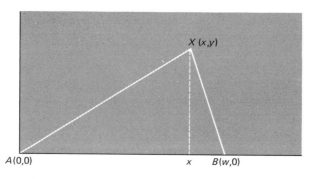

Reilly's Law may now be stated as

$$y^2 + x^2 = m(y^2 + x^2 - 2x\cdot w + w^2)$$

$$y^2(1-m) = -x^2(1-m) - 2xmw + w^2m$$

(1)
$$y^2 = \frac{w^2m}{1-m} - \frac{2xmw}{1-m} - x^2$$

Let

(2)
$$z = x + \frac{mw}{1-m}$$

Then

$$z^2 = x^2 + \frac{2xmw}{1-m} + \left(\frac{mw}{1-m}\right)^2$$

$$-x^2 = -z^2 + \frac{2xmw}{1-m} + \left(\frac{mw}{1-m}\right)^2$$

Substituting in (1),

$$y^2 = \frac{mw^2}{1-m} - \frac{2xmw}{1-m} - z^2 + \frac{2xmw}{1-m} + \left(\frac{mw}{1-m}\right)^2$$

$$y^2 = \frac{mw^2 - m^2w^2 + m^2w^2}{(1-m)^2} - z^2$$

$$y^2 + z^2 = \frac{mw^2}{(1-m)^2}$$

This is the equation of a circle with radius

$$\left|\frac{w\sqrt{m}}{1-m}\right|$$

The center of the circle is at $z=0$. Substituting in (2),

$$x = mw/(m-1)$$

The distance of the center of the circle from A is thus $m/(m-1)$ times the distance w from A to B. If $m>1$ (that is, if A has the larger population), the center will then be to the right of B in the diagram, by a distance $mw/(m-1) - w = w/(m-1)$.

In the special case of equal populations $(m=1)$ there is no circle, but a straight-line boundary, the perpendicular bisector of the line AB. Its equation is $x = w/2$.

APPENDIX 6-2

Conditions Determining the Existence and Size of Trading Areas
(See pages 125–127 and 145–147)

The following analysis applies to a highly simplified central-place system, with only one central-place activity. Demand for its product is uniform over the whole area, sales per unit of area being $g(h-m)$ where m is the delivered price and h is the price above which no one will buy; g reflects the "market density." Transport costs are uniformly t per unit quantity and distance. Each producer's total costs are $f + qc$, where f is fixed cost, c is unit variable cost (= marginal cost), and q is volume of output. To simplify the analysis still further, trading areas are treated as if they were circular in all cases. Distance of a buyer from the selling center is denoted by r, and the trading area radius by R.

Martin Beckmann[29] has shown that a monopolistic seller, in the situation described, can maximize his profits by setting prices as follows:

	No freight absorption (uniform f.o.b. price)	Full freight absorption (uniform delivered price)	Optimum discrimination (50 percent freight absorption)
Net (f.o.b.) price	$(h+3c)/4$	$-rt + (3h+c)/4$	$(h+c)/2$
Delivered price	$rt + (h+3c)/4$	$(3h+c)/4$	$(h+c+rt)/2$
Trade area radius[30]	$3(h-c)/4t$	$3(h-c)/4t$	$(h-c)/t$

It will be observed that the optimum radius is greatest with 50 percent freight absorption, and is $\frac{3}{4}$ that size (that is, the *area* is $\frac{9}{16}$ as large) under either zero or 100 percent freight absorption.

---

[29] *Location Theory* (New York: Random House, 1968), pp. 32, 51, 52. Beckmann's formulas have been translated here into my notation. He assumed $t=1$, and wrote a/b where I have h, and b where I have g.

[30] In the f.o.b. and optimum-discrimination cases, delivered price rises with increased distance from the market and at the edge of the market is equal to h (the price at which *buyers stop buying*). It is assumed that in the case of flat delivered price, the seller will *refuse to sell* to buyers beyond the trading area boundary: Though they would be willing to buy, he could not cover his variable cost and transfer cost on such sales.

The maximum profits attainable by the monopolist are:

(1) *With uniform f.o.b. price:*

$$\int_{o}^{R} 2\pi rg\,(p-c)\,(h-p-rt)\,dr - f$$

where p=f.o.b. price. This reduces to

$$\frac{9\pi g}{256}\,[\,(h-c)^4/t^2\,] - f = .110g[\,(h-c)^4/t^2\,] - f$$

(2) *With uniform delivered price:*

$$\int_{o}^{R} 2\pi rg\,(m-c-rt)\,(h-m)\,dr - f$$

where m=delivered price. This reduces to

$$\frac{9\pi g}{256}\,[\,(h-c)^4/t^2\,] - f$$

the same as in the case of uniform f.o.b. price.

(3) *With optimum discrimination:*

$$\int_{o}^{R} 2\pi rg\left(\frac{h-c-tr}{2}\right)^{2} dr - f$$

This reduces to

$$\frac{\pi g}{24}\,[\,(h-c)^4/t^2\,] - f = .131g[\,(h-c)^4/t^2\,] - f$$

It appears, then, that the returns applicable to fixed costs (that is, profits + f) for any given set of cost and demand conditions will be about $131/110 = 1.19$ times as large under optimum discrimination as under either uniform f.o.b. or uniform delivered pricing.

The threshold conditions that have to be met in order for any trade areas or centers to exist at all are shown by setting maximum profits at zero. These conditions are as shown below:

	Maximum permissible fixed cost (f)	Minimum permissible demand density (g)	Maximum permissible transfer rate (t)
Under either uniform f.o.b. or uniform delivered pricing	$.110g \ (h-c)^4/t^2$	$9.05ft^2/(h-c)^4$	$.332(h-c)^2\sqrt{g/f}$
Under optimum discrimination	$.131g \ (h-c)^4/t^2$	$7.64ft^2/(h-c)^4$	$.363(h-c)^2\sqrt{g/f}$
Effect of pricing system—under optimum discrimination	Maximum is 19% higher	Minimum is 16% lower	Maximum is 9% higher

It is clear from these results that the chances for the *existence* of trading areas are favored by (1) lower fixed costs, (2) higher market density, (3) cheaper transfer, and (4) the exercise of rational price discrimination.

The *size* of trade areas, once they exist, is another question. The first table in this appendix shows that, for a *monopolist,* the most profitable trade area will be larger when transfer is cheaper (R is inversely related to t) and is independent of both fixed costs and demand density. When there is competition among sellers, trading areas will be larger if fixed costs (f) are greater, or if demand density (g) is lower, but depend in a more complex way upon the levels of t, h, and c and the kind of pricing system the competitors use.

APPENDIX 6-3

Concentration of U.S. Manufacturing Industries by City-Size Class
(See page 141)

On page 141, a possible locational categorization of activities was suggested, according to whether the activity tends to locate predominantly (1) in large cities, (2) in small cities, or (3) without regard to city size. Some tabulations of Census data by the U.S. Department of Commerce provide the basis for such a categorization of all *manufacturing* industries on the rather detailed 4-digit level of the Standard Industrial Classification. The data are from the *Census of Manufactures,* 1954.

For each of the several hundred 4-digit industries, total U.S. employment was broken down according to the city-size class in which the establishment was located. The percentage breakdown of *the industry's employment* by city-size class was then compared with the percentage breakdown of *population* by city-size class, and the differences between corresponding percentages were summed, to obtain a *location quotient* for each industry in each city-size class. (See the explanation of location quotients in connection with Table 8-3, pp. 209–211.)

The set of location quotients for any given industry gives a profile of that industry's location pattern in relation to city-size class—for example, if the quotients are high for the larger city-size classes, we can say that the industry in question tends to be more proportionately represented in large cities.

Table 6-A-1 presents some illustrative findings. For each city-size class, a few industries have been picked out that most clearly show the specific concentration pattern indicated. It is interesting to note that all of the first group of industries (concentrated in the largest cities) appear also in the list of "external-economy industries" highly concentrated in New York

TABLE 6-A-1. Selected U.S. Manufacturing Industries Showing Especially High and Especially Low Concentration in Particular Size Classes of Urban Places, 1954

Industries, by city-size class of greatest concentration (highest location quotient)	Location quotient in city-size class of greatest concentration	Number of employees, U.S. total (thousands)	Percentage of U.S. employment located in Standard Metropolitan Statistical Areas
500,000 or more			
Fur goods	5.39	10.0	97.8
Miscellaneous bookbinding work	4.97	3.3	99.2
Tucking, pleating, stitching	4.90	6.5	98.0
Embroideries, exc. Schiffli-machine	4.70	5.7	98.1
Millinery	4.31	20.2	94.9
Men's and boys' neckwear	4.21	9.5	95.9
Dolls	4.21	15.1	95.5
Bookbinding	4.20	17.2	96.3
Typesetting	4.19	14.6	98.4
100,000–499,999			
Photographic equipment	4.28	58.1	95.1
Optical instruments and lenses	3.97	12.7	97.4
Jewelers' findings	3.97	5.4	98.5
Tires and inner tubes	3.77	92.7	86.0
Costume jewelry	3.40	27.7	98.4
Cigars	3.19	38.5	88.2
50,000–99,999			
Chewing and smoking tobacco	6.34	7.5	90.5
Electrical measuring instruments	4.59	33.0	88.8
Transformers	4.10	41.0	89.7
Malleable iron foundries	3.71	23.4	52.1
Schiffli-machine embroideries	3.53	5.7	98.1
Steel foundries	3.31	55.1	88.0
Motor vehicles and parts	3.19	649.3	91.2

Industries, by city-size class of greatest concentration (highest location quotient)	Location quotient in city-size class of greatest concentration	Number of employees, U.S. total (thousands)	Percentage of U.S. employment located in Standard Metropolitan Statistical Areas
10,000–49,999			
Fur-felt hats and hat bodies	4.11	8.2	59.9
Professional furniture	3.76	5.5	51.2
Internal combustion engines	3.76	51.8	59.5
Pressed and blown glassware, n.e.c.*	3.61	41.9	32.7
Mineral wool	3.57	10.2	42.4
Carpets and rugs, exc. wool	3.29	11.5	32.3
Engine electrical equipment	3.28	46.3	39.2
2,500–9,999			
Work shirts	5.50	7.0	16.7
Fabric work gloves	3.94	10.1	22.3
Wood office furniture	3.42	5.5	61.4
Concentrated milk	3.39	13.3	13.4
Tractors	3.25	64.7	92.6
Full-fashioned hosiery mills	3.12	60.2	51.6
All other places			
Beet sugar	2.28	11.0	12.9
Raw cane sugar	2.18	3.1	0.0
Logging camps and contractors	2.13	75.5	6.3
Lime	2.11	8.0	16.9
Structural clay products, n.e.c.	1.79	5.0	27.7
Industries not concentrated by city size†			
Paper bags	1.35	33.3	69.7
Canned seafood	1.41	15.1	55.4
Plastic products, n.e.c.	1.52	92.0	78.9
Primary metal industries, n.e.c.	1.57	25.1	94.1
Nonferrous foundries	1.68	73.5	78.4
Pickles and sauces	1.69	21.9	64.9
Machine shops	1.69	103.7	77.1

* n.e.c.: not elsewhere classified.

† Location quotient between .80 and 1.70 for every city-size class from 2,500 up.

SOURCE: Stanford Research Institute, School of Planning and Architecture, *Costs of Urban Infrastructure for Industry as Related to City Size in Developing Countries: India Case Study* (Menlo Park, Cal.: Stanford Research Institute, 1968), Table B-2. Based on U.S. Department of Commerce, Office of Area Development, *Metropolitan Area and City Size Patterns of Manufacturing Industries, 1954,* Area Trend Series No. 4 (Washington, D.C.: Government Printing Office, June 1959), 12–21.

(Table 4-3). The table also includes (at the end) a list of industries that seem to be located without regard to city size, since their location quotients for the different size classes are all within a comparatively narrow range.

INTRODUCTION

The importance of manpower supply as a locational factor is suggested by the sheer magnitude of labor costs as an element in the total outlays of productive enterprises. Even in such an industrialized country as the United States, wage and salary payments account for about three-fifths of the gross national product, and this does not include the earnings of self-employed people and business proprietors (for example, farmers, store owners, free-lance professionals) which mainly represent a return to their labor. Accordingly, we should expect to find many kinds of activities locationally sensitive to differentials in the availability, price, and quality of labor.

Labor's role as a purchased input, however, is only one aspect of the locational interdependence of people and their economic activities. People in their role as consumers of the final output of goods and services affect the locational choices of market-oriented activities. They play still another role as users of residential land, and in urban areas residence is by far the largest land use. Finally, and most importantly, the purpose of the whole economic system is to provide a livelihood for people. Regional economics is vitally concerned with regional income differences, the opportunities found in different types of communities, and regional population growth and migration.

The present chapter is devoted to integrating and exploring these various aspects of "the location of people."

A LOOK AT SOME DIFFERENTIALS

Differentials in Pay Levels

Rates of pay in any specific occupation can differ widely from one place to another and even within the same labor market area. For example, the union wage scale for local truck drivers in 1967 averaged $3.59 an hour for some 70 cities surveyed by the U.S. Bureau of Labor Statistics, with the rate in individual cities ranging from a high of $4.33 in Sacramento, California, to a low of $2.91 in New Orleans.[1]

7

The Location of People

---

[1] U.S. Department of Labor, Bureau of Labor Statistics,

The differentials among cities are not entirely erratic: Some evidence of an underlying pattern appears in Tables 7-1 and 7-2, both of which refer to comparisons among metropolitan labor markets in recent years. Table 7-1 suggests that, in each of three broad types of occupation, the South is

TABLE 7-1. Relative Pay Levels in 80 Standard Metropolitan Statistical Areas: Averages by Region, 1964–1965 (Average for all 80 SMSAs for each occupation group = 100)

	Office clerical workers	Skilled maintenance workers	Unskilled plant workers
Northeast	99	96	103
North Central	101	103	107
South	93	96	79
West	107	106	112

SOURCE: U.S. Department of Labor, Bureau of Labor Statistics, *Wages and Related Benefits,* Bulletin No. 1430-83, Part II: Metropolitan Areas, United States and Regional Summaries, 1964–65 (Washington, D.C.: Government Printing Office, May 1966), 3–5. The regions used here are mapped in Fig. 8-2 on page 202.

TABLE 7-2. Relative Pay Levels by Region and Size of Metropolitan Area, 1966–1967 (227-area average pay level for each occupational group = 100)

Region and population size class	Office clerical workers	Skilled maintenance workers	Unskilled plant workers
Northeast			
1,000,000 or more	100	100	105
250,000–1,000,000	92	91	96
Less than 250,000	84	88	90
North Central			
1,000,000 or more	98	103	108
250,000–1,000,000	98	102	108
Less than 250,000	96	92	108
South			
1,000,000 or more	99	96	79
250,000–1,000,000	91	94	79
Less than 250,000	86	84	68
West			
1,000,000 or more	108	107	118
250,000–1,000,000	97	104	102
Less than 250,000	92	*	100

* No data.

SOURCE: U.S. Department of Labor, Bureau of Labor Statistics, Bulletin No. 1600, *Handbook of Labor Statistics 1968* (Washington, D.C.: Government Printing Office, 1968), Table 72, pp. 138–139. Each index figure shown here is the median of the indices for all areas in that region and size class as given in the source table.

Bulletin No. 1600, *Handbook of Labor Statistics 1968* (Washington, D.C.: Government Printing Office, 1968), Table 78, 151–162.

the region with the lowest pay levels; the Northeast, North Central, and West regions paying successively higher average rates. Table 7-2 provides some further detail, based on a larger number of metropolitan areas by size class; the same general pattern of interregional differentials appears. In addition, we see a consistent tendency, within each region and occupational group, for rates to be higher in the larger metropolitan areas. Such scanty data as are available for nonmetropolitan labor markets indicate that the positive relation between pay levels and size of place applies there as well. Finally, it can be noted in both tables that the interregional disparities are somewhat wider for the unskilled workers than for the two other groups. This feature of the pattern will be explained later.

Although the figures cited are based on careful comparisons of the standard earnings rates in (as nearly as possible) identical jobs, they do not give a complete picture of relative advantages for either the employee or the employer. No account is taken of the increasingly important fringe benefits (vacations, overtime pay, sick leave, pensions, and so on) or of differences in the cost of living. Further, these comparisons do not give us any indication of differentials in the productivity of workers, which also play a part in determining the employer's labor cost per unit of output.

Income Differentials

These likewise show a discernible pattern according to region and city size. The difference in per capita or per family incomes between two areas is, of course, determined not only by relative earnings in specific occupations, but by differences in the occupational and industry structure of the areas, the degree of labor force participation, and unemployment rates. For example, the median income of American families in 1966 was $7,436. By regions the corresponding figures were as follows:[2]

Region	Median income	Percentage of national median
Northeast	$7,878	106
North Central	7,893	106
South	6,233	84
West	8,089	109

The relation of income to type and size of the place of residence is shown in Table 7-3. The highest income levels are characteristically found in the smaller suburbs of the larger cities; intermediate income levels

[2] U.S. Department of Commerce, Bureau of the Census, *Current Population Reports: Consumer Income,* Series P-60, No. 53 (Washington, D.C.: Government Printing Office, December 28, 1967).

TABLE 7-3. Median Incomes of Families and Unrelated Individuals by Size and Type of Community, 1959

			Urban fringe	
			Incorporated places of 2,500 or more	Other places
	Total	**Central cities**		
In urban areas of				
3,000,000 or more	$5,831	$5,183	$6,790	$7,042
1,000,000 to 3,000,000	5,656	4,807	6,411	6,938
250,000 to 1,000,000	5,170	4,646	5,867	6,306
less than 250,000	4,903	4,674	5,311	5,709
	Total	**Inside SMSAs**		
Outside urban areas, in places of				
25,000 or more	$4,441	$4,658		
10,000 to 25,000	4,327	5,085		
2,500 to 10,000	4,328	5,347		
Rural nonfarm	4,013	5,106		
Rural farm	2,951	4,139		

SOURCE: Department of Commerce, Bureau of the Census, *United States Census of Population, 1960,* Report PC(3)-1B (Washington, D.C.: Government Printing Office, 1964), Table 1, pp. 10–12.

characterize cities proper, with income positively related to city size; and the lowest income levels are in nonmetropolitan small towns and rural areas.

Differentials in Real Income

From the standpoint of the worker, the possible advantage of working in a high-wage or high-income area partly depends on how expensive it is to live there. Most of us are aware that there are considerable differences in the cost of living in different parts of the country and different sizes of community.

Although it is impossible to measure relative living costs comprehensively so as to take into account all the needs and preferences of an individual, a useful indication is provided by surveys of the comparative cost, in different locations, of securing a specific "standard family budget" of goods and services. Table 7-4 summarizes the results of a 1966 survey of this type.

A fairly distinct pattern of differentials appears. In each region, living costs are consistently higher in metropolitan areas than in smaller nonmetropolitan places for all major items except possibly transportation.

TABLE 7-4. Indices of Comparative Living Costs in Urban Areas Based on the City Worker's Family Budget, Autumn 1966

	Total budget costs*	Food	Housing	Clothing and personal care	Trans- portation	Medical care
Percentage of total budget costs (for urban U.S.)	100	23	24	11	9	5
Cost relative to U.S. urban average = 100						
United States						
Metropolitan areas (average)	102	101	103	102	100	103
Nonmetropolitan areas	91	94	86	93	100	88
Northeast						
Metropolitan areas (range)	97–111	103–111	88–123	99–105	90–112	80–106
Nonmetropolitan areas	98	102	96	95	101	94
North Central						
Metropolitan areas (range)	93–106	93–103	92–115	98–104	95–109	86–103
Nonmetropolitan areas	93	93	76	96	97	85
South (excluding Washington, D.C.)						
Metropolitan areas (range)	85–96	92–95	76–91	92–98	99–110	91–102
Nonmetropolitan areas	85	90	76	88	99	84
Washington, D.C.†	102	100	105	98	101	99
West (excluding Honolulu)						
Metropolitan areas (range)	97–108	95–106	87–109	101–111	106–113	102–134
Nonmetropolitan areas	97	95	91	102	104	94
Honolulu†	122	119	129	99	122	100

* Includes, in addition to the categories shown, other items of family consumption, gifts, life insurance, personal income taxes, social security deductions, and occupational expenses such as work clothes and union dues.

† Shown separately because the cost indices for this city were markedly different from those of other reported areas in the region.

SOURCE: Phyllis Groom, "A New City Worker's Family Budget," *Monthly Labor Review,* 90, 11 (November 1967), Tables 1 and 2, pp. 3 and 5.

Although there is a wide range of living costs among individual metropolitan areas within any one region, those in the South tend to be somewhat lower. The major cost item with the widest variations is housing: Examination of the indices for individual areas reported in the survey suggests that high housing costs are significantly associated with large size, recent rapid growth, or rigorous climate.

An impressionistic picture of relative real income levels in metropolitan areas of the four major regions can be obtained by dividing the 1966 median family income index, cited earlier, by the median family budget cost index, for metropolitan areas in each region.[3] Results are as follows:

	(1) Income	(2) Budget cost	(1) ÷ (2) "Real income"
Northeast	106	101	105
North Central	106	101	105
South	84	92	91
West	109	102	107

It is worth noting that the differences in budget costs are generally in the same direction as those in incomes and pay rates but are smaller. Consequently, *real* pay rates and incomes tend to be higher where *money* rates, incomes, and budget costs are higher. Spatial differences in real income are narrower than those in money income or pay rates. There is some evidence that this relationship also applies when we compare places of different size,[4] though it is impossible to compare adequately the psychic satisfactions and costs that people get from living in large cities rather than in smaller places.

The persistence of the broad pattern of income differentials is remarkable. Lower incomes in smaller towns and cities, lower incomes in the South, and higher incomes in the West have prevailed for many decades—longer, in fact, than the period covered by any adequate measurements.

It is also to be noted that areas with higher levels of income are generally areas of rapid growth in population and substantial net inward migration. One explanation is that people migrate in the direction of higher income levels; another conceivable explanation is that rapid population growth

---

[3] Derived from the indices for individual metropolitan areas reported in the source for Table 7-2.

[4] For example, a study of workers' hourly earnings and living costs in Swedish industrial towns and cities showed a consistently positive relationship, with roughly twice as great a range of variation in earnings as in living costs. The same study found consistently higher living costs in larger communities and in regions more distant from food-producing areas or with especially rigorous climatic conditions. Bertil Ohlin, *Interregional and International Trade* (Cambridge, Mass.: Harvard University Press, 1933), 215–218.

stimulates an area's economy so that it advances rapidly in welfare and productivity. We shall have occasion later to consider both hypotheses.

THE SUPPLY OF LABOR
AT A LOCATION

To understand the causes and effects of wage and income differentials between locations, we shall follow tradition by separately examining the factors affecting the supply and the demand for labor at any given location.

The aggregate supply of labor in a community may be quite inelastic in the short run, since it can change only through migration or changes in labor force participation. For a single activity or occupation within the labor market area, the supply is more elastic because it can be affected by workers changing their activities or occupations as well as by migration and changes in the labor force. The labor supply as seen by an individual employer is still more elastic, and perhaps in a large labor market almost perfectly so.

Work Location Preferences and
Labor Mobility

There are many reasons for preferring a job in one area to the same kind of job in another area. First, it may pay better—not necessarily just in terms of the basic wage but when all fringe benefits are considered. Second, a community with cheaper living costs might be preferred in the absence of any pay differential. Third, various aspects of the quality of the job, such as security and prospects of advancement, may be considered. Choosing a location can represent a sizable commitment, and calls for foresight. Finally, other aspects of the desirability of the community as a place to live can include, for example, climate, cultural and social opportunities, and access to other places that one might like to visit.

"Spatial mobility" refers to people's readiness to change locations in response to some measurable set of incentives, identified in practice as "real income" or simply as money wage rates deflated by a cost-of-living index. If mobility in this sense were perfect and real wages thus equal everywhere, there would be differentials in money wages paralleling the differentials in living costs. A labor market where the living costs were 10 percent above average would pay wages 10 percent above average, but real wages there would be the same as anywhere else.

The term "equalizing differentials" has been applied to this kind of money wage or income differential.[5] The pattern of actual money differen-

---

[5] *Ibid.*, p. 212. The term "equalizing" has also been applied to wage differences explainable by differences in the attractiveness of occupations.

tials is then made up of two components: (1) equalizing differentials, which would exist even in the absence of any impediments to labor mobility, and (2) "real" differentials, representing differentials in *real* incomes and, thus, presumably caused by such impediments. Referring back to Table 7-1, we see roughly a 15 percent difference for the earnings of office clerical workers in Western metropolitan areas compared to Southern metropolitan areas. The index of family budget costs (as shown in the last text table) was about 11 percent higher in Western than in Southern metropolitan areas. Accordingly, we could break down the 15 percent money earnings advantage of the West into two components: an equalizing differential of 11 percent and a real differential of 4 percent.

The relevance of this distinction is that *workers* can logically be expected to choose locations and to move in response to *real* differentials; while *employers* looking for cheap labor will logically be guided by the total *money* wage differential (thus in the present case, finding a 15 percent advantage in locating in the South).

These concepts of real and money wages, cost of living, and equalizing and real differentials help us to understand some basic motivations underlying the locational choices of employees and employers; but unfortunately they are not very sharp tools. We have already mentioned the impossibility of including in indices of income and living costs all the considerations affecting the desirability of a location. For example, such indices take no account of the attractions of a mild and sunny climate (except as reflected in housing costs), the dirt and discomforts of life in a large industrial city, the social pressures and cultural voids of a small town, or the advantage to a research worker of being stationed where the action is in his field. As a result of our inability to measure real income fully, we are also unable to measure mobility fully. If a family, for example, likes the physical and social climate of its surroundings and refrains from moving to another area where the pay is higher both in money terms and as deflated by a conventional family budget cost index, should we ascribe its failure to move to a lack of mobility?

A further difficulty with the simple concept of real and equalizing differentials is the implicit assumption that migration is not merely motivated by real income differentials but tends to eliminate them. Under certain conditions it is possible for migration, even when so motivated, to leave the differential unchanged or even to widen it. We need to look further into both the causes and the consequences of migration.

Who Migrates: Why, When, and Where?

Migration is influenced by three conditions: the characteristics of both the origin and destination areas, the difficulties of the journey itself, and the characteristics of the migrant.

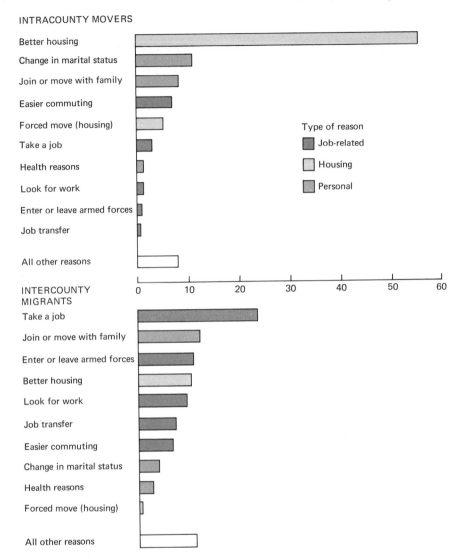

Fig. 7-1. Reasons for Moving or Migrating Given by Males Aged 18–64 Who Changed Residence between March 1962 and March 1963 (Length of bars shows percentage of all reasons given)

SOURCE: U.S. Department of Commerce, Bureau of the Census, *Current Population Reports: Population Characteristics,* Series P-20, No. 154 (August 22, 1966), Table E, p. 4.

REASONS FOR MOVING. It is a drastic oversimplification to explain migration simply on the basis of response to differentials in wage rates, income, or employment opportunity. Fig. 7-1, which refers to males aged 18–64 who changed their residences in the United States in the 12-month interval from March 1962 to March 1963, indicates the variety of reasons given. Presumably, the responses would be quite different for other sex or age groups and would also vary according to such "background" factors as the level of unemployment and the state of the housing market.

Subject to these qualifications, we see that those men who only moved within the same county were predominantly influenced by housing considerations. Since all of a county is generally regarded as being in a single labor market or commuting range, job changes are related only to a minor extent with intracounty moves: most such movers are not changing jobs.

For those who moved to a different county—whom the Census defines as *migrants*—the picture is quite different, with employment changes (including entry to or exit from military service) emerging as the major reasons for migrating. This reflects the fact that an intercounty migration generally involves shifting to a different labor market beyond the commuting range for the former job.

CHARACTERISTICS OF ORIGIN AND DESTINATION AREAS. The characteristics most obviously affecting attractiveness to the individual migrant have already been suggested. In addition, we should expect that a larger place would have more migrants arriving and departing than a smaller place, more or less in proportion to size. But size itself can significantly affect the appeal of a place for the individual. Historically, migrants have responded to the greater variety of job opportunities in larger urban centers by migrating to them in numbers somewhat more than proportional to their size.

Rather than thinking of migration as being motivated simply by net advantages of some places over others, it is useful to separate the "pull" of attractive characteristics from the "push" of unattractive ones. Clearly, many people migrate because they do not like it where they are, or perhaps are even being forced out by economic or political-social pressures. The basic decision is to get out, and the choice of a particular place to migrate to is a secondary and subsequent decision, involving a somewhat different set of considerations. On the other hand, some areas can be so generally attractive as to pull migrants from a wide variety of other locations, including many who were reasonably well satisfied where they were.[6]

---

[6] Separation of the push from the pull effect is obviously a tricky business, and there has been much controversy about how much weight to attach to each with respect to specific historical or current migrations. It has been argued that the migrations from European countries to the United States in the latter part of the nineteenth century were primarily motivated by pull, because they fluctuated from year to year in harmony with fluctuations in American business conditions but did not significantly vary in response to business cycles in specific European countries. See Richard A. Easterlin, "Long Swings in United States Demographic and Economic Growth: Some Findings on the Historical Pattern," *Demography*, 2 (1965), 497–500.

Recent studies on migration using detailed data on flows in both directions (rather than just net flows) have considerably revised earlier notions
of push and pull. Rather surprisingly, it appears that in most cases the
so-called push explaining out-migration from an area is not primarily the
economic characteristics of the area (such as low wages or high unemployment) but the demographic characteristics of the population of the
area. Areas with a high proportion of well-educated young adults have
high rates of out-migration regardlesss of local economic opportunity. The
pull factor (that is, the migrant's choice of where to go) is, however, primarily a matter of the economic characteristics of areas. Migration is
consistently heavier into prosperous areas. Accordingly, the observed net
migration losses of depressed areas generally reflect low in-migration but
not high out-migration, and the net migration gains of prosperous areas
reflect high in-migration rather than low out-migration.[7]

DIFFICULTIES OF THE JOURNEY. Within a country, distance is perhaps
the most obviously significant characteristic of the migration journey, and
virtually all analyses of migration flows have evaluated the extent to which
migration streams attenuate with longer distance. Thus, a simple "gravity
model" of migration shows that the net annual migration from A to B
will be proportional to the populations of A and B and to the size of some
differential (say, in wage rates) between A and B, and inversely proportional to the square of the distance from A to B, as follows:

$$M_{ab} = \frac{g P_a P_b (W_b - W_a)}{D^2_{ab}}$$

(where the P's represent populations, the W's wage rates, D the distance,
M the number of migrants per unit of time, and g a constant of proportionality). This basic migration flow model has been modified in various ways
in the attempt to make it more realistic. It has already been suggested that
in many circumstances at least, there is a "scale effect" upon migration,
which could be accounted for in the model by giving the populations an
exponent greater than 1. Any relevant factor of differential advantage that
can be quantified (for example, unemployment rates, mean summer or
winter temperature, percentage of sunny days, average education or income
level of the population, percentage of housing in good condition, crime
rates, insurance rates, or atmospheric dust content) can be introduced,
with whatever relative weighting the user of the model deems appropriate.
   The distance factor in the model likewise can be assigned a different

[7] See Ira S. Lowry, *Migration and Metropolitan Growth: Two Analytical Models*
(San Francisco: Chandler, 1966).

exponent to fit the circumstances (there is nothing special about the *square* of the distance, except for the law of *physical* gravitation) and elaborated in various ways. Actually, distance per se is a very rough measure of the difficulties attending migration. The factors involved are actual moving costs (which can sometimes be the least important obstacle), uncertainty, risk and investment of time involved, restrictions upon migration per se, and what is sometimes called "social distance," suggesting the degree of difficulty the migrant may have in making adequate social adjustment after he arrives. As an example of this last, a model designed by W. H. Somer- meijer to explain Dutch internal migration flows included a term that measured the difference in the Catholic-Protestant ratio between the two areas; this substantially improved the model's explanatory power.[8]

Social distances depend partly, of course, upon the individual migrant. But wide social distances between communities and regions (that is, great heterogeneity) tend to restrict migration flows to those individuals who can most easily make the required adjustments. With the improvement of communications and travel, social distance in space tends to lessen; but it is still a factor, for example, between French and English Canada, between the North and the Deep South in the United States, or between farm and city.[9]

Another feature of migration paths is that they seem to be subject to economies of volume of traffic along any one route. Well-beaten paths become increasingly easy and popular for successive migrants. This is so for a variety of reasons. Sometimes (as in the case of earlier transatlantic and more recent Puerto Rico-to-mainland migrant travel) transport agen- cies give special rates or in other ways favor the still further increase of migrant travel on the most frequented routes. Perhaps more generally applicable and more important is the fact that migrants try to minimize uncertainties and risks by choosing places about which they have at least a little information and where they will find relatives, friends, or others from their home areas who will help them to get a foothold. This tendency is particularly important, of course, when the social distance is large. It goes far to explain the heavy concentration of late nineteenth-century European migrants to the United States in a few large cities and the even more remarkable concentration of particular ethnic and subethnic groups in certain cities and neighborhoods, which even now retain unto the third

---

[8] H. ter Heide, "Migration Models and their Significance for Population Fore- casts," *Milbank Memorial Fund Quarterly,* 41, 1 (January 1963), 63–64.

[9] "Functional distance" is a still broader concept, wrapping up in one index a measure of all factors impeding migration between a given pair of points. Functional distance can be evaluated by comparing actual migration flows with the flows that would be expected to occur simply on the basis of, say, the populations of the points in question. Functional distance can then be correlated with actual distance and other suspected determinants in order to break it down into components.

generation some of their special character. The most recent ethnically distinctive waves of migration to American cities—blacks and Puerto Ricans—have in the same fashion followed a few well-beaten paths. It has been established that Southern black migrants to Chicago, for example, mainly come from certain sections of the South, while those going to Washington, D.C., or Baltimore originate in other Southern areas, and those going to the West Coast come from still other areas.

A recent analysis of labor mobility in the United States between 1957 and 1960, based on Social Security records, gives striking evidence of the beaten-path effect where migration of blacks is concerned. For white workers, both male and female, migration flows were significantly related to earnings differentials (positively) and to distance (negatively) as we might expect. For black men, however (and to a lesser extent for black women), earnings differentials and distance appeared to be less important determinants than either the number of blacks or the proportion of blacks in the work force of the destination area. In other words, blacks (or at any rate, black males) were selectively attracted to labor markets in which there already was a high proportion of blacks.[10]

The tendency of migration to channelize in well-beaten paths provides part of the explanation for another characteristic of migration streams which at first sounds quite unreasonable; namely, that places with high rates of inward migration tend to have high rates of outward migration as well. This so-called counterstream effect was noted as long ago as the 1880s in Ravenstein's pioneer statement of migration principles, and has been amply verified since.[11]

The point here is that a well-beaten path eases travel in *both* directions. Migrants generally come to a place with incomplete knowledge, and many of the disappointed ones simply retrace their steps. Also, a city that offers especially favorable adjustment opportunities for migrants is likely to serve as a "port of entry" for migrants coming into that region or country. New York has historically been the entry place for transatlantic immigrants, and Chicago has functioned as an important first destination for Mexicans migrating to the American Midwest. In such cases, many of the migrants move out again (either to other places in the region or perhaps back to their place of origin), so the out-migration rate of such an entry point or staging area is likely to be high. More generally, it is plausible to assume that people who have just migrated are especially mobile by circumstances

---

[10] Lowell E. Galloway, *Geographic Labor Mobility in the United States, 1957 to 1960*, U.S. Department of Health, Education and Welfare, Social Security Administration, Office of Research and Statistics, Research Report No. 28 (Washington, D.C.: Government Printing Office, 1969).

[11] E. G. Ravenstein, "The Laws of Migration," *Journal of the Royal Statistical Society*, 52 (June 1889), 241–301. See pages 178–180 below for further discussion of the relation between incoming and outgoing migration streams.

or taste and hence more likely than others to swell the outward flow.

Migration flows over long distances within the same country have historically involved a considerable amount of what is sometimes called "chain" migration. Most of the migrants move relatively short distances, but the moves are predominantly in one direction to form a "stream." As people move from *B* to *A,* they are replaced in *B* by other migrants from *C,* who in turn are replaced by others from *D.* It has been established that most of the massive redistribution of population in England during the Industrial Revolution was carried out in such fashion by short-distance moves cumulating toward the new industrial towns.[12] The same process was included as one of the basic principles of migration in Ravenstein's analysis. It may be surmised that chain migration is becoming relatively less important in the United States, since the difficulties of moving almost certainly depend less than they once did upon the sheer physical distance involved.

CHARACTERISTICS OF THE MIGRANT. Some people are far more prone to migrate than are others. This is often expressed as a difference in the mobility of different groups, but we really cannot explain all of the difference in that way since the *incentives* to migrate are not the same. For example, a young scientist fresh out of school is confronted with a quite different set of pushes and pulls than is an aging farmer, an unskilled laborer, or a wealthy widow.

The most conspicuous differences in migration rates are those experienced by the individual as he passes through successive stages of his life. As a very young child, he is relatively portable. After he enters school and has older, more settled parents (and probably more brothers or sisters), his probability of moving declines. The rate rises suddenly when he is ready to look for a job or choose a college and remains high until after he is married and has children of his own. As his stake in his job and community grows, and as his and his family's local ties develop, he becomes less and less likely to move. His mobility recovers somewhat at the stage when all of his children are on their own, and again at retirement. Finally, the decline of migration rates with increasing age can once again be interrupted by the death of the spouse.

Most of these characteristic life-cycle variations are manifest in Fig. 7-2, showing United States moving and migration rates by age and sex. The pattern is blurred in the aggregate, of course, by the fact that not all people enter the labor force, marry, or retire at the same ages. But age remains the characteristic most distinctly associated with migration-rate differentials. Most of the migration that occurs (except in massive displacements of

---

[12] Arthur Redford, *Labour Migration in England, 1800–1850* (Manchester, 1926; 2nd ed., New York: A. M. Kelley, 1968).

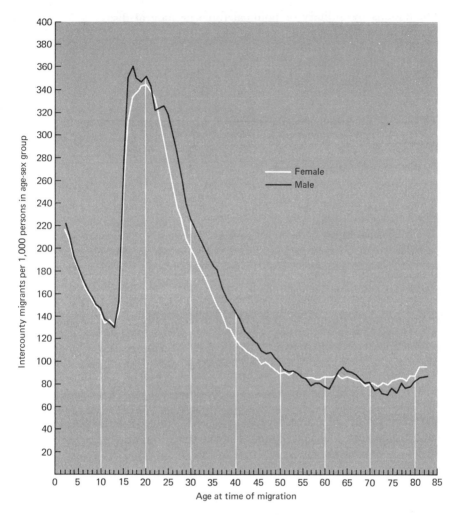

Fig. 7-2. Rates of Migration by Sex by Single Years of Age: United States, 1955–1960

Note: In the source, based on Census tabulations, rates were shown in terms of the respondent's age in 1960. Since the migrations were spread over the interval 1955–1960, the best estimate of the age at the time of migration is 2½ years less than the 1960 age. Accordingly, I have shifted the age scale 2½ years to the right.

SOURCE: Everett S. Lee and G. Putnam Barber, "Differentials in Spatial Mobility," in H. G. Beard, ed., *National Vocational-Technical Education Seminar on Occupational Mobility and Migration,* Center Seminar and Conference Report No. 2 (Raleigh, N.C.: North Carolina State University at Raleigh, Center for Occupational Education, 1966), p. 134.

populations by military or political force or natural disaster) is done by people in the "young adult" age groups.

Certain other individual characteristics also substantially affect migration rates. The most important are marital status, parenthood, and level of education. Table 7-5 shows migration rates for men in three mature age

TABLE 7-5. U.S. Intercounty Migration Rates per 100 for Males, by Age, Education, and Occupational Status, 1966–1967

	25–34	35–44	45–64
By years of schooling completed			
College (1 year or more)	15.7	8.8	4.5
High school (4 years)	9.6	5.7	3.5
High school (1 to 3 years)	9.9	5.4	2.8
Elementary (8 grades or less)	9.1	5.6	3.1
By occupational status			
White collar	12.8	6.6	3.2
Manual	9.1	4.9	2.3
Service	7.7	1.8	3.2
Farmers and farm managers	3.3	2.2	0.4
Farm laborers and foremen	12.5	12.8	9.3

SOURCE: U.S. Department of Commerce, Bureau of the Census, *Current Population Reports: Population Characteristics,* Series P-20, No. 171 (Washington, D.C.: Government Printing Office, April 30, 1968). Based on a sample survey.

groups (that is, after their schooling was probably completed and occupational status established) according to level of education and occupational status, which are of course highly correlated. We see that, in general, education seems to enhance mobility. The extremely high rates for farm laborers are a conspicuous exception, reflecting their precarious search for a livelihood.[13]

In addition to such regularly recorded characteristics as we have considered, individuals have many other personal characteristics that influence their propensity to migrate. Some people are simply more footloose, more adventurous, more easily dissatisfied, or more ambitious than others, or in countless other ways more mobile.

These wide differences in migration rates among different kinds of people mean, of course, that those who migrate are almost never a representative cross section of the population of either their area of origin or their area of destination. A migration stream substantially alters the makeup of the population and the labor force in both areas.

---

[13] These and almost all other such tabulations record migrants' characteristics as they were *after* the move. Many migrants move in conjunction with a change of occupation, and to that extent these figures are inaccurate in measuring migration probabilities of persons in particular occupation groups.

The selectivity of migration is greatest when the journey is difficult, when the areas of origin and destination are in sharp contrast, and when the population itself is highly diverse in such characteristics as education, income level, occupational experience, and ethnic or racial background. Migrants generally seem to be somewhat above the average of the *origin* area in terms of energy, ability, and training; this suggests that the direct effect upon the remaining population is to lower its average "quality." One of the oldest clichés regarding emigration, in fact, is that it tends to drain the best people out of an area and leave the dregs, thus damaging the prospects for industrialization or other economic development.

A recent intensive study of the occupational status of American men aged 20–64 came to these conclusions:[14]

> ... migration has become increasingly selective of high potential achievers in recent decades.
> ... the careers of migrants are in almost all comparisons, clearly superior to those of nonmigrants. . . . Whether migration between regions or between communities is examined; whether migration since birth or only after adolescence is considered; whether migrants are compared to nonmigrants within ethnic-nativity groupings or without employing these controls; whether education and first job are held constant; and whether migrants are compared to natives in their place of origin or their place of destination—migrants tend to attain higher occupational levels and to experience more upward mobility than nonmigrants, with only a few exceptions.
> ... Migrants from urban places, though not those from rural areas, enjoy higher status than the natives in the community to which they have come, regardless of its size.

These findings go well beyond the traditional folklore about selective migration in that they suggest (1) that migrants (except from rural areas) tend to be superior to the population of the *destination* area as well as the origin area, and (2) that selectivity may be *increasing,* contrary to the expectation that more general literacy and other trends enhance the mobility of an increasing proportion of the population.

Another study, relating to migrants to the industrial metropolis of Monterrey, Mexico, between 1940 and 1960[15] gives a rather different picture. Migration appears to have become much less selective with respect to populations of origin in that interval. Early in the period only a few of the more highly educated ventured the move to the city; later, mobility increased so that villagers of all educational and income levels became able and willing to move. As a result, the migrant stream became more nearly

[14] Peter M. Blau and Otis Dudley Duncan, *The American Occupational Structure* (New York: Wiley, 1967), 271–272.

[15] Harley L. Browning and Waltraut Feindt, "Selectivity of Migrants to a Metropolis in a Developing Country: A Mexican Case Study," *Demography,* 6, 4 (1969), 347–357.

representative of the population of its areas of *origin,* while at the same time it was becoming increasingly different from (educationally inferior to) the population of the urban *destination* area.[16]

Migration selectivity, then, can depend to a large extent on the state of development of the regions involved and can change in character fairly rapidly. It has already been suggested that a broadening of education and economic opportunity in less-developed regions can reduce selectivity. Finally, Lee has proposed a plausible but not easily verifiable hypothesis: that migration motivated by pull tends to be "positively selective" (that is, the more productive people are the ones who go), whereas migration motivated by push tends to be negatively selective.

> Factors at origin operate most stringently against persons who in some way have failed economically or socially. Though there are conditions in many places which push out the unorthodox and the highly creative, it is more likely to be the uneducated or the disturbed who are forced to migrate.[17]

INWARD, OUTWARD, AND NET MIGRATION: THREE HYPOTHESES. The typical age selectivity of migration is sometimes an important factor accounting for the observed tendency that places with high in-migration rates have high out-migration rates as well. The most mobile age groups (and perhaps also the individuals most mobile by temperament or other characteristics) are present in abnormally high proportion in a growing area with high recent and current in-migration; and such local demographic characteristics play a large part in determining how many people leave an area.[18]

We have learned that the relationships among inward, outward, and net migration are more complex than one would suspect. Let us review them in terms of three hypotheses or "laws of migration," using Fig. 7-3 as a graphic aid.

The naive or common-sense expectation regarding migration into and out of an area is that if the area is attractive as a place to work and live,

---

[16] Where the quality (education, skills, income, or whatever) of a stream of migrants is, as in the Monterrey case, intermediate between that of the origin and the destination populations, the curious result is that the immediate effect of the migration is to lower the average quality in *both* areas, although at the same time it usually improves the quality of the migrants and of the populations of the two areas combined! A similar apparent paradox is involved in the case of the legendary student who flunked out of Harvard and transferred to a rival New England institution (which shall be nameless), "thus raising the average scholastic level of both universities."

[17] Everett S. Lee, "A Theory of Migration," *Demography*, 3, 1 (1966), 56. This article represents a thorough revision and amplification of Ravenstein's much earlier "Laws of Migration," *op. cit.*

[18] See Lowry, *op. cit.*

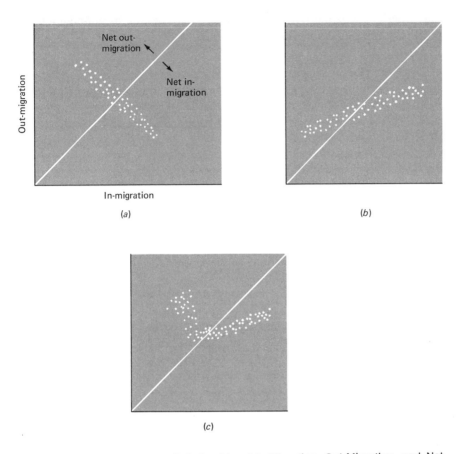

Fig. 7-3. Three Views on the Relationship of In-Migration, Out-Migration, and Net Migration Rates

there will be a net inward flow reflecting large inward and small outward migration; while if the area is unattractive, there will be a net outflow reflecting large outward and small inward migration. This hypothesis is represented diagrammatically in the first panel (*a*) of Fig. 7-3, where the dots represent different labor market areas, or perhaps the same area at different times. In-migration and out-migration rates are measured on the horizontal and vertical axes respectively. The 45-degree line represents zero net migration. The various areas show a pattern of negative correlation of out-migration with both inward and net migration: "Attractive" areas are those in the lower right part of the scatter and "unattractive" areas are those above and to the left of the diagonal.

The second panel (*b*) depicts the contrasting relationship, previously suggested on the basis of migration selectivity and other factors, which we might designate as the Lowry hypothesis. Here the rate of out-migration is *positively* correlated with both inward and net migration.

A still more recently developed view is that shown in the third panel (c), which we may call the Beale hypothesis.[19] Using 1955–1960 data for the 509 state economic areas into which the Census Bureau divides the United States,[20] Beale discovered a relationship schematically resembling that of Fig. 7-3c. He found that high gross out-migration can be associated with either high net in-migration or high net out-migration. The net rate is mainly determined by out-migration when the net is negative, and by in-migration when the net is positive. We may interpret this as meaning that the "Lowry effect" dominates in relatively prosperous and growing areas, whereas in areas that are seriously depressed the predominant effect is the common-sense one: Poor prospects both discourage inflow and encourage outflow, and economic factors exert both pull and push.

The significance of this issue is far from trivial, as Beale points out and as we shall more fully appreciate in the context of Chapters 8 and 9. If migration out of seriously depressed or backward areas is assumed to be affected only by demographic characteristics of the population and not by the level of unemployment or income, then measures to stimulate activity in such areas would not reduce out-migration (in fact, according to the Lowry hypothesis they would eventually increase it). The Beale findings suggest, however, that such stimulus may, in some cases at least, retard out-migration. In choosing among policy decisions regarding aid to depressed or backward areas, it is of some importance to try to gauge this possible impact.

CHANGES IN MIGRATION RATES. One of Ravenstein's Laws is that people become more and more mobile, and most observers of migration have similarly noted a tendency for migration rates to increase secularly. Lee accounts for this on several grounds: increasing diversity of the opportunities afforded by different areas, increasingly diverse specialization of people's capabilities and preferences, the beaten-path effect already mentioned, and the increasingly wide knowledge and experience of other locations that is brought by better communication, education, more income, and leisure to travel. These seem to be valid points; but it does not appear that there has been any trend either upward or downward in the migration rate of the American population since systematic annual sample surveys

---

[19] Calvin L. Beale, "Demographic and Social Considerations for U.S. Rural Economic Policy," *American Journal of Agricultural Economics,* 51, 2 (May 1969), 410–427. A fuller account of Beale's findings appears in an unpublished paper, "The Relation of Gross Outmigration Rates to Net Migration" (presented at the meetings of the Population Association of America, Atlantic City, N.J., April 1969).

[20] Lowry's study was restricted to major *metropolitan* labor market areas.

were instituted soon after World War II.[21] It seems quite possible that, at least in this recent period in the United States, regions have become more alike rather than more diverse, so that in some respects the *incentives* for migration may have lessened. Regional income levels do tend to converge toward the national average. Reduced migration incentives could offset increased personal mobility in such a way as to leave the migration rate substantially unchanged.

Despite the lack of any apparent trend in the proportion of people who migrate, it does appear that the *range* of migration in the United States has been increasing. A study by Tarver and McLeod, in which interstate migration distances were roughly estimated on the basis of the distances between population centers of states, disclosed that the average interstate move increased from 606 miles in 1935–1940 to 689 miles in 1949–1950 and 756 miles in 1955–1960. In each period, however, the most frequent range of distance was between 100 and 200 miles. Nonwhite interstate migrants tended to move only about 74 percent as far as whites in 1935–1940, but the difference narrowed rapidly—by 1955–1960, the nonwhites were moving about 90 percent as far as the whites.[22]

Migration rates show marked seasonal and cyclical variations. In general, prosperity favors migration because opportunities are more plentiful, risks of unemployment at the new location are less, and the migrant himself is in a better financial position. In periods of economic recession or depression, people tend to look for the place with the best economic security. This may mean staying where they are or (in the case of fairly recent migrants) returning to their last place of residence. Thus the long-term migration stream toward places with better long-term prospects is temporarily interrupted or even reversed by severe recessions. For example, in the worst years of the Great Depression of the 1930s, the long-standing net flows of migrants from farm to nonfarm areas and from foreign countries to the United States were both reversed.

THE EFFECTIVENESS OF MIGRATION. When people migrate they are seeking to better their lot. How well does migration accomplish that purpose, and how does it affect people other than those who migrate?

The answer obviously depends in part on how accurately people size up the prospects when they decide to move (or not to). The better informed they are, the greater the probability that migration will justify itself and will contribute to a more efficient allocation of human resources

---

[21] Results of these surveys, covering migration and other population characteristics, are published by the U.S. Bureau of the Census in its *Current Population Reports,* Series P-20.

[22] James D. Tarver and R. Douglas McLeod, "Trends in Distances Moved by Interstate Migrants," *Rural Sociology,* 35, 4 (December, 1970).

in the economy as a whole. Thus, public policy with regard to migration should, first, help potential migrants to get the information they need for rational choice. Beyond this rather obvious point, the question of the effectiveness of migration can be examined on three different levels.

(1) The "efficiency of migration" between any two areas is sometimes defined as the ratio of the net flow to the total gross flow in both directions. In other words, if all migrants go in the same direction, the efficiency is 100 percent, in the sense that there is no crosshauling of migrants: the net flow equals the gross flow. At the other extreme, if the flows in the two directions just balance so that there is no net movement at all, the efficiency is said to be zero.

This measure may be useful in suggesting to us the degree to which a net migration figure can be misleading as an indicator of the amount of movement; but it has little to do with efficiency in any meaningful sense. People are not simply interchangeable units of manpower as the efficiency ratio implies. Those moving in one direction may be presumed to differ qualitatively from those moving in the other; with each stream believing, and perhaps correctly, that it is going in the right direction. Accordingly, a situation in which two opposing flows largely cancel out in terms of numbers of people is not necessarily indicative of any "lost motion" in terms of either the welfare of the individual migrants or the socially desirable spatial allocation of manpower resources.

(2) A different and somewhat more sophisticated question about migration is to ask whether it seems to be going to the right places so far as the immediate economic benefit to the migrant is concerned. If we find people moving predominantly from places of lower incomes to places of higher incomes, or from areas of heavy unemployment to labor shortage areas, we surmise that they know what they are doing. If they go the other way, or simply in all directions without any apparent regard to income or employment differentials or any other obvious index of advantage, we have to surmise either that the migrants are ignorant about the alternatives or that we are ignorant about their real motivations.

Actually, most migration flows do fit a "rational" pattern in relation to observable differences in earnings levels, unemployment rates, and such other easily identified variables as climate and the level of public assistance benefits. Even the migration of poor blacks from Southern farms to Northern city ghettos with high unemployment and dismal living conditions can make sense in terms of improvement in the income of the person involved —despite a variety of possible adverse effects on the individual's state of social adjustment and on the communities involved.

In relating migration to indices of community economic welfare (for example, wage or income levels) we cannot assume that the migrant immediately fits into the pattern of the area and receives the average pay, employment security, and other perquisites of the residents in his age and occupational category. Migrants are no more representative of the populations of their destination areas than they are of the populations of their areas of origin. Some of their differential characteristics are subject to modification, so that if they stay they will tend to become more similar to their new neighbors. This tendency toward assimilation applies not only to skills but also to consumption patterns, ratings on most kinds of "intelligence" tests, desired number of children, and social behavior.

(3) Finally, we can judge migration on the basis of how much it contributes to aggregate output or, more broadly, to general social welfare. This is the appropriate level of judgment for public authorities and public-spirited citizens to try to use. It calls for assessing the effects of migration not just upon the migrants but upon the communities they leave and enter.

This is by no means a simple criterion to apply. On the face of it, the transfer of manpower to places where its productivity is higher seems likely to raise national per capita output and increase "aggregate welfare," if that term has any meaning. And differentials in real earnings rates reflect, roughly at least, differentials in the marginal productivity of labor. But migration (particularly highly selective migration) can have important side effects (externalities) upon the areas involved, in terms of the costs of public services, the prospects for future economic development, and the quality of life. The discussion of these problems will be taken up in later chapters where we come to grips with the processes of regional growth and change.

It will be recalled that interregional migration of black males in the United States tends to be dominated by the beaten-path effect—in other words, such migrants are inclined to go where their predecessors have already congregated. The author of the report cited on page 173 above, which documented this tendency, derived therefrom a rather gloomy implication. The labor markets in which there is a high proportion of blacks tend to be (because of discrimination barriers that split a local labor market into white and black submarkets) those where the color differential in earnings is widest. Black migrants are being drawn to those areas where they are at the greatest relative disadvantage, which implies socially inefficient migration and a potential inclination toward cumulative regional concentration of the urban black population. The pessimistic implications should not be exaggerated, however, so long as black migrants do improve their economic position by migration.

THE DEMAND FOR LABOR
AT A LOCATION

Our discussion of mobility and migration has shed some light on what determines the supply of labor at different places. To the extent that people move to places offering more jobs or higher earnings, the labor supply adjusts to the spatial pattern of labor demand. In areas where demand has grown relative to supply and there are hindrances to inward migration, a tight labor market is manifest by low unemployment rates and relatively high earnings; in places where labor demand has declined or has failed to keep pace with the growth in the labor force (resulting in part from natural increase of the population) and outward migration is not easy, we find labor surplus manifest in high unemployment rates and relatively low earnings rates. This is, of course, a somewhat simplified picture; many areas, at any given time, do not fit wholly into either of these two contrasting categories.

On the demand side, we envisage employers of labor as being concerned about its costs and seeking to make profitable adjustments to such labor cost differentials as they are aware of.

What, then, will employers do if labor is expensive (relative to its productivity) in a specific location? They have three possible ways of economizing on this expensive labor: by changing their production techniques so as to substitute other inputs (for example, labor-saving machinery) for manpower; going out of business; or moving to a different location where labor is cheaper. Where the last two alternatives are seriously considered, we can say that the activity in question is locationally sensitive to labor supply, or to some degree is "labor oriented."

The degree of labor orientation varies widely among activities. In one extreme case (activities tightly tied to a locality by market orientation, orientation to inputs other than labor, or some other compulsion), labor costs may have no significant locational effect at all—the employer's demand for labor at that location is highly inelastic. Retail trade and local services illustrate this category of locally bound industries essentially unaffected by labor cost differentials. If, for example, drug store clerks were paid twice as much in Milwaukee as in Akron, this would not induce Milwaukee drug store proprietors to relocate to Akron. Their market is entirely local: they are not in competition with Akron in any sense and only need to assure themselves that they are not paying their clerks more bounteously than their Milwaukee competitors. There would, however, be a stronger incentive in Milwaukee than in Akron to skimp on labor and substitute other inputs if possible. In the case assumed, we might expect Milwaukee drug stores to be quicker to install such things as vending machines, change-making cash registers, and display layouts facilitating self-service.

At the other extreme, we have strongly labor-oriented activities whose demand for labor at any particular location is highly elastic—unless labor is cheap, they will close down or go elsewhere. Normally, these are activities that are rather "footloose" with respect to locational factors other than labor supply. A change of location makes relatively little difference in their costs of transfer, level of sales, or outlays for other local inputs per unit of sales, while their labor costs do vary markedly from one location or region to another. Historically, the manufacture of textiles and standard clothing has been strongly oriented to low-wage labor, while labor-intensive activities requiring scarce special skills have been strongly oriented to the few places where such skills are available.

Until rather recently, most activities oriented to cheap labor as such mainly employed unskilled or semiskilled blue-collar workers; but nowadays there are numerous instances of firms moving to places where there is cheap white-collar clerical labor. This is partly the result of the rapidly increasing proportion of white-collar to total employment; but the locational effect also reflects the increased availability of qualified clerical help in small communities.

THE RATIONALE OF LABOR COST DIFFERENTIALS

Having briefly considered the location of manpower from both the supply side and the demand side, we now have some insight into the rather complex set of interrelations shown schematically in Fig. 7-4. This diagram may be useful in reminding us of the interdependencies and in tracing the repercussions of different kinds of change. For example, the mechanism implied by the concept of equalizing differentials in wages (that is, the tendency of migration to eliminate real income differentials) involves the simple feedback sequence of effects shown by the *solid* lines in the diagram below.

A more complex and realistic model of the equalization process, taking into account the fact that the price of labor affects living costs through the price of locally produced goods and services, would include in addition the effects shown by *dashed* lines in the same diagram. In either model, the equalization effect is finished when there are no longer any real income differentials (that is, equilibrium has been reached, as far as the employee

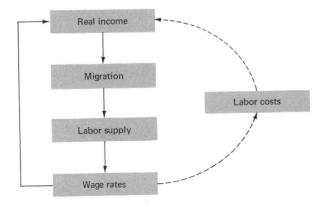

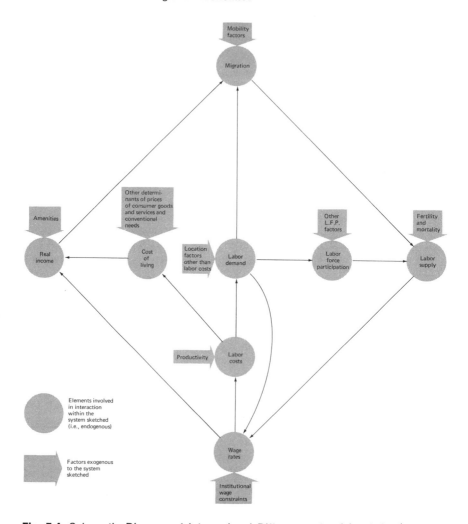

Fig. 7-4. Schematic Diagram of Interregional Differences Involving Labor*
* I am indebted to Mr. Robert D. Lang for major improvements in the presentation of this diagram.

is concerned). The reader may find it useful to trace out in a similar fashion, using Fig. 7-4 as a guide, what happens as labor-oriented employers shift their hiring to areas of low labor cost.

Where Are Labor Costs Low?

What are the types of location to which a labor-oriented activity is attracted? There is no single, simple answer to this question, mainly because different activities and individual firms are seeking different kinds of labor cost economy. In some jobs, one worker can perform as well as another. For such a job, labor is a rather homogeneous input, and the wage rate is a good measure of labor cost. In other occupations, skills and aptitudes vary widely, and a poor worker is not a bargain at any wage. In some activities, the nature of the product and the work and the volume of output are highly changeable, and the employer wants to be able to arrange with a minimum of difficulty for changes in job specifications, short layoffs, overtime, and other changes. In such an activity, good labor supply locations may be those where the local pool of labor is large, where the average age and seniority of workers is low, or where union bargaining has not built up a rigid structure of work rules.

Each activity, then, will have its own preferences among labor supply locations, determined by the relative emphasis it puts upon low wages, skill or trainability, and flexibility.

Low wages are most often found in relatively backward areas where the demand for labor has not kept up with the natural increase of the labor force. Obviously, these are areas where manpower is impounded, as it were, by its imperfect outward mobility. Less obviously, such areas tend to develop certain characteristics that impede out-migration.

Many such areas heavily specialize in kinds of employment for which the demand has grown slowly or declined (for example, general farming or coal mining). This may, in fact, be the chief reason why they are areas of labor surplus. But this specialization also means that their labor force lacks experience in more dynamic industries or occupations, which is a disadvantage in seeking work elsewhere. There are attitudinal barriers, too, to giving up an occupation in which one has acquired age and seniority in order to start near the bottom in a new trade. Derelict coal mining villages in Appalachia are full of middle-aged and older ex-miners who are slow to consider any alternative line of work, even though it may be clear that the local mine is closed for good. Finally, the very existence of labor surplus and low wages helps to lower the cost of such major budget items as shelter and services, and this helps to diminish the economic incentive to move out.

The advantages of experience and skill in a labor supply are most often found in areas where the educational level is high and where activities requiring some special skills have been concentrated for a long time. The supply of some types of highly paid and scarce manpower (such as scientific and other specialists, or persons of high artistic capability) is coming to be located increasingly in areas and communities of high physical and cultural amenity, since those types of people are in such demand that they can afford to be quite choosy about where they are willing to live. It is no accident or whim that has located so much research-oriented activity in pleasant places near large cities or major universities.

Flexibility and diversity of labor supply is most likely to be found in a large labor market in an intensively urban region. In some of these labor markets, however, the potential labor economies of size and diversity are partly offset by the greater rigidity of union work rules and bargaining practices and the greater age and seniority of the work force that characterize an area where an activity has developed a mature concentration.

The different kinds of labor cost advantage (low wage rates, skill, and flexibility and diversity of supply) are unlikely to be found in the same places, because to some extent they reflect contrasting area characteristics. Thus, low wage rates are associated with small towns in relatively undeveloped and slow-growing farm areas with low living costs. Experience and diversity of supply are associated with the opposite type of location: large urban areas in advanced industrialized regions with relatively high living costs. Any given area, then, tends to be classified according to the aspect of labor supply in which it has the greatest comparative advantage.

Indirect Advantages of Labor Quality

The cost savings involved in the use of highly productive (that is, skilled and/or adaptable) manpower are sometimes underestimated, because not all of them show up in labor cost per se. Recall the case of Harkinsville and Parkston discussed on page 18 above. Harkinsville workers work faster, and get correspondingly higher hourly wages, than those in Parkston. Thus, there is no difference in labor cost per hour. Nevertheless, it will be recalled, Harkinsville is a better location for the employer. For example, if the output of the firm is to be 1,000 units a day at whichever location is chosen, the production worker payroll will be the same at either location; but the plant can be smaller at Harkinsville. This means a smaller investment in land and buildings, a smaller parking lot and cafeteria, fewer rest rooms and facilities and drinking fountains, a smaller work load for payroll accounting and personnel management, and so on. Only such cost items as are geared directly to the volume of output and not the number of men working will be as large in Harkinsville as in Parkston: for example, production materials, shipping containers, motive power and fuel for processing, and loading and handling facilities.

Institutional Constraints on Wages and Labor Costs

To an increasing extent in most countries, the supply of labor to an individual employer at one location is affected by bargaining procedures and constraints involving other employers and other locations as well. In activities where the employing firms are few and large and where a strong labor organization includes a major fraction of the workers, key negotiations can set a quasi-national pattern of fringe benefits and work rules subject to only minor local differences. Examples include the steel and automobile industries and rail and air transportation. In still other activities, agreements cover major sections of the activity (such as the East Coast ports with respect to handling ship cargo).

Multi-area bargaining introduces a strong additional equalization element into the wage pattern. Even more generally, labor organizations with aspirations for nationwide power try to work toward elimination of regional wage differentials. Lower wages in areas of weaker organization are viewed as a threat to employment in the areas of stronger organization and higher wages, since employers are naturally tempted to move to save labor costs. And employers not contemplating such a move are, of course, in favor of higher labor costs for their competitors. Both parties, then, may well favor extension of the geographical area of wage bargaining and the enactment of federal and state minimum-wage laws, which still further limit differentials.

There are often pressures toward similarity of pay rates and fringe benefit levels among different activities and occupations within a single labor market. This means that if there are important high-wage activities in an area, they tend to some extent to set the tone for related types of employment in the same area, and to make it generally a higher cost area than it might otherwise be.

It is easy to see how this works between occupations calling for similar qualifications, so that the various activities in the community are competing in a common pool of available workers with those qualifications. For example, steelworkers are relatively highly paid; as a result, a community dominated by steel making is likely to have relatively high wage scales in construction and in other kinds of male employment not too different in their requirements from the jobs of many steel mill employees. There would be no such direct effect, however, upon wage rates for women or for sales or clerical workers.

Furthermore, unions of the dominant industry in a community generally organize a number of other industries as well, the jurisdictional lines being rather loose. Thus in Pittsburgh, metal fabricating plants are mainly organized by the steelworkers' union, while similar plants in Detroit have locals of the automobile workers' union. Though such a union does not necessarily find it feasible or desirable to extend the wage and benefits pattern in the dominant industry to the other industries it has organized in the same community, there is certainly some pressure in that direction, and a consequent reinforcing of the tendency toward intra-area wage level conformity.[23]

This tendency is not area-wide, as a rule. For example, in the Pittsburgh labor market area the upward wage pressures arising from the importance

---

[23] On this and related questions, see Pittsburgh Regional Planning Association, *Region in Transition*, Economic Study of the Pittsburgh Region, Vol. I (Pittsburgh: University of Pittsburgh Press, 1963), Ch. 4, especially pp. 106–109.

of some tightly organized and high-paying industries are essentially restricted to blue-collar male occupations, which heavily predominate in the major industries involved. Until very recently, however, Pittsburgh wages in retail trade and for women's jobs generally tended to be a little lower than those in cities of comparable size in the same part of the country. Presumably, this reflected the relatively slow growth of the area as a whole and the relative surplus of employable women arising from the predominance of male jobs in the area. It is interesting to note that in the late 1950s the differentials began to disappear, perhaps reflecting vigorous local growth in office employment and no growth in heavy industry employment.[24]

It has been observed that the "wage spread" or "skill margin" among different occupations within a single labor market is generally wider in less-developed and slower growing regions. This has been explained in terms of the lower educational standards and the smaller proportion of semiskilled manufacturing jobs in such areas, since education and the availability of an accessible "ladder" of skill development both enhance occupational mobility and make the labor market more competitive.[25]

A further explanation lies in the tendency for people of higher occupational, educational, and earnings levels to be geographically more mobile. As a result, regional differentials in their earnings are narrower than is the case for lower status people.[26] In an area of labor surplus and out-migration, it is the people in the better paid occupations who move out most readily; a relatively larger differential is required to move the unskilled. The wage spread in such a labor market is consequently wide compared to that in a more prosperous and active place.

Table 7-6 provides an illustration, comparing earnings levels by major occupation groups in California, a state with heavy net in-migration, with corresponding levels in West Virginia, a state that in recent decades has experienced predominantly outward migration. As we go down the occupational and income scale, the California–West Virginia differential tends to increase. And in West Virginia, most occupations are further

---

[24] *Ibid.*

[25] ". . . one would expect that, within the United States, the South—where semiskilled manufacturing jobs are relatively infrequent, minimum educational standards are low, and racial prejudice acts as a barrier to substitution of unskilled negroes for skilled whites—would be an area where the skill margin would be relatively high. In the Far West where minimum educational standards are relatively high, where negroes and foreign immigrants are relatively infrequent and where females and children are an unusually small part of the work force, one would expect to find a relatively high degree of substitutability between skilled and unskilled labor and, consequently, a narrow skill margin. And, as is generally known, the skill margin is higher in the South and lower in the Far West than in any of the other parts of the United States." Melvin W. Reder, "The Theory of Occupational Wage Differentials," *American Economic Review*, 45, 5 (December 1955), 846–847.

[26] This relationship was noted earlier in connection with Table 7-2.

TABLE 7-6. Median Family Incomes, by Occupation of Head of Family, in California and West Virginia, 1959

Occupation group*	Median income		Calif. as percentage of W. Va.	Percentage deviation of median income for specific occupation group from overall median for state	
	Calif.	W. Va.		Calif.	W. Va.
All occupations	7,284	5,317	137	0	0
Professional, technical, etc.	9,232	7,525	122	+27	+41
Managers, proprietors, etc. (nonfarm)	9,412	7,136	132	+29	+34
Craftsmen, foremen, etc.	7,512	5,911	127	+3	+11
Sales workers	7,973	5,663	140	+9	+7
Clerical and kindred workers	6,556	5,622	117	−10	+6
Operatives and kindred workers	6,461	5,008	129	−11	−6
Laborers (nonfarm)	5,577	3,915	142	−23	−26
Service workers	5,801	3,716	156	−20	−30
Farmers and farm managers	5,562	2,188	254	−24	−59
Farm laborers	3,794	1,854	204	−48	−65
Private household workers	2,456	1,535	160	−66	−71

* Ranked in order of West Virginia income level.

SOURCE: U.S. Department of Commerce, Bureau of the Census, *United States Census of Population, 1960,* Vol. I: Characteristics of the Population, Part 6 (California) and Part 50 (West Virginia) (Washington, D.C.: Government Printing Office, 1963), Table 145.

above or further below the overall state median than is the case in California. In fact, the only exceptions are in occupational categories that are not much above or below the overall state median in either state.

Complementary Labor

Different categories of labor are to some extent jointly supplied: that is, the supply of one kind of labor in an area depends on how much of the other kind is there. A local population or potential labor force is almost always an assortment of people of different ages, sexes, and physical and mental capabilities. If most of the jobs available in the area call for superior aptitude, the area is likely to have a surplus of people with more pedestrian abilities, and these may represent a bargain in labor supply for an activity with less exacting requirements. Conversely, if all the jobs in an area involve rugged manual labor, there is likely to be a surplus of not quite so rugged individuals, who might represent a bargain labor supply for an activity not requiring physical strength.

We have to consider, then, as another kind of advantageous labor location for an activity, places where there is a heavy demand for some contrasting and complementary kind of labor. This principle assumes, of course, that mobility is quite imperfect, so that all the different types of workers are not able to seek out the locations where their own kind of work is best rewarded.

The most important basis for such restriction is inherent in family ties. In a family's choice of location from the standpoint of income, the most important consideration is opportunity and earnings for the principal earner, usually the head of the family. His wife, and any other full or partial dependents of working age, are then part of the potential labor supply in the area where he locates, and usually represent capabilities quite different from his. Accordingly, a labor market heavily specialized in activities employing men is likely to have a plentiful and relatively cheap female labor supply, and a labor market heavily specialized in activities employing mature adults is likely to have a plentiful and relatively cheap supply of young labor of both sexes.

Historically, many industries have owed their start in certain areas to a complementary labor supply generated in such a way. A classic case is the making of shoes in colonial days in eastern Massachusetts. The coastal area north of Boston was heavily specialized in the male occupations of sailing and fishing; this created a large complementary labor surplus of wives and daughters, who were able to supplement family incomes by making shoes at home, and later in small factories.[27] At a later period, the anthracite mining area of eastern Pennsylvania attracted a substantial amount of the silk weaving industry on a similar basis. As late as the 1920s, it was observed that in the anthracite area about 60 percent of the silk weavers were women, while in the previous center of that industry (in and around Paterson, New Jersey) 60 percent were men. The manufacture of cheap standard garments, cigars, and light electrical equipment and components has also been significantly attracted to areas well stocked with what have been picturesquely styled "by-product women."[28]

---

[27] See E. M. Hoover, *Location Theory and the Shoe and Leather Industries* (Cambridge, Mass.: Harvard University Press, 1937), pp. 109, 215–217, and sources cited therein.

[28] R. M. Haig, "Toward an Understanding of the Metropolis," *Quarterly Journal of Economics,* 40, 1 (February 1926), p. 195.

THE LOCATION OF PEOPLE
WITHIN A LABOR MARKET AREA

Up to this point, we have been looking at the location of people and differentials in earnings and labor costs on a macrogeographic scale, comparing labor markets as units. A quite different set of considerations come to the fore when we adopt a microgeographic focus and look at preferences and differentials inside the individual labor market area. A few points may be noted here for later reference in the last three chapters, which will deal specifically with questions of location inside urban areas.

Residential Location Preferences

The choice of location for an individual or a family within a single labor market area can be largely or even wholly a matter of *residential* preference, since by definition a labor market area is supposed to lie within feasible commuting range. Consequently, wage or income differentials are unlikely to determine the choice. Some other location factors that are important for interregional location choice also drop out of the picture when we consider location within a given labor market area. For example, the costs of food and utility services are unlikely to vary much. The main factors determining how much people are willing to pay for residential space are (1) access, measured primarily in terms of travel time, and (2) quality of the site and neighborhood.

Access advantage is measured largely, but not wholly, in terms of the time and money cost of the *journey to work*. This is the largest single category of local trips as reported in urban transportation surveys.[29] Shopping trips are next in volume; but this may exaggerate the importance of access to retail stores and shopping centers as a factor in residence choice, in view of the wide dispersion of food stores and other outlets that account for the bulk of the shopping journeys. Trips to school and trips for cultural and recreational purposes make up the rest of the pattern.

The quality of the site and neighborhood means, of course, different things to different people, according to their personal tastes. Most of us, however, would agree on preferring quiet, spacious, and orderly living areas with good public services and populated by people of about the same income and style of living as ourselves. Few people like to live in really high-density neighborhoods unless they provide offsetting advantages of access or service.

---

[29] For relevant reference material, see J. R. Meyer, J. F. Kain, and M. Wohl, *The Urban Transportation Problem* (Cambridge, Mass.: Harvard University Press, 1965). For a primarily bibliographical survey of the whole question of access, see Gunnar Olsson, *Distance and Human Interaction: A Review and Bibliography* (Philadelphia: Regional Science Research Institute, University of Pennsylvania, 1965).

Residential choice in urban areas is further constrained by competition for space and by pressures for neighborhood homogeneity, as we shall see in greater detail in a later chapter. First, people have to choose among the alternatives that they can afford, which means that the latitude of choice narrows drastically as we go down the income scale. Second, the site they pick must, with few exceptions, be similar in character to the other developed sites in the same neighborhood. Most of the residential choices that are made in an urban area involve dwellings already built, in neighborhoods whose physical and social pattern is already established. Even the few (mainly in the upper-income groups) who can select new houses on the suburban fringe will be choosing mainly among developments whose physical and social pattern is predetermined by the developer's plan and the local zoning constraints. Neighborhood homogeneity is still further strengthened by the forces of ethnic and racial segregation reflecting attitudes both within a segregated group and among other groups.

These neighborhood homogeneity constraints imply that individual choice (particularly for lower-income and minority groups) is narrowly restricted. Neighborhoods are shaped and reshaped only in response to the demands of rather large groups of individuals of similar preferences and incomes, expressed over substantial periods of time. If large numbers of well-to-do people have a strong preference for living close to the center of a city, an old and decaying area may in time be upgraded into a posh high-income neighborhood of small single-family homes (such as the Georgetown district of Washington, D.C.) or high-rise luxury apartments. If there is a sufficiently strong and persistent demand for living quarters that can be made by dividing old mansions into cheap apartments, a neighborhood once characterized by high-income levels, prestige, and low density can gradually change into a slum. But in both cases, the transition is a gradual and massive one, encountering strong inertia and resistance, and well beyond the influence of any individual's specific residence choice.

Labor Cost Differentials and Employer Locations

Although labor market areas are in principle defined in terms of a feasible commuting range, people prefer short work journeys to long ones; thus, the supply of labor to an employer is not really ubiquitous throughout such an area. Differential advantages of labor supply within a single labor market area are particularly significant when the employer wants a special type of labor or a large supply of job candidates, and in large labor market areas where residential areas are sharply differentiated in character.

Thus, if an activity mainly employs a class of people dependent on public transportation to get to work (for example, very low income people or married women whose husbands preempt the family car for their own commuting), it may have difficulty in recruiting an adequate work force in the less accessible suburban areas. Even if there is not an absolute shortage of applicants, there may not be enough of a surplus of applicants to allow much freedom of selection.

In the late 1950s, a study was made of the recruiting experiences of business firms in the Boston metropolitan area which had relocated to sites along a circumferential suburban freeway.[30] Most of the establishments in the sample canvassed were sizable manufacturing plants, with electronics equipment the most numerous category. Every firm in the sample had made an advance survey of the residence and commuting patterns of its employees in an effort to anticipate any recruitment problems that the new location might involve. Several of the firms took explicit account of employee residence locations in choosing the specific section of the highway on which to relocate. Every firm found it necessary to establish a plant cafeteria at the new location.

The survey's findings on recruitment problems were summed up as follows:

> A summary of the observations of personnel managers interviewed indicated a general, but not universal, conclusion that Route 128 locations in comparison with the downtown areas definitely eased recruitment of engineering, professional and administrative staff, but neither helped nor hindered recruitment of skilled labor. Recruiting difficulties arose especially when the firms sought young, female clerical workers, male unskilled workers, and seasonal workers, both male and female, particularly in the higher income suburbs of the western subarea of Route 128. The type of recruitment problem mentioned most frequently was that of the younger, unmarried female, clerical workers.
>
> The most serious of the recruitment problems was that of unskilled production labor, both male and female, but especially male, for seasonal work. Although this problem did not arise frequently, the need for a seasonal expansion of employment could cause a major headache for the personnel department, and to indicate [sic] very sharply the lack of casual labor market in the suburbs. At a downtown location, a firm could readily draw unskilled male and female workers with a "Help Wanted" sign in the window for seasonal employment. At a Route 128 location, this type of labor was scarce, and intown labor found commuting to the plant time-consuming and costly for low-paying jobs on a seasonal basis.
>
> . . . the existence of a circumferential highway or of a few long-distance commuters does not lead to the conclusion that there is also a circumferential labor market, in which a firm at any one location can draw equally well from any other part of the area. On the contrary it would appear as if suburban firms tend to draw from areas nearby, and lose those workers who live at abnormally long distances away.
>
> . . . relationship of a firm to the immediate local labor supply seems to be crucial. Where the local supply is already committed, or of the wrong composi-

---

[30] Everett J. Burtt, Jr., "Labor Supply Characteristics of Route 128 Firms," Research Report No. 1-1958 (Boston: Federal Reserve Bank of Boston, 1958; mimeographed). The excerpts quoted above appear in a somewhat altered sequence.

tion to meet the demands of the firm, the company will be forced to rely on longer-distance commuters. If this means extension of commuting beyond the normal range, or direction, for that type of labor, the firm will be likely to have major labor supply difficulties.

This and other studies show that, despite the enhancement of worker mobility provided by the private automobile, distance is still an important consideration in the location of both employers and employees within large labor markets. One of the most serious aspects of the present-day problem of adequate opportunity for the residents of urban slums is that an increasing proportion of the kinds of jobs that they might fill has shifted to distant suburban locations with little or no public transportation available, while very few employers have been willing to accept some obvious disadvantages of a slum location for the sake of closer access to that labor supply.

SELECTED READINGS

Richard A. Easterlin, "Regional Income Trends, 1840–1950," in Seymour Harris (ed.), *American Economic History* (New York: McGraw-Hill, 1961), Ch. 16.

Larry Sjaastad, "The Costs and Returns of Human Migration," *Journal of Political Economy,* 70, 5, pt. 2 (October 1962), 80–93.

Julian Wolpert, "Behavioral Aspects of the Decision to Migrate," *Papers of the Regional Science Association,* 15 (1965), 159–169.

Everett S. Lee, "A Theory of Migration," *Demography,* 3, 1 (1966), 47–57.

Ira S. Lowry, *Migration and Metropolitan Growth: Two Analytical Models* (San Francisco: Chandler, 1966).

Gunnar Olsson, *Distance and Human Interaction,* Bibliography Series No. 2 (Philadelphia: Regional Science Research Institute, 1966).

John Lansing and Eva Mueller, *The Geographic Mobility of Labor* (Ann Arbor: Survey Research Center, University of Michigan, 1967).

Lawrence A. Brown, *Diffusion Processes and Location,* Bibliography Series No. 4 (Philadelphia: Regional Science Research Institute, 1969).

Harry W. Richardson, *Regional Economics* (New York: Praeger, 1969), Ch. 12.

INTRODUCTION

Statistically, the economy of a region represents the sum of its activities, just as a tree represents an aggregation of different kinds of substances. But to understand how either a tree or a region develops we have to look at it in functional terms, finding out how each part serves or affects other parts. Any living organism is much more than the sum of its parts.

From earlier chapters we have gained some understanding of the ways in which different activities, in the proximity and interdependence associated with sharing a regional location, affect one another's development. Thus, within any region there is a vast amount of transference of goods and services among activities. A furniture factory buys locally its electricity, labor services, public services, and at least some of its materials and supplies. A wholesale firm supplies retailers in the region and gets its labor, public services, and some of its other inputs from inside the region. Nearly everyone in a region is in fact both a buyer from and a seller to someone else in the region and thus helps to support the presence of various other activities.

In addition to this interdependence through local purchases and sales of goods and services, regional activities affect one another by competing for space and other scarce local resources, such as water. Some of these relationships were explored in Chapter 5.

In Chapter 4 we examined other ways in which activities in a region affect one another by mutually creating external economies of agglomeration, and in Chapter 6 we saw how agglomerative forces give rise to urban concentrations of various sizes and functional characteristics. Chapter 7 referred to some of the ways in which the demand and supply of labor in a region affect and are affected by the region's activities and growth.

Although nobody can fully comprehend the interdependencies in a regional economy, we are well aware that they exist. A normal attribute of a region is a general consciousness of a common regional interest; this is fortunate because it makes possible some rational collective efforts to improve regional welfare.

8
Regional Economic Structure and Growth

The aim of the present chapter is to develop a fuller understanding of how and why a region changes in size and structure. Viewing regions as organisms, we are concerned with their anatomy and physiology, as preparation for an inquiry in Chapter 9 into their health, pathology, and therapy.

SOME BASIC MEASURES OF REGIONAL ACTIVITY IN THE UNITED STATES

Before inquiring into the reasons for regional structure and growth, it is useful to have some general background on American regions and metropolitan areas. We shall look briefly at measures of overall growth, income level, and structure.

Relative Regional Growth

Fig. 8-1 shows the differences in the population growth rates of the Census divisions of the United States over the last century or so.[1] We are not concerned here with the absolute sizes of the divisions' populations, but only with the question of which areas have shown faster growth than others. Accordingly, the chart is plotted on a logarithmic or ratio scale, so that the slope of a line on it represents the *percentage* rate of population growth per annum, and the different divisions are simply stacked in an arbitrary order on the chart for comparison. We are interested not in the vertical position of these lines but only in their relative slopes.

It is immediately apparent that, although all divisions have increased in population throughout the period, the rates of growth have been quite different for various divisions at various times. The earliest settled Eastern areas have grown slower than the others. The West North Central displayed above-average growth until 1890 but has since lagged, while the West South Central had a rapid growth period lasting until 1910, and since then has just about kept pace with the rest of the country. The Far Western divisions, especially the Pacific, have grown faster than the national average throughout the period. The 1940s, the decade of World War II, brought sudden surges of population to the Pacific and South Atlantic and declines to the Middle Atlantic and West North Central.

It is also apparent that there has been a gradual tendency for the growth rates to become more alike, as the pioneer stages of development have passed and the country has become more fully settled and more evenly industrialized. The fastest-growing parts of the country in recent years have been the Pacific Coast, the Southwest, and the Gulf Coast, while the central plains area has tended to lose ground.

---

[1] The areas involved are mapped in Fig. 8-2.

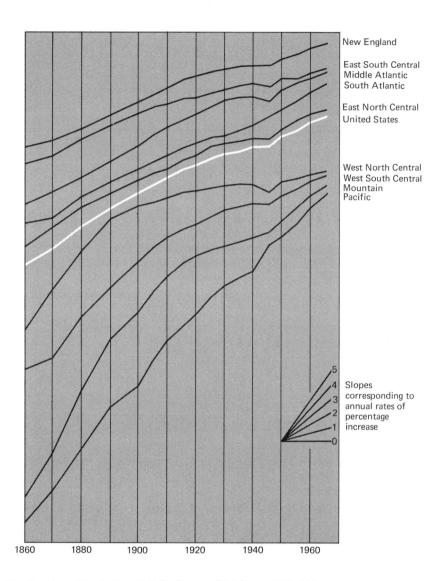

New England

East South Central
Middle Atlantic
South Atlantic

East North Central
United States

West North Central
West South Central
Mountain
Pacific

Slopes
corresponding to
annual rates of
percentage
increase

Fig. 8-1. Resident Population of U.S. Census Divisions, 1860–1965

Note: The sharp changes between 1940 and 1950 primarily reflect movements of military personnel and defense workers within the U.S. and overseas.

SOURCE: U.S. Department of Commerce, Bureau of the Census, *Long-Term Economic Growth, 1860–1965* (Washington, D.C.: Government Printing Office, 1966), pp. 218–219.

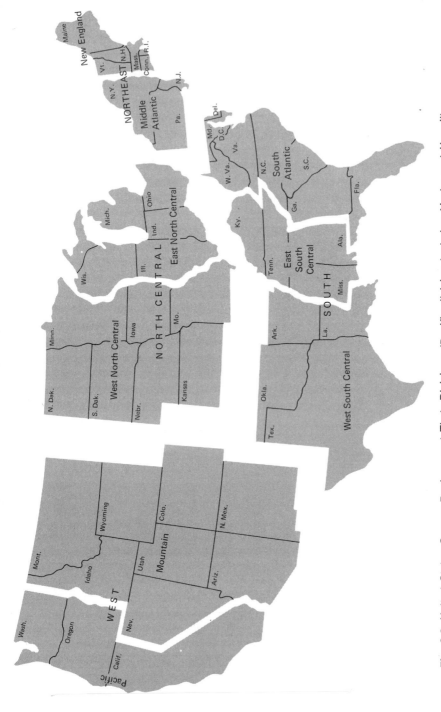

Fig. 8-2. United States Census Regions and Their Divisions (Pacific division includes Alaska and Hawaii)

SOURCE: U.S. Department of Commerce, Bureau of the Census, *Statistical Abstract of the United States, 1957* (Washington, D.C.: Government Printing Office, 1957).

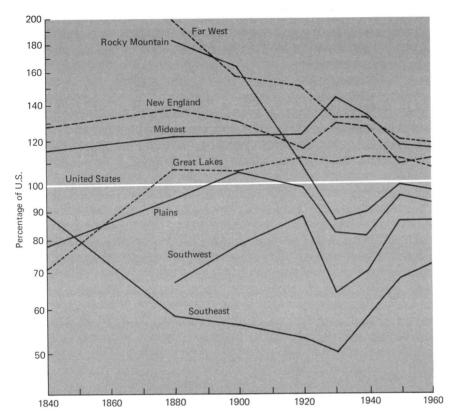

Fig. 8-3. Personal Income per Capita in U.S. Regions as Percentage of U.S. Personal Income per Capita, 1840–1960

SOURCE: Hugh O. Nourse, *Regional Economics* (New York: McGraw-Hill, 1968), Table 6-5, p. 146. "Southwest" excludes Oklahoma in 1880. Alaska and Hawaii are included in "Far West" in 1960.

Regional Trends and Differentials in per Capita Income

Fig. 8-3 portrays the changes in the *relative* levels of regional per capita income that have taken place since 1840, though the estimates for the earlier years are quite rough. Each region's per capita income is shown, at each date, as a percentage of the national average. The regional breakdown used here is not the same as in Figs. 8-1 and 8-2 but is that shown in Fig. 6-1 on p. 122 above.

We notice once again the persistently higher income level of the West and the persistently lower level of the South. After 1880, there is a trend toward convergence: the regional disparities become narrower as time passes. People generally assume that such convergence is desirable on social, political, and economic grounds, but there are some qualifications,

TABLE 8-1. Relative per Capita Incomes in Metropolitan and Nonmetropolitan Areas and by Regions, Selected Years, 1929–1966

	1929	1940	1950	1959	1966
Total United States	100	100	100	100	100
SMSA counties/U.S.	132	129	117	114	112
Non-SMSA counties/U.S.	57	59	72	73	75
Non-SMSA counties as percentage of SMSA counties	43	46	62	64	67
New England					
SMSA counties/U.S.	130	135	112	112	113
Lowest SMSA as percentage of highest	57	51	56	69	62
Highest in 1929 and 1966	Boston, Mass.				New London-Groton-Norwich, Conn.
Lowest in 1929 and 1966	Lewiston-Auburn, Me.				Lewiston-Auburn, Me.
Mideast					
SMSA counties/U.S.	149	143	124	121	118
Lowest SMSA as percentage of highest	44	45	57	51	53
Highest in 1929 and 1966	Paterson-Passaic, N.J.				Paterson-Passaic, N.J.
Lowest in 1929 and 1966	Johnstown, Altoona, and Erie, Pa.*				Johnstown, Pa.
Great Lakes					
SMSA counties/U.S.	139	135	126	118	118
Lowest SMSA as percentage of highest	43	48	59	61	69
Highest in 1929 and 1966	Chicago, Ill.				Chicago, Ill.
Lowest in 1929 and 1966	Terre Haute, Ind.				Terre Haute, Ind.
Plains					
SMSA counties/U.S.	122	119	118	115	112
Lowest SMSA as percentage of highest	57	63	71	65	63

	1929				1966
Highest in 1929 and 1966	Des Moines, Iowa				Cedar Rapids, Iowa
Lowest in 1929 and 1966	Springfield, Mo.				Springfield, Mo.
Southeast					
SMSA counties/U.S.	84	89	92	92	94
Lowest SMSA as percentage of highest	29	25	38	59	56
Highest in 1929 and 1966	Miami, Fla.				Richmond, Va.
Lowest in 1929 and 1966	Huntsville, Ala.				Tuscaloosa, Ala.
Southwest					
SMSA counties/U.S.	94	95	102	96	93
Lowest SMSA as percentage of highest	28	32	31	40	34
Highest in 1929 and 1966	Midland, Texas				Midland, Texas
Lowest in 1929 and 1966	McAllen-Pharr-Edinburg, Texas				McAllen-Pharr-Edinburg, Texas
Rocky Mountain					
SMSA counties/U.S.	112	111	109	105	99
Lowest SMSA as percentage of highest	37	41	53	62	58
Highest in 1929 and 1966	Denver, Colo.				Denver, Colo.
Lowest in 1929 and 1966	Provo-Orem, Utah				Provo-Orem, Utah
Far West					
SMSA counties/U.S.	141	142	124	123	118
Lowest SMSA as percentage of highest	42	47	63	62	60
Highest in 1929 and 1966	San Francisco-Oakland, Sacramento and Stockton, Calif.*				San Francisco-Oakland, Calif.
Lowest in 1929 and 1966	Eugene and Salem, Ore.*				Salem, Ore.
Anchorage, Alaska/U.S.	—	—	—	133	120
Honolulu/U.S.	—	—	—	104	108

* Combination of 2 or more SMSAs for which separate data were not available.

SOURCE: Robert E. Graham, Jr., and Edwin J. Coleman, "Metropolitan Area Incomes, 1929–66," *Survey of Current Business*, 48, 8 (August 1968), Table 1, 32–37.

which we shall be examining in Chapter 9, in connection with regional goals and policies.

Table 8-1 gives more detail on income differentials for the period 1929–1966, focusing also upon the nation's Standard Metropolitan Statistical Areas (SMSAs). The trends over the 37-year period are rather striking.

First, we observe in Table 8-1 that in the United States as a whole, per capita income levels have been consistently higher in metropolitan counties, but the gap has become progressively narrower. People in nonmetropolitan areas in 1929 had per capita incomes only 43 percent as high as those in metropolitan areas; by 1966, the ratio had risen to 68 percent.

Looking at the data for the various regions shown in Table 8-1, we see once again the familiar differentials in favor of the West and Northeast and against the South, and also a progressive narrowing of the interregional differentials. Per capita incomes in every region except the Southwest were closer to the national average in 1966 than in 1929. In 1929, the incomes in metropolitan areas of the poorest region were less than 60 percent of those in the richest region; this ratio had risen to 79 percent by 1966.

Finally, within each region we see a surprisingly large range of per capita incomes for individual SMSAs. In a majority of regions, in fact, there was more than a 2-to-1 spread among SMSA income levels in 1929. Here again, substantial convergence seems to have taken place between 1929 and 1966 within nearly every region. Individual SMSAs ranking low or high within their regions tended to keep that position: in fact, there were only a few changes in the top and bottom positions as noted in the table. It is observable that the richest SMSA in a region was, in most cases, much larger than the poorest. In general, there is still a positive association of per capita income with size among metropolitan areas, though the differentials seem to be narrowing.

Regional Structural Differences

The growth of regions and the kind of opportunities they provide for their residents depend to a large extent on the mix of activities they have. We can characterize regions or locations as being narrowly specialized in a limited range of activities, or as being diversified in structure.

To illustrate this differentiation let us consider the metropolitan areas of the United States. Table 8-2 shows a structural grouping made by the U.S. Department of Commerce on the basis of the sources of income of residents of each SMSA in 1966. "Manufacturing" SMSAs (97 in all) were defined as those in which earnings from manufacturing employment accounted for an above-average fraction of total personal income. In each of the 28 SMSAs in the "manufacturing-intensive" category, this fraction was 40 percent or higher. Nearly all of those 28 are in the Mideast and Great Lakes regions.

TABLE 8-2. Percentage Distribution of Sources of Personal Income, by Type of SMSA, 1966

	Total personal income	Earnings of persons employed in						Property income and transfer payments less personal contributions to social insurance
		All activities	Govt.	Mfg.	Agri.	Mining	Residentiary*	
United States, total	100.0	80.8	13.0	24.4	3.2	.9	39.3	19.2
All SMSAs	100.0	81.5	12.4	25.5	1.0	.5	42.1	18.5
Outside of SMSAs	100.0	79.3	14.9	20.9	10.3	2.0	31.2	20.7
Type of SMSA								
Manufacturing-intensive	100.0	84.0	7.3	43.9	1.3	.2	31.3	16.0
Manufacturing-moderate	100.0	82.1	9.1	33.0	.7	.3	39.0	17.9
Government-military-oriented	100.0	83.2	35.8	10.9	1.3	.5	34.7	16.8
Government-other	100.0	82.0	28.8	10.7	1.5	.4	40.6	18.0
Agriculture	100.0	79.2	19.5	9.7	12.4	1.9	35.7	20.8
Mining	100.0	79.3	9.1	14.2	.6	12.5	42.9	20.7
Recreation	100.0	77.6	11.4	8.8	1.0	.3	56.1	22.4
Retirement	100.0	68.9	11.2	11.0	2.2	.8	43.7	31.1
Regional center	100.0	83.6	9.1	19.9	1.1	1.6	51.9	16.4
National center	100.0	79.7	10.2	22.2	.2	.2	46.9	20.3
Mixed	100.0	81.0	13.6	20.5	1.2	.8	44.9	19.0

* Construction, transportation, communication, public utilities, trade, finance, insurance and real estate, and services. Personal income from local government, which also should be classed as a residentiary activity, was combined with income from state government in the source table, and has been included here under "Government."

SOURCE: Robert E. Graham, Jr., and Edwin J. Coleman, "Metropolitan Area Incomes, 1929–66," *Survey of Current Business*, 48, 8 (August 1968), p. 29.

SMSAs with at least 20 percent of personal income derived from government (compared with 12.4 percent for all SMSAs) were put in the "Government" category. In 26 of these, military payrolls bulk large (at least 10 percent of personal income); in the other 21, government civilian payrolls are relatively more important.

There were 10 SMSAs classified as agricultural, since each had at least 10 percent of its personal income (that is, more than the average for all *non*metropolitan areas!) derived from agriculture. This classification reflects the fact that SMSAs, being generally made up of whole counties, contain substantial amounts of rural farm territory, usually intensively developed.

In 5 SMSAs, mining is a major source of personal income. In 4 of these, in Texas, Oklahoma, and Louisiana, the specialization is in oil and natural gas production, and property incomes also bulk large in their sources of income; the fifth is the Duluth-Superior SMSA, specializing in iron ore mining.

Recreational and retirement SMSAs (there are 4 of each) are characterized by low proportions of income derived from manufacturing, rather high proportions derived from property, and (in the case of the retirement SMSAs such as Tampa-St. Petersburg and Tucson), by high proportions of income derived from transfer payments, principally pensions.

There are 16 SMSAs classed as regional or national centers because an above-average share of their incomes is derived from typically "residentiary" types of activity. This reflects the fact that in these areas some of the typical residentiary activities such as transportation, communications, finance, trade, and services are really export activities serving an unusually far-flung region. The 4 national centers are New York, Los Angeles, Chicago, and San Francisco, ranking first, second, third, and sixth in population in 1966. It is interesting to observe that Philadelphia and Boston (ranking fourth and fifth in size) do not appear as national centers; since they are so close to New York, their areas of influence are curtailed.

The residual group of 40 "mixed" SMSAs comprises those lacking any of the marked specializations of structure that characterize the other categories.

In similar fashion, larger geographical areas such as states or multistate regions exhibit different specializations of function and structure. Regional specialization in some specific activity generally implies that the region is a net exporter of the product of that activity, although in some cases it can reflect instead a distinctive pattern of demand in the region itself. Thus, Michigan's specialization in motor vehicle production and Washington, D.C.,'s specialization in government are associated with heavy exports of cars and government services from those areas; but the unusually high proportions of health and recreational service activities in retirement areas are primarily accounted for by the local demand.

Should we expect that regions become more alike, or more differentiated and specialized, as development proceeds? The answer is not obvious. On the one hand, improved transport, communication, affluence, and mobility are conducive to a greater uniformity in tastes and demand patterns in different regions. Interregional convergence of levels of income also works toward uniformity. And as more regions and urban centers mature and grow to a sufficient size to support a wider variety of activities, their attractions as production and residence locations may become more nearly alike. On the other hand, improved transport and communication make it easier for any one area to serve others over longer distances and to develop export specialties. Adam Smith's dictum that the division of labor depends on the extent of the market is relevant here, and we have already noted that historically, the great improvements in overland transport in the nineteenth century increased the geographical concentration of individual industries. Today, improvements in air transport and communication are leading to greater concentration of some types of activities like public and private administrative offices and research laboratories.[2] On this basis, we might expect to see more specialization among areas rather than less, so far as those activities are concerned.

Some Quantitative Measures

There is also the question of how we measure the degree of specialization of a region, or its opposite, diversification. Such a measure must imply some assessment of the degree of dissimilarity of activities, which is more qualitative than quantitative.

In one respect, however, the direction of the trend over the last several decades is clear. The regions of the United States have become progressively more similar in their degree of industrialization as measured by manufacturing employment per 100 persons. Table 8-3 documents this trend, as well as illustrating a handy analytical measure known as the "location quotient."

In 1899 in the United States as a whole, 6.49 percent of the population were employed in manufacturing industries. In New England, the percentage was 16.3, which was 241 percent of the national average. This 241 percent is the location quotient for manufacturing employment relative to population in New England and normalized to the United States in 1899. It tells us that New England had 2.41 times as much manufacturing employment as it would have had on a pro rata basis with manufacturing distributed in the same geographical pattern as population. Referring to

---

[2] For an excellent discussion of the effects of transport changes upon industry location and regional concentration in the United States, see Benjamin Chinitz, "The Effect of Transportation Forms on Regional Economic Growth," *Traffic Quarterly*, 14, 2 (April 1960), 129–142, and *Freight and the Metropolis* (Cambridge, Mass.: Harvard University Press for the Regional Plan Association, 1960).

TABLE 8-3. Location Quotients for Manufacturing Employment with Respect to Population by Census Divisions, Selected Dates, 1899–1964*

	1899	1929	1949–1953 average	1964
Total, United States	100	100	100	100
New England	241	183	157	143
Middle Atlantic	168	139	134	126
East North Central	110	140	147	136
West North Central	43	51	63	73
South Atlantic	69	76	77	85
East South Central	37	51	59	81
West South Central	28	34	43	55
Mountain	43	39	32	41
Pacific	82	83	76	83
Ratio of largest regional quotient to smallest	8.6	5.4	4.9	3.5

* Each figure represents the percentage ratio of manufacturing employment per 100 population in the Census division to manufacturing employment per 100 population in the United States at the same date.

SOURCE: U.S. Department of Commerce, Bureau of the Census, *Long-Term Economic Growth, 1860–1965* (Washington, D.C.: Government Printing Office, 1966), p. 77.

Table 8-3, we see that in the same year the West South Central region had a location quotient of only 28 percent, indicating a marked "underrepresentation" of manufacturing in that region.

As we read across to the later years, we see New England's coefficient dropping. The region's overrepresentation in manufacturing was diminishing, and New England was becoming more like the rest of the country in its degree of industrialization. The Middle Atlantic region, another area of relatively early industrial development, showed a similar trend; while the East North Central region became more specialized in manufacturing until around 1950 and then less so. Most of the regions that were less industrialized than the rest of the country in the earlier period have had rising location quotients for manufacturing, so that the overall trend is strongly in the direction of equalization. Manufacturing has come to be distributed among regions in a pattern more and more similar to the pattern of population. This is brought out by the bottom row of figures, which shows the range of variation of the quotients consistently narrowing.

The location quotient can also be applied to individual activities or other characteristics, comparing different areas or the same area at different times. For example, in an economic study of the Pittsburgh region in the early 1960s, the manufacturing industries in which that region specialized most intensively were identified on the basis of location quotients. For each industry the location quotient was calculated as:

$$\frac{\text{Employment in Industry } A \text{ in Pittsburgh}}{\text{Total employment in Pittsburgh}} \div \frac{\text{Employment in Industry } A \text{ in U.S.}}{\text{Total employment in U.S.}}$$

An industry with a location quotient greater than 100 percent could be considered as overrepresented in the Pittsburgh labor market, and in that sense it was a Pittsburgh specialty.[3] The highest quotients (for industries on the 3-digit level of the Census industry classification) were:[4]

Industry	Location quotient (percentage)
Blast furnaces, steel works, and rolling and finishing mills	1230
Railroad equipment	840
Glass and glassware, pressed or blown	510
Electric transmission and distribution equipment	490

The coefficient of specialization, a more general type of measure, can be used to gauge the degree to which the mix of a region's economy differs from that of, say, the nation as a whole, or the same region at an earlier date. The calculation of this measure is illustrated in Table 8-4.

The first two columns of numbers are the percentage distributions of value added by manufacture in 1963 according to broad industry groups in the United States and New England respectively, and the last two columns contain the differences between the national and the New England percentages. If the industrial mix in New England were identical to the national mix (that is, if New England had just the same share of the national total in every industry group), all these differences would be zero.

The sum of the differences is in any case zero, since the pluses exactly offset the minuses. But if we add up just the positive differences (or just the negative ones, which would give the same sum) we have a measure of the degree to which the New England mix differs from the national. This is the coefficient of specialization. A coefficient of zero indicates no specialization at all, with the region's mix just matching the national or other standard mix. The maximum value of the coefficient would be close to 100 percent, and would correspond to a situation in which the region in question is devoted entirely to one industry that is not present in any other region.

If we similarly apply this measure to other regions as well, we have the set of specialization coefficients presented in Table 8-5. According to this measure, the "most specialized" region (that is, most different from the

---

[3] Alternatively, the same coefficient could be calculated as the ratio of Pittsburgh's fraction of national employment in Industry A to Pittsburgh's fraction of total national employment in all activities.

[4] Pittsburgh Regional Planning Association, *Region in Transition* (Pittsburgh: University of Pittsburgh Press, 1963), Table 4, p. 19. Two other industries (flat glass and hydraulic cement) were combined in the Census reports to avoid disclosure of data for individual establishments, and had a combined location quotient of 640 percent.

TABLE 8-4. Example of Calculation of a Coefficient of Specialization:* New England Relative to U.S. Value Added by Manufacture by Industry Groups, 1963

| Industry group | Percentage of total value added in all industries | | Difference between New England and U.S. percentage | |
	U.S.	New England	New England greater than U.S.	New England smaller than U.S.
Food and kindred products	12.0	9.6		−2.4
Tobacco manufactures	0.1	0.1		
Textile mill products	2.3	4.3	2.0	
Apparel and related products	9.1	6.7		−2.4
Lumber and wood products	11.6	10.8		−0.8
Furniture and fixtures	3.4	2.7		−0.7
Paper and allied products	1.8	2.6	0.8	
Printing and publishing	12.3	9.8		−2.5
Chemicals and allied products	3.8	3.1		−0.7
Petroleum and coal products	0.6	0.4		−0.2
Rubber and plastic products, n.e.c.†	1.8	2.6	0.8	
Leather and leather products	1.3	3.9	2.6	
Stone, clay, and glass products	5.1	3.2		−1.9
Primary metal industry	2.1	2.5	0.4	
Fabricated metal products	8.6	10.2	1.6	
Machinery, except electrical	10.8	12.1	1.3	
Electrical machinery	3.2	4.0	0.8	
Transportation equipment	2.3	1.9		−0.4
Instruments and related products	1.3	1.6	0.3	
Miscellaneous manufacturing	4.7	6.6	1.9	
Ordnance and accessories	0.1	0.1		
Administrative and auxiliary	1.7	1.2		−0.5
Totals	100.0	100.0	12.5	−12.5

* Coefficient of specialization for New England = 12.5 percent.

† n.e.c.: not elsewhere classified.

nation in its industrial mix) is the East South Central, while the "most diversified" is the Pacific region.

This coefficient, too, has a fairly wide range of applications. For example, we could use it to determine which areas most nearly have a cross section of the national population in terms of age groups or ethnic categories; or whether a given region's employment pattern diverges more from the national pattern in years of recession than in prosperous years; or whether two areas are more like each other than either is like some third

TABLE 8-5. Coefficients of Industrial Specialization for Census Divisions, 1963 (Relative to U.S. distribution of value added by industry groups)

Division	Coefficient (percentage)
East South Central	22.6
Mountain	21.6
South Atlantic	20.8
Middle Atlantic	18.8
West North Central	17.2
East North Central	15.3
West South Central	14.2
New England	12.5
Pacific	10.0

area (which might be useful in delimiting larger regions on a basis of homogeneity).

Finally, one other closely related measure should be mentioned: the coefficient of concentration, which measures how closely one locational distribution (for example, that of population, income, or employment in a specific activity) matches another locational distribution (for example, that of total employment or land area). Thus, if the distribution of population by counties in the United States just matched the distribution of land area among counties, we should say that the population was evenly distributed (at the county level); while if the locational pattern of the rubber industry is radically different from that of population or total employment, we can say that the rubber industry is spatially concentrated.[5]

The coefficient of concentration is calculated in much the same way as the coefficient of specialization, except that we line up two columns of figures representing *location patterns* (that is, each is a percentage distribution by areas), take all the positive or negative differences, and add. Such a coefficient could be calculated from the same body of basic data as was used for the coefficients in Table 8-5; namely, the 1963 distribution of value added by manufacture by region and industry group. The results are shown in Table 8-6. It appears that the "least concentrated" industry group (that is, the one whose regional location pattern most closely resembles that of manufacturing activity as a whole) is food and tobacco products, while the "most concentrated" group is textiles and leather products.

Though location quotients and coefficients of concentration and specialization are useful summary measures, their limitations must be kept in mind. In particular, their values depend partly on the arbitrary decisions we make regarding demarcation of both activities and areas. Thus, the coefficients of concentration shown in Table 8-6 would be larger if we used

---

[5] Sometimes the terms "localization" and "localized activity" are used to describe such a situation of concentration. These terms are best avoided, however, since they have both been used with other meanings and are consequently ambiguous.

TABLE 8-6. Coefficients of Concentration for Manufacturing Industry Groups, 1963 (Based on distribution of value added by manufacture, for Census divisions)

Manufacturing industries, total	14.7
Durable goods industries	20.8
Instruments and related products	37.4
Lumber and wood products	31.1
Machinery, except electrical	29.5
Primary metal industries	28.6
Transportation equipment	28.4
Fabricated metal products	25.1
Electrical machinery	24.6
Furniture and fixtures	18.7
Stone, clay, and glass products	9.6
Nondurable goods industries	9.1
Textiles and leather products	40.0
Apparel and related products	31.8
Petroleum and coal products	31.3
Rubber and plastics	27.1
Printing and publishing	22.2
Chemicals and allied products	14.8
Paper and allied products	11.7
Food and tobacco products	6.6

SOURCE: "Regional Patterns of Industrial Activity and Freight Transportation in the United States," in Federal Reserve Bank of Cleveland, *Economic Review* (September 1968), Table II, p. 15; based on data from U.S. Bureau of the Census and Federal Reserve Bank of Cleveland.

states rather than Census divisions as the areal unit, or if we classified the industries more finely; and the same is true of the coefficients of specialization in Table 8-5.

WHAT CAUSES REGIONAL GROWTH?

Regional change and growth entail complex interactions among activities within the regional economy, so it is not reasonable to expect that any single initial "cause" of such change and growth can be identified. Useful explanations mainly consist of analyses of the ways that an impetus of change is passed from one regional activity or location factor to another, and we shall first examine in some detail these impacts. However, some theories of growth emphasize certain kinds of change as more independent, exogenous, primary, or causal than others. In particular, we shall see that the external demand for the region's exports and the region's supply of labor and other production inputs have been stressed as prime movers by some widely accepted theories of regional development.

RELATIONS OF ACTIVITIES
WITHIN A REGION

A simple classification of relationships will be helpful here. We shall consider separately (1) "vertical" relationships, (2) "horizontal" relationships, and (3) "complementary" relationships. As has been brought out in previous discussion, the locational relation between two activities can involve either mutual attraction (sometimes called a "positive linkage") or mutual repulsion.

Vertical Relationships

When outputs of one activity in a region are inputs to another activity, transfer costs are reduced by proximity of the two activities, and the presence of either of these activities in a region enhances to some degree the region's attractiveness as a location for the other activity. Thus, vertical linkages normally imply mutual attraction.

Rarely, however, is such attraction equal in both directions. We can distinguish between cases where the linkage is predominantly "backward" and cases in which it is predominantly "forward."

Backward linkage means that the mutual attraction is important mainly to the *supplying* activity. In other words, a market-oriented activity is attracted by the presence of an activity to which it can sell. This is called backward linkage because it involves transmission of an effect to an activity further back in the sequence of operations that transforms such primary inputs as natural resources and labor into products for final consumption.

An example of backward linkage is the case of a Pittsburgh printing firm that specializes in producing annual reports for large corporations. In 1968 a number of large corporations with national headquarters in Pittsburgh were merged into firms with headquarters in other cities; so that Pittsburgh lost, for the time being at least, its position as the third largest center of corporate headquarters activity. As a result, the printing firm is reported to have lost a number of its larger contracts, since corporations prefer to have their annual reports printed locally if possible (in other words, the business of printing annual reports is rather closely oriented to corporate headquarters locations).

Backward linkage is extremely common, because so much of the activity in any region is, in fact, producing for and oriented to the regional market. The larger the region (in terms of total area, population, or employment), the greater the relative importance of the internal market is likely to be. The residentiary category of activities in a region (including nearly all retail and most wholesale trade, most consumer and business services, local government services, public utilities, construction, and the manufacturing of such perishable or bulky products as ice cream, bread, newspapers, soft drinks, gravel, and cement blocks) is likely to be stimulated by any increase in aggregate regional employment and income and, thus, is the recipient of backward linkage effects.

Forward linkage means that an impact of change is transmitted to an activity further along in the sequence of operations. The activity affected by a forward linkage must be locationally sensitive to the price or supply of its inputs (that is, input oriented). One class of forward linkage involves activities which use by-products of other activities in the same region: for example, glue or fertilizer factories or tanneries in areas where there is a large amount of activity in fish canning, freezing, or meat packing. The supply of by-products from coke ovens is similarly an inducement to establish a considerable range of chemical processes in steel-making centers; sometimes, but not necessarily, by the same firm that operates the coke ovens. The presence of steel rolling and finishing facilities is usually regarded as a significant factor in the choice of location for heavy metal-fabricating industries, since it means cheaper steel and probably quicker service.

In addition, many of the external economies of agglomeration, discussed in Chapter 4, involve the locational advantages of a local supply of some inputs such as materials, supplies, repair or equipment rental services or, last but not least, specialized manpower. The importance of a good local supply of business services for regional growth, and particularly for the establishment of new lines of activity in a region, has become increasingly recognized in recent years.[6] There has also been marked emphasis on the vital role of "infrastructure" (the supply of basic public facilities and services) in the development of backward, low-income regions both in our own country and overseas. In all these situations, forward linkages are the key factors.

Horizontal Relationships

The role of horizontal relationships has already been discussed in some detail in Chapter 4. These relationships involve the competition of activities, or units of activity, for either markets or inputs. The locational effect is basically one of mutual repulsion, in contrast to the mutual attraction implied in vertical linkages.

Particularly significant for regional growth and development is the rivalry of different activities for scarce and not easily expansible local

---

[6] See Benjamin Chinitz, "Contrasts in Agglomeration: New York and Pittsburgh," *Papers and Proceedings of the American Economic Association,* 51, 2 (May 1961), 279–289. Chinitz argues that a center like Pittsburgh, heavily specialized in a few industries and dominated by large plants and firms, is likely to be deficient in various business services needed by small and new firms, because the dominant firms are big enough to provide such services internally for themselves.

resources (such as particular varieties of labor, sites on riverbanks or with a view, clean and cool water, or clean air). The entrance of a new activity using such local resources tends to raise their costs and may thus hamper or even preclude other activities requiring the same resources. The region as a whole has much at stake in this rivalry. A relevant and important question of regional policy, for example, is whether to let the region's water and waterside sites be preempted and polluted by water-using industries or to reserve them in part for residential, institutional, or recreational use. Again, should regional efforts to enhance employment opportunities take the form of trying to attract new activities with the largest number of jobs, regardless of character, or should priority be given to new activities that pay high wages, provide opportunities for individual learning and advancement, and attract a superior grade of in-migrants? Should a community's last remaining tract of vacant level land be given over to an airport, a strip-mining operation, a high-class low-density suburban development, a low-income housing project, a missile-launching site, or an industrial park? How much smoke is the community willing to tolerate for the sake of the income earned by the smoke producers and the taxes they pay? These are all familiar issues that must be faced by citizens, responsible authorities, and planners of a city or larger region; and they all arise because of horizontal linkage in the form of competition of rival uses for scarce local resources. Regional objectives and policy will be the subject of our next chapter.

Complementary Relationships

We have already noted, in previous chapters, complementary relationships among activities in a region, particularly in connection with external economies in Chapter 4. The locational effect is mutual attraction: that is, an increase of one activity in a region encourages the growth of a complementary activity.

MUTUAL ATTRACTION AMONG SUPPLIERS OF COMPLEMENTARY PRODUCTS. Examples of this attraction are found in fashion goods and other "shopping goods" industries. As additional producers come into a region, they help those already there by building up the region's status as a Mecca for buyers of those products or services, because the buyer is looking for a variety of offerings and a chance to compare and "shop around." The manufacture of sportswear in some large cities in California and Texas in recent years has developed largely on this basis.

This is really a two-step linkage, which can be broken down into (1) a forward linkage effect, whereby the coming of an additional producer attracts to the region more buyers of the product, and (2) a backward linkage effect, whereby the greater demand from those buyers enhances the attractiveness of the region for still more producers.

Such effects are, however, not entirely restricted to shopping goods. Another example from the Pittsburgh region is pertinent here. In recent years, various civic leaders have urged Pittsburgh to develop major league status as a designer and producer of urban transit systems to meet the projected growing demand from large urban areas in the United States and other countries. A wide variety of inputs is needed to feed into this line of activity: the manufacture of components and supplies, designers knowledgeable in transport technology and urban planning, urban and regional economists, and specialized research facilities and consultants. To the extent that the main effort succeeds and Pittsburgh firms do get more orders for transit systems, local suppliers of the various inputs cited above will also flourish and multiply, and their availability and expertise can further enhance the capabilities and reputation of the prime contractors.

MUTUAL ATTRACTION AMONG USERS OF JOINTLY SUPPLIED PRODUCTS. This second kind of complementary linkage (also with an effect of mutual locational attraction) is basically the converse of the complementary linkage just discussed. Many activities (perhaps most) turn out not one but several different products, those of least importance or value being called by-products. A regional activity that furnishes a market for one of these by-products helps the supplying activity, and this can make the supplier's other outputs more easily or cheaply available to some third activity which uses them. All three of the activities are then in a situation of mutual assistance and attraction.

There are many examples of this effect in the chemical industries, which by their nature usually turn out combinations of products. Producers of coke for blast furnaces also turn out gas and a variety of hydrocarbon chemicals that can serve as building blocks for a still wider range of products, like synthetic rubber, synthetic gasoline, dyestuffs, and pharmaceuticals. The presence in the same region of industries using any of the first-stage outputs of the coal distillation process enhances the returns of the coke producer and may even be a significant factor in his decisions to expand or relocate. If he does expand output, this means a still larger (and perhaps cheaper and more dependable) regional supply of other coal distillation products, which in turn makes the region more attractive as a location for industries using these products.

Like the complementary linkage among sellers of jointly demanded products, discussed earlier, this complementary linkage can be broken down into two separate links. There is a backward linkage effect if additional demand from a new synthetic rubber producer, for example, leads coke producers to expand their output. Then there is a forward linkage if the resulting increased regional supply of coal distillation products from the ovens attracts still other users of these products (for example, producers of pharmaceuticals or dyestuffs) to the region.

Horizontal Linkage (negative—mutual repulsion among competitors)

Drug stores

Simple One-Way Vertical Linkages (attraction toward a market or an input source)

(a) "Backward"

(b) "Forward"

Complementary Linkages, with formation of clusters through external economies of agglomeration (two or more vertical linkages involved)

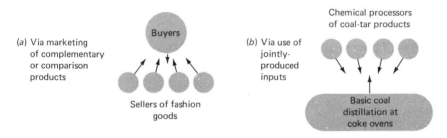

(a) Via marketing of complementary or comparison products

(b) Via use of jointly-produced inputs

Fig. 8-4. Types of Spatial Linkage (In each case, the arrow shows the direction in which the locational unit is pulled)

The complementary linkages we have described are, of course, valid regardless of whether the complementary processes are engaged in by separate firms or within the same firm. In the case of the steel producer and his coke ovens, for example, he may elect to process his distillation outputs for one or more additional stages or even down to the final consumer product, rather than selling them to other firms.

In case the reader is slightly bewildered by now with the nomenclature of linkages, he may find some surcease in Fig. 8-4, where they are all schematically diagrammed and illustrated.

COMPLEMENTARY LINKAGES AND THE ECONOMIES OF SCALE AND AGGLOMERATION. The external economies of agglomeration, discussed in Chapter 4, represent in part complementary linkages among users of jointly supplied products. Manufacturers of fashion garments and many other typical external-economy industries identified by Lichtenberg (see pp. 79–84) have a strong tendency to cluster because they draw on both kinds of complementary linkage: among suppliers of complementary products and among users of jointly supplied products. For example, fashion garment manufacturers find a clustered location pattern profitable both (1) because such clustering gives the location the advantage of variety of offerings, which attracts buyers, and (2) because in such a cluster many kinds of inputs can be secured quickly and cheaply from specialized suppliers who could not economically exist without the volume supported by a large cluster. We see, then, that external economies of agglomeration can be broken down into internal economies of scale plus two kinds of complementary linkage; each of which, in turn, can be broken down into backward and forward linkages.

Self-Reinforcing and Self-Limiting Effects in Regional Growth

Our examination of the various kinds of linkages among firms and activities in a region has brought to light some effects of a cumulative or "chain-reaction" character. Both vertical and complementary linkages are generally of this type. Thus, external economies of agglomeration (the expression of complementary linkages) attract firms and activities of a similar nature, and this further enhances the agglomeration economies so that still more firms and activities are attracted, which leads to still more agglomeration economies.

Vertical linkages per se have cumulative effects. If Detroit can increase its automobile sales to other areas, Detroit's automobile manufacturers will buy larger quantities of inputs locally. Each of the supplying activities will then increase its own local purchases of inputs (for example, automobile workers will spend some of the increased payroll on housing, consumer goods, and services, and Detroit public utilities will need more labor and other inputs). Some of the additional spending in Detroit will take the form of increased purchases of automobiles, which further contributes to the repercussions of the initial stimulus.

It appears, then, that vertical linkages of activities in a region, and also complementary linkages (which are really combinations of vertical linkages) have self-reinforcing effects. An initial change in the level of activity in the region leads to still further change in the same direction and affects a broader range of activities. This applies to decline as well as to growth.

This being the case, how does it happen that regions do not normally expand in an explosive chain-reaction fashion, or wither away to the vanishing point? What are the forces that provide some constraint and stability, by setting up counterreactions to an initial change and thus limiting its total effects?

Part of the answer lies in the horizontal linkages among activities, which, as we have seen, are characteristically negative, or locationally repulsive in their effects. In other words, activities in a region are always competing for some scarce local inputs (land, labor, and others); and, particularly in the short run, increased demand raises the cost of these inputs. Other constraints upon explosive growth or decline will appear as we look further into the mechanics of regional adjustment.

Demand and Supply as Determinants of Regional Development

The various kinds of linkages represent ways in which some impetus to regional change is transmitted from one activity to another within the regional economy, leading to overall growth or decline. The next question, then, is where can such impetus originate? What really initiates change?

Here as in almost any other economic problem, the dichotomy of supply and demand appears. Regional activity requires both inputs and a market for outputs, and it does not make sense to argue that either supply or demand is the sole determinant of growth.

If we look to demand for the explanation of regional growth, we first inquire where the demand comes from, and then trace its impact through the regional economic system. This approach will emphasize *backward* linkages among regional activities, since such linkages are the way in which a demand for one regional output (say, automobiles) gives rise to demand for other regional activity (say, the making of automobile parts or paint, the generation of electricity, or the employment of labor).

If we look to supply for the explanation of regional growth, we inquire where inputs come from, and in what way the supply of, say, mineral resources, capital, or labor in a region leads to regional activity generating a regional supply of, say, coal, electricity, automobile parts, or automobiles. The approach from the supply side will emphasize *forward* linkages.

Clearly, both approaches are relevant and necessary parts of an adequate theory of regional change and development. Complementary linkages and external economies of agglomeration, as we have seen, involve both backward and forward vertical linkages; and in evaluating the factor of competition for scarce local inputs, both demand and supply have to be considered. Far more attention has been devoted to the demand approach, and we shall take this up first.

THE ROLE OF DEMAND

Economic Base Theory and Studies

One approach to an explanation of regional growth is that of the so-called economic base. The essential idea is that some activities in a region are peculiarly "basic" in the sense that their growth *leads and determines* the region's overall development; while other ("nonbasic") activities are simply *consequences* of the region's overall development. If such an identification of basic activities can really be made, then an explanation of regional growth consists of two parts: (1) explaining the location of basic activities and (2) tracing the processes by which basic activities in any region give rise to an accompanying development of nonbasic activities. The usual economic base theory identifies basic activities as those which bring in money from the outside world, generally by producing goods or services for export.[7]

The argument advanced for this approach is that a region, like a household or a business firm, must earn its livelihood by producing something that others will pay for. Activities that simply serve the regional market are there *as a result of* whatever level of income and demand the region may have achieved: They are passive participants in growth but not prime movers. A household, a neighborhood, a firm, or a region cannot get richer by simply "taking in its own washing," but must sell something to others in order to get more income. Consequently, exports provide the economic base of a region's growth.

A regional economic base study[8] generally seeks (1) to identify the regional export activities, (2) to forecast in some way the probable growth in those activities, and (3) to evaluate the impact of that additional export activity upon the other, or nonbasic, activities of the region. The result is not only a projection of the region's prospective growth and structural change but also a model that can be used in evaluating the effects of alternative trends of export growth.

A region's export activities can be determined with various degrees of precision. The simplest and crudest procedure is simply to assign whole industries or activity groups to the export or nonexport category without making any specific local investigation. Thus, retail trade, utilities, local government, and services may be classed *en bloc* as nonexport, while manufacturing is considered wholly an export activity.

A more sophisticated approach is to recognize that almost all activities in a region produce partly for export and partly for the regional market and to try to estimate how much of each activity is for export. The sim-

---

[7] Exporting in this sense does not necessarily imply that the goods or services are sent out of the region by their producers. They may instead be consumed in the region by outsiders who occasionally come for that purpose. Selling of recreational and other services to tourists from outside is a major export activity in some regions. What is relevant for the region's development is the income, rather than the movement of the output.

[8] For a careful and readable description of the purposes and techniques of such studies, see Charles M. Tiebout, *The Community Economic Base Study*, Supplementary Paper No. 16 (New York: Committee for Economic Development, December 1962).

plest way to make such estimates is by using the location quotient measure discussed earlier. For example, in 1963 North Carolina produced 3.8 percent of the national output of work clothing, while total personal income in North Carolina was estimated at about 1.9 percent of the national total. The location quotient is $3.8/1.9 = 2$; from this we might surmise that half of the North Carolina production of work clothing is for export to other areas and half for consumption within the state. Accordingly, we could assign half of the state's work clothing industry to the basic or export activity category.

This conclusion, however, rests on the rather tenuous assumption that a region's personal income is a good measure of its purchases of work clothing. If we wanted to use the location quotient approach to estimate how much of the Toledo SMSAs output of metal-working machinery is for export, we would do better to base the location quotient not on personal income or population but on some statistic presumably more indicative of the demand for such machinery: for example, value added by manufacture in metal-working industries.

Location quotients are likely to lead to an underestimate of a region's exports, since they are necessarily applied to whole industries or even industry groups. Within any industry classification (or for that matter, within any single firm or establishment), there are different specific products, and the region may be importing some and exporting others. Since the quotient estimates only the *net* surplus of output over regional consumption, it may seriously understate the total exports of products of that industry.[9]

The location quotient method, however, does have the advantage of taking account of "indirect" as well as direct exports:

> A community with a large number of packing plants is also likely to have a large number of tin can manufacturers. Even though the cans are locally sold, they are indirectly tied to exports. Location quotients will show them as exports . . .[10]

A more painstaking procedure is to get information on actual shipments of goods and services out of the region. In recent years, rapid progress has been made by the Census in collecting and organizing data on manufac-

---

[9] See Tiebout, *ibid.,* Table 10, p. 49, for a series of examples of such understatement, involving 8 different industry groups and 6 different community economic base studies. In each case, a questionnaire survey of business firms provided the more accurate data against which the location quotient estimate was checked.

More generally, there is an aggregation effect involving the offsetting of "surpluses" and "deficits" that restricts the comparability of location quotients. As a rule, the use of a finer activity classification or a smaller region will make quotients larger, whereas a coarser classification or larger region permits more offsetting and reduces the quotients.

[10] *Ibid.,* pp. 48–49.

turers' shipments between large regions. For some time, however, there will continue to be a dearth of information on exports from smaller regions such as individual SMSAs or counties; and exports of some services pose additional data problems. Many economic base studies have canvassed at least a sample of the firms that are believed to be involved in exporting, in order to get a reasonably accurate measure of the region's external trade.

Projection of the future trend of exports from a region involves a series of studies of the prospective national growth and interregional location trends of each of the activities concerned, and an evaluation of whether the region's competitive position is likely to get better or worse. The kinds of location factors to be taken into account in such studies have already been discussed in earlier chapters.

Given some prospective change in the level of export or basic activity in the region, how much overall regional growth in income and employment is implied? This determination requires the tracing of linkage effects. Specifically, it involves the estimation of a "multiplier," which tells us how much increase in total regional income (or sales, or employment) to expect as a result of each additional dollar of export sales or income, or each additional man employed in producing for export.

At this stage too, there are alternative procedures of varying degrees of sophistication. The simplest method is to derive the multiplier from the "basic ratio." If, for example, one-third of the region's employment is in basic activities, we simply assume that that proportion will be maintained. Accordingly, every man added to basic employment will indirectly lead to the employment of two additional men in nonbasic activities: the multiplier is 3.

Such a procedure is too easy to be convincing. There is really no reason to assume that the ratio will remain unaffected by export growth, and such ratios vary rather widely. There is a discernible tendency for export multipliers (whether derived by this or by more sophisticated analysis) to be larger with increasing regional size and diversity.[11]

Regional Input-Output Analysis

The economic base approach has been described in its simplest terms. Actually, various types of models of regional economic interaction have been developed to trace the impact of demand upon a region's income and employment. They all involve some framework of "regional accounts"

---

[11] For a series of estimated export multipliers for a dozen cities of assorted sizes, see Charles L. Leven, "Regional Income and Product Accounts: Construction and Applications," in Werner Hochwald (ed.), *Design of Regional Accounts* (Baltimore: Johns Hopkins University Press for Resources for the Future, 1961), Table 1, p. 179.

describing transactions between the region and the outside world and
among activities within the region; and nearly all include some type of
multiplier ratio that sums up the relation between an initial increase in
demand and the ultimate effect upon regional income or employment.
Some of these procedures are primarily relevant to short-term variations
while others are more relevant to long-term regional growth trends. We
shall confine attention here to models using an input-output or interindustry framework.

The essence of the input-output schema is a set of accounts representing
transactions among the following major economic sectors:

Intermediate—private business activities within the region. This sector is
  broken down into individual industries or activities (such as mining, food
  processing, construction, chemical products). It is sometimes referred to
  as the interindustry sector because much of the detail of the input-output
  statement refers to transactions among the separate industries within the
  sector.

Households—individuals and families residing or employed in the region,
  considered both as buyers of consumer goods and services and as sellers
  (primarily of their own labor).

Government—state, local, and national public authorities, both within and
  outside the region.

Outside world—activities (other than government) and individuals located
  outside the region.[12]

Capital—the stock of private capital, including both fixed capital and inventories.[13]

These are, of course, transactions both between sectors and among the
activities within each sector (for example, between households, or between
different processing activities in the region, or between different units of
government, or different activities and regions in the "outside world"). But
not all categories of transactions are of equal interest to us in analyzing a
given region. The form of account illustrated in Table 8-7 represents a
usual abridgment, where the lower right–hand portion is not filled in. What
we have, then, is simply an itemization of the inputs and the outputs of
each of the designated activities in the Intermediate sector.

In order to express all these transaction flows in a common unit, they
are stated in terms of money payments for the goods or services trans-

---

[12] The example to be given here is the simplest input-output table applicable to a
region and is identical in form to the table for a whole country. For more penetrating
regional analysis the exports, the imports, or both are broken down in terms of the
various other regions with which there are substantial transactions. In such a table,
there would be several outside world columns and rows.

[13] In practice, the entries involving this sector comprise sales to and purchases
from firms (both inside and outside the region) *on capital account.* The outside
world entries refer to export or import transactions with nongovernmental parties
on current account.

TABLE 8-7. Simple Form of Regional Input-Output Table

		Intermediate sector, by industry				Households (consumer goods sales in region)	Government (sales to governments)	Outside (exports)	Capital (gross private investment, including additions to inventories)	Output totals
		A	B	C	D					
Intermediate sector, by industry:	A	300	400	100	500	1600	500	200	700	4300
	B	50	200	1000	300	100	200	100	900	2850
	C	1000	200	100	700	100	300	200	500	3100
	D	0	800	200	500	700	0	0	400	2600
Primary supply sectors										
Households (labor services)		1900	300	1000	400					
Government (public services)		200	100	200	100					
Outside (imports)		200	300	300	0					
Capital (capital consumption and withdrawals from inventories)		650	550	200	100					
INPUT TOTALS		4300	2850	3100	2600					

Final demand sectors

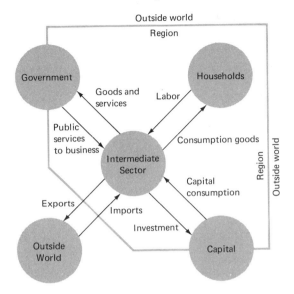

Fig. 8-5. Intersector Flows of Goods and Services in a One-Region Input-Output Model

ferred. Thus, the purchase of labor services from the Household sector is shown as wages and other payroll outlays; inputs from the Government sector are represented by taxes and fees paid to public authorities; and inputs from the Capital sector are represented by depreciation accruals plus inventory reductions.

The accompanying schematic chart, Fig. 8-5, may help in understanding the mechanics of the input-output model. The flows shown there are goods and services passing from one sector to another; money payments for those goods and services go in the opposite direction. The solid line represents the regional boundary; as noted earlier, the Government and Capital sectors are partly inside and partly outside the region.

Activities within the Intermediate sector engage in interindustry transactions with one another (and also each with itself, since each activity includes a variety of firms with somewhat different kinds of output). Sales by the Intermediate sector to *other* sectors are called sales to "final demand." At this point, the outputs are considered to be in their final form, not destined for further processing, and ready for their final stage of use as far as the region is concerned; namely, export, delivery to household consumers or the public sector, or incorporation into the stock of capital. They are *leaving* the region's stream of current processing activity. The counterpart to final demand on the input side is "primary supply": imports and the services of labor, capital, and public authorities are *entering* the region's processing system for the first time.

The abridged set of accounts in Table 8-7 shows total receipts and payments for only the activities in the Intermediate sector, since transactions among all the other sectors are ignored. Thus, we cannot read total regional personal income from a table like this, since it omits the incomes that individuals receive from government jobs, pensions, property ownership, or sources outside the region. Nor does this table show total regional exports or imports of goods and services, since interregional transactions by the Households, Government, and Capital sectors are omitted.

This kind of input-output table is particularly useful, however, in tracing and evaluating certain cumulative effects of vertical linkages in the region. It is easy to construct a set of "input coefficients" (see Table 8-8)

TABLE 8-8. Input Coefficients for Activities in the Intermediate Sector (Calculated from illustrative data in the preceding table)

Purchases (in dollars) from:	Per dollar's worth of gross output in:			
	A	B	C	D
Intermediate sector				
A	.070	.140	.032	.192
B	.012	.070	.323	.115
C	.233	.070	.032	.269
D	0	.281	.065	.192
Primary supply sectors				
Households	.442	.105	.323	.154
Government	.047	.035	.065	.038
Outside	.047	.105	.097	0
Capital	.151	.193	.064	.038
Totals*	1.000	1.000	1.000	1.000

* Columns do not always add exactly to totals, because of rounding off.

showing that for each dollar's worth of output of Industry A in the region, that industry buys 1.2¢ worth of Industry B's output, 23.3¢ worth of Industry C's output, and so on.

Now let us suppose that Industry A increases its sales outside the region by $1,000. To furnish this added output, Industry A will (according to Table 8-8) need to spend $12 more on inputs from Industry B, $233 more on inputs from Industry C, $442 more on labor payrolls, and so on. But Industry C's sales have now increased by $233, so it will have to spend $233×.032 for additional inputs from A, $233×.323 for additional inputs from B, $233×.097 more for imported inputs, and so on. As each of the activities in the Intermediate sector feels the impact of the increase in demand for its outputs, its own purchases in the region will increase. The chain of repercussions, or "indirect effects," is in principle endless; but this does not mean that the initial $1,000 increase in A's sales will snowball into an infinitely large growth in the region's activities. The total effect, in fact, will be at most only a few times the size of the initial final demand increase. The ratio in this case is called the regional "export multiplier."

The reason that the multiplier is not infinitely large is that there are so-called demand leakages from the regional economy. Each time one of the Intermediate activities experiences an increase in sales, it has to allocate part of the extra revenue to purchasing inputs not from other Intermediate activities but from primary supply sectors. Money paid for additional imports leaves the region, and its stimulus to regional demand is ended. Similarly (in the simplified model portrayed by our input-output accounts), disbursements for payroll, taxes, and depreciation simply drop out of the stream of "new money" that is being circulated among the processing activities. The stream gets smaller at each round and finally peters out altogether.

We can, in fact, gauge exactly what the total stimulus will be, on the basis of our hypothetical input coefficients. Table 8-9 shows the amount by

TABLE 8-9. Total Direct and Indirect Effects of an Increase in Final Demand (Calculated from illustrative data in the preceding table)

Total added sales (in $) by Intermediate activities	Per dollar of increased sales to final demand by:				
	A	B	C	D	A, B, C, D combined*
A	1.118	.289	.157	.359	.661
B	.126	1.234	.439	.352	.439
C	.297	.284	1.171	.501	.477
D	.068	.452	.247	1.400	.400
Total	1.609	2.259	2.014	2.612	1.977
Added purchases (in $) by all Intermediate activities from primary supply sectors:					
Households	.614	.419	.532	.427	
Government	.079	.092	.108	.086	
Outside	.095	.171	.167	.059	
Capital	.215	.317	.193	.179	

* Figures in this column show the impact of an added dollar of aggregate final demand sales by all Intermediate activities, apportioned in the same proportions as these activities shared in the final demand sales shown in Table 8-7. Specifically, this means added final demand sales of 46¢ by A, 20¢ by B, 17¢ by C, and 17¢ by D, totalling $1.00.

which each processing activity's sales are increased as the *ultimate* result of a dollar's increase in the final demand sales of any Intermediate activity, including the whole sequence of multiplier effects described above.[14]

---

[14] For an explanation of the calculations, see Appendix 6-1 or any general reference on input-output analysis, such as William Miernyk, *The Elements of Input-Output Analysis* (New York: Random House, 1965). For any table of substantial size, such calculation is best done on a high-speed computer.

These effects are naturally largest for the activity experiencing the initial final demand increase, since that increase is part of the total increment. This explains why the figures on the diagonal of the table are especially large. In the case we assumed (an initial $1,000 increase in export sales by Industry A), we see that as a result A gets a total direct and indirect increase of sales amounting to $1,118, while B, C, and D come out with smaller increments: $126, $297, and $68 respectively.

The total increase in sales for the whole Intermediate sector is $1,609 ($1,000 times the sum of the figures in the first column of Table 8-9). Since all this resulted from an assumed initial $1,000 increase in A's sales to final demand, we could identify here a multiplier of 1.609. This is a specific multiplier ratio, evaluating the effects of an initial increase of *final demand sales by Industry A*.[15]

This estimate of the multiplier, however, is almost certainly too small. Our evaluation of indirect effects took into account only the vertical linkages implied by transaction relationships among activities within the Intermediate sector. A more sophisticated estimate would have to allow for vertical linkages involving other sectors, as well as for the positive effects of complementary linkages and the negative effects of horizontal linkages.

Perhaps the most obvious omission involves the Household sector. With all this increase of Intermediate sector output, payrolls must also increase, and it would be unrealistic to assume that all the added pay will be saved, or spent outside the region. Instead, we should expect a roughly proportional increase in consumer demand for the outputs of the region's Intermediate sector, and this in turn would be magnified in its ultimate effect by the workings of the multiplier.

It is somewhat less certain that increased purchases from Government and increased use of the region's fixed capital and inventories would automatically induce either increased purchases in the region by Government or a step-up in investment activity. And it seems rather unlikely that

---

[15] So far, we have a whole set of specific regional multipliers, since the assumed initial impact that gets multiplied can be taken as an increase in final demand sales of any of the several Intermediate sector activities. Sometimes it is desirable to settle on a single overall regional multiplier figure. Such a figure can be derived by starting from an "across-the-board" unit increase in final demand; that is, each Intermediate activity's final demand sales rise by the same proportion. The last column in Table 8-9 illustrates this calculation, giving an overall multiplier of 1.977.

These and other types of regional multipliers have been estimated at different times for many regions. Although, as we might expect, there is considerable variation, there is a rather consistent tendency for multipliers to be greater for larger and more fully diversified regions. This is logical: such a region "takes in more of its own washing," and the sequence of indirect and induced effects is subject to less demand leakage than would be the case in a smaller or more narrowly specialized region. Presumably, the minimum multiplier (1) would be most closely approached in a community, such as a mining camp, devoted to a single exporting activity.

increased imports would lead (through raising incomes in other regions) to any significant increase in the demand for the region's exports.

The upshot of these considerations is that final demand (except perhaps for the export component) is not really independent of primary supply, as our abridged set of input-output accounts assumed. The modifications or adjustments that might be called for would depend on the particular regional situation. But we might well decide that it would be more realistic to assume an automatic "feedback" from Household supply to Household demand than to assume no feedback at all. To incorporate this new assumption, we could simply take Households out of final demand and primary supply and put them into the Intermediate sector as an additional, fully interacting activity. Referring to Table 8-7, this would mean supplying numbers to fill out the presently incomplete Households row and column.[16] The successive steps and results are set forth in Appendix 6-2.

The possibility of shifting Households out of the final demand category makes it clear that the decision about what activities to include in final demand (and primary supply) is not preordained or arbitrary but reflects our judgment about what relationships are important and relevant to the question at hand. Final demand in the input-output accounts framework really has the same implications as *basic* in the simple economic base model, and an input-output model with export demand as the only final demand category can be thought of as a more detailed description of an export-determined regional economy.

The inclusion of Government in final demand does not represent any major departure from economic base principles. Government is a basic source of income if public expenditures in the region vary independently from total regional income. This is true at least of federal and state government expenditures.

The role of investment in regional economic change is not really spelled out in the simple form of input-output that we have been considering; since by convention, sales to the Capital sector of final demand include all sales of capital goods, whether within the region or outside or to governments. There are other, more complex, varieties of input-output tables, as well as more general systems of regional income and product accounts, that do lend themselves to analysis of the mechanisms of saving, investment, and interregional capital flow. These will not be discussed here;[17]

---

[16] There are alternative ways of allowing for the multiplier effect via household income and expenditure. In any case, it is customary to refer to this effect as "induced" to distinguish it from the indirect effects resulting from interindustry transactions in the narrower sense.

[17] There is a large recent literature on systems of regional accounts and models for analysis and policy guidance; for a well-rounded and up-to-date treatment, see Harry W. Richardson, *Regional Economics* (New York: Praeger, 1969).

but it is appropriate to ask whether investment in a region should more logically be considered an exogenous factor initiating growth of regional income and output or a response to other changes in the regional economy.

The answer depends on whether we are concerned with the short run or the long run. In the short run, rates of investment can vary widely and suddenly relative to levels of output, and decisions by major firms in the region to make extensive additions to their facilities can almost immediately convert a depressed region into a prosperous one. The question in the short run is the degree to which existing regional labor and productive facilities are fully employed, and changes in investment outlays can be a major determining factor. Thus, a short-run regional model should certainly treat investment as primarily an exogenous or basic element.

For the long-run development of a region, however, it is reasonable to regard investment at least partly as a *reflection* of regional size and growth, rather than a sufficient explanation in itself.

The Need for a Broader Approach

The prevalent view of export demand as the prime mover in regional growth raises some interesting questions that indicate the need for a more adequate explanation.

Consider, for example, a large area, such as a whole country, that comprises several economic regions. Let us assume that these regions trade with one another, but the country as a whole is self-sufficient. We might explain the growth of each of these regions on the basis of its exports to the others and the resulting multiplier effects upon activities serving the internal demand of the region. But if all the regions grow, then the whole country or "super-region" must also be growing, despite the fact that it does not export at all. The world economy has been growing for a long time, though our exports to outer space have just begun and we have yet to locate a paying customer for them. It appears, then, that *internal* trade and demand can generate regional growth: a region really *can* get richer by taking in more of its own washing.

Let us next look at the role of imports. In the mechanism of the regional export multiplier, expenditures for imports represent demand leakage from the regional income stream. The greater the proportion of any increase in regional income that is spent outside the region, the smaller is the multiplier.

It follows that if a region can develop local production to meet a demand previously satisfied by imports, this "import substitution" will have precisely the same impact upon the regional economy as an equivalent increase in exports. In either case, there is an increase in sales by producers within the region.

It is quite incorrect, then, to identify a region's *export* activities exclusively as the basic sector. It would be more appropriate to identify as basic activities those which are *interregionally footloose* (in the sense of not being tightly oriented to the local market). This definition would admit all activities engaging in any substantial amount of interregional trade, regardless of whether the region we are considering happens to be a net exporter or a net importer. Truly basic industries would be those for which regional location quotients are either much greater than 1 or much less than 1.

This necessary amendment to the export base theory, however, exposes a more fundamental flaw. We are still left with the implication that a region will grow faster if it can manage to import less, and that growth promotion efforts should be directed toward creating a "favorable balance of trade," or excess of exports over imports. Let us examine this notion.

If a region's earnings from exports exceed its outlays for imports, the region is a net investor, or exporter, of capital. Its people and businesses are building up equities and credits in other areas. By the same token, if imports exceed exports the region is receiving a net inflow of capital from outside.

It is patently absurd to argue that the way to make a region grow is to invest the region's savings somewhere else, and that an influx of investment from outside is inimical to growth. If anything, it would seem more plausible to infer that a region's growth is enhanced if its capital stock is augmented by investment from outside—which means that the region's imports exceed its exports.

In any event, regional development is normally associated in practice with increases in both exports and imports. There was, in fact, a tendency among United States regions between 1929 and 1959 for increases in both per capita and total income to be greater in capital-importing (import-excess) regions,[18] though there is no reason why this need always be the case.

We shall come back to this relationship later. The important point here is that explanations of regional growth based exclusively on demand lead to absurd implications, so that a broader approach is called for.

THE ROLE OF SUPPLY

In the basic accounts structure illustrated in Table 8-7, the Intermediate sector is shown as delivering outputs to the various final demand sectors and receiving inputs from those same sectors in their capacity of primary suppliers. Money payments for these goods and services flow in the reverse

---

[18] See J. Thomas Romans, *Capital Exports and Growth Among U.S. Regions* (Middletown, Conn.: Wesleyan University Press, 1965), p. 118.

direction, from final demand sectors to the Intermediate sector and then to primary supply.

In tracing changes, we can follow the flow of money payments "backward" from purchaser to seller, or we can follow the flow of goods and services "forward" from producer to user. The scheme is symmetrical with respect to supply and demand, or input and output. It does not indicate whether we should look for the initiating causes of regional growth and change in final demand, in primary supply, or within the Intermediate sector; and we might reasonably infer that change can originate in any of these three areas.

In view of this basic symmetry, it is striking that the techniques of input-output and multiplier analysis have nearly always been applied in just the backward direction, tracing the effects of changes from final demand to the Intermediate and primary supply sectors.[19] The implication in locational terms is that market orientation and backward linkage are all-important, with no attention being paid to input orientation or to forward and complementary linkage effects.

Input-Output Analysis in Reverse: Supply Multipliers

Since the input-output table is a comprehensive and "neutral" image of a regional economy, we can use it as a point of departure for the consideration of supply factors as well as demand factors. Earlier, we emphasized final demand, backward linkage, multipliers of demand, and market orientation of activities. We shall now shift the emphasis to primary supply, forward linkage, multipliers of supply, and input orientation of activities.

---

[19] Probably one reason for this overemphasis on the role of demand in regional growth is that modern regional growth theory and input-output and multiplier analysis have been influenced by the contemporary development of Keynesian theories of what determines the degree of utilization of given resources in the short run. A more balanced approach, taking into account long-term growth factors on both the supply and the demand sides, appears in some of the more recent theoretical work; notably in Horst Siebert, *Regional Economic Growth: Theory and Policy* (Scranton, Pa.: International Textbook Co., 1969); Romans, *op. cit.;* and G. W. Borts and J. L. Stein, *Economic Growth in a Free Market* (New York: Columbia University Press, 1964).

One of the first regional economists to question the primacy of exports and call for a balanced theory was Charles M. Tiebout, "Exports and Regional Economic Growth," *Journal of Political Economy,* 64, 2 (April 1956), 160–164. His article was prompted by a forceful statement of the export doctrine by Douglass C. North, "Location Theory and Regional Economic Growth," *Journal of Political Economy,* 63, 3 (June 1955), 243–258. The whole North-Tiebout controversy, including both these articles, North's subsequent reply, and Tiebout's final rejoinder, is reprinted in John Friedmann and William Alonso (eds.), *Regional Development and Planning* (Cambridge, Mass.: M.I.T. Press, 1964), 240–265. Another good statement emphasizing supply factors is Richard T. Pratt, "Regional Production Inputs and Regional Income Generation," *Journal of Regional Science,* 7, 2 (Winter 1967), 141–149.

When considering the effect of demand on regional activity, we assumed that supplies of inputs would automatically be forthcoming, at no increase in per-unit cost, to support any additional activity responding to increased demand—in other words, supplies of inputs, such as labor, capital, imports, and public services, were taken to be perfectly elastic and consequently imposing no constraint on regional growth. If export demand for a region's steel output increased, the region could freely import as much additional fuel and iron ore as might be needed; if the demand for labor exceeded the region's labor force, more workers would move in from other areas.

Conversely, a "supply" model of regional growth takes demand for granted (that is, it assumes that there is a perfectly elastic demand for the region's exports), and thus makes regional activity depend on the availability of resources to put into production.

Accordingly, the starting point in the input-output table is now primary supply rather than final demand. Availability of labor, capital, imported inputs, and government services (infrastructure) makes possible certain Intermediate activities that require such primary inputs. The products of these activities are used within the region by other activities in the Intermediate sector, enabling them to turn out more of their own kinds of output. Each increase in output by one activity that sells in the region leads to further increases by other activities which use its output, giving rise to an indirect effect through a supply multiplier. There is an induced effect through the Household sector as well: additional consumer goods delivered to the Household sector elicit an increased labor supply. The supply multiplier effect is limited by the existence of supply leakages—at each stage, some of the increase in regional outputs is drained off into exports, investment, or deliveries to governments.

This whole process is recognizable as the exact inverse of the process by which, in the more conventional input-output and multiplier analysis based on demand, an initial increase in final demand gives rise to indirect and induced growth of income and employment in the region and increased drafts upon primary supply.[20]

Thus, it is possible to manipulate the input-output table to derive various supply multipliers that show the direct and indirect effects upon the regional economy arising from an assumed increase in some component of primary supply. Results are shown in Tables 8-10 and 8-11 (using the same basic data as for the earlier tables).

---

[20] Since input-output analysis conventionally refers to the analysis of impacts eventuating from initial changes in final demand, it may be convenient to apply the term "output-input analysis" to this inverse approach that begins with changes in primary supply.

TABLE 8-10. Output Coefficients for Activities in the Intermediate Sector (Calculated from illustrative data in Table 8-7)

Per dollar's worth of inputs into:	Deliveries (in dollars) to:								
	Intermediate activities				Final demand sectors				
	A	B	C	D	House-holds	Govern-ment	Outside	Capital	Totals*
A	.070	.093	.023	.116	.372	.116	.046	.164	100.0
B	.018	.070	.351	.105	.035	.070	.035	.316	100.0
C	.323	.064	.032	.226	.032	.097	.064	.161	100.0
D	0	.308	.077	.192	.270	0	0	.154	100.0

* Rows do not always add exactly to totals because of rounding off.

External Growth Determinants Based on Supply

It will be recalled that in the analysis of effects of final demand, there was some latitude in choosing what kinds of demand to consider as "final." There is a corresponding latitude in the analysis of effects of changes in primary supply. We can identify certain types of primary supply as more independent, causal, exogenous, primary, or basic than others (in the present context, all these terms have substantially the same meaning).

If the provision of additional public services is considered to be a regional growth stimulant and is not regarded as being determined by the regional private sector's delivery of goods and services to governments, Government is appropriately included as a primary supply component and we can try to measure the impact of such provision of public services through some kind of supply multiplier calculation. The same applies to the Capital sector. If immigration is regarded as leading to expansion of regional activity by easing labor supply, and if the labor supply is regarded as changing in response to factors other than household income in the region, then Households can appropriately be regarded as another originating point for regional growth, and the impact of added manpower can be evaluated through a supply multiplier calculation.

Finally, we may regard the supply of some inputs of imported privately produced goods or services as growth originators rather than merely responses to regional demand. For example, if an oil field is opened up in a nearby region, the cheaper supply of crude oil available to the region can give rise to refining activity and perhaps a variety of associated chemical processing activities. In this case, the growth stimulus originates in the "outside world" or Imports sector of primary supply, and affects the region's economy directly and indirectly through a supply multiplier.

In some respects, the "supply-determined" input-output model we have been examining is clearly unrealistic in its assumptions. But similar criticisms can be raised against the more orthodox "demand-determined" model:

TABLE 8-11. Total Direct and Indirect Effects of an Increase in Primary Supply (Calculated from illustrative data in the preceding table)

Per dollar of increased purchases from primary supply by:	Total added purchases (in $) by Intermediate activities					Added sales (in $) by Intermediate activities to final demand			
	A	B	C	D	Total	Households	Government	Outside	Capital
A	1.118	.237	.113	.216	1.684	.486	.157	.067	.310
B	.020	1.526	.476	.316	2.338	.161	.155	.085	.611
C	.412	.323	1.171	.418	2.324	.315	.184	.105	.423
D	.112	.613	.113	1.398	2.236	.444	.067	.034	.446
A, B, C, D combined*	.629	.542	.459	.397	2.028				

* Figures in this row show the impact of an added dollar of aggregate primary supply purchases by all Intermediate activities, apportioned in the same proportions as these activities' shares in the primary supply purchases shown in Table 8-7. Specifically, this means added primary supply purchases of 45.4¢ by A, 19.2¢ by B, 26.2¢ by C, and 9.2¢ by D, totalling $1.00. The overall "primary supply multiplier" is 2.028. This row is the counterpart of the last column in Table 8-9.

if one is more unrealistic than the other, it is a matter of degree. Each gives a limited, one-sided picture. The purpose of our discussion was to show that both final demand and primary supply conditions are important as external determinants of regional growth, though in certain situations one may deserve the greater emphasis.

REGIONAL DEVELOPMENT AND INTERREGIONAL MOVEMENTS OF CAPITAL AND LABOR

Growth Stages and "Maturity"

The development of a region is a complex economic and social phenomenon involving all aspects of life. But certain basic trends are so universally associated with development that they almost define it. These are:

1. A structural change in the region's activity pattern, with extractive industries (especially agriculture) shrinking in importance and industrial and service activities playing a larger part[21]
2. Increased urbanization
3. Higher levels of per capita income
4. Accumulation of capital, with property income accounting for an increasing share of total personal income

The concept of regional economic "maturity" implies that there is a limit to at least some of the structural changes associated with development. For example, there is clearly a limit to the industrialization and urbanization of the farm population: we simply run out of farmers.[22]

The Role of Interregional Capital Flows and Migration

A mature region normally becomes an exporter of capital as the supply of savings outruns local investment opportunity. Savings rise more than proportionally with increased income. At the same time, the supply of labor to nonfarm activities is restricted as the dwindling agricultural sector

[21] This aspect of development was particularly stressed by Colin Clark, *The Conditions of Economic Progress* (London: Macmillan, 1940), who viewed the development process mainly in terms of the evolution from dependence upon "primary" (extractive) activities to specialization in "secondary" (processing and fabricating) industries and finally to specialization in "tertiary" (exportable service) activities. The rigidity of this 1-2-3 sequence has since been questioned; North, *op. cit.*, and others have shown that some regions have successfully developed secondary and even tertiary specialization without going through a stage of specialization in primary production for export.

[22] The United States as a whole appears to be coming close to that limit. The farm population is now down to about 5 percent of total population, and the net migration from farms that has persisted for most of our history has virtually come to an end.

can no longer supply as many farm-to-city migrants as it formerly did. Finally, development and urbanization usually reduce birth rates and thus retard the growth of the labor force.

Capital from mature regions seeks more profitable investment opportunities in the less-developed regions, where the reverse conditions hold; namely, a cheap and plentiful labor supply augmented by recruits from a large and prolific farm population, a shortage of savings, and large opportunities for the investments needed for the transition to an urban and industrial economy.

This interregional flow of capital helps to speed the development of the less-developed regions and thus works in the direction of more similar regional economic structures and levels of development. This is also one of the mechanisms whereby regional differentials in per capita income are progressively narrowed (that is, income levels tend to "converge"), as was noted early in this chapter. In the low-income regions, income growth is stimulated by the influx of capital from mature regions, which provides the basis for a greater demand for labor and, at the same time, by the development process itself, which normally entails a shift from low-income agriculture to higher-income nonfarm activities and development of an increasing variety of productive capabilities.

At the same time, labor migration in the opposite direction (from low-income, labor surplus regions to high-income, labor shortage regions) also furthers the convergence of regional structures and income levels. This is true despite the fact that the migrant from the low-income area is unlikely to get as high an income in the high-income region as the people already there, who have the advantage of greater skills and education and whose income average is substantially swelled by returns on property.

Both the capital flows and the labor flows can persist over long periods of time, since (1) neither labor nor capital is perfectly mobile among regions, even within a single country, and (2) levels of regional development only change slowly and require massive amounts of investment and redeployment and retraining of manpower.

The effect of capital and labor flows upon regional growth in *aggregate* terms (population or total income), and thus upon the interregional distribution of population and activity, depends at least partly on the relative mobilities of capital and labor. If capital is highly mobile but labor highly immobile, most of the adjustment will take place through capital flow, and the low-income, capital shortage regions will grow much faster in aggregate terms. On the other hand, if capital is highly immobile and labor highly mobile, the high-income, labor shortage regions will show faster growth in population and aggregate output. We should be wary of making any universal judgment about which of these situations will prevail. But Romans' analysis of United States regions between 1929 and 1959 disclosed that the mature, high-income, capital-exporting regions generally had slower growth in aggregate income; this should be expected if capital is more interregionally mobile than labor.[23]

Convergence of Regional
per Capita Incomes

It is not difficult to find plausible explanations for the convergence of regional income differentials among regions (as noted earlier in this chapter). Such convergence would seem to be.a natural result of the gradual development and maturation of areas once on the frontiers of settlement; the greatly reduced relative importance of farming as a means of livelihood; the improvement of transport and communications and the enhanced mobility of both capital and labor; and the rise of more activities not closely oriented to natural resources and consequently enjoying a wider choice of possible locations.

Actually, however, the story is not quite this simple, and we cannot infer that convergence will always be the order of the day. There seem, in fact, to have been two periods in United States history in which the interregional income differentials either widened or remained about the same; namely, 1840–1880 and 1920–1940. In the earlier period, the development of railroads brought rapid concentration of industrial activity in larger plants and larger industrial centers, and an increase in regional specialization. This raised incomes in the Northeast, where the bulk of the industrial activity was concentrated, compared to the basically agricultural parts of the country. In the period 1860–1880, the disruption of the Southern economy by the Civil War dramatically widened the gap between Southern and Northern incomes. Between World Wars I and II, there were at least two special reasons for divergent regional income levels. One was the low level of farm product prices and the consequently depressed condition of agriculture.[24] A major part of the regional income differentials, especially in that period, simply reflected differences in the relative importance of agriculture in the various regions. In addition, the virtual cutting off of the influx of cheap immigrant labor after World War I removed a constraint on rising wage levels in the industrial areas that had previously been employing the bulk of that labor.

The inevitability of convergence can be questioned on more general grounds. To be sure, migration flows predominantly in the direction of higher income levels and seems to be, on balance, an equalizing factor; though as we have suggested earlier, it is not always true that in-migration

---

[23] See Romans, *op. cit.* This is another demonstration of the inadequacy of the naive export base theory of regional growth, which would imply that regions with net exports should grow faster than others.

[24] The farm price parity ratio (index of prices received by farmers to prices paid by farmers, on the base 1910=100), averaged 104 in 1911–1920; 88 in 1921–1930; 76 in 1936–1940; and 107 in 1941–1950. U.S. Bureau of the Census, *Historical Statistics of the United States, Colonial Times to 1957,* Series K-138 (Washington, D.C.: Government Printing Office, 1960), p. 283.

from a region tends to lower income levels (and even less sure that out-migration tends to raise them). Increased interregional trade resulting from improved transport can also promote convergence by permitting regions to share to a greater extent the benefits of the production economies of other regions.

But shifts of employing activities (involving interregional capital flows) are an equalizing factor only to the extent that the activities are primarily oriented to labor supply. Consequently, changes in production and transfer technology, availability and use of resources, economies of agglomeration, and other location factors can either narrow or widen income differentials according to circumstances. The same is true of changes in the makeup of demand for goods and services: the effect on income differentials can be in either direction. For example, the practically universal tendency of demand for agricultural products to grow more slowly than demand for manufactured products and services in a progressive economy seems more likely than not to *widen* the differential between incomes in farming areas and those in industrialized and urban areas. Easterlin concludes:

> ...it is by no means certain that convergence of regional income levels is an inevitable outcome of the process of development. For, while migration and trade do appear to exert significant pressure towards convergence, they operate within such a rapidly changing environment that dynamic factors may possibly offset their influence. One may argue, of course, that migration and trade may become progressively more important during growth, as a result, for example, of improvements in transportation, and hence that the pressures towards convergence will tend increasingly to predominate. But whether this is generally the case cannot be settled on a priori grounds . . .[25]

Consideration of all the factors influencing regional income inequalities leads to an interesting hypothesis relating convergence and divergence systematically to the stages of the development process. Specifically, the early stages of national economic development are associated with increasing regional income disparities, while regional income levels tend to converge in a more maturely developed national economy.

In the present age, the crux of what we call development and attainment of self-sustaining progress is the transition from an agrarian economic basis to a basis of secondary and tertiary activities, with accompanying urbanization. A wide gap exists between the new and the old in terms of income levels, ways of life, and locational factors.

---

[25] Richard A. Easterlin, "Long Term Regional Income Changes: Some Suggested Factors," *Papers and Proceedings of the Regional Science Association,* 4 (1958), 325. See also Easterlin, "Interregional Differences in Per Capita Income, Population, and Total Income, United States, 1840–1950," *Trends in the American Economy in the Nineteenth Century,* Vol. 24, Conference on Research in Income and Wealth, Studies in Income and Wealth (New York: National Bureau of Economic Research, 1960), and Easterlin's chapter, "Regional Income Trends, 1840–1950," in Seymour Harris (ed.), *American Economic History* (New York: McGraw-Hill, 1961), 525–547.

When industrialization is in its early stages, most of the rise in overall productivity and per capita income comes from the change of mix—that is, the increasing importance of the nonagricultural sector relative to the agricultural. The new activities cannot take root everywhere at once, but are highly concentrated at first in a few key cities—generally the places with the most active contact with more advanced countries and the largest and most diverse populations. (The generative role of such cities was discussed near the end of Chapter 6.) At this stage of development, most regions still lack the necessary local market potential and the necessary local inputs to engage in the new and unfamiliar types of activity. Migration is likely to be heavy from the backward areas to the industrializing cities. This migration is highly selective (see the discussion of migration selectivity in Chapter 7), and on the whole this selectivity is prejudicial to the areas of out-migration. The result is the next stage: progressive agglomeration of modern industry in the principal urban areas and an accentuation of regional differences in economic structure, productivity, and income. Such conditions appear to have prevailed in the United States during the divergence period 1840–1880, which was probably lengthened by the destructive effects of the Civil War upon the economy of the South.

As development proceeds, more and more regions acquire the market potential, attitudes, and access to capital and know-how required to surmount the threshold of industrialization. A stage of interregional convergence in economic structure, productivity, and income sets in. This convergence may be made cumulative because migration is likely to become less selective, and national government policies will be less preoccupied with the objective of getting industrialization started in the country as a whole and more sensitive to the political pressures arising from regional inequality.[26]

EXTERNAL AND INTERNAL FACTORS IN REGIONAL DEVELOPMENT

We have seen that the development of a region—in terms of its size, income level, and structure—is affected by external conditions of two types: (1) demand for the region's outputs, or, more broadly, external sources of income for the region, and (2) supply of inputs to the region's

---

[26] See J. G. Williamson, "Regional Inequality and the Process of National Development: A Description of the Patterns," *Economic Development and Cultural Change,* 13, 4, pt. 2 (July 1965), 3–45; reprinted in L. Needleman (ed.), *Regional Analysis* (Baltimore: Penguin, 1968). Williamson presented and substantiated the hypothesis described here, using nineteenth and twentieth century data for a number of countries both cross-sectionally and in terms of changes over time. He also investigated the degree of income inequality among counties within states in the United States and established that its changes have been closely correlated with changes in interstate income inequality.

productive activity. We have also seen that the impact of these external factors is conditioned by the size and maturity of the region and by the internal relationships of its various activities in the form of vertical, horizontal, and complementary linkages.

Since all regions (except the pure homogeneous type) contain a variety of activities, it is to be expected that some of these activities will be determined mainly by external conditions based on demand (such as export markets) while others will be particularly sensitive to supply conditions. The regional economy as a whole, then, is always subject to a variety of growth determinants. Although there may be some one principal factor affecting its overall level of activity (for example, the nationwide demand for automobiles is the principal factor affecting the prosperity and growth of Flint, Michigan), there is never just one single determinant.

How much influence upon a region's development can be exercised from within the region itself? This question is basic to the discussion of regional objectives and policies in the next chapter. As far as growth determinants in the form of final demand are concerned, the latitude for regional initiative is ordinarily limited. But perhaps export demand in some lines can be stimulated by sales promotion campaigns, or the region can better its access to external markets by lobbying or other pressure to get more favorable freight rates or transport services for its exports, improved waterways, or high-speed highways. Improvement of the region's own terminal and port facilities may also have some effect on export demand and thus on regional growth. Houston, with its ship canal to the sea, is a dramatic illustration of a successful effort of this type.

A region also has some leverage on primary supply inputs. By persuasion, pressure, and subsidy it may secure better and cheaper inbound transport for its imported materials and may be able to attract activities with strong forward linkages that will have a supply multiplier effect. Governmental and private research centers and universities are increasingly valued as local suppliers of services, people, and ideas providing the basis for new growth industries. Regions where demand for labor tends to exceed supply can stimulate immigration by campaigns of advertising and recruitment, publicizing both job opportunities and the pleasures of living that the region has to offer.

Finally, regional growth can be significantly affected through changes in intraregional input supplies and interactivity relationships, which are more immediately subject to local choice and action. The quality of the labor supply can be enhanced by a variety of education and training programs and by removal of barriers to occupational mobility and technical change (including racial discrimination, restrictive work rules, and job-entry requirements). The region's limited land and other natural resources can be managed so as to increase their contribution to productivity. Local public services, an important input to almost all activities, can be made more efficient and conducive to productivity and amenity. The region's economies of agglomeration can be enhanced by appropriate action involving both public and private sectors (for example, in the planned development of new and improved office centers, regional shopping centers, produce markets, health centers, research parks, and the like).

In the next chapter we turn to a consideration of how these and other ways of influencing regional development are used in the pursuit of objectives involving regional structure and growth.

SELECTED READINGS

Otis Dudley Duncan and others, *Metropolis and Region* (Baltimore: Johns Hopkins Press, 1960).

Walter Isard and others, *Methods of Regional Analysis: An Introduction to Regional Science* (Cambridge, Mass., and New York: Technology Press and Wiley, 1960).

Charles M. Tiebout, *The Community Economic Base Study*, Supplementary Paper No. 16 (New York: Committee for Economic Development, 1962).

G. H. Borts and J. L. Stein, *Economic Growth in a Free Market* (New York: Columbia University Press, 1964).

John Friedmann and William Alonso, *Regional Development and Planning* (Cambridge, Mass.: M.I.T. Press, 1964).

J. Thomas Romans, *Capital Exports and Growth Among U.S. Regions* (Middletown, Conn.: Wesleyan University Press, 1965).

Wilbur R. Thompson, "Urban Economic Growth and Development in a National System of Cities," Philip M. Hauser and Leo F. Schnore (eds.), *The Study of Urbanization* (New York: Wiley, 1965), 431–490.

Theodore Lane, "The Urban Base Multiplier: An Evaluation of the State of the Art," *Land Economics*, 42, 3 (August 1966), 339–347.

Allen R. Pred, *The Spatial Dynamics of U.S. Urban-Industrial Growth, 1800–1914* (Cambridge, Mass.: M.I.T. Press, 1966).

Richard T. Pratt, "Regional Production Inputs and Regional Income Generation," *Journal of Regional Science*, 7, 2 (Winter 1967), 141–149.

Horst Siebert, *Regional Economic Growth: Theory and Policy* (Scranton, Pa.: International Textbook Co., 1969).

Harry W. Richardson, *Regional Economics* (New York: Praeger, 1969), Chs. 9–13.

APPENDIX 8-1

Further Explanation of Basic Steps in Input-Output Analysis
(See pages 228–229)

The input coefficients (Table 8-8) are derived from the information on interactivity purchases and sales (Table 8-7) as follows. The total output of activity A is 4300 (dollars per month, or other appropriate money/timeunits). A purchases 50 units of input from B. Therefore, for each unit of A's output, 50/4300 or .012 units of B output is called for. In similar fashion, we find that each unit of A's output involves the following further purchases by A:

From *A* itself (that is, sales from one *A* firm to another): 300/4300=.070
From *C:* 1000/4300=.233
From *D:* none
From Households: 1900/4300=.442
From Government: 200/4300=.047
From Outside: 200/4300=.047
From Capital: 650/4300=.151

Similarly, every unit of output by *B* involves purchases by *B* from *A* amounting to 400/2850=.140 units, and so on. In this fashion, we can derive the rest of the coefficients in Table 8-8.

The figures in Table 8-9 (total direct and indirect effects) are derived as follows from the input coefficients in Table 8-8. Let us denote the outputs of activities *A, B, C,* and *D* simply by these letters. Then we can write the entire *distribution* of *A*'s output as follows:

$$A = .070A + .140B + .032C + .192D + F_A$$

where F_A represents *A*'s sales to final demand sectors. The above equation can be restated more simply as:

(1) $$.930A - .140B - .032C - .192D - F_A = 0$$

and, applying the same procedure to the other three Intermediate activities, we get

(2) $$.930B - .012A - .323C - .115D - F_B = 0$$

(3) $$.968C - .233A - .070B - .269D - F_C = 0$$

(4) $$.808D - .281B - .065C - F_D = 0$$

We now have four simultaneous equations (1–4) which can be solved for the output levels *A, B, C,* and *D* in terms of the final demand sales levels F_A, F_B, F_C, and F_D. This solution ("matrix inversion") of the simultaneous equations is laborious (for even as few as four equations) if done by hand, but it can be done quickly and cheaply on a computer. The solution is as follows:

(5) $$A = 1.118F_A + .289F_B + .157F_C + .359F_D$$

(6) $$B = .126F_A + 1.234F_B + .439F_C + .352F_D$$

(7) $$C = .297F_A + .284F_B + 1.171F_C + .501F_D$$

(8) $$D = .068F_A + .452F_B + .247F_C + 1.400F_D$$

These coefficients are entered in the upper part of Table 8-9.

The figures in the lower part of Table 8-9 are obtained as follows, taking the first figure (.614) as an illustration. From the table of input coefficients (Table 8-8), we see that Households sell .442 units to A for every unit of A's output. From (5) above (or from the first figure in Table 8-9), we see that A must produce 1.118 units for each extra unit that A sells to final demand. Consequently, each unit that A sells to final demand will require purchases by A from Households amounting to .442×1.118 units. But (as we see from 6, 7, and 8 above, or from Table 8-9), each unit of A's sales to final demand calls for the following further purchases by A:

From B: .126
From C: .297
From D: .068

For every unit that B produces, B buys (Table 8-8) .105 units from Households; there is thus an additional indirect demand *via* B for .126×.105 units. Similarly for C and D. The *total* additional sales by Households resulting from a one-unit increase of final demand sales by A is therefore

$$(.442 \times 1.118) + (.126 \times .105) + (.297 \times .323) + (.068 \times .154) = .614 \text{ units,}$$

which is entered as the first figure in the lower part of Table 8-9.

APPENDIX 8-2

Example of Input-Output Table with Households Included as an Endogenous Activity

As indicated in the text (page 231), Households may be included as another activity in the Intermediate sector, if we care to assume that household expenditures are linearly related to household receipts. This first requires filling in some additional cells in Table 8-7 on page 226, and we shall use the following figures:

	Household sales to:	Household purchases from:
Households	200	200
Government	500	1200
Outside	300	1100
Capital	600	200

Table 8-7 will now appear as follows, using H to denote Households:

	Intermediate sector					Final demand sectors			
	A	**B**	**C**	**D**	**H**	**Govt.**	**Outside**	**Capital**	**Total**
A	300	400	100	500	1,600	500	200	700	4,300
B	50	200	1,000	300	100	200	100	900	2,850
C	1,000	200	100	700	100	300	200	500	3,100
D	0	800	200	500	700	0	0	400	2,600
H	1,900	300	1,000	400	200	500	300	600	5,200
Govt.	200	100	200	100	1,200				
Outside	200	300	300	0	1,100				
Capital	650	550	200	100	200				
Totals	4,300	2,850	3,100	2,600	5,200				

The only new figures are those in italics.

From the figures in the foregoing table, the input coefficients can be calculated in the same fashion as was done for Table 8-8. The revised version of Table 8-8 (with headings abbreviated) will look like this:

	A	**B**	**C**	**D**	**H**
A	.070	.140	.032	.192	.308
B	.012	.070	.323	.115	.019
C	.233	.070	.032	.269	.019
D	0	.281	.065	.192	.135
H	.442	.105	.323	.154	.038
Govt.	.047	.035	.065	.038	.231
Outside	.047	.105	.097	0	.212
Capital	.151	.193	.064	.038	.038
Totals	1.000	1.000	1.000	1.000	1.000

Here again, the only new figures are in italics.

Finally, the total direct and indirect effects of an increase in final demand are derived in the same way as for Table 8-9. The revised Table 8-9 is shown below. In it *all* the figures are new. All the ratios are much larger than in the original version of Table 8-9 (see p. 229), since the new calculation includes a large additional multiplier effect involving feedback through the Households sector (additional employment induces additional household expenditure for local products, imports, capital, and taxes). No such effect was allowed for in the original version of Table 8-9, in which Households were a final demand sector.

	A	B	C	D	H	A, B, C, D, H combined
A	1.482	.537	.473	.699	.593	.797
B	.233	1.307	.532	.452	.174	.528
C	.466	.400	1.318	.659	.276	.574
D	.270	.590	.422	1.589	.329	.482
H	.906	.618	.786	.846	1.476	.963
Subtotals	3.357	3.452	3.531	4.245	2.848	3.344
Govt.	.328	.262	.324	.347	.405	
Outside	.331	.332	.373	.324	.386	
Capital	.343	.405	.304	.327	.209	
Totals	4.359	4.451	4.532	5.243	3.848	

9

Regional Objectives and Policies

In the previous chapter we gained insight into processes of regional economic development involving the initiation and transmission of changes. We saw, also, that economic change within a region is determined partly by external forces beyond the influence of parties within the region itself and partly by decisions and actions that can be taken by such parties.

The present chapter will take up the question of what directions of change are desirable or desired: the *objectives* of regional economic policy. We shall look also into the *pathology* of regional development: what situations arise in which there is an urgent need for corrective action. Finally, we shall look into the *prophylaxis and therapy* aspects of regional development policy: what appropriate means exist for influencing development in desired directions, and how they can be used most efficiently.[1]

These questions are definitely in the spotlight today. A vast amount of talk and action, and a substantial amount of thought, are directed at urgent problems of regional development (including but not limited to the special problems of urban life covered in Chapters 10–12).

Such concern is relatively recent; as late as 1948 it seemed fair to state that:

Although governments have a large stake in the results of locational development, great power to influence that development, and a correspondingly heavy responsibility for influencing it in socially desirable directions, few governments have ever followed any coherent policy in regard to location.[2]

The "few governments" referred to certainly did not include the United States.

---

[1] Some of the material in this chapter is adapted from my paper "Some Old and New Issues in Regional Development" (presented at the International Economic Association Conference on Backward Areas in Advanced Countries held in Varenna, Italy, August–September 1967). The conference proceedings were published in E. A. G. Robinson (ed.), *Backward Areas in Advanced Countries* (London: Macmillan, and New York: St. Martin's Press for International Economic Association, 1969).

[2] E. M. Hoover, *The Location of Economic Activity* (New York: McGraw-Hill, 1948), p. 242.

But a radical change in thinking was already brewing. In Britain even before World War II, it had become clear that the depressed economic position of the northern and Welsh industrial areas presented an intractable problem, and controversy was rife on which national policies might or might not work. Since the 1950s, we have been observing with some frustration that the so-called developing countries do not seem to catch up automatically with the more advanced ones, even with continued and massive international assistance of various types.

Moreover (as was noted in the previous chapter) economic statisticians and historians who had been investigating interregional disparities of income within the United States found reason to question the inevitability of convergence. One basis of concern and desire for better understanding and policies has been a realization that regional stagnation or depression can be quite persistent.

Another basis for increasing concern stems from urbanization and the declining relative importance of agriculture. Unemployment in urban areas is more visible and more unsettling for both the individual and the community than is rural underemployment. In the United States the rapid shift of black population from rural to urban slums[3] has intensified this change; and along with a complex of other problems of urban adjustment, it has vastly increased the number of local areas calling for external economic aid. Problems of traffic congestion and environmental pollution (particularly in and around urban areas) have stimulated a search for more rational use of space and resources.

Fiscal pressures on local and state governments in the United States are part of the picture too. With increased demands for all kinds of public services, the principal revenue sources of those jurisdictions (primarily the real property tax at the local level) have not kept up with rapidly rising demands, and states and local communities are rightly fearful that higher taxes will drive away or deter business investment. As a result, there has been increasing though sometimes reluctant reliance on the more ample and flexible taxing powers of the federal government to finance programs in aid of local public services (such as education, health, and highways), and still more broadly to provide unrestricted grants to the states for use at their discretion. This channeling of public money through the national treasury naturally brings to the fore rival regional claims upon federally collected funds and the problem of just and efficient allocation.

Still another factor arousing interest in the policy problems of regional development is the disillusionment with the effects and objectives of the more naive forms of local and regional self-promotion. As more localities participate in this competitive game, more of the total effort is recognized as simply cancelling out (that is, each community is driven to promotional efforts in self-defense by the activity of rival areas). And more and more

---

[3] The nonwhite population is now more urban than the white population.

questions are raised about whether growth itself is a sensible standard of community interest and objective of public action at the local level.

Next, it appears that there has been a significant shift in the attitude of the general public, and of most economists, toward population growth on a local, regional, national, or world basis. In the 1920s and 1930s, the American credo of the beneficence of population growth was unquestioned, and leading economists and statesmen were pointing with alarm to the perils of economic stagnation that would beset us if we did not get busy breeding more young consumers. Malthus' gloomy nineteenth-century warnings were dismissed as a discredited fantasy.[4]

This attitude has changed considerably. In part, the change came from the frustration of seeing hard-won output gains in so many of the underdeveloped countries cancelled out by mushrooming population growth. Meanwhile at home the postwar baby boom, the all too evident pressures of population growth in urban and outdoor-recreation areas, the generally inflationary bent of the economy, and the relatively high fertility of people low on the economic and education ladder, all helped to undermine the venerable New World tradition of the blessings of increasing population. Today, thinking and policy are much more directed toward welfare objectives, such as fuller employment and higher per capita income, rather than to the misleading standard of aggregate growth.

Still another contributing factor in the shift toward more enlightened approaches to regional promotion is what might be called the dilution of provincialism. We now find it normal that an individual makes his home in several different communities and regions during his lifetime,[5] and that he travels often and widely. This more varied exposure is conducive to more objective feelings about programs that may benefit one region at the expense of another.

Finally, there have occurred (and are occurring) a number of important changes in the factors determining location choices of producers and consumers. These changes, arising mainly from changes in technology and increased income and leisure, really underlie many of the developments already mentioned, and have certainly played a significant part in the rethinking on regional development. These changes in location determinants have been mentioned in previous chapters, and can be briefly recapitulated as follows:

---

[4] The best-known statement of this concern over the implications of slow population growth in America is Alvin Hansen's presidential address to the American Economic Association in 1938, "Economic Progress and Declining Population Growth," *American Economic Review*, 29, 1, Pt. I (March 1939), 1–15. However, Hansen, unlike some of the other contributors to that discussion, did not advocate incentives to higher fertility as a solution.

[5] Census sample surveys indicate that each year about 1 American in 5 moves to a different house, and 1 in 15 to a different county or state. These proportions have remained rather stable since the late 1940s.

1. In terms of linkages between industries and their sources of materials and markets, the cost of physical transport of heavy and bulky goods is less important, and increased importance attaches to the speedy and flexible transportation of high-value goods and above all to communication—that is, the transmission of intangible services and information.
2. Access to markets has increased in importance for most industries compared to access to sources of raw materials and energy sources.
3. More and more importance is attached to amenity factors such as good climate, housing and community facilities, and access to recreational and cultural opportunities. This change reflects rising standards of income and leisure, the increased importance of white-collar employment, and the fact that industries in a dynamic growth stage require a high proportion of well-trained and educated people who are in short supply and so can afford to be choosy about where they will live and work.
4. There is an increasing degree of dependence of particular industries on various services locally supplied by other industries, institutions, and public bodies. Thus, we hear more about the external economies of a location well supplied with such services and facilities. We hear more of the importance of an adequate regional or community infrastructure, supplying such things as local utility services, police and fire protection, schools, hospitals, reference libraries, and the like as a necessary basis for development of profitable enterprises producing goods and services for outside markets.

Concern, controversy, and experience have brought into focus some basic issues of regional development objectives and policy, to which we now turn.

OBJECTIVES

Individual and Social Welfare Criteria

The ultimate objectives of regional economic policy run in terms of promotion of individual welfare, opportunity, equity, and social harmony. It would seem obvious, then, that economic policy in regard to a region should promote higher per capita real incomes,[6] full employment, wide choice of kinds of work and styles of life for the individual, security of income, and not too much inequality among incomes. The relative importance of these goals is, of course, something that economics cannot tell us. Each of us has his own values and can try through the political process to influence the objectives of social policy so as to reflect those values.[7]

---

[6] See the discussion in Chapter 7 on measurement of real income.

[7] For a more detailed discussion on regional policy objectives, see Charles L. Leven, "Establishing Goals for Regional Economic Development," *Journal of the American Institute of Planners,* 30 (1964), 99–105; Thomas Wilson, *Policies for Regional Development,* University of Glasgow Social and Economic Studies, Occasional Paper No. 3 (Edinburgh and London: Oliver & Boyd, 1964); Wilbur R. Thompson, *A Preface to Urban Economics* (Baltimore: Johns Hopkins Press, 1965), Ch. 5; Benjamin Chinitz, "Appropriate Goals for Regional Policy," *Urban Studies,* 3, 1 (February 1966), 1–7; and Harry W. Richardson, *Regional Economics* (New York: Praeger, 1969), Chapter 14.

The aspect of equity raises some difficult questions in connection with the application of these criteria to programs and policies affecting diverse groups of people such as the inhabitants of a region. Any action—such as spending public funds for improved services, subsidizing the establishment of new industries in the region, or imposing restrictive controls on land uses—is sure to help some people more than others, and may well help some at the expense of others. There is general agreement, however, on the guiding principle of the so-called Pareto optimum,[8] which says that a change is desirable so long as it helps somebody without hurting anybody else. In practice, some of the benefits conferred on individuals by a change (for example, building a new highway) can be taxed away from these beneficiaries so as to compensate those who otherwise would suffer by the change; and the real question is whether the Pareto criterion is satisfied after feasible compensatory transfers of this sort have been made.

This guiding principle is much easier to propound than to apply. The very essence of a region is interdependence of activities and interests, and these interactions become particularly crucial in a high-density urban region within a city or neighborhood. Any change in one activity produces externalities and neighborhood effects upon a variety of other activities, and these effects can be either helpful or harmful. Thus, the building of a sports stadium can help the merchants of an area by bringing in more visitors and purchasing power, while at the same time it can spoil the surrounding residential neighborhood by creating traffic congestion, noise, and litter.

An important task for regional economists is to devise ways of "internalizing" the externalities involved in regional change. Take, for example, a chemical plant whose operations pollute a river. The pollution imposes a variety of injurious externalities upon other residents of the area. Thus, other industrial plants and water supply systems downstream will have to incur extra costs for water treatment preparatory to use; businesses based on recreational use of the river, or fishing, will suffer diminished patronage, higher costs, or both; and there is a still broader injury to the community in terms of loss of recreational opportunity and amenity, and possible health hazards. In principle, it might be possible to set a fee or tax upon the chemical plant to reflect all these social costs, whereupon the costs of pollution would become internal costs of the chemical firm. These costs having been properly internalized, or placed where they belong (that is, imposed upon the party that causes them), the chemical firm will have to reconsider its profit calculus. It can (1) choose a different location altogether; or (2) invest some money in effluent treatment to reduce or eliminate the pollutant, and thus get relief from the special tax; or (3)

---

[8] Named after the Italian economist and sociologist Vilfredo Pareto (1848–1923), a pioneer analyst of economic welfare.

continue the pollution and pay the tax, whereupon the community gets the money to use for downstream water treatment or for compensating in some fashion the various parties injured by the pollution. Any one of these three outcomes is, of course, preferable to the original situation in which the chemical plant's activities imposed social costs borne by other parties. This holds true regardless of whether the polluting firm absorbs or passes on to its customers the added costs imposed upon it.

We can also speak of internalization in the opposite case, in which some individual activity yields external *benefits* to other parties but cannot feasibly collect directly from them in return. In such a case, the socially optimum scale of this activity is greater than the scale on which it will be led to operate on the basis of its costs and returns. Internalization of the social benefits will then be in the general interest. This is the rationale for the granting of various forms of subsidies, inducements, and exemptions to activities that are believed to have beneficial external effects. Thus, a chamber of commerce or a neighborhood merchants' association may raise money from its members to help build a convention hall, park, or other facility which they believe will eventually help their businesses; or a municipality or a state may use general tax funds to subsidize new industries, or give them tax exemptions, on the theory that such subsidy is a sound investment for the taxpayers as a group.

Regional Economic Growth as a Goal

What has been said above applies to economic objectives and policies for the welfare of a group of people. But a region is not, except at an instant in time, a definite group of people—it is an area populated by a changing group of people. In any region of consequence, there are probably some new arrivals (by birth or migration) and some departures every day.

This continual turnover of a region's population complicates the question of policy goals. What is to be maximized, say, over the next 10 years? The welfare of the present inhabitants of the region, regardless of where they may be in 10 years' time? The welfare of those who will be living in the region 10 years hence, regardless of where they are now? Should it be counted as a regional gain if some people move in whose incomes are above the regional average, so that the average rises with their advent? If so, should one of the aims of regional policy be the out-migration of its poorer inhabitants? Is a region improved if its population and total income increase at equal rates, with per capita income unchanged?

Our preferred objective for a region's development depends, of course, on where we sit. In addition to differences of interest among groups within a region, there is an important difference between the optimum for any single region and the optimum pattern of regional growth rates in relation to national welfare.

Is simple regional growth (in aggregate terms, without regard to per capita income or welfare levels) a sensible objective? On the face of it, such a criterion sounds quite irrelevant. Yet in practice we find that regional promoters and governments spend a great deal of money and effort in the avowed pursuit of a bigger regional economy—that goal is put forward without apology as something worth striving for.

How can this be explained? Partly, perhaps, by emotion and tradition. The idea that "bigger is better" has been a remarkably enduring component of American ideology, although it is no longer such a universal article of faith.

There is an even more basic explanation, however. A substantial part of the business and political interests in a region are, in locational terms, oriented to the local demand, and thus have a direct stake in the overall population and income of the region. Department stores, banks, utility companies, real-estate owners and speculators, and local political leaders have vested interests in aggregate growth. Their fortunes depend not so much upon how well off the region's people are as upon the size and growth rate of the population. Net in-migration is good from their standpoint even when it is accompanied by a reduction in per capita income and other aspects of individual welfare; accordingly, population losses are viewed with alarm.[9]

Quite logically in terms of their own interests, therefore, these groups are active promoters of and contributors to any programs and policies that promise to expand the regional economy. It is they who support chambers of commerce and local or regional booster associations; firms primarily involved in export business have little or nothing to gain from such participation. With respect to regional programs aimed at improving individual rather than total income, however, these two groups may be about equally public-spirited.

Regional Objectives in a National Setting

Regions are not self-contained nor independent of one another. Accordingly, a true concern for human welfare calls for evaluating development and framing policy goals on a multiregional or national basis.

NATIONAL HIGH-EMPLOYMENT POLICY AND REGIONAL ECONOMIC ADJUSTMENT. Experience has taught us that we cannot expect any satisfactory

---

[9] A challenging and brilliant discussion of the actual and supposed benefits and costs of regional growth is in E. J. Mishan, *The Costs of Economic Growth* (London: Staples Press, 1967). An illustration of the conflicting interests involved in regional prosperity is the report that in June 1969, an association of residents of Hawaii implored convention visitors from the mainland to curb their spending, because such spending raises living costs for the resident consumer.

solution to the problem of regional unemployment or arrested development except in the context of a prosperous national economy. In a depression period, businesses are doing relatively little capacity expansion, and have little difficulty in locally finding labor, services, and space for such expansion as they want to undertake. Their investment is more likely to take the form of cost-cutting improvements in existing plants, and this may well involve closing down some branch facilities at the more marginal locations. Moreover, in slack times, the surplus manpower in any area has literally no place to go and fewer resources to go anywhere; we cannot look to labor migration for any significantly useful adjustment.

We have found also that the national monetary and fiscal authorities have great powers to increase the nation's money supply and disposable income, and thus to stimulate spending and investment in the aggregate. Such action helps to maintain the necessary buoyant climate in which constructive regional adjustments by people and industries can occur.

EFFICIENCY, EQUITY, AND STRUCTURAL UNEMPLOYMENT. Some feel that maintaining a high level of employment and demand in the economy is as much as the national government should do in regard to regional economies. There are, however, two distinct arguments for other, and more specifically region-oriented, national policies and programs.

The first argument invokes the criterion of *efficiency,* claiming that there are other ways besides fiscal and monetary policy for facilitating effective allocation of resources among regions and the necessary dynamic adjustments. The second argument is based on *equity,* claiming that the national government has a responsibility for helping disadvantaged regions as such.

The efficiency argument largely rests on the idea of "structural unemployment" and the problem of fully utilizing resources without destructive inflation. In a prosperous economy, inflation is always just around the corner if not banging on the door, and keeping an economy prosperous is truly an art of brinkmanship. In the United States, for example, it has not been possible to push the economy hard enough to provide jobs for more than about 95 or 96 percent of the labor force without getting ominous symptoms of inflation.

This comes about largely because there are wide disparities in the employability of different groups in our labor force. There is a poor matching between the kinds of labor that are in demand and those that are available, and there is insufficient mobility and interchangeability within the labor force. This makes it inevitable that we run into shortages, rising costs, and consequently inflation while millions of the less employable are still out of work. Obviously, any policies that will reduce these wide disparities and make manpower more mobile and interchangeable will have the good effect of shifting the inflationary brink closer to the ideal of full employment.

There is, then, a strong case for public programs involving education and worker training and retraining, and for more direct aids to spatial and occupational mobility: for example, improved information about job opportunities, assistance to migrants, and removal of racial and other discrimination in employment. It is also clear that such efforts ought to focus on upgrading the least advantaged types of workers and reducing their competitive handicaps. Such emphasis is, of course, in accord with equity objectives as well.

HELPING REGIONS AND HELPING PEOPLE. When it comes to translating this policy into geographical terms, we pass from consensus into controversy. It is tempting to argue that if public policy should specifically help the less-advantaged classes of *people* to find jobs, then it should by the same token seek to underwrite the prosperity and growth of all *communities.*

Such a view has been aptly characterized as substituting "Place Prosperity" for the more fundamental objective of "People Prosperity."[10] In its more naive expressions, the Place Prosperity doctrine represents merely false analogy: an unreasoning assumption that whatever is true of individuals must also apply to areas. On a more rational level, it is possible to suggest Place Prosperity as a pragmatic *proxy* for the ultimate ideal of People Prosperity—on the hypothesis that the best way to help a person is to promote the overall prosperity of the area in which he happens to live.

The Place Prosperity doctrine will figure importantly in later discussion in this chapter. For now, it is enough to indicate two of its shortcomings. The first lies in ignoring the fact that a region does not correspond, for any length of time, to a fixed set of people. Since people have some mobility, the best way to help disadvantaged people who are living in a particular region may be to encourage them to move. Migration can, in fact, serve both the objective of efficient use of resources and the objective of interpersonal equity and distribution of opportunity.

A second criticism of the Place Prosperity approach is that in practice it is wastefully nonselective in its assistance. In any community or region where there are unemployed and needy people, there are also employed and prosperous people. Increased employment and income for the area as a whole may help those who need it most; but a large part of its local benefits will come to those who do not need it. Those surest to benefit, as suggested earlier, are generally property owners and the operators of established locally oriented business, such as utilities, banks, and commercial and consumer service firms. Growth of aggregate area income and

---

[10] Louis Winnick, "Place Prosperity vs. People Prosperity: Welfare Considerations in the Geographic Distribution of Economic Activity," in *Essays in Urban Land Economics,* in honor of the 65th birthday of Leo Grebler (Los Angeles: University of California, Real Estate Research Program, 1966).

employment does not automatically mean improvement in per capita income or the reduction of unemployment, and generally injures some while helping others. Such considerations suggest that attacking human hardship and lack of opportunity solely through Place Prosperity might be like using a shotgun to kill flies.

REGIONAL RIVALRY AND THE NATIONAL INTEREST. The benefits of growth in a region are directly and strongly felt by certain influential interest groups, while the costs are likely to be more diffused and less well perceived. Most regions, consequently, devote some effort to furthering their own economic growth by attracting additional activities.

Regional rivalry, like other forms of competitive promotion and warfare, can be in large part self-defeating, or a "zero-sum game," contributing nothing to the national welfare. One region's gain is another's loss. This is especially true when the regions are small and when the primary weapons are persuasion and subsidy.

Actually, however, some significant net benefits can accrue from regional rivalry. Enlightened efforts to enhance a region's growth potential can take the form of upgrading the region's human and natural resources and public services, protecting and improving amenities, stimulating entrepreneurship and innovation, fostering cooperation among various business, social, and political elements, and discovering the true comparative advantages of the region for further development. All these effects favor better utilization of resources and are clearly in both the national and the regional interest. A logical national policy with regard to regional development should include some effort to channel the growth urge of regions into these constructive paths.

But it is also true that regional rivalry in development can be something *worse* than a zero-sum game if it distorts the efficient allocation of resources. This danger is inherent in a use of local subsidies, and most of all with respect to the use or abuse of natural resources and the neglect of externalities.

> Competitive regional and urban development are clearly suboptimal. They may involve regions in a competitive race to offer up for private exploitation their air and water quality. The resulting resource deterioration involves transfer of income from local residents to business firms. Competitive tax concessions to attract development may also result in relative weakening of the public sector. Competitive regional development may involve serious external diseconomies resulting from failure to treat environmental units, such as river basins, as planning units. The larger the planning region, the more adequately externalities can be assessed.[11]

---

[11] John H. Cumberland, "A Regional Interindustry Model for Analysis of Development Objectives," *Papers of the Regional Science Association,* 17 (1966), 93.

We see, then, that national policy in terms of the development of specific regions can help to achieve more efficient use of natural resources as well as to reduce regional unemployment and broaden human opportunity.

REGIONAL PATHOLOGY: THE
EMERGENCE OF "PROBLEM AREAS"

Regions, like people, want a doctor only when they are sick. When a region is enjoying full employment or high and rising employment, there is no great disposition to examine its situation and prospects in detail and search for ways to gild its robust health. National attention is directed only to those regions that are in trouble, and there always are enough of them to worry about. We assume, in other words, that in healthy regions the workings of the market economy under existing constraints are relatively satisfactory.

To focus on regional pathology is both politically and economically rational. Our diagnostic and therapeutic resources are limited enough, and we are more likely to find something helpful to do for regions with obvious ailments than to improve comparably an already good situation. The only risk is that we may thus overlook opportunities to nip unwelcome developments in the bud.

Our main concern here is with situations where things have definitely gone awry. Regional economic growth is not a smooth, straightforward process. The persistence of efforts to explain development in terms of successive "stages" attests to the existence of important discontinuities. We do not by any means know what all these are, how to foresee them, or how to deal with them. But we do know that the development of a region, like that of a nation, encounters from time to time crucial situations in which its future course can be significantly influenced by major planning decisions and policies. Alternative paths appear; one of the alternatives may be a further growth along some new line, and the other may be stagnation, arrested development, or even regression.

These crucial situations present the biggest challenge to our insight into growth-determining factors. The stakes are highest and the rewards for correct decisions, in terms of economic progress, are at a maximum.

Backward Regions

A familiar case is that of underdeveloped nations poised on the threshold of industrialization and threatened by a genuine Malthusian peril of overpopulation. Much effort has gone into defining the conditions necessary for a successful surmounting of the threshold, the so-called takeoff into a self-sustaining growth process.

Most if not all of the so-called advanced countries also include one or more backward regions, which seem to be hung up at a threshold on the road of development and have not kept pace with the structural changes and the rising income and opportunity levels of the more fortunate regions of the country. In the United States, Appalachia, a huge zone characterized by rural poverty, straddles the eastern highlands from New York State to Mississippi. Five other large areas (each extending into more than one state) have been officially designated by the federal government for special developmental attention and now have regional commissions to study and plan for their needs.[12] Many smaller pockets of relative poverty and apparently arrested development exist in still other parts of the country. In Canada, the extreme eastern part of the country (the Maritime Provinces) is regarded as the chief area of concern of this type; in Italy, it is roughly the southern half of the country *(Mezzogiorno)*; in Sweden, it is the far north.

Developed Regions in Recession

A second and quite different type of problem area is the mature industrialized urban region afflicted by stagnation. In Britain, the industrial areas of southern Scotland and Wales and northern England entered this phase in the 1920s. In the United States at about the same time, migration of the textile industry to the South laid heavy blight on the industrialized region of southern New England, and real rejuvenation with new industries did not set in for more than 20 years. In the Pittsburgh region, slow growth or decline in the leading industries caused fears of stagnation and regression that gave rise to a major community effort to reverse the trend after World War II.[13]

Symptoms of this particular syndrome are easily recognizable. The ailing region's rate of growth has been increasingly subnormal for many decades. Unemployment is high and chronic. Out-migration is heavy. The area appears to have somehow lost the dynamic growth character that had brought it to its peak importance in days gone by. There is a feeling that unless something really decisive happens, stagnation will prevail indefinitely.

---

[12] See map below, Fig. 9-1 on page 289.

[13] See Pittsburgh Regional Planning Association, Economic Study of the Pittsburgh Region, 3 vols. (Pittsburgh: University of Pittsburgh Press, 1963). The first volume, *Region in Transition,* traces the economic history of the region and diagnoses its position as of the time of writing. The second volume, *Portrait of a Region,* by Ira S. Lowry, focuses on population trends and the geographic patterns of activities within the region. The third volume, *Region With a Future,* assesses prospects for further change and suggests some appropriate directions for policy. A concise summary of the study's approach and findings is in E. M. Hoover, "Pittsburgh Takes Stock of Itself," *Pennsylvania Business Survey,* 5, 1 (January 1964), 4–9.

Such a situation can arise in a region whose economy is heavily based on a few activities that have themselves ceased to grow or have begun to decline. They are the activities of yesterday and today, but not those of tomorrow. But arrested growth in a region may also mean simply that the factors of interregional competition, in specific activities, have taken a trend adverse to that particular region. The region's difficulties are compounded if *both* of the above conditions apply, so that it finds itself with shrinking shares of declining activities.[14]

But in diagnosing the ills of such a region, it is not enough to determine the extent to which it is losing ground to other areas in major activities, or the extent to which its activities are no longer of the growth-industry type. After all, we could hardly expect that every activity would continue to grow forever, or that any given region could forever retain or increase its relative position in its principal activities. A healthy regional economy can absorb losses in its stride and shift its resources into new fields, getting a share of the emerging new rapid-growth activities to balance the inevitable decline of other activities. When a region fails to make such adjustment successfully, we must ask why. Perhaps it is simply because the degree of specialization in nongrowing activities was so intense. Perhaps it is because the loss of competitive advantage in some important activities has been so drastic. Or perhaps it is because the region has developed a sort of economic arthritis that inhibits its ability to adjust to rapidly changing conditions.

Whether regional analysts operate as full-fledged physicians ministering to the economic ills of sick regions, or more narrowly as diagnosticians, they have a special concern for cases in which the patient seems deficient in his resistance to infection and in his ability to recover. We have to look beyond the immediate symptoms to the less-obvious organic difficulties.

Excessive Growth and Concentration

In both types of problem regions thus far mentioned, a basic symptom is that employment opportunities have not developed (in amount, in variety, or in both) fast enough to keep pace with the size and aptitudes of the labor force. Resources are underutilized. Somewhat the opposite situation prevails in regions that undergo extremely rapid growth involving massive inward migration. The growing pains of such regions are felt as impairment of the quality of services, destruction of local resources and amenities through overuse, a high rate of obsolescence of facilities, neighborhoods, and institutions, and a general deterioration of the quality of life. The forestalling or mitigation of these effects through analytical foresight and advance planning poses a major challenge to regional specialists.

---

[14] See the illustration of "shift-share" analysis in Appendix 9-1.

The most widespread and obvious present-day examples of the perils of too rapid development appear in two types of areas. One is the suburban fringe of metropolitan areas, where many factors have combined to produce sudden and often unforeseen growth. The problems of these areas will be discussed in later chapters. The other type of area comprises beaches and other zones of special recreational amenity. The growth of population plus its increased mobility, leisure, and taste for outdoor pleasures add up to a formidable threat to our basically nonexpansible resources of open space, clean water, and privacy. This problem obviously is much more serious than temporary "growing pains."

Related to, but distinct from, the question of too rapid growth is the problem of excessive spatial concentration of development, specifically in gigantic metropolitan centers. Concern on this score is felt in nearly every country. In the less-developed countries, the problem is seen as exclusive concentration of modern industrial development, business, and population in the chief city. In France and England, the concentration of growth in Paris and London has been officially deplored and combatted for a generation or more. And although in America we are reluctant to worry about anything being too big, with the possible exception of the federal government, there is a rapidly growing anxiety about the prospect of our largest metropolitan centers getting even larger.

The question whether our largest cities are "too big" defies any easy answer. Part of the difficulty lies in the variety of possible criteria. Large cities have been variously assailed as hotbeds of vice, breeders of psychological and political disorder, and hazards to health and safety, and have been extolled for equally diverse virtues. With respect to economic criteria, it is often argued that the rising costs of housing, public services, and similar items make large cities uneconomical as places to produce or to live. These diseconomies of size are said to outweigh, in very large cities, the positive advantages of urban agglomeration that we discussed earlier.

Such empirical evidence as is available suggests that there are strong net economies in the provision of infrastructure and public services for middle-sized cities as compared to small ones, but that the curve relating such costs (per capita) to city size flattens out somewhere in the 100,000 to 500,000 population bracket, with a possibly rising trend thereafter.[15] On this limited basis, there is no "economic optimum size" of city, though we might refer loosely to a "minimum efficient size." In any event, costs of

---

[15] Niles M. Hansen, *French Regional Planning* (Bloomington: Indiana University Press, 1968), 16–17 and Ch. 2; "The Structure and Determinants of Local Public Investment Expenditures," *Review of Economics and Statistics,* 67, 2 (May 1965), 150–162; *Rural Poverty and the Urban Crisis* (Bloomington: Indiana University Press, 1970), Ch. 10. See also G. M. Neutze, *Economic Policy and the Size of Cities* (Canberra: Australian National University, 1965).

public services are only one element in the comparative economic advantages of different sizes of cities.

Many regional economists see hidden disadvantages in very large cities, justifying a public policy of diverting growth from such cities to medium-sized ones. They argue that there are important *external diseconomies* (such as added costs of housing, congestion, and environmental spoilage) that do not enter into the calculations of the firms or individuals who contribute to city size by establishing themselves there—in other words, these costs should, but do not, work to limit urban growth. For example, an additional urban freeway commuter adds to congestion and causes losses to all the other commuters whom he slows up, but he does not have to pay for the added costs inflicted on the others.

Such externalities are real enough, and we shall have occasion to consider them further in Chapter 12. But their existence does not necessarily imply a net bias toward excessive city size, as is frequently alleged. First, the usual argument assumes too readily that the external diseconomies of large city size outweigh the external economies. Further, it implicitly assumes that the adverse externalities fall upon parties that have no recourse—that is, they are "locked in" and can neither leave the city nor raise the prices of their services in order to compensate themselves for the injuries suffered.

By and large, this assumption is unwarranted. Individuals and firms subjected to such external diseconomies as air pollution, traffic delays, long commuting journeys, high taxes, expensive housing, or noise can (and do) decide that they will not stay in such an environment unless they are paid extra to do so. Urban populations are characteristically mobile, and pay rates do run higher in large metropolitan areas than elsewhere, as we saw in Chapter 7. This suggests that at least some of the disutilities that urban life imposes on the individual are being passed back to employers in the form of higher wage costs, which of course affect their locational decisions.

It would seem to follow that—unless we could establish that personal and business migration from large cities is somehow more inhibited than the contrary flow, or that state and national governments are consistently subsidizing locations in large cities at the expense of taxpayers elsewhere—the external diseconomies argument proves nothing about whether cities in fact tend to grow uneconomically large. Although the diseconomy may be external to the unit or activity causing it, it is internal to the city economy as a whole, and does fall upon firms and households whose decisions affect city size.

The foregoing comment is not intended to dismiss concern about adverse externalities as such, or concern about the many serious problems attending urban growth, which do in fact tend to be most aggravated in very large cities. Such problems are, in fact, the subject of our final chapter. We shall see that the way in which urban public services are *priced* can be extremely important.

A Comparison of Characteristics of
Problem Areas

Table 9-1 summarizes the results of a classification of "problem areas" (mainly on a county-by-county basis) made by Benjamin Chinitz in 1967, along lines similar to those suggested above. The table is largely self-explanatory in the light of previous discussion, but the inclusion of the "high income, fast growth" category (I) comes as a surprise. A substantial number of cases of fairly severe unemployment do occur from time to time in basically flourishing labor markets, such as San Diego. Often these are transitory situations reflecting cutbacks in federal defense contract employment in the area, and in some cases the unemployment is mainly seasonal; but distress may be more chronic in areas that attract large numbers of migrants by their amenities.

Regional Structure and Economic Health

Both a region's growth and the quality of opportunity it offers depend not merely on external influences and location but also to a large extent on the mix of activities that the region has. Some of the relationships are simple and obvious, others less so.

As explained in some detail in Appendix 9-1 at the end of this chapter, it is possible to separate statistically the component of a region's growth in any time interval that reflects the activity-mix of the region from those components that reflect overall national growth rates and changes in the region's competitive position. Other things being equal, a region will grow faster if it is specialized in "growth industries," just as it will tend to have a low wage level if it is specialized in low-wage activities or a high skill level if it specialized in high-skill activities. But shift-share analysis does not really tell us much about why regions grow or improve. It says nothing about the important question of how a region's ability to hold its share of existing activities or to attract new ones is affected by the region's economic structure. Here we need to look into some less simple and obvious relationships.

"Regional economic balance" or, in somewhat more definite terms, "diversification" has for a long time been viewed as a "healthy" structural feature worth striving for. The grounds for this view, however, have not been clearly articulated.

Thus, it is sometimes assumed that a region with a diversified structure (many different kinds of activities and an absence of strong specialization) is necessarily less vulnerable to cyclical swings of general business conditions and demand. Actually, this is neither true nor logical, as was shown quite a long time ago by McLaughlin.[16] Diversification per se is roughly

---

[16] Glenn E. McLaughlin, "Industrial Diversification in American Cities," *Quarterly Journal of Economics,* 45 (November 1930), 131–149.

TABLE 9-1. Socioeconomic Characteristics of 5 Types of U.S. Problem Areas, 1965

	(I) High income, fast growth	(II) High income, mature	(III) Rural, not very poor*	(III-A)	(IV) Poor de-pressed rural	(V) Appalachia
Number of areas	38	37	492	105	441	253
Unemployment (percentage)	6.8	7.6	8.6	7.6	4.0	8.7
Population per area (thousands)	300	461	26	37	14	17
Population per square mile	282	3,728	68	131	27	31
Population growth, 1950–1960 (percentage)	+44.7	+7.2	−1.1	+44.8	−10.7	−10.8
Percentage of population nonwhite	8.6	7.2	7.8	11.9	27.9	21.6
Median family income, 1959 (dollars)	6,014	5,602	4,437	5,037	2,322	2,392
Median school years completed, persons 25 and older	10.9	10.4	9.6	10.2	8.0	7.9
Percentage of labor force in agriculture	4.8	3.7	12.8	9.3	30.1	21.3
Percentage of labor force in manufacturing	25.0	30.0	19.0	8.8	16.9	15.9

* Chinitz distinguishes III-A from III on the basis of population growth rates.

SOURCE: Benjamin Chinitz, "The Regional Problem in the U.S.A.," in E. A. G. Robinson (ed.), *Backward Areas in Advanced Countries* (London: Macmillan, and New York: St. Martin's Press for International Economic Association, 1969), Table 1, p. 53. Chinitz identifies two other types of problem area, the large city ghetto and the Indian reservation, but does not provide corresponding data for them.

neutral in its effect on cyclical stability. What really makes a region especially vulnerable to cyclical swings is specialization in cyclically sensitive activities (mainly, durable goods industries and especially those making producers' equipment and construction materials and components). Thus, a specialized steel-making center like Youngstown naturally has greater cyclical ups and downs of employment than either tobacco-processing centers like Winston-Salem or Durham or a broadly diversified manufacturing center like Philadelphia. Analogously, a community or region highly specialized in seasonal recreation (like Atlantic City or the coast of Maine) shows much more seasonal variation in employment than the average area, while a region specialized in some nonseasonal activity may be more seasonally stable than the average.

It is a different story, however, when we consider stability and other desirable attributes over a longer period. In time, any of a region's activities will suffer arrested growth and perhaps decline or even extinction, either because the product itself becomes obsolete (as in the famous case of buggy whips, which sorely affected Westfield, Massachusetts, the principal whip-making center of the country) or because the region loses out competitively (as, for example, New England lost to the South in textile manufacturing, and Pittsburgh in the nineteenth century successively lost out as a leading producer of salt, wagons, cotton textiles, and refined petroleum products).

If a region is narrowly specialized, such a loss can be at least temporarily disastrous; in a diversified region, it is unlikely that a major proportion of the total activity will suffer at any one time. Equally significant is the fact that a narrowly specialized region is likely to show less resilience in recovering its stride by developing new activities to take the place of those lost.

This attribute of resilience is an extremely important aspect of regional economic health. It depends to a large extent on diversification, since diversity of employment develops a wide variety of skills and interests in the labor force and also among business entrepreneurs, bankers, and investors, and a wider array of supporting local business services and institutions. In such a setting, there is clearly a better chance for new kinds of business to get a start and to survive the hazardous years of infancy.

Diversity is not the only factor affecting resilience. The inhibiting effects of high specialization are compounded if the region is specialized in activities characterized by large producing units, large firms, and absentee ownership. Such large units are relatively self-sufficient with respect to most kinds of business services that smaller units tend to buy from others; consequently, a region heavily specialized in, say, steel making fails to develop a broad base of such supporting services. In addition, its business leaders and sources of local finance have a more restricted outlook and interest. The range of local external economies is underdeveloped, and the whole climate for new and small businesses and new lines of activity is much less favorable than it is likely to be in a region of similar size where the firms and production units are smaller, more numerous, and less self-contained.[17]

Finally, a region's resilience partly depends on the amount of overall growth momentum it has at the time the loss is experienced. If the rest of the region's activities are growing vigorously, even a sizable loss may produce only a short spell of abnormal unemployment. Fluctuations from a sharply rising trend may not involve much absolute decline; distress is

---

[17] A cogent discussion of the effects of specialization and business unit size on regional economic resilience is Benjamin Chinitz, "Contrasts in Agglomeration: New York and Pittsburgh," *American Economic Review,* 51, 2 (May 1961), 279–289.

most meaningfully measured in terms of how long and how far the region's employment is below the previous peak, rather than how long and how far it is below a trend line.

Moreover, a region that has been growing rapidly has a number of characteristics favoring resilience. The labor force is relatively young because much of it has been recruited through recent migration, and young adults move the most readily. Thus, the labor force is likely to be more occupationally mobile and adaptable, and less afflicted by seniority and tradition. The same applies to employers. Facilities are newer. A greater proportion of the population has had the broadening experience of living in other places. There is a more buoyant community climate of expectation of growth and favorable change.

Such considerations as these help to explain why Pittsburgh, for example, took in its stride the losses of such important specialties as textile and vehicle manufacturing and oil refining during its dynamic growth period in the nineteenth century, but was very slow to recover from losses of preeminence in such specialties as steel, glass, electrical equipment, and coal mining after about 1920.[18]

THE AVAILABLE TOOLS

Mention has been made of some of the ways in which a region can influence its structure and development from within. Also, it was suggested earlier in this chapter that a national government can do a great many things to assist healthy regional adjustment and development, even without having to make any decisions as to which regions should be favored or why. In general, this involves the provision of information and the improvement of the quality and mobility of productive resources including labor, capital, and land. Aid to education and vocational training, improvement of communications and money markets, preparation and distribution of statistical and technical information, improved labor market information and placement services, and a wide variety of other programs help to reduce the structural underutilization of labor and other resources in all regions. We also noted that maintenance of a high national level of demand makes it easier for labor and capital to find their most productive uses.

Nearly all national governments nowadays take the important additional step of designating certain regions for special attention. In a few special cases (for example, Greater London, Paris, and some recreational areas such as the National Seashores in the United States) the purpose is to restrict further private development in an area judged to be overcrowded.

---

[18] For details on this story, see Pittsburgh Regional Planning Association, *Region in Transition*, vol. 1 of the Economic Study of the Pittsburgh Region (Pittsburgh: University of Pittsburgh Press, 1963).

Much more often, the immediate purpose is to increase employment and income in a backward or otherwise "distressed" area. Let us give a quick look at some of the means that can be used for such ends.

One line of action involves easing the supply of capital to encourage growth of employment in an area. Federal, state, and local funds are made available at low interest rates, generally on a matching basis, to establish or expand business facilities. A wide variety of tax exemptions and incentives (such as deferment of taxes, allowance of larger write-offs against income before taxation, and special low assessments on real property taxes) further encourage private investors. Public authorities (often working through local development associations) also encourage business expansion in certain areas by direct investment involving the purchase and assembly of land, clearing of sites, and construction and operation of "industrial parks" provided with all the necessary utilities and sometimes with buildings that can be adapted or leased by private firms.

In the contrasting case of areas in which development is to be restrained, public policy is implemented by imposing restrictions on further private investment or land use.

Another policy lever involves transport costs and services and the construction or licensing of new routes. In regulatory decisions on freight rates, the regional effects are given some weight, and the regions that stand to gain or lose by the decision often mobilize impressive and costly efforts to protect their interests. Both private and public leaders in the Pittsburgh region, for example, have in recent years battled persistently and effectively against Buffalo and Youngstown in favor of adjustments in freight rates on flour-mill products and against the construction of a canal connecting the Ohio River with Lake Erie. Authorization for United States participation in building the St. Lawrence Seaway was preceded by decades of controversy, with different regional interests aligned pro and con.

Another tool is the regional allocation of procurement contracts (particularly the defense contracts of the federal government). The procurement agencies themselves are not particularly interested in conferring regional stimuli except as a way of pleasing influential congressmen; but they have, from time to time, been adjured to follow policies of greater decentralization, or of preference to areas of high unemployment. A region especially can sometimes effectively increase the demand for some of its products by sales promotion in outside markets or protective measures designed to restrict imports, and some states have been quite ingenious in setting up interstate trade barriers for certain commodities, such as milk.

A region can sometimes be effectively aided in development by subsidized technological progress or technical assistance leading to more efficient and profitable ways of using some special regional resource. Thus, federally supported research on new uses for coal may play a significant part in improving the economic status of Appalachia. In such types of research and development efforts, the state governments, universities, and private foundations in the region are generally active as well.

A region's development can also be guided along more effective lines through support of general analysis of the region's economic situation and potentialities and through the formulation of integrated development plans. Modest but significant amounts of federal funds and technical assistance have been made available in recent years for planning activity and demonstration projects.

Allocation of federal funds to improve local public services and utilities has become, at least in terms of expenditure, a substantial element in regional assistance recently, particularly in Appalachia. This includes, in addition to schools, health services, and roads, the construction of water supply and sewerage facilities, libraries, and some kinds of recreation facilities. The Tennessee Valley Authority operation, instituted in 1933, represents one of the earliest large efforts to use federal funds systematically to develop a particular region; the project emphasized control of water resources and electric power but also embraced a wide variety of other forms of development assistance.

Finally, and probably most important, are programs to upgrade and mobilize human resources through education, vocational training and retraining, easing of ethnic discrimination and other kinds of restrictions on employment, and assistance in job finding and relocation in search of employment opportunity. Such programs were mentioned earlier as being in the national interest in all areas; but the need for them is obviously greater in regions where skills and mobility are particularly restricted and where there is a particularly poor match between labor supply and the demand for labor.

BASIC ISSUES OF REGIONAL DEVELOPMENT STRATEGY

As soon as a national government assumes responsibility for the geographical impact of its actions, it needs to decide which areas merit its favorable attention. The answer is inevitably determined in part as the net resultant of political pressures, but it is clearly in the national interest to formulate and apply some more objective social and economic rationale.

We note an interesting shift in the use of terms to describe areas to which national public development assistance programs are directed. In the 1920s and 1930s, the British used to refer to their "depressed areas." Later, these same objects of solicitude were rechristened under the curiously neutral term of "special areas." Still more recently, they have come to be referred to as "development areas." In our own country in the 1930s, we used to refer to "problem areas," or "stranded areas"; later, to "redevelopment areas"; and now to "development areas," and to "growth centers" within them. As to our less fortunate brethren across the seas, we used to refer to them as simply "poor" or "backward," or "low-income" countries. Later they became "undeveloped" and then "underdeveloped." Nowadays, it is considered more tactful to speak of the "less-developed" or, better still, the "developing" countries.

Does this curious trend reflect anything besides euphemism—that is, a growing squeamishness about offending the sensitivities of people in the areas in question? Not necessarily; but perhaps we can read into the new terms a growing emphasis on the positive, and a belief that any and every region can and should be made to develop faster. We may descry also a disquieting indication that the ideal of Place Prosperity is enlisting greater support.

The Four Issues

Actually, three more strategy issues come to light here in addition to Place Prosperity versus People Prosperity. One is whether we consider aid to regions as charity or as investment. Should we select areas on the basis of the greatest degree of distress (what has aptly been called the "worst-first" rule of priority) or on the basis of how much additional income and employment opportunity can be generated per dollar of aid? A further issue involves the spatial focusing of aid to areas: that is, what size area is a proper "development unit," what is the role of urban focal points within such areas, and should aid be concentrated at a few points or widely spread? The final issue concerns the appropriate choice of means of assistance from among the large variety of available devices sketchily catalogued in the previous section of this chapter.

These four issues (Place Prosperity versus People Prosperity, distress versus development potential, concentration versus diffusion, and the choice of means of assistance) will recur often in the discussion that follows. We shall find that they are closely interrelated, and that none of them can be resolved as categorically as the word "versus" might imply.

Should Jobs Move to People, or People to Jobs?

If manpower is scarce in some areas while jobs of similar types are scarce in other areas, the situation can presumably be improved either by moving some jobs or moving some people or both. Both kinds of adjustment do take place spontaneously, though not by any means to the extent that would be necessary to eliminate regional structural unemployment. Both can be assisted or impeded to some extent by public policies. The question of which policy should be emphasized is a perennial one, and was debated with particular heat over a generation ago when the British government was trying to decide what to do about certain depressed industrial areas. It is a crucial question today in every country that is seeking to improve regional adjustment, and it particularly involves the two issues of (1) People versus Place Prosperity and (2) need versus development potential.

The answer depends on our judgments about the footlooseness of people on the one hand and that of investment and employment opportunity on the other. If we believe that people are reluctant to move, that we should not try to induce them to do so, and that practically any populated area can be made attractive to new employers, then it follows that the proper cure for a region with high unemployment is to induce more employers to go there. Consistent with this view is an emphasis on degree of distress as the criterion for allocation of assistance to regions, since it is assumed that people have to be helped *in situ,* and that every region has adequate development potential. By this approach, Place Prosperity is equivalent to People Prosperity. Finally, this view would imply that assistance should be given to individual small areas and should be widely diffused, since people are assumed to be tied to their labor market areas. To sum up, the elements of this position are: Place Prosperity, allocation on the basis of need to a large number of quite small areas, and inducements to employers as the principal means of assistance other than straight charity.

If on the other hand we judge that people can reasonably be induced to move, and that some regions lack the potential for eventually self-sustaining growth in employment, the strategy implications are the opposite of those just described. We conclude that many of the unemployed people will best be served by moving to some area with better opportunities, and draw a sharp distinction between their welfare (People Prosperity) and Place Prosperity. Assistance logically takes the form of improving the employability and mobility of the people affected, facilitating their relocation, and increasing employment opportunities in the areas of greatest potential. Thus, the elements of this position are: People Prosperity, stimulation of development on the basis of growth potential, and stress on the up-grading of human resources. Job creation does not have to be stimulated on a diffused basis in a large number of individual areas, since people are prepared to move to one of a smaller number of growth centers.

Which of the above two positions is the more correct? Clearly, neither is wholly right or wrong, since both people and employment activities are partially footloose. A few observations are in order, however.

First, certain emotions and prejudices seem, on balance, to impart bias toward the view first mentioned (namely, that jobs must move to people). Because of local pride as well as vested interest in their community or region, most regional spokesmen are reluctant to admit that their region lacks development potential or to see its population decline. As we noted earlier, most of the active and articulate spokesmen and leaders in regional development are those who do have a vested economic interest there in the form of large property ownership, a business depending on local markets, or a political position whose importance and perquisites depend to some extent on the region's size and growth. Quite naturally, they are ready to invoke ethical and cultural arguments in support of their economic interests and loyalties.

It is an article of faith among many that no one should have to move in order to better himself, any more than he should have to change his religion, political affiliation, or skin color. A presidential advisory commission in 1967 endorsed "a national policy designed to give residents of rural America equal opportunity with all other citizens. This must include access to jobs, medical care, housing, education, welfare, and all other public services, without regard to race, religion, *or place of residence.*"[19]

Reinforcing this bias is a general tendency to overrate the footlooseness of activities with which one is not directly familiar. In particular, the complex and subtle economies of agglomeration that favor major urban areas as locations are not well understood. Moreover, the consideration of efficient interregional allocation of resources and output, from the standpoint of national welfare, has few spokesmen. That faceless individual, the consumer and taxpayer, is here again the forgotten man.

In view of this considerable bias, it is not surprising that official policies and public statements have generally soft-pedaled migration as an instrument of regional policy, have paid a great deal of deference to the Place Prosperity strategy and the criterion of need, and have favored spreading assistance among an increasingly large number of claimant areas rather than concentrating it.

How mobile are people in areas of high unemployment, and can their mobility be expected to increase? A number of excellent recent studies have addressed themselves to these questions.[20] First, it appears that unemployed people (regardless of area) are more likely to *want* to migrate than are employed people of the same occupational or age group. But these desires tend to be frustrated in the case of the less educated, the less skilled, and the black. Lansing and Mueller conclude that:

> . . . unemployment constitutes a "push" which leads people to move if they are young, well-educated and trained, or live in a small town. In the absence of such characteristics, unemployment is highly unlikely to overcome the reluctance

---

[19] *The People Left Behind*, Report of the President's National Advisory Commission on Rural Poverty (Washington, D.C.: Government Printing Office, 1967), p. xi (italics added). Professor Mary Jean Bowman justly observes that the inclusion of the italicized words could make this recommendation "a prescription for national disaster." "Poverty in an Affluent Society," in Neil W. Chamberlain (ed.), *Contemporary Economic Issues* (Homewood, Ill.: Irwin, 1969), p. 99.

[20] Notably John B. Lansing and Eva Mueller, *The Geographic Mobility of Labor* (Ann Arbor: Survey Research Center, University of Michigan, 1967).

to move, unless the unemployment is prolonged, the income loss substantial, and the family has no alternative local source of support.[21]

Thus the labor force groups most prone to unemployment are also the least mobile (quite naturally, because they have the least to offer in relation to labor demands and the least likelihood of finding a job if they do move). Out-migration is highly selective in favor of the better trained and more educated. This has two serious implications. First, even assuming continuous prosperity, we cannot presently count on migration alone to solve all the problems of distressed areas by draining away their unemployed. Second, such migration from distressed areas as does occur results in a lowered "quality mix" of the labor supply of those areas, which may further handicap them in any competition for new employers.

But if migration is inadequate, the remedy is not to discourage it as some would propose. It is quite possible and certainly more appropriate to upgrade the less productive and less mobile groups so that they will be better able to migrate and also will be more attractive to potential employers wherever they are. One of the great virtues of a strategy of human resources development, improved job information, and placement services is this double-action impact. It helps people to move to jobs and helps jobs to move to people. The danger in practice is that part of the benefit may be thrown away by misguided efforts to restrict migration—for example, by training people only for the kinds of jobs existing in their home areas, or by pension plans, union restrictions, and relief eligibility rules[22] that discriminate against newcomers in areas of in-migration.

The long-term prospects—or at least the possibilities—seem good for some continued increase in the mobility of the disadvantaged groups in labor surplus areas; this should diminish migration selectivity and allow migration to contribute more effectively to regional adjustment.

The mobility of employment locations is the other important aspect relating to the issue of bringing jobs to people or the reverse. It is commonly said that manufacturing industries have become much freer in their choice of locations than they were in the age of coal and steam, and this is almost certainly true as *among regions*. It is not at all obvious, however, that employers are becoming increasingly indifferent about whether they locate in a sizable urban area or in a small-town or rural location. A

---

[21] *Ibid.*, p. 77. See also the reference to the "Beale hypothesis" on p. 180 above.

[22] In April 1969, the U.S. Supreme Court ruled that a state may not impose residency provisions "for the purpose of inhibiting migration by needy persons into the state." Up to that time, most states had denied welfare assistance to applicants with less than a year's residence. There are still large differentials in the level of such benefits, which substantially affects interregional migration. But public and political support seems to be growing for a nationally uniform basic level of welfare services financed with federal funds.

reasonably plausible case might, in fact, be made for the proposition that size of place is becoming a more important consideration than choice of region.

In any event, there seems to be ample evidence that an attempt to solve problems of regional employment by bringing new industry to every community or labor-market area would be wasteful and futile. Henry Ford I in the 1920s, and many others before and after, have thought it possible and desirable that industrial employment be diffused to every small town and village, and the first Indian Five-Year Plans after independence put substantial reliance on developing small-scale village industries. In no country, however, has such an attempt really succeeded. On the contrary, there is a progressive drift of population and employment to major urban areas and out of small towns and the countryside. This reflects in part the growing importance of tertiary activities, the declining importance of agriculture, the improvement of long-distance communication and people transport,[23] larger scale production and management units, greater demand for urban-type amenities, and proliferation of the external economies of agglomeration and urbanization. All these factors have been discussed in previous chapters.

Some Conclusions

Where does all this leave us in terms of the basic strategy issues for regional development assistance? The points raised thus far suggest these conclusions:

1. Migration can, does, and should play a substantial role in effecting desirable regional adjustments. Its effectiveness tends to grow and can be greatly enhanced by programs of education, training, retraining, equal opportunity, open entry,[24] job information, and placement services especially directed at the least employable and least mobile manpower groups in areas of labor surplus. Programs more explicitly directed at the encouragement of migration can also play a substantial role.[25]

---

[23] Relevant also is the increasing *nonlinearity* of costs of transfer with respect to distance—resulting from the relatively greater speeding of long-distance transport and communication and the increasing importance of time as an element in costs of transfer for goods, people, services, and information. With respect to communication, personal travel, and shipment of an increasing range of goods, the added time required for an additional several hundred miles is often less than the time required for the first 10 miles.

[24] Equal opportunity here basically refers to the removal of employment discriminations based on color, sex, or any other personal characteristics not relevant to work performance. Open entry refers to the removal of inappropriate restrictions on occupational or geographic mobility imposed by union rules and employment agreements regarding hiring, apprenticeship, union membership, or transfer of seniority and pension rights.

[25] For a survey and appraisal of such programs in Western Europe, the United States, and Canada, see U.S. Congress, Joint Economic Committee, *Programs for Relocating Workers Used by Governments of Selected Countries*, Economic Policies and Practices, Paper No. 8, 89th Cong. 2 Sess. (Washington: Government Printing Office, 1966).

2. Employment is not fully footloose: there are important differences in the development possibilities of different areas, especially between small-town or rural areas and sizable urban areas. It would not be feasible to bring employment (except of the work relief type) to each and every labor market area.
3. Accordingly, Place Prosperity is an inadequate and misleading goal; development assistance should be allocated on the basis of the *needs* of people and the *development potential* of areas; such assistance should be at least to some extent focused on particularly promising locations; and human resources programs of the type outlined in (1) above should play a major role.
4. Strong political pressure is to be expected in the direction of the use of local distress as a priority guide, discouragement of emigration, and diffusion of assistance to more and more areas.

THE ROLE OF GROWTH CENTERS

One of the four basic issues of regional development assistance strategy concerns the focusing of such assistance upon a relatively small number of selected growth centers[26] at which there exist or can easily be created the necessary conditions for expanding employment opportunity, and especially the public infrastructure and the external economies that most activities require. Such growth centers are then expected to attract commuters and migrants from surrounding areas of labor surplus, and at the same time to stimulate secondary growth of employment in some of those areas.

Applicability of the Growth Center Strategy to Different Types of Problem Areas

The problem of choosing growth centers arises only in certain of the problem areas characterized on pages 261–267. There has been a tendency, in assistance programs, to lump together indiscriminately the backward areas and the developed-but-distressed areas.

These two types of areas have, of course, certain common symptoms of maladjustment. Both suffer essentially from obsolescence of the bases for

---

[26] The theory and policy of growth centers was developed in Europe and particularly in France, in the 1950s, before attaining much currency in the United States. The broader term "growth poles" does not always have a spatial meaning and is quite loosely used. It refers sometimes to larger development regions that include centers and sometimes to specific industry complexes, activities, or even single large installations that play a strategic role in sparking new development. Two titles from the large recent literature on this subject are: J. R. Boudeville, *Problems of Regional Planning* (Edinburgh: University Press, 1966), and Hansen, *French Regional Planning, op. cit.* For further references and a penetrating discussion of growth center concepts and development strategy, see Harry W. Richardson, *Regional Economics* (New York: Praeger, 1969), 415–428, and Gordon C. Cameron, "Growth Areas, Growth Centres and Regional Conversion," *Scottish Journal of Political Economy,* 17, 1 (February 1970), 19–38.

their former economic viability; both need help in making a structural shift to a new base in response to changes that have occurred in demand, resources availability, and competition from other areas. For both, a successful transition calls for modernizing human and capital resources and infrastructure (including institutions and attitudes) so that they can effectively grasp new opportunities provided by technological and economic change and thus become more resilient, self-reliant, and generative.

But at this point, the similarity ends. With respect to needs for education, the two kinds of areas are likely to differ substantially. The population of a distressed developed area may show no particular deficiencies in all-round literacy and capability for productive industrial or tertiary employment. Internal and external transport and communication facilities in such an area are also likely to be adequate or better. There are substantial local resources of capital and at least some relevant industrial know-how. The basic elements of growth centers are already there, and the problem is essentially one of modernization—reorienting the local labor force, business community, infrastructure, and public sector toward the opportunities of today and tomorrow.

By contrast, for truly backward areas with little industrialization or urbanization, the necessity of finding or creating specific growth centers is of major concern. It is primarily to this kind of region that we refer here.

Justification for Focusing Employment Stimulus in Growth Centers

The next question that concerns us is the role the growth center is supposed to play vis-à-vis the surrounding area. On both economic and political grounds, it is vital to have an acceptable answer to this question, if only to justify the denying of direct aid to places that are not growth centers. Justification is needed because these other places cannot be expected to like being left out of the distribution of largesse, and because the growth centers are likely to be relatively well off and growing places and thus apparently the least in need of any help. "Unto every one which hath shall be given" is scarcely a policy to evoke the enthusiastic support of a hath-not area.

Two elements appear in the case usually made for the growth center strategy. The first argument stresses availability of infrastructure and the external economies of urban size as prerequisites for competitive survival in a modern economy. Concentration of public investment at growth centers is justified on the ground that those are the *only* locations where adequate public services can be provided at reasonable cost, and where there is a prospect that prosperity and growth can eventually be self-sustaining without permanent subsidy.

This basis of strategy is clearly involved, for example, in a project proposed by the Québec provincial government in late 1969 for the Gaspé Peninsula, where 11 backwoods villages were slated to be wiped off the map. The residents would be given cash incentives to relocate in larger coastal towns where schools, hospitals, and vocational training centers could be made available. The project is described as merely the initial experimental stage in a larger development program for the backward rural areas of the province.[27]

Were this the only rationale for the growth center approach, it would imply that the peripheral backward areas outside of the centers have no prospects of survival except as charity cases, and that they should be vacated as fast as is humanely possible. But there is a second argument in this case; namely, that some of the effects of economic improvement initiated in growth centers will trickle out to their less-urban hinterlands or "zones of influence." This implies that the best way to help these hinterlands may not be by either uprooting or direct assistance, but indirectly through promoting the progress of accessible growth centers. Let us see how this "trickle-out" effect may be expected to work.

There was mention in Chapter 6 of the manifold ways in which an urban center can provide a focal point of leadership in the development of its region. The reader may wish to refer again here to that earlier discussion (particularly pages 148–151). All the considerations mentioned are relevant to the growth center strategy, but we still do not know a great deal about how to measure or control the effects in question. Most of our quantitative knowledge is in terms of the two familiar frameworks of central-place and input-output analysis. Each of these approaches is only helpful to a limited extent in articulating the impact of a growth center on its zone of influence.

The central-place model is designed, in fact, to describe essentially the inverse relationship; namely, the dependence of the urban center upon demand in its tributary area. Central-place analysis is concerned only with a limited set of consumer-serving activities that are stringently market oriented. The spatial distribution of consumer demand is taken as given, and it determines the extent to which various orders of central places can develop appropriate ranges of consumer-serving activities.

Despite the fact that the roles of the central place and the growth center are so different, the analysis of a region's system of central places may be helpful in suggesting likely growth center locations. First, the central-place analysis will indicate something about minimum size constraints:

---

[27] *The New York Times,* November 8, 1969. Some of the same considerations are involved in current programs in Pittsburgh and other cities to eliminate isolated pockets of settlement on steep hillsides where costs of maintaining streets and other public services are inordinately high. The properties are acquired by the city and all structures removed, with appropriate landscaping and planting.

it can establish that cities or towns below some specified population are unlikely to contain certain trade and service activities that may play an essential role in the operations of a growth center. Second, the tributary trading area of a central place, being based largely on the feasible range of frequent travel, may be a rough indicator of the zone of influence that that place would have as a growth center.

The relations described by the input-output model are more directly relevant to the role of a growth center, particularly if we think of a model embracing as separate subregions the growth center and the zone of influence. In its usual application, the input-output model traces direct, indirect, and induced impacts of some initial change via backward linkage, and this is, of course, one of the mechanisms by which a growth center can stimulate its tributary zone. For example, manufacturing and other exporting activities in the growth center will purchase local materials and services, some of them from the zone of influence. A food-processing plant illustrates the direct effect: by its presence in the growth center, it provides a market for farmers in a surrounding agricultural area. In Chapter 8 we explored the nature and measurement of the subsequent indirect effects (through local purchases by business firms) and induced effects (through local purchases by households). For as much of the zone of influence as constitutes the commuting field of the growth center, the most obvious impact of growth at the center upon the surrounding area is likely to be the direct, indirect, and induced demand for *labor*.

In principle, as was suggested in Chapter 8, input-output analysis can be directed alternatively to the evaluation of forward linkages. But input-output analysis is severely constrained in the extent to which it can express the role of growth centers because, for operational reasons, it ignores the scale economies and the external economies of agglomeration that are basic to the whole growth center strategy. Nor does the input-output approach, as developed so far, take into account growth-initiating factors, such as the supply of capital, enterprise, and specific public services, or the progressive improvement of productivity through education, health, training, and informational services.

It is clear that growth centers exert their influence in many ways that elude the usual quantitative models and systems of accounts. In particular, there is a recognized need for more adequate techniques for dealing with those growth center effects that operate through supply rather than through demand.

It is difficult in principle to make a meaningful distinction between forward-linkage effects and external-economies effects of growth center development; since in both cases an activity initially established in the center provides cheaper and more accessible inputs that make possible the nearby establishment or expansion of other activities dependent on access to such inputs. Generally, we seem to prefer to speak of external economies when the initially established activity is of a so-called threshold type, normally associated (because of scale economies) with a certain minimum size of urban or industrial concentration, and when it provides products or service inputs to a wide variety of other activities in the same locality. We are more likely to refer simply to a forward linkage when those conditions do not hold and when the initially established activity supplies inputs to just one or a few activities locationally oriented to sources of that input. But both cases involve a similar principle of input orientation or forward linkage. Finally, terms such as infrastructure or "social overhead" generally denote services supplied by the public sector or by public utilities, such as schools, hospitals, water supply, and communications.

The transmission of growth effects outward from a growth center via forward linkages involves only those kinds of outputs that can be transferred from the center to the people in the tributary region. This would not ordinarily include fire protection, elementary schools, or garbage disposal. It does, however, include a wide variety of public services (technical schools, colleges, research libraries, and hospitals) and a similarly wide variety of business services (commercial research and testing laboratories, banks, data processing centers, and so on).

Size and Number of Growth Centers

Adoption of the strategy of growth centers already implies a substantial degree of geographical focusing of development assistance. But should the growth centers be few and large, or numerous and small?

There are a number of possible approaches to this question. For example, we can examine the past growth records of urban areas of various sizes, to see whether size seems to affect growth potential in any important way. Thompson has observed that American metropolitan areas of 250,000 population or more rarely show actual declines of population from one Census to the next; his "urban size ratchet" hypothesis is based on various advantages of agglomeration and proposes that when a metropolitan area attains a size of about 250,000 its structural characteristics "may almost ensure its continued growth and fully ensure against absolute decline."[28] As we go further down the size range, vulnerability increases, and the smallest types of settlements are preponderantly in stagnation or decline. These facts suggest that a great proliferation of small growth centers would be risky and expensive, and that cities with populations in the six-figure range are likely to offer the greatest assurance of self-sustaining growth.

Another approach is to try to estimate the costs of providing basic public services or infrastructure in cities of various sizes, to see whether we can

---

[28] Wilbur Thompson, *A Preface to Urban Economics* (Baltimore: Johns Hopkins Press, 1965), p. 24. See also Neutze, *op. cit.*

identify urban size economies and an optimum size or a minimum efficient size of city with regard to such costs. Here we get some limited guidance, to the effect that middle-sized cities (say from 200,000 to 1 million population) tend to have lower unit public service costs than smaller places, and (with somewhat less certainty) lower costs than the still larger places (see page 264). This is quite consistent with the pattern of growth rates identified in the previous paragraph. But some difficult problems are involved in making legitimate comparisons of such costs between one city and another. (Just how, for example, do we measure the cost per unit of output of a police force or a park system?) More importantly still, the costs and efficiency of public services (even if we could measure them accurately) would be only one element in the comparative social costs and effectiveness of different sizes of cities viewed as agents for the development of surrounding zones of influence. There is no reason to suppose that the optimum size of growth center coincides with the minimum-cost size of city from the limited standpoint of measured public service costs. Thus, all that we really get out of this approach is, once again, a warning that when we dip down into, say, the five-figure population range, the potential growth center is increasingly likely to be handicapped.

Still another approach leans on central-place theory and data and attempts to define a viable growth center in terms of the range of central-place activities represented there. Leaders in developing this approach are Karl Fox and Brian Berry. The range of the center's influence as a purveyor of consumer goods and services and the range of its influence as an employer of labor are tied together in the concept of a "fundamental community" or "functional economic area" demarcated on the basis of both commuting and shopping distances and having a sufficiently full line of central-place activities to be relatively self-contained.[29]

If the area radius is assumed to be large and if we are willing to accept quite small cities as nuclei of functional economic areas, the network of such areas can be spread out to cover the bulk of the population of the United States. For example, Berry constructed a set of such areas that

[29] Berry's report for the Upper Great Lakes Regional Commission is listed among the suggested readings at the end of this chapter. Fox's ideas are set forth extensively in *Functional Economic Areas: A Strategic Concept for Promoting Civic Responsibility, Human Dignity and Maximum Employment in the United States* (Ames: Iowa State University, Department of Economics, January 10, 1969). Briefer statements are in his "Agricultural Policy in an Urban Society," *American Journal of Agricultural Economics*, 50, 5 (December 1968), 1135–1148, and in "A New Strategy for Urban and Rural America," *Appalachia*, 2, 10 (August 1969), 10–16. Fox's proposal is to use functional economic areas of the order of a quarter of a million population not only as units into which to aggregate small communities and rural territory for planning, development, and administrative purposes, but also as units into which large metropolitan areas might be subdivided. In short, he argues that "our metropolitan areas are too large and our rural communities too small for effective government, a creative social life and an efficient community."

included in their boundaries 96 percent of the 1960 population. The radius in this case was based on 1 hour's driving time as the limiting factor, with an assumed average speed of about 50 miles an hour. Many of the central cities were well below 50,000 population.[30]

In the Fox-Berry conception, it is not the size of the central city or growth point that matters, but the population of the whole commutation and trading area including it. Such an area is regarded as constituting a single community, and Fox has suggested that something like 250,000 might constitute a viable size for self-sustaining growth. This figure is roughly the same as suggested by Thompson, Hansen, and others as the critical minimum size at which a metropolitan area passes the "urban size ratchet" and becomes fairly protected from decline.

It does not yet appear established, however, that a population of 250,000 spread over 7,900 square miles (the area of a circle of 50 miles radius) and lacking any city of more than 25,000 population would have the same growth potential as the usual SMSA of 250,000—which generally comprises a single county with an area of just a few hundred square miles and contains a central city of 60,000 to 150,000 population. In fact as we have seen already, other evidence strongly suggests that an area lacking a really sizable urban focus is at a disadvantage under present conditions. Small cities and towns show slower and less stable growth than do middle-sized cities; they have lower income levels; and they are apparently more costly to provide with infrastructure and urban public services.

All this discussion of growth center strategy suggests that a major policy problem is how to avoid yielding to the pressures for too much proliferation of growth centers and spatial diffusion of development investment. Gordon Cameron's discerning study of current American regional policies emphasizes this point:

> With a few notable exceptions, the efforts of small urban areas and rural counties to stem structural decline and to prevent continuous out-migration have been signally unsuccessful. Once again a few statistics will clarify the dimensions of the problem. In July 1966, 885 counties out of a total of 3,134 in the U.S. were qualified by the Federal Economic Development Administration as being distressed either on grounds of heavy unemployment or because of low income and heavy out-migration or low income alone. Significantly, the proportionate qualifications were far heavier amongst the smaller counties of under 50,000 inhabitants, than for the larger counties. . . .
>
> Another way of showing this is to compare the degree to which small, medium and large labour markets have responded to the fast growth of the national economy over the last few years. In 1963, 528 areas were qualified as distressed

---

[30] Brian J. L. Berry and others, *Metropolitan Area Definition: A Re-evaluation of Concept and Statistical Practice.* U.S. Department of Commerce, Bureau of the Census, Working Paper No. 28 (Washington, D.C.: Government Printing Office, June 1968).

on grounds of their substantial and persistent unemployment. Four years later, when the rate of national unemployment was steady at around 4 per cent, approximately two-thirds of these large and medium-size labour markets had been removed from the list of qualified areas because of the drop in their unemployment level. However, at the same date almost 57 per cent of the smallest size group remained qualified. In general then, high redevelopment potential seems to be a function of the size of the community, so that the prospects for small communities distant from major urban centres, appear to be distinctly unfavourable.[31]

Migration to Growth Centers

The growth center strategy is sometimes presented as an alternative to migration from backward rural areas and small towns. Nevertheless, it would appear that migration does and should play an important role in a successful growth center strategy.

First, "commuting range" is a somewhat elastic concept. The 50 miles suggested by Fox is certainly feasible with automobiles and good highways; but most people prefer not to commute that far if they can avoid it. Growth of employment opportunity in a growth center, then, normally will attract from such distances people who initially commute but eventually move closer. Some local inward migration *within* the zone of influence of a growth center is, then, a part of the development sequence.

Second, it would be entirely unrealistic to expect a regional development strategy to eliminate incentives and need for migration *among* zones of influence of various urban centers. No development plan can or should aspire to make the growth of employment opportunity in each region or labor market area exactly match the natural increase rate of the working-age population.

Finally, our consideration of the apparent size requirements for a viable growth center strongly suggests that in many poorer and less-developed regions substantial areas will lie outside of even a 50-mile range of any urban center of sufficient size and promise to merit growth center status. Though no one would propose the blanket evacuation of all such areas, it seems clear that most or all of their natural increase of population, and perhaps also some of their existing population, will need to move out in order to find adequate opportunity for self-supporting employment.

An assumption implicit in the growth center strategy is that people in backward regions will migrate more readily to a growth center in their own region than they will to places outside that region. Distance is assumed to be an important determinant of migration flow.

Proximity does indeed seem to encourage migration—thus bearing out one of Ravenstein's Laws and the deductions of theorists. The actual costs

---

[31] Gordon C. Cameron, "The Regional Problem in the United States—Some Reflections on a Viable Federal Strategy," *Regional Studies,* 2 (1968), 216.

of moving are probably less important in this connection than the "social distance" involved in moving to an area with very different characteristics and climate and in which there is a smaller probability of knowing someone (see the beaten-path principle cited in Chapter 7).

But the big hurdle to be overcome in inducing migration from backward areas to employment centers involves the initial decision to move at all. The social distance from any farm or village to a sizable city is enormously greater than that separating different rural areas or different urban places of similar size, and many people in backward areas suffer special disabilities of lack of education, training, and information. The evidence does suggest that such people will probably move more readily to a growth center within, say, 100 miles from home than they would to an entirely different part of the country; and, therefore, the creation of more jobs in such growth centers will help them in getting employed. But clearly the strategy must also involve measures to improve mobility and employability as such, and to facilitate entry into productive employment at the growth center.[32]

The implication of focusing attention on employment in rather few growth centers, all of substantial size, is that many or perhaps most such centers will lie outside the boundaries of regions demarcated on the basis of such indices as high unemployment, low income, or slow growth. Measures aimed at stimulating employment by improving infrastructure and inducing private investment may thus be most effective when applied in places already relatively well off, active, and prosperous; while measures applied to less-urbanized and poorer areas may be confined largely to human resources development and to income supplements for people who, because of age or disability, cannot be expected to solve their problems by migrating.

---

[32] The Appalachian Regional Commission (see p. 288) made a sample survey of the gross migration of workers (using Social Security records) between 1960 and 1964, and found that ". . . the migrant workers displayed a distinct tendency to move relatively short distances. Most migrants from the center of Appalachia migrated to nearby areas, still within Appalachia. Migrants from the fringes of Appalachia were more likely to move to the ring of territory surrounding the Region, or to other parts of the United States. . . . all outmigrants increased their income substantially, especially those leaving the central part of Appalachia, where hardcore unemployment has been most severe." *Appalachia,* 2, 8 (May 1969), 14–15.

The Executive Director of the Appalachian Regional Commission observed in 1967 that there are large colonies of recent migrants from Appalachia in Chicago, Cleveland, Cincinnati, and a number of other cities outside the region, while "there are no Appalachian neighborhoods in Pittsburgh despite the fact that it is the only major metropolis in the area." Some explanation for this surprising fact, as he pointed out, lies in the structure and relative low growth rate of the Pittsburgh economy. But this example is useful in suggesting that centers well outside the boundaries of a depressed or backward area can provide employment opportunities to people living in such an area. Ralph R. Widner, "Experiment in Appalachia," *Pittsburgh Business Review,* 37, 3 (March 1967), 1–15.

MAJOR UNITED STATES REGIONAL
DEVELOPMENT PROGRAMS

The foregoing discussion has disclosed the main policy issues involved in national efforts to assist regional development as a means of improving people's welfare; it has suggested solutions with which the reader may or may not wholly agree. It has likewise noted. some of the administrative and political difficulties complicating strategy decisions and their implementation.

Let us now see how these problems have been handled in the major programs of regional development assistance in the United States in recent years. We shall not try to deal with the strategies and programs (many of them quite similar) that have been developed in other countries. Nor shall we go into much detail regarding the American experience, since this field of public concern and action is in a state of flux and any account of current programs or accomplishments would be quickly outdated.

The Area Redevelopment Administration
and the Economic Development
Administration

The Economic Development Administration (EDA) was set up in the U.S. Department of Commerce by the Public Works and Economic Development Act of 1965 to replace a predecessor agency, the Area Redevelopment Administration (ARA). Both were empowered to help local public authorities to build or improve public service facilities (such as sewer systems) by grants or loans, to provide part of the financing for construction of private commercial or industrial facilities, and to aid areas in development analysis and planning through technical assistance in kind or through grants to support such work. The purpose of this assistance is to increase employment opportunity in the specific areas where aid is given by making those areas more attractive to private investors in terms of the availability of capital and public services.

Areas of eligibility are defined at three different levels of size. For projects of very local significance, the unit is the "redevelopment area," which can be as small as a county, a city, an Indian reservation, or, in certain cases, even smaller. Eligibility can be established on the basis of either "substantial and persistent unemployment" or markedly low income level.[33]

The EDA operation, as described so far, is similar to its ARA predecessor. The policies of Place Prosperity, worst-first, and reliance on stimuli to employment-creating investment appear dominant. One of the reasons

---

[33] Special eligibility categories are provided for Indian reservations and for areas experiencing or threatened by "unusual and abrupt rise in unemployment"; and there is the interesting stipulation that each state must always have at least one redevelopment area regardless of the other criteria.

for the new 1965 legislation, however, was dissatisfaction with the exclusive emphasis on such an approach under which ARA operated. An important feature of the EDA program is the creation of a set of larger units, known as economic development districts. Each such district must contain at least two redevelopment areas plus at least one "economic development center" (growth center), and those centers are eligible for assistance of the types already described. Local initiative to form development districts is stimulated by a provision for extra funding for redevelopment areas that are part of development districts. The economic development center must have "sufficient size and potential to foster the economic growth activities necessary to alleviate the distress of the redevelopment areas within the district," but must not have a population of more than 250,000.

The stated purpose of this application of the growth center concept is "that economic development projects of broader geographical significance may be planned[34] and carried out." Although size and potential are recognized as criteria for aid to the growth centers, and the latter are recognized as useful in helping the distressed areas, the act makes no mention of the possibility that people in the redevelopment areas might be helped by migrating to the growth centers. Our earlier discussion suggested that such migration is probably the principal way in which the growth centers can help, and that quite different strategies are appropriate in growth centers and in distressed outlying areas respectively. But EDA's mandate appears to assume that the same kinds of assistance are appropriate in both places.

Another point to be noted is that there is no specific minimum population size for growth centers, though there is a maximum of 250,000 (corresponding to what has been suggested by some regional economists as a *minimum* for self-sustaining growth!). The standards provided in the law do not provide much resistance to the predictable local pressures for designation of an ever-increasing number of small development districts and centers, since a combination as small as just two poor counties and a town could be designated as a district.[35]

The Regional Commissions

The same Public Works and Economic Development Act of 1965 also provided for designation of still larger areas called economic development regions, extending into two or more states. Each such region has a regional

---

[34] As a condition of eligibility, both redevelopment areas and economic development districts are required to prepare approved plans for their development.

[35] A redevelopment area can be eligible with as few as 1,500 people (or 1,000 in the case of an Indian reservation).

commission made up of a representative of each of the states involved plus a federal representative with veto power. The prototype was the Appalachian Regional Commission, established under separate legislation in 1965, but with similar purposes and powers. For our purposes, we can consider them all together, including Appalachia.

Economic development regions are defined on the basis of

1. High unemployment
2. Low income
3. Low levels of "housing, health and educational facilities"
4. Dominance of the regional economy by "only one or two industries, which are in a state of long-term decline"
5. Substantial out-migration of labor, capital, or both
6. Low growth rate of aggregate output
7. Adverse effects from changing industrial technology or changes in national defense facilities or production

The regional commissions are primarily designed to secure interstate cooperation and a broader perspective for development planning and action within areas much larger than development districts. They are expected to produce plans for a coordinated attack on the economic problems of their respective regions through all kinds of existing and proposed federal and state programs. They are, of course, in competition with one another for federal assistance, though some respect for the general national interest is expected to be introduced by the federal co-chairman of each commission. Each regional commission has advisory functions regarding the initiation and coordination of economic development districts.[36]

Fig. 9-1 shows the location and extent of the development regions established up to October 1969. All of them meet the criterion of relatively slow growth and substantial net outward migration, and all of them with the striking exception of New England are undeveloped, low-income, primarily rural areas with little industrialization or urbanization (that is, backward regions). By contrast, New England is the patriarch of American regions in terms of industrial and urban development, has an income level comparing favorably with the national average, and does not have especially high unemployment. If it is a "problem area" at all, it cannot be rated as such on the basis of underdevelopment or poverty as can the others.[37] The inclusion of New England probably reflects instead a positive factor: the region has been ahead of others in achieving a sense of common regional interest and developing effective interstate cooperation. This

---

[36] Except in Appalachia, where the commission itself exercises the functions performed by the EDA for the other economic development regions.

[37] What is said here applies to New England as a whole and to the 3 southern states of that region where four-fifths of its people live. Much of northern New England, by contrast, does share many of the economic characteristics of backward low-income rural areas in other parts of the country.

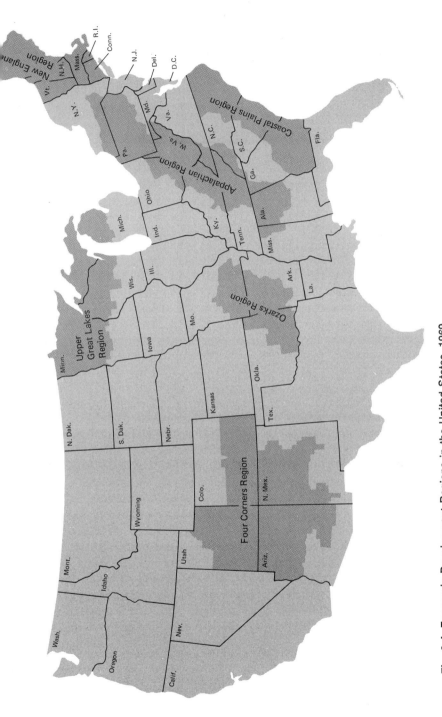

Fig. 9-1. Economic Development Regions in the United States, 1969
SOURCE: *Manpower Report of the President* (Washington, D.C.: Government Printing Office, 1968), Chart 23, p. 139. Prepared by U.S. Department of Labor on the basis of data from the U.S. Department of Commerce; modified by present author to show subsequent extension of the Appalachian Region into Mississippi.

early start reflects the facts that the challenge of industrial stagnation came early in New England, reaching almost crisis proportions in the 1920s with the loss of the textile and other industries, and that the New England states are very small in size compared with those in other parts of the country.

The establishment of New England as an economic development region suggests, in fact, that it would be appropriate to carve up the whole country into development regions instead of using them as special devices for recognizably sick areas of wide extent. It is questionable, at best, whether a homogeneous region defined in terms of backwardness and distress is a proper unit for constructive and efficient development policy.

Appalachia, for example, is not a region at all in the sense of an area with strong internal linkages. Appalachians in Pennsylvania or West Virginia may resemble Appalachians in Alabama with respect to income level, education and training, style of life, and attitudes, but they are not linked to them by any significant flows of trade or migration. A conspicuous characteristic of Appalachia, in fact, is the lack of facilities for internal movement. Much more meaningfully, Appalachia should be regarded as a succession of hinterlands to various major centers located mainly outside the region as officially defined: a row of back yards, as it were. We are led to the view that

> . . . a good part of Appalachia's development effort should be concentrated outside the region, and . . . the region itself should be restructured and, as it were, apportioned among the metropolitan regions on its perimeter.[38]

Similar statements could be made about some of the other economic development regions as well.

It is true that development assistance in Appalachia has heavily emphasized roads with the avowed intention of "opening up" the region to the outside world and to such cities as it contains. But there is no evidence of any effort to encourage out-migration from this or the other economic development regions. On the contrary, loss of population is stipulated as one of the criteria of eligibility for development assistance; and by implication at least, as one of the conditions to be corrected.

If the most promising areas of future growth are metropolitan centers with populations in six figures (as comparative growth trends and surveys of infrastructure costs and people's living preferences strongly suggest), then the appropriate units for programs of employment creation are regions with such centers as focal points. Establishment of a nationwide set of development planning and action regions should not be too long de-

---

[38] John Friedmann, "Poor Regions and Poor Nations: Perspectives on the Problem of Appalachia," *Southern Economic Journal*, 4 (April 1966), 472.

layed, because it will have to overcome the inertia and vested interests of the existing problem area jurisdictions.

A further argument for redesigning development regions so as to give a more positive role to moderately large urban growth centers throughout the country is that it could put us in a better position to restrain excessive concentration of population and employment in the large megalopolises. For reasons already stated, it can be expected that an effort to absorb the surplus manpower of backward areas by forcing the growth of hundreds[39] of growth centers of inadequate size and promise will not be particularly effective. Migrants from such areas are now attracted in large and probably excessive numbers to the slums of the giant cities. If some of this flow could be diverted to intermediate-sized cities (mostly outside of the present economic development regions) by migrant guidance and by stimuli to employment growth in such centers, we should be getting growth where it is most productive and at the same time easing the population growth pressures and related urban problems of the places where such problems are most evident. These aspects of urban adjustment are taken up in Chapter 12.

Finally, the organization of regional planning and development efforts in regions built around major growth centers with demonstrably high potential would have important political and administrative advantages over the long run. Such regions would have the internal economic cohesion that is missing in an area like Appalachia and would have the growth potential and the resources to plan and implement efficient development strategies on their own.[40] The combination of recognized intraregional interdependence, greater consciousness of a common regional interest, and financial and technical strength could check the trend toward ever-increasing dependence upon federal initiatives, decisions, and specific subsidies. The federal role could be less paternal and philanthropic, and could con-

---

[39] As of June 1969, 69 planning and development districts had been designated in Appalachia alone. Their populations ranged from 8,202 to 2,826,400. *Appalachia,* 2, 9 (June–July 1969), 36. Many districts contain more than one designated center.

[40] Gordon Cameron concludes, on the basis of a penetrating analysis of development trends in U.S. regions: "All of these factors suggest that every *region* [he refers to the 9 Census Regions] is capable of sustaining a satisfactory rate of growth in employment, and that some regions which are especially well endowed with natural and environmental features, have particularly favourable opportunities for rapid expansion. This thesis tends to be confirmed both by the marked convergence in the ratio of manufacturing employment to population among the various regions of the country, and by the small deviation in regional growth rates from the national growth rate, during the period of full employment and fast expansion in the 1960's. . . .

"And yet the crucial point is that growth is not spread evenly within each region. All the evidence suggests that it is the large metropolitan areas which have increasingly dominated U.S. production, sucked in an ever-growing share of U.S. population, and outpaced the growth of the spatial regions which contain them." *Op. cit.,* p. 216.

sist mainly of maintenance of high overall levels of demand, provision of information and aggregate national development guidelines, and design of programs to improve the quality and mobility of human resources.

SELECTED READINGS

Committee for Economic Development, *Distressed Areas in a Growing Economy* (New York: Committee for Economic Development, 1961).

John E. Moes, *Local Subsidies for Industry* (Chapel Hill: University of North Carolina Press, 1962).

John Friedmann and William Alonso, *Regional Development and Planning,* Part IV, "National Policy for Regional Development" (Cambridge, Mass.: M.I.T. Press, 1964).

Thomas Wilson, *Policies for Regional Development,* University of Glasgow, Social and Economic Studies, Occasional Paper No. 3 (Edinburgh and London: Oliver & Boyd, 1964).

John H. Cumberland, "A Regional Inter-Industry Model for Analysis of Development Objectives," *Papers of the Regional Science Association,* 17 (1966), 65–94.

John Friedmann, *Regional Development Policy: A Case Study of Venezuela* (Cambridge, Mass.: M.I.T. Press, 1966).

E. J. Mishan, *The Costs of Economic Growth* (London: Staples Press, 1967).

Niles Hansen, *French Regional Planning* (Bloomington: Indiana University Press, 1968).

E. A. G. Robinson (ed.), *Backward Areas in Advanced Countries* (London: Macmillan, 1969).

Horst Siebert, *Regional Economic Growth: Theory and Policy* (Scranton, Pa.: International Textbook Co., 1969).

Harry W. Richardson, *Regional Economics* (New York: Praeger, 1969), Chs. 14–15.

Upper Great Lakes Regional Commission, *Growth Centers and Their Potentials in the Upper Great Lakes Region* (Washington, D.C.: Upper Great Lakes Regional Commission, May 1969; report prepared by Brian J. L. Berry).

Niles Hansen, *Rural Poverty and the Urban Crisis: A Strategy for Regional Development* (Bloomington: Indiana University Press, 1970).

Gordon C. Cameron, "Growth Areas, Growth Centres and Regional Conversion," *Scottish Journal of Political Economy,* 17, 1 (February 1970), 19–38.

APPENDIX 9-1

The Shift-Share Analysis of Components of Regional Activity Growth
(See pages 263 and 266)

The overall growth rate of a region's activity (as measured, say, by total employment or total value added) is, of course, a weighted average of the growth rates of the separate sectors or activities making up the region's economy. If the region's growth rate is compared with that of some other area (for example, the entire nation), it is possible to "explain" the difference in growth rates statistically in terms of two components, which for convenience can be styled "mix" and "competitive." Quantitative analysis of comparative regional growth rates along these lines is sometimes referred to as the "shift-share" approach.[41]

An example of a regional growth differential arising exclusively from mix would be the case of a region in which each activity grows at exactly the same rate as in the nation as a whole. In other words, the region's *share* of the national total for each industry remains unchanged over the time interval in question. But the national growth rates for some activities are higher than those for others. If our region contains mainly fast-growing activities and relatively few of the slow-growing activities, it can be said to have a "favorable growth mix" of activities and its overall percentage growth rate will exceed that of the nation. On the other hand, if slow-growing industries are more than proportionally represented in the region's mix, the region's overall growth rate will be slower than the national growth rate. This is an example of the pure mix effect.

We can evaluate the competitive component by imagining the case of a region that has exactly the same mix of activities as does the nation: its percentage share of the national total is the same for all activities. This region will have an overall growth rate higher than that of the nation if it increases its shares (that is, if each activity grows faster in the region than in the nation). Such a case represents the competitive component in isolation.

In any real situation, of course, it is nearly certain that the relative growth rates of region and nation will show the effects of some combination of mix and competitive components. Either effect, and the net result, can be either positive or negative for the region.

A drastically simplified numerical example will serve to show the way in which shift-share analysis determines the effect to be imputed to each

---

[41] This approach was apparently first used by Daniel B. Creamer in 1942 in U.S. National Resources Planning Board, *Industrial Location and National Resources* (Washington, 1943) and was expounded and used on a large scale by Edgar S. Dunn, Jr., in Harvey S. Perloff, E. S. Dunn, Jr., E. E. Lampard, and R. F. Muth, *Regions, Resources, and Economic Growth* (Baltimore: Johns Hopkins Press, 1960). The basic exposition of the method is in Ch. 5, 63–74, of that source. What we are calling the "mix component" corresponds to Dunn's "net proportionality shift," and our "competitive component" corresponds to his "net differential shift." The method was later applied still more extensively in the U.S. Department of Commerce by Dunn and others, and comprehensive tabulations have been prepared and published for U.S. Census regions and smaller areas. See Lowell D. Ashby, *Growth Patterns in Employment by County, 1940–50 and 1950–60* (Washington, D.C.: Government Printing Office, 1965).

The logic and usefulness of the shift-share approach were attacked by David B. Houston, "The Shift and Share Analysis of Regional Growth: A Critique," *Southern Economic Journal*, 33, 4 (April 1967), 577–581. A rejoinder in defense was given by Lowell D. Ashby in the same journal, "The Shift and Share Analysis: A Reply," 34, 3 (January 1968), 423–425. A more recent critique is H. James Brown, "Shift and Share Projections of Regional Economic Growth: An Empirical Test," *Journal of Regional Science*, 9, 1 (April 1969), 1–18.

component. Let us take the following Census data on manufacturing employment (in thousands) : [42]

	United States		Pennsylvania	
	1958	**1963**	**1958**	**1963**
All industries	15,800	16,715	1,331	1,320
Durable goods	7,680	8,418	718	709
Nondurable goods	8,120	8,297	613	611

From these data we see that manufacturing employment in the United States increased by 5.79 percent (from 15,800 to 16,715 thousand) in the five-year interval. If manufacturing employment in Pennsylvania had registered this same rate of increase, it would have risen from 1,331 to 1,408 thousand persons. Actually, the 1963 employment in Pennsylvania was only 1,320 thousand, so there is a total difference of -88 thousand to be explained.

To evaluate the mix component, we can eliminate the competitive one by assuming that each of the two kinds of industries grew at the same rate in Pennsylvania as in the nation (that is, durable goods industries 9.61 percent and nondurables 2.18 percent). Had those sectoral growth rates applied in Pennsylvania, the state's manufacturing employment in 1963 would have been $718 \times 1.0961 = 787$ thousand in durables and $613 \times 1.0218 = 626$ thousand in nondurables, or a total of 1,413 thousand. So the mix effect operating in the absence of any competitive effect would have raised Pennsylvania's manufacturing employment to 1,413 thousand, or 5 thousand more than what would have been achieved by simply keeping pace with national growth. We can express this result by saying that Pennsylvania had a favorable growth mix compared to the nation (in this case, meaning a higher proportion of durable goods industries in its mix), and the 5 thousand figure is a measure of that advantage, or the mix component of growth.

But as noted earlier, Pennsylvania's actual growth fell 88 thousand short of what would have been achieved by keeping pace with the nation. The competitive component, then, must be $-88 - 5 = -93$ thousand. This figure is a measure of the result of the fact that Pennsylvania's *share of the national total* dropped in both durable and nondurable goods industries; that is, Pennsylvania industries lost out to that extent in competitive position vis-à-vis the rest of the country.

---

[42] Industry Group 19 (ordnance and accessories) has been omitted here, since data for Pennsylvania are not available. Minor adjustments in the totals have been made to take account of rounding-off errors in adding up the figures for individual industry groups to arrive at the subtotals for durable and nondurable goods industries. Basic data were taken from the 1963 U.S. Census of Manufactures reports.

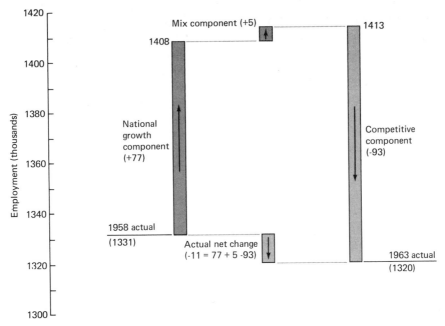

Fig. 9-A-1. Components of Change in Pennsylvania Manufacturing Employment, 1958 to 1963, According to Shift-Share Analysis

The results of this dissection of growth components are diagrammed in Fig. 9-A-1. All the figures are expressed in absolute terms (thousands of employees), since they are additive. In comparing the mix and competitive shifts of different regions, however, it might sometimes be preferable to express them in relative terms (for example, as percentages of the initial employment in the respective region).

The observed changes in Pennsylvania employment in each industrial sector can be split into two components. If durables employment in Pennsylvania had increased at the national rate of 9.61 percent it would have grown to 787 thousand in 1963 (an increase of 69 thousand). Similarly, Pennsylvania nondurables employment would have increased by 13 thousand if the state's share of the national total had been maintained. The entire set of results can be summarized as follows for this illustrative case (all figures in thousands):

	Total manufacturing	Durable goods industries	Nondurable goods industries
Total change	−11	−9	−2
National growth	+77	+69	+13
Competitive	−93	−78	−15
Mix	+5		

INTRODUCTION

The remainder of this book is concerned with spatial relations within the special type of region represented by the individual urban or metropolitan area.[1] Such an area includes a principal city with a relatively dense core or downtown area (the central business district) and a surrounding fringe of suburbs and satellites linked to it by trade, commutation, and other socioeconomic interaction.

An increasing majority of the population in advanced countries lives in areas of this type. In the United States, roughly six-tenths of the total population lives in Standard Metropolitan Statistical Areas with populations of more than 250,000 and another tenth in SMSAs smaller than 250,000.

Patterns of location, locational preference, and land use in urban areas are continually shifting. "Urban problems" emerge from these changes and from the intense interaction that characterizes the urban setting. Some of these problems will be examined in the final chapter, but we first need to get a clear picture of the factors determining urban spatial patterns and their changes.

LOCATION FACTORS

One important feature of location in urban areas is the large role that *movement of people and direct face-to-face contact* play in access and transfer relations. A crucial function of cities is to make it possible for large numbers of people to make contact easily and frequently for work, consultation, buying and selling, negotiating, instruction, and other purposes. People are more expensive to transport than almost anything else, mainly because their time is so valuable.

Accordingly, intracity locations are governed by powerful linkage attractions operating over short

10
The Spatial Structure of Urban Areas

---

[1] Much of the content in this chapter and parts of Chapters 11 and 12 are taken or adapted from my article "The Evolving Form and Organization of the Metropolis," in Harvey S. Perloff and Lowdon Wingo, Jr. (eds.), *Issues in Urban Economics* (Baltimore: Johns Hopkins Press for Resources for the Future, 1968), 237–284.

distances and emphasizing speed of travel. Time costs are more important than money costs in most urban linkages.

Another feature of urban locations is the intense *interdependence* caused by proximity and by competition for space and other nontransferable inputs. Every activity affects many neighbors, for better or for worse: external economies and diseconomies and neighborhood effects are always strong. The cost of occupying space is a major factor in location, and the relevance of the line of analysis set forth in Chapter 5 is correspondingly high.

Central-place concepts also are relevant to the determination of activity patterns within urban areas. The various concentrations of consumer-serving activity are the counterpart of the hierarchy of major and minor trade centers in a region. The downtown area, or central business district, plays a special role as the apex of the central-place hierarchy, and has a number of other unique features. It characteristically represents the highest peak of the urban rent gradient; the most important nexus of transport routes; the location with the largest variety of external economies; and the place with the highest density of daytime population and the most congestion of movement.

When we try to construct a conceptual scheme or model describing the way in which various residential and nonresidential activities are spatially distributed in an urban area, we find a vast web of interdependence. Shopping centers locate primarily on the basis of access to consumers; people like to live close to their work, schools, shopping areas, and other types of facilities that they have occasion to use; business firms are variously attracted by access to labor supply, other related firms, or transportation facilities. In many kinds of urban activities, like seeks like: there are strong pressures for neighborhood homogeneity as such, as illustrated by the exclusive suburb, the garment district, and the automobile row. Finally, every user of space also has to consider its price, and that will depend on how desirable the site is to other users.

Independent Locations

There are, however, some kinds of locations within an urban area that can be regarded as independently determined, and which, therefore, make a convenient starting point for an understanding of the whole pattern. In fact, there are two distinct bases for exogenous determination of locations in an urban area. For some activities, certain topographical or other natural site features are essential; this means that the lay of the land narrows the choice to one or a very small number of locations. Ports for water traffic illustrate this, and there are some urban areas where the topography limits jet airport sites almost as drastically; in the past, considerations of defense played a major part in locating the heart of the city and the city itself. Localized recreational features such as beaches also illustrate this kind of factor, and in a few urban areas extractive industries (mainly mining) occur and are, of course, limited to certain special sites.

There is a further type of exogenously determined location where the independent influence arises not from site features as much as from the fact that the activity requires contact with the outside world. Not just water ports but all kinds of terminal and interarea transport activities come under this head. Since there are great economies of scale in inter-regional transport and in terminal handling of goods, the urban area's gateways to and from the outside world constitute a set of focal points, whose locations within the area help to determine—rather than just being determined by—the other activities of the area. This does not mean, of course, that such terminal locations are absolutely and permanently unresponsive to the changing pattern of other activities in the area served. Such terminals are from time to time shifted so as to improve local accessibility or to make way for more insistent claimants for the space. But the terminal locations do play an active role in shaping the pattern and are to be viewed as part of the basic framework around which other activities are fitted.

The Center

There is also a strong element of exogenous determination in the location of the point of "maximum overall accessibility" within the urban area. If we think of this, for example, as the place where all the people of the area could assemble with the least total man-miles of travel, it is the "median center of population" and would seem to depend simply upon the location of the various types of residence. But travel is cheaper and faster along developed routes, and the cost and layout of these routes are affected by scale (traffic volume) and topography. Thus, evaluated in terms of travel cost and time, the focal maximum-access point can be regarded as a rather stable datum, even though the extent and importance of its access advantage over other points can change radically. In major American urban areas, despite great overall growth, far-reaching change, and redistribution of activities, the focal point, in this sense, has usually shifted only a relatively short distance over periods measured in decades and generations, and the earlier central foci are well within what we currently recognize as the central business district.

This concept of a single "most central" focal point in an urban area is then significant and useful in developing simplified bases for understanding the overall pattern. Obviously, it has its limitations, some of which will be discussed now and others later. First, there is really a variety of distinguishable central points of this sort, depending on what kinds of people or things we are imagining to be assembled with a minimum of total expense or effort. The employed workers of the area are not distributed in quite the same pattern as the total population, the shopping population, the school-attending population, the office workers, the industrial blue-collar workers, the theater-going or the library-using population; there might be a different optimum location from the standpoint of access to each of these types of people. Where goods rather than people are moving (for example, in the case of wholesale activity or production serving local needs such as daily newspapers or bread), the transport conditions are different, and this may again mean a different optimum-access point. Finally, we have to recognize that, in varying degrees, the concept of one single point serving as the origin or destination for all flows of a specified type is unrealistic, and defensible only as a convenient fiction. Thus, if we identify some central point as having best access to the homes of the entire clerical office force of an urban area, this does not imply that all offices should logically be concentrated there. What it does imply is that, solely from the standpoint of commuting access for the clerical workers and ignoring claims of alternative use of space, it would make sense for the density of clerical employment to peak at that point.

The Access Factor

Since the function of an urban concentration is to facilitate contacts, the most important class of location factors shaping the spatial pattern involves the advantage of physical proximity as measured by money and time saved. This applies to cases in which such costs are substantially increased by added distance; where they are not, they have nothing to do with urban concentration. For example, information in a broader sense (including not only the printed word but sounds, computer signals, and various types of pictures) can now be transmitted electronically over long distances just as quickly as over short distances, and sometimes just as cheaply to the user. This kind of contact, then, does not in itself depend upon, or help to maintain or explain, intraurban concentration.

Most relevant to the urban pattern are types of access for which costs are high and increase very rapidly with distance within the intraurban range of distances (ranging from "next door" to a few dozen miles). Access involving human travel belongs to this category. Human beings require more elaborate and expensive vehicles (in dollars per ton of "freight") than does almost anything else. And in particular, the time cost generally becomes even more important than the actual transport cost.

The various kinds of access linkage that tie together the urban complex can be meaningfully classified in many ways: for example, by mode of transport or communication, or according to whether the incentive toward proximity is thought to influence predominantly the location of the sender or the receiver of whatever is being transported. A useful classification can be based on the distinction between households and other decision units—that is, between residential and nonresidential activities.

Access linkages *among nonresidential activity units* involve in part "interindustry" transactions such as those recorded in an input-output table. Thus, business firms have an incentive to locate with good access to their local suppliers and their local business customers. Some important interbusiness linkages, however, do not directly involve such transactions at all. Local branch offices or outlets of a firm are presumably located with an eye to maintaining good access to the main local office, while at the same time avoiding overlap of the sublocal territories served by the branches (for example, the individual supermarkets of a chain or branch offices of a bank). There are strong access ties between the central office of a corporation and its main research laboratory, involving the frequent going and coming of highly paid personnel.

Linkages *among households* are also important. A significant proportion of journeys from homes are to the homes of others. Such trips are by nature almost exclusively social, and thus involve people linked by family ties or similar tastes and interests. This suggests that the value of inter-household access can also be expressed fairly accurately in terms of homogeneity preferences. However, as we shall see later, the pressures toward neighborhood homogeneity include other factors besides access.

Linkages *between residential and nonresidential units* are by far the most conspicuous type in the urban pattern. The entire labor force, with minor exceptions, is concerned with making the daily journey to work as quick and painless as possible, and work trips are the largest single class of personal journeys within any urban area.[2] Shopping trips are another major category. The distribution of goods and services at retail makes mutual proximity an advantage for both the distributors and the customers. Trips to school, and cultural and recreational trips, make up most of the rest of the personal trip pattern. There is mutual advantage of proximity throughout. The nonresidential activities dealing with households are most advantageously placed when they are close to concentrations of population, and at the same time residential sites are preferred (other things being equal) when they provide convenient access to jobs, shopping districts, schools, and other destinations.

Agglomerative Factors

Access considerations involve a mutual attraction between complementary parties: store and customer, firm and employee, school and pupil. But there are also economic incentives favoring the concentration and

---

[2] For relevant reference material, see J. R. Meyer, J. F. Kain, and M. Wohl, *The Urban Transportation Problem* (Cambridge, Mass.: Harvard University Press, 1965) and Louis K. Loewenstein, *The Location of Residences and Work Places in Urban Areas* (New York: Scarecrow Press, 1965). Also, for a primarily bibliographical survey of the whole question of access, see Gunnar Olsson, *Distance and Human Interaction: A Review and Bibliography*, Bibliography Series, No. 2 (Philadelphia: Regional Science Research Institute, 1965).

clustering of identical or similar units of activity. The simplest case of this is perhaps that of scale economies. A large electric power plant is more efficient than a smaller one. A large store can, in addition to possible cost savings, provide more variety and thus enhance its attractiveness to buyers. As already suggested above and in Chapter 6, some kinds of activities (such as opera performances) are subject to scale economies to the extent that only in the largest cities can more than one establishment be supported. Business corporations as a rule find that they can best concentrate their research laboratories at one location, and the same applies more obviously to their central offices.

The tendency to clustering of similar or related activities subject to external economies of agglomeration was analyzed in Chapter 4. Since most of these economies require close and frequent contact (personal movement and face-to-face interaction), they tend to bring units together not merely in the same city but in the same district of the city.

Neighborhood Externalities

Proximity can have unfavorable as well as favorable effects. "Neighborhood character" in terms of cleanliness, smells, noise, traffic congestion, public safety, variety interest, and general appearance is important in attracting some kinds of use and repelling others. Prestige types of residence or business are, of course, particularly sensitive to this kind of advantage, which often is more important than any access consideration as such. A high-income householder may be willing to lengthen his work journey greatly for the sake of neighborhood amenity or agreeable surroundings.

As was suggested earlier, the usual effect of this type of consideration is to make neighborhoods more homogeneous within themselves, and more unlike other neighborhoods: a tendency toward areal specialization by uses, or "segregation" in the broad sense. With few exceptions, a given type of activity finds advantage in being in a neighborhood devoted to reasonably similar kinds of uses, and disadvantage in being in violent contrast to the neighborhood pattern. Zoning controls and planned street layouts play a part in reinforcing this tendency.

The Price of Land

Most of the relationships thus far mentioned are pulls or positive linkages—they involve a mutual locational attraction among complementary or similar units of activity. This reflects the underlying rationale of a city as a device promoting close contact and interaction on a grand scale.

But every land use needs some space or elbowroom in which to operate, and the sites with best access or environmental features command a high scarcity value. The real-estate market mechanism works, albeit imperfectly like most markets, to allocate locations to uses and users who can exploit them to best advantage, as measured by what they are willing to bid for their use. As the discussion in Chapter 5 suggested, von Thünen's simplified model of the patterns of rural land use arising from the competition of various activities for space is applicable in some degree to urban land use patterns, but with substantial modifications.

SYMMETRICAL UNICENTRIC MODELS OF URBAN FORM

Bases of Simplification

The various determinants of location in an urban area have been catalogued above in some detail. But basically there are three kinds of considerations that determine the relative desirability of locations for particular decision units, such as households or business establishments. These are (1) environmental characteristics, (2) access, and (3) cost. They reflect the fact that the user of a site is concerned with it in three distinct ways. He *occupies* it, as resident or producer, and is thus concerned with its "site and neighborhood," or immediate environmental qualities. He and other persons and goods and services *move* between this site and others, and he is therefore concerned with its convenience of access to other places. Finally, he has to *pay* for its use and is therefore concerned with its cost.

Considerable simplification along these lines makes possible the useful step of building a schematic picture, or model, of the spatial structure of an urban economy. For example, in such a model we can reduce the complex factor of "access" to the simple form of proximity to a single focal point, as if all intraurban journeys were to or from downtown and all shipments of goods also passed through downtown.

We can eliminate all differentiation of sites with respect to topography, amenity, and environmental advantage. These two simplifications also imply ignoring, for the time being, the manifold types of external economy effects and environmental attractions and repulsions that have been discussed. In effect, we envisage each type of activity as independently attracted (by access considerations) toward the urban center. The only interdependence among the locations of the various activities arises, then, from the fact that they are bidding against one another for space.

With the above simplifications and still others, it is possible to develop workable frameworks of analysis for urban spatial patterns. Most such models are "partial" in the sense that they attempt to explain or predict the location of one type of activity in terms of its adjustment to given or assumed locations of the other activities, including transportation services. Thus, a retailing location model may analyze the way in which retail stores locate in response to the advantages of access to the homes of consumers; a residential location model may analyze the way in which residences locate in response to the desire to shorten the journey to work; and so on.

The Density Gradient

Perhaps the most elementary aspect of an urban pattern is the way in which intensity of land use varies with distance from the center, assuming a symmetrical circular pattern. Implicit here is the concept of a city as a multitude of space-occupying activity units seeking close contact. If these activity units are affected by more or less the same kind of access attraction (as, for example, households are affected by the desire to shorten the journey to work), and have some leeway in the amount of space they occupy, we should expect their density (intensity of space use) to be at a peak at the center (the optimum total-access point) and to fall off in all directions with increasing distance from the center. Such a tendency can be described by a density gradient, where density is a negative function of radial distance.

In this simple scheme the decline of density with distance depends (1) on the rate at which the area's noncentral activity units (households, in a purely residential journey-to-work model) are willing to trade off spaciousness of home sites against a quicker or cheaper journey to the center, and (2) on the time and money cost of transport. Obviously, a variety of circumstances—such as better transport in some directions than in others and variations in site quality—can complicate this neat symmetrical picture in the real world.

As Colin Clark demonstrated, the gradient of population density with respect to radial distance, in a wide selection of large modern cities, has a consistent shape, identifiable as an exponential function. In any specified city, residential density tends to fall by a uniform percentage with each unit increase in distance from the center. Any such gradient can therefore be specified by two parameters: D_0, the peak density at the center, and b, a slope factor, in the following formula:

$$D_x = D_0 e^{-bx}$$

where x represents radial distance and e is 2.718 . . . , the base of natural logarithms.[3] Several actual gradients are shown in Fig. 10-1.

---

[3] Colin Clark, "Urban Population Densities," *Journal of the Royal Statistical Society,* Series A, 114 (1951), 490–496.

This same form of density gradient can alternatively be expressed in terms of the *logarithms* of the densities as follows: $\ln D_x = \ln D_0 - bx$. The logarithm of density is thus linearly related to distance and the gradient can be plotted as a straight line on a chart if a logarithmic (ratio) scale is used for density. The percentage rate of decline in density per unit of distance is equal to $100/e^b - 100$.

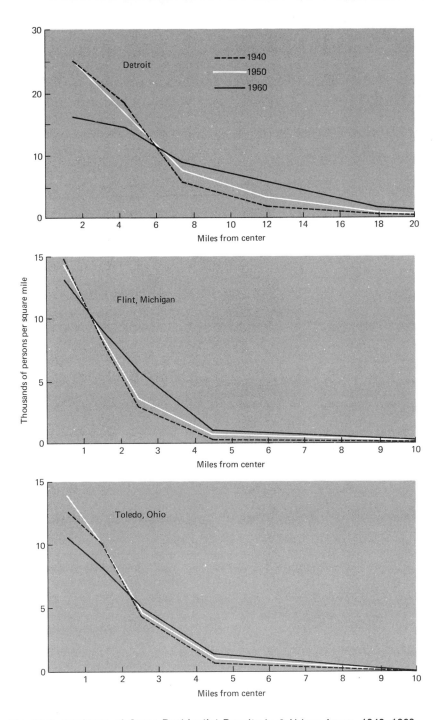

Fig. 10-1. Gradients of Gross Residential Density in 3 Urban Areas, 1940–1960

SOURCE: C. A. Doxiadis, *Emergence and Growth of an Urban Region* (Detroit: Detroit Edison Co., 1967), Vol. 2, p. 116; based on U.S. Census of Population data for census tracts.

Since this particular conformation describes *residential* density, it fits in only those parts of the urban area that are primarily residential. The "peaking" of residential densities actually resembles a volcano more than a sharp conical mountain peak, with a crater of lower gross density in the innermost zone preempted mainly by nonresidential activities. The D_0 parameter in the gradient formula is thus fictional, representing an extrapolation to what the gross residential density would theoretically be at the center if nonresidential uses did not preempt that location.[4] Alternatively, it is possible (though more difficult in terms of data availability) to construct the gradient on the basis of *net* residential density.[5]

Clark noted that the slope (b) of his density gradient varied considerably from one city to another, and showed a consistent downward time trend for any given city. It was not clear, however, whether this reflected increasing size, increasing age, or some combination of the two.

More recent analysis by Muth, Berry, Alonso, Mills, and others has confirmed the prevalence of this exponential form of residential density gradient, and has developed and begun to test some useful explanatory hypotheses about its determinants so that more reasoned projections of changes in density patterns can be made.[6]

In brief, it appears that:

1. Larger cities have, in addition to higher central densities, lower (flatter) slope coefficients.
2. In developed countries, a city's gradient flattens as the city grows.[7] (See Fig. 10-1.)

---

[4] Newling has proposed a more sophisticated formula that does provide for a "central crater" and lends itself to a dynamic model of urban growth in which the zone of peak density moves outward over time. Bruce E. Newling, "The Spatial Variation of Urban Population Densities," *Geographical Review,* 59, 2 (April 1969), 242–252.

[5] Net residential density means population per acre of land actually in residential use. It has been shown that in the Chicago area the fit of the gradient formula is better for net than for gross residential density. Carol Kramer, "Population Density Patterns," *CATS* (Chicago Area Transportation Study) *Research News,* 2 (1958), 3–10; and *Chicago Area Transportation Study, Final Reports,* Vols. 1–2 (1959–1960).

[6] See particularly Richard F. Muth, *Cities and Housing: The Spatial Pattern of Urban Residential Land Use* (Chicago: University of Chicago Press, 1969); William Alonso, *Location and Land Use* (Cambridge, Mass.: Harvard University Press, 1964); Brian J. L. Berry, J. W. Simmons, and R. J. Tennant, "Urban Population Densities: Structure and Change," *Geographical Review,* 53, 3 (July 1963), 389–405; and Brian J. L. Berry, "Research Frontiers in Urban Geography," in Philip M. Hauser and Leo F. Schnore (eds.), *The Study of Urbanization* (New York: Wiley, 1965), 403–430.

[7] The parameters of the residential density gradient for the Chicago urban area are presented for all decennial years, 1860–1950, in Berry, Simmons, and Tennant, *op. cit.,* p. 399. The central density rose to a peak in 1900 and 1910 and declined thereafter; the slope (b) showed an uninterrupted decline from 0.91 in 1860 to 0.18 in 1930. Clark, *op. cit.,* traces the steady flattening of the London density gradient from 1801 to 1941, with central density also showing signs of a decline in the more recent decades. Fig. 11-1 on page 326 pictures the flattening of density gradients in a group of U.S. metropolitan areas after 1920.

3. The observed decline of population per acre with increased distance from the city center is actually a combination of at least three different gradients. As we go outward from the center, the number of housing units per acre falls, and so does the proportion of people living outside of households (for example, in institutions, hotels, and rooming houses); but the declining density effect of those two variables is partially offset by rising household size.

4. The central density is largely determined by conditions (such as transport, communication, production technology, income levels, and occupation structure) during the period when the city became established. Once set, the basic form of the city (particularly in the central area where investment in structures is heaviest) is subject to considerable inertia. At any given time, then, the *age* of a city (definable in terms of the date at which it attained some specified minimum size, such as 50,000) is highly correlated with its central density. The familiar dichotomy between newer American "auto-oriented" cities like Phoenix and older "pre-automobile" cities recognizes this effect. Berry concludes, "knowing the population of a city and its age, it is possible to predict fairly closely the population densities within it."

5. The central density in specific cities has generally been declining in this century,[7] presumably responding to some of the factors that explain flattening of the gradient slopes, and suggesting that those factors have, in the period covered, outweighed the density-increasing effects of growth per se.

Perhaps the most intensive statistical analysis of urban residential density gradients is in Richard Muth's work. After a series of statistical tests of the relation of distance to gross residential density figures in 46 U.S. cities in 1950 (based on samples of 25 Census tracts in each city), he concluded that ". . . the negative exponential function in distance from the CBD [central business district] alone fits population density data for American cities in 1950 rather well."[8] This held true despite the fact that there were numerous deviations from regularity and that the exponential formula as a regression equation accounted for only about half of the observed intracity variation of density (among tracts within any city). The fitted density gradients varied widely in their slopes, with b ranging from 0.18 to 1.2. These b values correspond to density declines of 17 percent and 70 percent respectively for each mile of distance.

Muth then looked for factors to explain why some cities had steeper density gradients than others. He found that flatter gradients (that is, lower values for b) were significantly associated with each of the following characteristics of the urban area:

High automobile ownership
High income level
High proportion of nonwhite to total population
Large size (population) of urban area

---

[8] Muth, *op. cit.*, p. 184.

Low degree of concentration of the SMSAs manufacturing employment in the central city

Low quality (in terms of condition and plumbing facilities) of housing in the central city

Finally, he found by further analysis that ". . . the distribution of population between the central city and its suburbs and the land used by the urbanized area are largely governed by the same forces influencing the population distribution within the central city." Two main qualifications to this general statement appeared. First, an influx of lower-income persons into the central city is apparently associated with a greater degree of suburbanization of population, whereas *within* the central city the effect is in the opposite direction (a steeper density gradient). This, as Muth suggests, makes sense considering that the central city is a separate fiscal unit and the presence of a larger low income group tends to make the tax burden heavier for the upper income groups and for business firms, whose incentive to escape to other jurisdictions is thereby increased.[9]

Various empirical investigations have brought to light similar fairly consistent density gradients for certain nonresidential types of land use as well. Duncan presents a gradient of manufaoturing employees per thousand square feet of land occupied (that is, net manufacturing employment density) for Chicago in 1951, showing a reasonably good fit to the exponential formula, with a slope substantially flatter than that of the typical residential density gradient.[10] Daytime population likewise shows the same kind of gradient. In this case, the slope is much steeper, and the central density much higher, than for residential population. Finally, it appears that the gradient of land values in urban areas also follows the same general exponential form. Fig. 11-1 on page 326 shows the changes in the slopes of density gradients for manufacturing, trade, and service activity over several decades.

Analysis of the behavioral factors underlying these gradient patterns poses many complications. If all households could be assumed alike in preferences, and place of work, the form of the gradients of residential densities and rents could be read as representing the individual household's tradeoff between more space and quicker access. But it is not so simple. We know that this tradeoff is affected by income level. Higher income families tend to live farther out than lower income families, particularly if allowance is made for presence or absence of young children. This means that the observed overall residential density and land value gradients represent in part the gradation of tradeoffs; the analysis of residential distributions involves an additional dimension. Similarly for "man-

---

[9] *Ibid.,* p. 183.

[10] Otis Dudley Duncan, "Population Distribution and Community Structure," *Cold Spring Harbor Symposia on Quantitative Biology,* 22 (1957), 357–371.

ufacturing employment density": in the case of the employment density gradient referred to earlier, a breakdown of manufacturing into 25 industry groups disclosed that they displayed very different degrees of centrality, associated with employment density. A still finer breakdown would, of course, show the same kind of differentiation within an industry group.

Land Use Zones

It is clear that to go beyond such elementary explanations some explicit attention must be paid to the heterogeneity of both residential and nonresidential land uses in a more complicated conceptual scheme.

The "Burgess zonal hypothesis" is a schematic model developed along these lines in the 1920s.[11] Its kinship with von Thünen's much older zonal model of rural land uses around an urban focal point (see Chapter 5) is obvious. Activities are grouped on the basis of concentration in successive distance zones from the center outward, in this order:

1. Central business district activities: department stores and smart shops, office buildings, clubs, banks, hotels, theaters, museums, organization headquarters
2. Wholesaling
3. Slum dwellings (in a zone of blight invaded from the center by business and light manufacturing)
4. Middle-income industrial workers' residences
5. Upper income single-family residences
6. Upper income suburban commuters' residences

It should be noted that this schema was based on empirical observation of patterns prevailing in the 1920s, and also that it was put forward as a simplified *dynamic* model. The Burgess hypothesis was that these land use zones preserve their sequence, but as the city grows each zone must spread and move outward, encroaching on the next one and creating zones of transition and "land use succession." He emphasized the transitional problem created in the third (blighted) zone.

In the Burgess model, we have an elementary classification of urban land uses by locational types that is still useful as a starting point. Downtown uses, light manufacturing, wholesaling, and three or four levels of residence characterized by income level are singled out as significantly different and important locational types. Finally, heavy industry is not in the Burgess model at all, which makes sense in the light of the location factors discussed earlier. Heavy industry requires large level sites with

---

[11] For a brief account of the Burgess model and models involving subcenters and sectors (discussed later in this chapter), and references to the original sources, see Chauncy D. Harris and Edward L. Ullman, "The Nature of Cities," in Harold M. Mayer and Clyde F. Kuhn (eds.), *Readings in Urban Geography* (Chicago: University of Chicago Press, 1959), 282–286.

good transport to and from the outside world, and access to the urban "center of gravity" is of little relevance since most of the inputs (except labor) and outputs are nonlocal.

The Residential Income and Color Gradients

INCOME. The Burgess model introduces an important generalization about residential location preferences in urban areas: the richer people are, the farther they live from the city center. How can this be explained rationally? Does higher income as such necessarily increase a household's demand for space relative to its demand for access?

First, we can say that there is no universal "law" of behavior in this regard. Although the pattern observed by Burgess had long been typical in America and still is, the reverse relationship between income and distance has prevailed in some other countries and in other historical periods. In those situations, the wealthy favor inner-city locations with good access, while the poor huddle in suburban slums. Many Latin American cities, such as Rio de Janeiro, illustrate this pattern;[12] and in preindustrial America, the mansions of the rich were generally found very near the center.

The presently prevailing outer-suburban orientation of upper income people as a class seems especially costly to them in terms of work access. Executives and other managerial personnel, and many types of high-income professional people, have job locations more highly concentrated in downtown areas than most other income or occupational groups, yet they tend to live farthest out. This is particularly striking considering that a person's valuation of the time he spends in commuting is positively related to his income.

---

[12] "In a Latin American city rural migrants and, in general, the proletariat are not customarily crowded into a blighted area at the urban core, as in the schema devised for the North American city by the sociologist E. W. Burgess; but they are scattered, often in makeshift dwellings, in peripheral or interstitial zones. The Latin American city center with its spacious plaza was traditionally the residence area for the wealthy and was the point of concentration for urban services and utilities. The quickening of commercial activity in this center may displace well-to-do residents without necessarily creating 'contaminated' and overcrowded belts of social disorganization. The poor are often not attracted into transitional zones by cheap rents; they tend to move out to unused land as the city expands, erecting their own shacks. The downtown area becomes converted for commercial uses or for compact and modern middle- and upper-income residences." Richard M. Morse, "Latin American Cities: Aspects of Function and Structure," *Comparative Studies in Society and History,* 4 (1962), 485. For a comprehensive discussion of such characteristic contrasts in urban form and their socioeconomic background, see Leo F. Schnore, "On the Spatial Structure of Cities in the Two Americas," in Hauser and Schnore (eds.), *op. cit.,* 347–398.

For some high-income groups, however, such as research scientists, suburban job opportunities have become important or even predominant, with the development of large research centers and scientifically oriented manufacturing establishments in peripheral locations, for reasons discussed in the next chapter. Moreover, some allowance can be made for the fact that upper income people can afford more expensive means of travel for the sake of speed and comfort. Thus, the suburban executive commuting to downtown may get to work about as expeditiously as the worker who lives in the city, despite the greater distance and greater cost involved.

There have been many attempts to rationalize the observed "income gradient" in American urban areas. Richard Muth has provided what appears to be the clearest explanation to date: Higher income increases the demand for space, but also increases the opportunity costs of the time spent in daily travel. The income elasticity of demand for housing has been empirically estimated as exceeding 1 and possibly running as high as 2—in other words, a 1 percent increase in income is associated with willingness to increase expenditure on housing by *more* than 1 percent. By contrast, the effect of additional distance upon real income (through imposition of added money costs and time costs of travel) is almost certainly *less* than 1-to-1. This is so because the money costs of a given journey do not depend on income at all, whereas the time costs may be assumed to vary roughly in proportion to income. Consequently, higher income is associated with increased willingness to sacrifice access for more spacious and better housing.[13] A simple illustrative case is worked out in Appendix 10-1.

From this formulation we can also understand why in other periods and cultures the income gradient in urban residential location can run the other way. An income elasticity of demand for housing in excess of 1 is not a law of human behavior but simply an observed characteristic of the present generation in America. If people's tastes were to change so that they preferred to spend additional income to a larger extent on, say, automobiles, boats, food, recreation, or education rather than on more and better housing, the income elasticity could be less than 1 and the prevailing income gradient might be reversed.

It seems that a considerable factor in the suburban preferences of the well-to-do is a preference for modernity as such. Some discussion of the locational effects of aging of structures and neighborhoods will be found

---

[13] See Muth, *op. cit.*, 29–34, for further details. He concludes that ". . . on a priori grounds alone, the effect of income differences upon a household's optimal location cannot be predicted. Empirically, however, it seems likely that increases in income would raise housing expenditures by relatively more than marginal transport costs, so that higher-income CBD [Central Business District] workers would live at greater distances from the city center" (p. 8).

in Chapter 11. A dislike of old houses and neighborhoods and a superior mobility help to explain the positive association between income and dispersion.

Such an association is especially prominent in families with school-age children, who are naturally more sensitive to differentials in school quality, neighborhood amenity and safety, open space, and neighborhood homogeneity. An analysis of residential patterns in the Greater New York area in the 1950s showed that well-to-do families with children under 15 showed relatively strong suburban and low-density preferences, while those without such children were more willing to accept the higher densities of close-in communities. Differences according to presence or absence of children were less evident for lower income families, whose latitude of choice of residential areas is narrower.[14]

COLOR. Some of the reasons for the persistent inner-city concentration of nonwhites are already evident from this discussion. As a relatively poor group, nonwhites live in more central, older, and denser neighborhoods. But additional considerations of racial identification are at least equally important. Not only have nonwhites been deliberately excluded from most new suburban communities even when they could afford such housing, but the nonwhite migrant to an urban area has a positive incentive to locate first in a nonwhite neighborhood where he has or can more easily develop helpful connections to make a place for himself, however unsatisfactory, in the urban scene. This factor of cohesion has been important in the settlement patterns of all ethnically distinct migrant groups, but is greatly heightened by the color distinction.

MULTIPLE DESTINATIONS AND THE
EVALUATION OF ACCESS

In the unicentric models of urban form discussed so far, it is implied that the access factor is a simple centripetal attraction, pulling all activities toward one central point. Those activities that can make most intensive use of space, and for which the access factor is strongest, are the successful bidders for the most central locations; other activities locate in outlying zones where land is cheaper.

This assumption, obviously, does not adequately describe reality. A considerable (and rising) proportion of journeys from homes are to destinations other than downtown; and for most nonresidential activities as well, the markets and input sources can be at many points other than

---

[14] E. M. Hoover and Raymond Vernon, *Anatomy of a Metropolis* (Cambridge, Mass.: Harvard University Press for the Regional Plan Association, 1959), Table 41, p. 180.

the city center. How, then, is access advantage to be more realistically evaluated as a factor influencing an activity's location preference within an urban area?

Let us consider this from the standpoint of measuring the relative job-access advantage of a residential location, assuming that jobs are available at a considerable number of points in addition to the central business district. We could, of course, construct such a measure by just summing up the total travel time that would be involved in going to all jobs in the labor market area. But this is unrealistic since it ignores attenuation with greater distances. In the real world, if a desired destination becomes harder to reach, more thought is given to economizing, by going there less often or by substituting some more convenient alternative destination.

The "access-potential" approach to interaction over distance, previously discussed in Appendix 2-1, is an empirically based attempt to introduce here a greater degree of realism. The value of access to a point varies positively with the desirable contacts or opportunities present there (for example, the number of jobs available in a center of employment), and negatively with distance or transport costs.

Urban transportation studies in recent years have accumulated voluminous data on how people respond to access opportunities in their choice of travel paths. To a much smaller extent, these data throw some light on the more basic question of how residential development patterns can be expected to respond to changes in transport facilities and in the locations of work places and other trip destinations.

For example, in the "potential" measure of the work access advantage of various residential locations, a key question is how heavily the various job locations are to be "discounted for distance." Do 1,000 jobs 10 miles away have the same attraction as 500 jobs 5 miles away? or only 250? Does the attraction attenuate in proportion to distance (or travel time) or in proportion to the square of the distance or some other function of distance?

Metropolitan transportation studies have provided many answers to this question. When the whole pattern of point-to-point travel flows is ascertained in such a survey, it can be compared with what the pattern of flows would be on an "expected" basis (that is, if travel time made no difference, and the mix of destinations were the same for every point of origin). When the deviations in actual and expected trip frequencies are regressed against travel time between points, we have an empirical measure of the inhibiting effect of travel time upon interchange. This differs according to trip purpose, type of traveler, and mode of transport; but, in general, for any specified kind of trips, the effect can be roughly expressed by a power function. That is, other things being equal, the number of trips between two points varies inversely as some *power* of the travel time. The exponent attached to travel time in this formula can be regarded, then, as a meaningful index of the importance attached to access for that particular kind of interchange.

It follows that if we want to map the relative job access advantage of various residential areas for a specified kind of people, an access potential index for each residential area can be constructed by dividing the number of jobs at each employment center by the travel time to that center from the area in question, raising the result to the indicated power, and summing for all employment centers within maximum commuting range.

As noted earlier, such formulas are called "gravity models," because of their analogy to the physical law of gravitation (the attraction between two bodies is proportional to their masses and inversely proportional to the square of the intervening distance). Investigators have devised numerous variants and elaborations of the basic form, and have applied gravity and potential measures to virtually every measurable type of human interaction involving distance.[15]

A comparison of the access-potential maps for different population groups shows the urban pattern of *comparative advantage* in terms of access. To the extent that access and the cost of space determine residential location, we should expect to find each population group predominantly concentrated in those parts of the urban area in which its comparative advantage of access is the highest.

The many empirical studies show that the exponent attached to distance (or travel time) varies significantly according to type of person, trip purpose, and type of destination. The exponent is relatively *low* for:

1. Trips to the central business district, for any purpose, compared with trips to other destinations within the urban area
2. Higher status white-collar workers, particularly in the professional and managerial category
3. Social-recreational trips, compared to work trips

The exponent is relatively *high* for:

1. Trips to destinations outside the central business district
2. Lower status blue-collar workers
3. Women
4. Trips to school (elementary and secondary), compared to work journeys

This kind of analysis of travel patterns and residential area differentiation has some value in describing and predicting transportation demands, residential development patterns, and locational choice for consumer-oriented activities (retail trade and services).[16]

---

[15] The large literature on the theory and application of gravity and potential measures is surveyed in Gunnar Olsson, *Distance and Human Interaction: A Review and Bibliography* (Philadelphia: Regional Science Research Institute, 1965).

[16] See, for example, T. R. Lakshmanan and Walter G. Hansen, "A Retail Market

DIFFERENTIATION BY SECTORS

Some approaches to the explanation of urban spatial patterns have stressed tendencies toward differentiation according to direction rather than distance from the center. The "sector theory" is associated especially with Homer Hoyt, and has been stated as follows: ". . . growth along a particular axis of transportation usually consists of similar types of land use. The entire city is considered as a circle and the various areas as sectors radiating out from the center of that circle; similar types of land use originate near the center of the circle and migrate outward toward the periphery."[17] Hoyt's formulation was mainly concerned with residential land use, and assigned a dominant role to the forces determining the direction of expansion of the highest class residential district.

In terms of the existing pattern at any given time in an urban area, it is easy to explain sectoral differentiation on the basis of such factors as (1) topographical and other "natural" variation, (2) the presence of a limited number of important radial transport routes, and (3) the previously discussed incentives toward a greater concentration of any one activity than a symmetrical concentric-ring layout would afford. But the Hoyt hypothesis is couched primarily in dynamic terms, as an explanation of persistent sectoral differences in the character of development. And in that context, it introduces two further useful concepts.

One of these concepts is that of succession of uses of a given site or neighborhood area. Except at the outer fringe of urban settlement, each type of land use as it expands is taking over from an earlier urban use; by and large, the growth process involves (as described earlier in the concept of the simple unicentric model) an outward encroachment of each type of activity into the next zone out. Some such transitions are cheaper or easier than others, and the extension tends to be in the direction of easiest transition. Thus, obsolete mansions are conveniently converted into funeral homes; row houses and apartments are easily converted, subdivided, and downgraded into low-income tenements; and obsolete factory

---

Potential Model," *Journal of the American Institute of Planners,* 31, Special Issue on Urban Development Models (May 1965), 134–143. In this study of shopping goods centers in the Baltimore metropolitan area, it was found that the actual sales at the various centers (or, in some cases, the number of shopping trips to those centers, estimated from transportation survey data) corresponded well to what would be predicted on the basis of an index of access to the homes of consumers (weighted by their total retail expenditures).

[17] Homer Hoyt, *The Structure and Growth of Residential Neighborhoods in American Cities,* U.S. Federal Housing Administration (Washington, D.C.: Government Printing Office, 1939). The quotation is from Harris and Ullman, *op. cit.,* p. 283. See also, in the same volume, Homer Hoyt, "The Pattern of Movement of Residential Rental Neighborhoods," 499–510. A handy collection of most of his writings over the period 1916–1966 is Homer Hoyt, *According to Hoyt* (Washington, D.C.: Homer Hoyt Associates, 1968).

space is easily used for wholesaling and storage. The "filtering" theory of succession of uses in the urban housing market implies gradual and continuous rather than abrupt change in residential neighborhood character.

The other useful concept might be called "minimum displacement." The growth process uproots all kinds of housing and business activities in the zones of transition, forcing them to seek new locations. Copious empirical evidence bears out the reasonable presumption that when these moves are made by householders or by small neighborhood-serving businesses, there is a strong preference for remaining as close as possible to the old location. This cohesion or inertia, which is quite rational in the light of both economic and social considerations, tends to perpetuate a sectoral differentiation and to cause a particular activity to move gradually outward along the line of least resistance, rather than into another sector.

SUBCENTERS

Although a city or metropolis generally has one identifiable main center, there are subordinate centers as well. Spatially, an urban area is multinuclear, and some models of urban spatial structure particularly stress the development of subcenters. Current and foreseeable trends, entailing the rapid sprawl and coalescence of originally discrete cities and towns into metropolitan and megalopolitan complexes, bring this multinuclear aspect increasingly into prominence as a basic characteristic of the urban pattern. Los Angeles today and the Boston-Washington megalopolis tomorrow are striking examples, as are the numerous "twin cities," "tri-cities," and even "quad-cities."[18] Even a small individual city usually contains a number of important business centers or other focal points outside the central business district.

The central-place principle discussed in Chapter 6 is the key to part of this phenomenon. Any consumer-serving activity that can attain its economies of scale and agglomeration without having to serve the entire urban area from a single center will increase its proximity to consumers by branching out into shopping centers, each serving a part of the whole area. Each shopping center is in turn a concentration of employment activity, a focal point for access for work, shopping, and recreational trips. The basic concentric patterns of access advantage, centripetal movement of people, and centrifugal movement of goods and services are replicated in each part of the urban area, albeit for a more restricted range of central-place functions than those represented downtown. Local peaks of the

---

[18] Of the 233 SMSAs recognized by the U.S. Bureau of the Census as of July 1, 1968, 33 had double names, such as Minneapolis-St. Paul, and 15 had triple names, such as Albany-Schenectady-Troy.

gradients of residential density, land values, intensity of land use, and access potential appear around each of these subcentral points, like hillocks on the shoulders of a mountain.

> . . . the aggregative [central-place] model and the attendant inequalities are applicable not simply to systems of urban centers, but also to systems of business centers within cities. The same basic relationships repeat themselves . . . referring to streetcorner, neighborhood, and community centers, respectively.[19]

But in terms of central-place functions this is only a partial explanation. It does not explain why subcenters of activity are functionally differentiated in some ways that have nothing to do with their relative size or their standing in the central-place hierarchy. The logic of this further subcenter basis is evident as soon as we recognize that, among the types of activity that usually do agglomerate in one place within an urban area, there are many for which the central business district is not an economic location. These activities are highly concentrated but typically off center.

For some, the basic reason is inherent in their production functions—they simply do not use space intensively enough to afford downtown land, but at the same time the internal-access requirements of the activity call for a more compact zone of occupation than a ring would provide. This case was examined on page 110 above, with a university campus as the example. Off-center cluster is the typical pattern for research centers, cultural centers, concentrations of automobile salesrooms, and, to an increasing extent, wholesale produce markets and other wholesaling activities with strong external economies of cluster but substantial space requirements.

There is an interesting exception to this principle of "blob rather than doughnut." The building of fast suburban beltways around major cities has made it more feasible for some activities (for example, electronics and other light industries) to assume a distribution along at least a sizable arc; that is, part of a doughnut.

Second, the tendency to concentration at the expense of symmetry is found in specific types of residential land use as well, reflecting among other things the preference for neighborhood homogeneity that acts like an agglomerative force for any particular class of residence (such as high-income single-family houses) even where low densities are involved.

A still further basis for off-center concentration appears in situations where the activity serves a market that is itself lopsidedly distributed in relation to the overall area. For example, if residential areas occupied by

---

[19] Brian J. L. Berry, "Research Frontiers in Urban Geography," in Hauser and Schnore (eds.), *op. cit.,* 407–408. Berry's article, in bibliographical notes appended on pp. 424–430, cites recent literature on both interurban and intraurban applications of central-place analysis.

higher income and educational groups are predominantly to the northwest of the city center, trade and service activities catering especially to those groups will find the point of maximum market access potential somewhere northwest of the city center. This pattern also applies for those activities that mainly serve markets outside their own urban area (such as export activities). Access considerations for such activities dictate location close to intercity transport terminals or major highways.

Finally, special topographical or other site features may make a particular off-center location optimal even though it does not have the best access. The availability of a large level tract amid generally hilly topography may well be the decisive factor for such uses as airports or major industrial developments.

Thus, a typology of urban subcenters might include:

1. "Central-place-type" retail shopping centers each serving a surrounding residential area
2. Subcenters based primarily on nodal advantages of transport—for example, at junctions of major traffic arteries or transit routes
3. Subcenters based essentially on a single large-scale unit, such as a major industrial plant or sports stadium
4. Subcenters that were formerly separate towns, now engulfed by the spreading metropolitan area
5. Subcenters based on transport terminals connecting to the outside world— for example, near airports
6. Subcenters based on special natural advantages of site

Any particular subcenter may, of course, qualify under more than one heading.

EXPLAINING URBAN FORM

We have discussed the location of activities within cities in terms of four simple schematic models: the density gradient, Burgess's concentric land use zones, sectoral differentiation, and systems of subcenters. Each of these throws into relief some recognizable features of urban patterns, though none provides by itself a really good likeness.

These simple analytical constructs are not to be regarded as rival, mutually exclusive theories of urban form. They are, in fact, mutually consistent and complementary, and each has something to contribute to our understanding of the whole pattern. Subcenters merely represent a replication of the basic concepts involved in the density gradient and concentric zone models; namely, an ordered sequence of land uses of different intensities and types around a common focal point. In the view that emphasizes sectoral differentiation, there is still the idea of an outward spread from a center and a recognition of the agglomerative tendencies of particular types of land use. Shifts associated with urban growth and change can be, as we shall see in the next chapter, analyzed in terms of all four basic constructs set forth in this chapter.

In real cities, spatial patterns are usually complex and seemingly haphazard. To explain them we have to analyze in depth the "natural" differentiation of sites and the neighborhood linkages between activities to which the sector and subcenter theories merely allude. We have to take into account the network and nodal structure of urban transport, which makes variation in access advantage less simple and continuous than smooth gradients and nice round concentric zones would suggest. Specifically in the case of retailing areas, we have to recognize the "ribbon" pattern wherein commercial areas sometimes extend for miles along a single major street in response to the attractions of access to a moving *stream* of customers rather than to a fixed residential or employment concentration. We must also recognize the locational effects of public decision making as embodied in zoning, housing finance, property taxation, and placement of public facilities.

Most importantly, an understanding of the spatial layout of a city requires some idea of the processes of change. Present locations and neighborhoods embody, to a large extent, decisions made in the past when conditions were different. The pattern is always behind the times and in a never-ending process of adjustment. Changes in urban patterns will be the topic of the next chapter.

SELECTED READINGS

Edgar M. Hoover and Raymond Vernon, *Anatomy of a Metropolis* (Cambridge, Mass.: Harvard University Press for The Regional Plan Association, 1960).

Jean Gottman, *Megalopolis: The Urbanized Northeastern Seaboard of the United States* (New York: Twentieth Century Fund, 1961).

Richard L. Meier, *A Communications Theory of Urban Growth* (Cambridge, Mass.: M.I.T. Press, 1962).

Werner Z. Hirsch (ed.), *Urban Life and Form* (New York: Holt, Rinehart, and Winston, 1963).

William Alonso, *Location and Land Use* (Cambridge, Mass.: Harvard University Press, 1964).

Leo F. Schnore, "On the Spatial Structure of Cities in the Two Americas," in P. M. Hauser and Leo F. Schnore (eds.), *The Study of Urbanization* (New York: Wiley, 1965).

Harold M. Mayer, "A Survey of Urban Geography," in P. M. Hauser and Leo F. Schnore (eds.), *The Study of Urbanization* (New York: Wiley, 1965).

Brian J. L. Berry, "Research Frontiers in Urban Geography," in P. M. Hauser and Leo F. Schnore (eds.), *The Study of Urbanization* (New York: Wiley, 1965).

Homer Hoyt, *According to Hoyt* (a collection of his writings, 1916–1966, mainly on urban land economics) (Washington, D.C.: Homer Hoyt Associates, 1968).

Edward T. Hall, *The Hidden Dimension* (New York: Doubleday, 1966; reprint, Anchor Books, 1969), Ch. XIII.

Ira S. Lowry, *Seven Models of Urban Development: A Structural Comparison* (Santa Monica, Calif.: RAND Corporation, 1967).

Harry W. Richardson, *Regional Economics* (New York: Praeger, 1969), Ch. 6.

Colin Clark, *Population Growth and Land Use* (New York: St. Martin's Press, 1969), Ch. IX.

Doris B. Holleb, *Social and Economic Information for Urban Planning,* 2 vols. (Chicago: University of Chicago, Center for Urban Studies, 1969).

Michael B. Teitz, "Toward a Theory of Urban Public Facility Location," *Papers of the Regional Science Association,* 21 (1969), 35–51.

Peter Scott, *Geography and Retailing* (Chicago: Aldine, 1970).

APPENDIX 10-1

Hypothetical Case to Illustrate the Effect of Income upon Residence Choice

Let us assume a household with an initial income of $10,000 per annum. The breadwinner values his commuting time at roughly his earning rate while at work: say, $5.00 an hour. This household is prepared to spend $2,000 per annum on housing.

We further assume that transportation bears a money cost of 15¢ a mile and has a speed of 20 miles an hour. Each added mile of distance between home and work place, then, will entail an additional money cost of 30¢ plus an additional 6 minutes in travel time for the daily round trip.

This household is offered two alternative sites, A and B. B is 1 mile farther from the work place than A, but the annual cost of housing at B is only 40¢ a square foot compared to 50¢ at A.

Considering the relative advantages of the two locations, our household will find that B would provide 1,000 square feet more space for the assumed $2,000 annual housing budget (that is, 5,000 square feet at B compared to 4,000 at A). Location at B would entail additional daily travel costs of 30¢ in money (2 miles at 15¢ a mile) plus time valued at 50¢ (6 minutes at $5.00 an hour); or in all, 80¢ a day more than at A.

Let us now suppose that under these conditions the household turns out to be *indifferent as between A and B*—in other words, a differential of 80¢ per work day in travel cost just balances a differential of 1,000 square feet in living space. This household, then, is willing to "trade off access against space" at that marginal rate: 80¢ travel cost for 1,000 square feet, or *.080¢ per additional square foot.*

Now let us increase this household's income by 10 percent, from $10,000 to $11,000, and see how its location preference may be affected.

We assume that the income elasticity of demand for housing is about 1.2; thus, this 10 percent increase in income will raise the housing expenditure by 12 percent, or from $2,000 to $2,240. The space that this outlay will buy at each location will be:

At B: $2,240/40¢ = 5,600 square feet
At A: $2,240/50¢ = 4,480 square feet
Difference in favor of B: 1,120 square feet

As to the travel costs, the added *money cost* of commuting from B rather than A will still be 30¢ per working day (1 mile each way, at 15¢ a mile). The added *time* entailed in commuting from B will still be 6 minutes a day. But since income has risen by 10 percent, the opportunity cost valuation put on that 6 minutes will now be 55¢ instead of 50¢. The daily travel cost saving in locating at A will amount to 85¢, compared to 80¢ at the original income level.

At the higher income level, then, the B location will offer 1,120 square feet more space in return for 85¢ more daily travel cost: this comes to *.076¢ per additional square foot.*

But as we noted earlier, this household is willing to pay up to .080¢ in added travel cost for each square foot of additional space. Accordingly, it will now definitely *prefer the more outlying location B,* rather than being indifferent between A and B as it was at the $10,000 income level.

The above case is offered as an illustration rather than a proof. For more rigorous theoretical analysis of the effect of income level on residence choice, see the Muth and Alonso references cited on pages 306 and 311 above.

Most of the urban problems that concern us today can be traced to underlying changes in land use, location, or locational advantage that make life or business survival more difficult for some group or groups. The regional economist rightly stresses the *spatial* origins and implications of such problems—where his peculiar talents are most likely to be relevant. The present chapter is concerned with the principal kinds of change that have been occurring and seem likely to occur in the spatial patterns of urban areas.

11
Changes in Urban Patterns

GENERAL EFFECTS OF URBAN GROWTH

In the previous chapter, highly simplified models of urban form were presented, primarily as static descriptions or rationalizations of spatial structure. Let us now put some of these models to work and see what they may be able to suggest regarding dynamic shifts in patterns. First of all, we shall ask them what may be expected to happen simply as the result of urban *growth.* The locational effects of rising levels of *affluence* and *new technologies* of production and transport will subsequently be examined in terms of specific types of urban activities.

One appropriate way to see the structural implications of pure size is to make cross-sectional comparisons among urban areas of different size classes in the same country at the same time. What differences, then, are associated with larger city size as such? Some of the most obvious ones can be rationalized in terms of the basic density gradient model. Increased total size has both intensive and extensive impacts. The "central densities" or other measures of peak central intensity rise, while at the same time development pushes farther out. Residential densities in any given zone increase, except that the central nonresidential crater expands. Increases in density are greatest, percentagewise, at the outer fringe of urban development.

We also envisage (as impacts of growth per se) the successive pushing out and widening of the various more or less concentric zones of activity already discussed in the context of the original Burgess model. An increase in the length of all types of journeys and hauls of goods is likewise to be expected.

But as such journeys and shipments become lengthier and more expensive with expansion of the area, there are partially compensatory adjustments, representing responses to the increased incentive to keep travel time and cost from being excessive. Subcenters for various single activities or for groups of activities play a growing role in a larger urban area, because the total market in the area, for more kinds of goods and services, becomes big enough to support two or more separate production or service centers at an efficient scale rather than just one. This is clearly pictured in the intra-urban central-place schema. Thus, the hierarchy of central places within a small town consists of a single order of activities, all concentrated on Main Street. In a larger place there may be two levels in the central-place hierarchy: downtown activities and neighborhood subcenters. In a still larger urban area there will be more levels—some kinds of activity being replicated in dozens or even hundreds of individual neighborhoods, others being replicated in a handful of big shopping centers each serving a whole sector of the area, and still others serving the whole area from a single location (which in the simplified central-place schema is, of course, the central business district).

The larger size of the area, with its expanded and more variegated manpower, services, materials, and markets, provides the basis for an increasing number of "non-central-place" subcenters as well—that is, off-center concentrations of nonresidential activity that are not simply oriented to the neighborhood consumer market but may serve the whole area and outside markets as well.

It would appear, then, that growth as such helps to account for the flattening of density gradients that has characteristically shown up as a trend in our cities—though, of course, there are other and perhaps more important reasons as well.

The picture of changing patterns in an urban area that is simply getting more populous, assuming no changes in the state of technology or level of income, is this: Development proceeds both vertically (that is, in terms of more intensive use of space) and horizontally (in terms of use of more space). Each specialized zone of activities widens and moves outward, encroaching upon its outer neighbor and giving way to its inner neighbor. New types of central-place activities arise in the central area. The variety of types of activity and occupance increases. Off-center foci of both central-place activities and other activities increase in number, size, diversity, and importance. The gradients of residential density and land value become higher but flatter. The average length of journeys and the total amount of travel and internal goods transfer increase, but not as much as if all nonresidential activity remained as highly concentrated at the center as it was originally. The pattern of transport flows becomes more complex, with more criss-crossing and more nonradial traffic. The larger the urban area becomes, the smaller will be the fraction of its total internal travel going to the central business district. (This expectation is borne out by traffic studies, and the effect appears to be more marked for nonwork journeys than for work journeys.[1])

With the increased variety of activities, occupations, and life styles represented in a larger area, and the proliferation of more and more orders and types of subcenters, it is clear that an urban area's growth is associated with a more elaborately differentiated pattern of land uses: more spatial division of labor and specialization of functions. This increased macroscale heterogeneity fosters, somewhat paradoxically at first sight, increased *homogeneity* within individual neighborhoods and other subareas, or segregation in the broad sense of the term. We have considered earlier the various pressures for microscale homogeneity within urban areas; and these pressures can operate to a much greater degree in the framework of a larger and more varied community complex. One manifestation of this is the magnitude of the problem of de facto racial segregation of schools (that is, reflecting neighborhood composition) in larger cities. Another is the problem (again, most evident in the larger cities) of accommodating intensely cohesive specialized business concentrations such as the Manhattan garment district and urban wholesale produce markets which are highly resistant to piecemeal moving or adjustment. A third problem, likewise more evident in the largest metropolitan areas, is the political and economic conflict between the main central city and the surrounding suburbs, which resist merger or basic coordination with the central city or with one another.

Thus, it appears that many of the most pressing problems of our larger urban areas today, ranging from traffic congestion to racial discord, city-suburb conflict, and the fiscal crises of central cities, can be traced in some part to sheer size and growth. They are implicit in even the simplest models of urban structure. More broadly still, it is clear that larger agglomerations must raise challenging problems of divergence of private costs and benefits from social ones (and local from overall), in view of the intensified proximity impacts: scarcity of space, pollution of water and air, environmental nuisances, and generally increased interdependence of interests. Such problems are part of what we must pay for the economic and social advantages of greater diversity of contact and opportunity that constitute the very reason for the city's existence.

This hypothetical and mainly deductive picture of trends of change in a single growing area conforms closely, as would be expected, with what we observe empirically in a cross-sectional comparison of urban areas of

---

[1] Richard B. Andrews, *Urban Growth and Development* (New York: Simmons-Boardman, 1962), Ch. 3, cites relevant evidence from U.S. Bureau of Public Roads, *Parking Guide for Cities* (Washington, D.C.: Government Printing Office, 1956), Table 26, p. 29, and D. L. Foley, "The Daily Movement of Population into Central Business Districts," *American Sociological Review*, 17 (October 1952), p. 541.

different sizes in one country at one time. Moreover, we recognize in this picture many familiar features corresponding to observed historical and current trends; and can infer that simple growth plays a part in accounting for them, and can be expected to exert a similar influence in the future.

But in some ways the picture does not fit. Conspicuously unrealistic in relation to observed trends, for example, is the implied rise in the central density parameter of the residential density gradient—as we have seen, this figure has characteristically fallen off in the present century, at least in urban areas in more developed countries. Influences other than growth per se must account for this phenomenon and for many other features of the actual evolution of urban spatial patterns.

CHANGES IN DENSITY GRADIENTS FOR MAJOR TYPES OF URBAN ACTIVITY

Fig. 11-1 indicates (in terms of progressively flattening gradients of density on distance from city center) the persistent trend toward suburbanization of manufacturing, wholesale, retail and services employment, and residence in a sample of six United States metropolitan areas. It appears

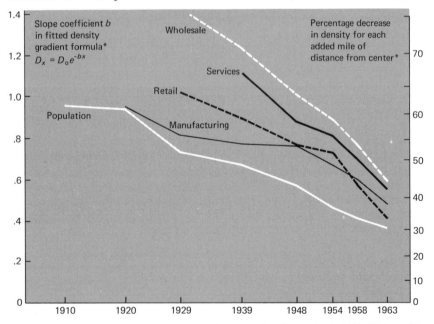

Fig. 11-1. Slope Parameters of Urban Density Gradients in 6 U.S. Metropolitan Areas, 1910–1963

Cf. p. 304.

SOURCE: Plotted from data in Edwin S. Mills, "Urban Density Functions," *Urban Studies,* 7, 1 (February 1970), Table 4, p. 14.

that trade and service activities (in these cities at least) were suburbanizing faster than residential population and at increasing rates, for at least three or four decades prior to 1963; and that manufacturing employment tended to suburbanize at a somewhat slower pace between 1920 and 1948 but quite rapidly thereafter.

It is convenient for the discussion that follows, to consider urban activities under four major types with distinctive locational characteristics: commodity-exporting, administrative and informational, residential, and consumer serving. For each of these we shall identify and try to explain the dominant trends of locational change.

LOCATION OF COMMODITY EXPORTING ACTIVITIES

Commodity-exporting activities are primarily manufacturing industries; though a few urban areas (see Table 8-2 above) export significant amounts of crops or minerals, and some wholesaling involves export of goods to a wider area than the city and suburbs. We have just noted some evidence of the suburbanization of both manufacturing and wholesaling.

An important instance of the outward shift of wholesaling is the transfer (in 1969) of the Paris produce market, which actually serves much of the rest of France as well, from Les Halles in central Paris to new quarters at suburban Rungis. Produce markets in many American cities (such as Pittsburgh and New York) have been similarly relocated, and wholesale establishments of other types as well are increasingly represented in suburban industrial zones.

In manufacturing at least, this suburbanization trend goes back even further than Fig. 11-1 shows. One of the earliest systematic investigations dates it from 1889:

> Between 1879 and 1889, manufacturing activity was growing more rapidly in most large metropolitan cities than in the surrounding districts. . . . Since 1889, manufacturing activity has grown more rapidly in the suburban sections, surrounding great manufacturing cities than in the manufacturing cities themselves.[2]

Improvements in Census data made possible Creamer's more detailed analyses for the period since 1899, which are summed up in Table 11-1. Because the data are not presented in precisely comparable terms by all censuses, and because the picture of location shifts is affected by changes in the classification of specific areas as they grow, three different time

---

[2] Glenn E. McLaughlin, *Growth of American Manufacturing Areas,* Monograph No. 7 (Pittsburgh: University of Pittsburgh, Bureau of Business Research, 1938), p. 186. His conclusions were based on U.S. Census data for the 13 largest Census Industrial Areas (composed of whole counties and groups of counties) and their central cities.

TABLE 11-1. Percentage Distributions of U.S. Manufacturing Employment by Type of Location, 1899–1958

	(A) Principal cities of industrial areas	(B) Satellite cities in industrial areas	(C) Suburbs in industrial areas	(D) Cities of 100,000 or more, outside industrial areas	(E) Remainders of counties containing D cities	(F) Other important industrial counties (10,000 or more mfg. jobs)	(G) Remainder of U.S.	U.S. total
Areas as defined in 1929								
Wage earners								
1899	39.5	3.7	14.6	5.9	1.1	8.4	26.8	100.0
1919	36.1	3.6	18.6	6.3	1.6	8.3	25.5	100.0
1929	35.1	2.9	18.2	6.9	1.6	9.3	26.0	100.0
Total employees								
1929	37.1	3.1	18.7	6.3	1.8	7.9	25.2	100.0
1939	33.4	3.0	19.9	6.2	1.8	7.8	27.8	100.0
1947	33.4	2.4	20.1	6.8	1.9	7.0	28.4	100.0
1954	30.2	2.4	21.4	7.2	2.5	6.6	29.7	100.0
1958	27.9	2.2	21.6	7.2	2.7	6.6	31.8	100.0
Areas as defined in current year								
Total employees								
1929	37.1	3.1	18.7	6.3	1.8	7.9	25.2	100.0
1939	33.5	3.0	19.9	6.4	1.9	8.7	26.6	100.0
1947	35.8	2.6	21.6	5.0	1.6	10.9	22.5	100.0
1954	33.6	2.7	24.3	4.6	1.7	11.0	22.1	100.0
1958	31.5	3.0	24.8	5.5	2.4	9.8	22.9	100.0
1963	27.9	2.9	26.3	5.6	2.9	10.8	23.7	100.0

SOURCES: Daniel Creamer, *Changing Location of Manufacturing Employment—Part I: Changes by Type of Location, 1947–1961,* Studies in Business Economics No. 83 (New York: National Industrial Conference Board, 1963), Table 2, p. 30, Table 4, p. 34, and Table 8, p. 53; Daniel Creamer, *Manufacturing Employment by Type of Location,* Studies in Business Economics No. 106 (New York: National Industrial Conference Board, 1969), Table 4, p. 17. The 1899–1929 figures originally appeared in Creamer's *Is Industry Decentralizing?* (Philadelphia: University of Pennsylvania Press, 1935), 10–11.

series are shown in this summary table. It is clear from each series, however, that location types *C* and *E* (suburban areas around important industrial cities) have shown faster industrial growth than those cities themselves (location types *A* and *D* respectively).[3] Suburbanization becomes increasingly apparent in the more recent years; by the 1960s, the popularity of outlying locations for new and expanded manufacturing plants was so obvious as hardly to require documentation. How can this tendency be explained?

More Extensive Plant Layouts

One important reason for this trend emerges from changes in manufacturing technology, relating particularly to the ways in which energy and goods in process are moved about within the plant. Comparing an old factory with a modern factory, one is immediately struck by the high, compact, almost cubical shape of the old and the low sprawling shape of the new. The old type dates back to the days when motive power was supplied by steam engines and transmitted by belts and shafting, calling for the closest possible proximity of the individual power-using units of equipment. Early in the twentieth century, there was a nearly universal shift to purchased electric power, transmitted to individual motors on each piece of equipment.[4] Since additional cable costs relatively little, much more extensive layouts became possible. This in turn contributed to the adoption of conveyors and assembly-line layouts in which machines bring the goods to the successive stages of processing or fabricating equipment.

Such considerations did not apply to any extent in heavy processing industries requiring tall structures and moving materials through pipes in liquid, gaseous, or powder form (such as oil refineries, primary chemical plants, smelters, cement plants, flour mills, distilleries, or breweries). Nor did they apply to small-scale light industries that could effectively operate

---

[3] Industrial Areas (location categories *A* + *B* + *C* in Table 11-1) and also selected other important industrial counties (category *F* in Table 11-1) were identified by the Census of Manufactures in 1929 and replaced by the Standard Metropolitan Areas concept in 1947. The Industrial Area was a unit based on concentration of at least 40,000 manufacturing wage earners in an important industrial city, its county, and adjacent important industrial counties. In 1929 there were 34 Industrial Areas; by applying the same criteria in later years, Creamer had 49 by 1963. This is obviously a more exclusive category than the present-day Standard Metropolitan Statistical Area, of which there were already 231 by 1966. The number of *B* cities (see Table 11-1) ranged from 12 to 23 in 1929–1963; the number of *D* cities and *E* counties, from 41 to 61; and the number of *F* counties, from 47 to 94.

[4] In U.S. manufacturing establishments, electric motors accounted for 4.8 percent of all mechanical horsepower in 1899, 55.0 percent in 1919, and 89.8 percent in 1939, *U.S. Census of Manufactures, 1954,* Vol. I (Washington, D.C.: Government Printing Office, 1957), Table 1, p. 207–2. See the discussion in Sam H. Schurr and Bruce C. Netschert, *Energy in the American Economy, 1850–1975* (Baltimore: Johns Hopkins Press, 1960), 185–189.

in rented upstairs space in loft buildings and were, in general, strongly dependent on external economies of cluster. But for nearly all other types of manufacturing, the attractions of a horizontal layout became large. With this increased desire for more spacious sites, the enticements of the cheaper land of the suburbs were naturally strong.

The desire for more space probably has had other bases as well, such as a growing tendency to anticipate expansion needs, increased emphasis on amenity and visibility, the need to provide parking space, and a fear of being hemmed in by surrounding development.

Impressive evidence of the increased appetite for space emerged from a comprehensive economic study of the Pittsburgh region in the early 1960s. Relevant findings were:[5]

[*Plants relocating within Allegheny County, 1957–1959*]
In the eleven cases in which the area of site and of buildings at both old and new locations were specified, the average site area per plant had increased from 4.6 to 19.6 acres, or 300 percent, and the average building area per plant had increased from 90,000 to 122,000 square feet, or 36 percent. (This sample consists primarily of rather large manufacturing plants.) The much greater expansion of site area than of building area indicates a desire for more open space for storage, loading and parking, and for subsequent expansion. *The site area per employee was at least doubled in each of these eleven relocations, and was increased by a factor of more than 20 in two cases.*

[*Plants that had not relocated but reported need for more space*]
The average estimate of additional space [site area] required was 153 percent, but the average estimate of increased employment associated with those requirements was only 38 percent. These figures imply a desire to *increase the amount of space per employee by 83 percent.*

[*Respondents, primarily occupying rented space in multitenant buildings, who reported need for more floor space*]
Although only fourteen of the respondents reporting inadequate floor space gave the requested information on amount of additional space needed and additional employment expected, in all but one of those cases the percentage increase in floor space was at least as great as the increase in employment. On the average, 138 percent more floor space was called for, with an associated increase in employment of only 44 percent. These figures imply a desire to *increase the amount of floor space per employee by 65 percent.*

Changes in Transport Technology

Another change contributing to the suburbanization of commodity-exporting activities comes from transport technology, and specifically

---

[5] Ira S. Lowry, *Portrait of a Region,* Vol. 2 of reports of the Economic Study of the Pittsburgh Region conducted by the Pittsburgh Regional Planning Association (Pittsburgh: University of Pittsburgh Press for Pittsburgh Regional Planning Association, 1963), p. 73. The three passages quoted here are from a section that I prepared. Italics have been supplied.

the improvement of motor vehicles and highways that has enabled a good part of the inputs of such activities and a still larger part of their outputs to be shipped by truck. This change became important only in the 1920s. It has most strongly affected wholesaling and the lighter types of manufacturing that ship high-value outputs in small consignments; but even steel rolling mills and other heavy industries have come to ship substantial parts of their output over the roads.

However, an interesting reversal occurred in the 1960s in the method of transport of new automobiles from factories and assembly plants. Statistics compiled by the Automobile Manufacturers' Association show that by 1959, 90 percent of such traffic was by road and only 8 percent by rail. The railroads then devised equipment and tariffs that made it more economical to ship by rail for medium and long distances, and in 1968 the rails carried about half of all the new cars shipped. Barge shipments of new automobiles, which had been nearly 8 percent of the total in 1949, had become insignificant by the mid-1960s.

The use of highway transport greatly widens the choice of locations, since the road network is many times finer than the rail network and offers an almost unlimited choice of stopping places. For direct shipment in whole truckloads, there is no need to be near any transport terminal, and many piggy-back loading yards have been conveniently placed for suburban access. An outlying plant location speeds the receipt and delivery of goods by obviating slow and expensive trucking through congested city streets.

Access to Labor Supply

A third factor contributing to industrial suburbanization is labor supply. Both the suburbanization and motorization of population have made it feasible to attract an adequate work force to locations outside of any major population center; and (as noted in the last section of Chapter 7) there is even a positive labor supply advantage in some suburban locations with respect to high-income professional personnel. Locations in beltway zones can provide quick access to labor from a sizable arc of the metropolitan circumference.

There remain serious problems of employment access for those who live in the central city and must engage in lengthy reverse commuting in order to reach the expanding suburban job market, particularly since these people include slum dwellers with the least marketable skills and the lowest degree of automobile ownership. This problem will be discussed in Chapter 12. From the employers' standpoint, however, the relative labor supply status of suburban locations has continued to improve; and any enhancement of the mobility of the urban poor would improve it still further.

This does not exhaust the list of reasons for the increased attractiveness of suburban locations for exporting activities. Business firms have become increasingly influenced by amenity, prestige, and public relations. A suburban location with attractively landscaped grounds, exposed to the view of thousands of daily travelers on a busy expressway, has an advertising value not to be underrated. Even new steel mills and fertilizer factories are now likely to be painted in pastel tints and to sport green lawns and signs proudly identifying the firm.

Finally, it is important to note that in the aggregate all of the forces motivating suburbanization acquire further importance from the changing composition of productive and distributive activities. Higher income levels and the proliferation of products, brands, and successive stages of processing mean an increasing proportion of the lighter types of activity, which involve relatively little weight loss or orientation to transported inputs and relatively high sensitivity to quick market access, environmental amenity, and local public relations.

LOCATION OF ADMINISTRATIVE AND OTHER INFORMATION-PROCESSING ACTIVITIES

A rapidly increasing proportion of activities produce intangible outputs that are delivered through personal contact or communication media, with little or no shipment of any actual goods.[6] Since new information obsolesces rapidly (yesterday's newspaper is trash, and last week's memo may only serve to clutter the files), and since human time is expensive, market access advantage for such activities is measured primarily in terms of time.

Technological advance has greatly speeded long-distance communication and personal travel, though in our times there has been relatively slight improvement for the short haul. The locational impact is clearly visible in the rapidly growing operations of administration, data processing, and research. Individual business corporations have been increasingly consolidating such operations at headquarters and reducing the relative importance of field offices. The unchecked trend toward business amalgamation, which in the 1960s involved a striking increase in "conglomerates," or multi-industry corporations, has played a part in this trend; for the acquiring firm customarily adds to its headquarters staff and drastically cuts the headquarters staff of the acquired firm even when the latter retains its name and the status of a division of the larger complex. New York and other headquarters cities have been frantically erecting new downtown skyscrapers since World War II to keep pace with an apparently insatiable demand for office space.

---

[6] See the discussion at the beginning of Chapter 2 regarding the transfer of commodities and information.

Headquarters offices have remained rather tightly concentrated in downtown areas because of the multifarious daily interfirm contacts involved (and also, to some extent, because of the prestige value of new skyscrapers and downtown addresses, and the stake that some large corporations and related financial institutions have in downtown property values).

At the same time, the suburbs hold strong attractions for office and informational activities that are least subject to the access needs and external economies of downtown cluster. As the "head office" activities of large firms have grown, they have at the same time tended to split into downtown and suburban (or even nonmetropolitan) categories. Routine data processing and other clerical work can fairly easily be shifted out of expensive downtown office space, leaving the "top brass" behind. The major concern in a split is access to adequate clerical manpower and womanpower in the suburbs. For research laboratories, the advantage of the suburbs is much more positive, and this is reflected in their customary location there. Suburbanizing factors include need for ample space, proximity to the preferred residential areas of professional workers and technicians, access to universities and scientific institutions, clean air, absence of undue noise, distraction, air pollution, vibration, and the like, and a degree of isolation from inquisitive competitors and from the distracting demands of the production divisions of the same firm for solutions to their day-to-day production problems. This last consideration may seem far-fetched, but was repeatedly stressed by responsible corporate officials in personal interviews with the author and his associates in connection with the Pittsburgh Regional Planning Association's Economic Study of the Pittsburgh Region in the early 1960s.

Table 11-2 provides some data on the two major categories of employment just discussed, covering only manufacturing firms. We first note the extremely rapid rates of growth of both central-office and research employment. The table also shows the still predominant but weakening concentration of central-office jobs within major industrial cities and the contrasting predominant concentration of research and testing jobs in suburbs. It is likely that the bulk of the latter category of jobs shown as located in cities were actually in establishments well outside the central business district.

Two other major categories of research facility are those of government agencies and commercial research firms. The locational considerations are quite similar to those already cited for research laboratories of manufacturing firms, except that there may be no separate downtown headquarters office.

> . . . the picking up of the research business coincided happily with the opening of the 65-mile, six-lane Beltway, which rings the District of Columbia about 10 miles from its center. Just as the small companies were beginning to outgrow their original quarters, the Beltway opened up to give swift access from any-

TABLE 11-2. Number and Percentage Distribution, by Type of Location, of Employees of Manufacturing Firms in Central Administrative Offices and Research and Testing Establishments, 1954–1963

	Central administrative offices			Research and testing		
	1954	**1958**	**1963**	**1954**	**1958**	**1963**
Number of employees	348,495	449,052	515,056	58,941	115,987	160,201
Percentage distribution, by type of location:						
U.S. total	100.0	100.0	100.0	100.0	100.0	100.0
A. Principal cities of industrial areas	69.2	61.5	54.5	28.3	16.7	16.3
B. Satellite cities in industrial areas	0.7	4.0	5.0	0.8	11.2	11.3
C. Suburbs in industrial areas	13.1	15.0	20.5	51.5	52.4	49.0
D. Cities of 100,000 or more, outside industrial areas	5.5	6.8	6.4	7.6	1.2	5.0
E. Remainders of counties containing D cities	1.4	1.2	1.2	4.1	7.6	2.0
F. Other important industrial counties	4.8	4.1	5.5	1.6	2.5	8.9
G. Remainder of U.S.	5.2	7.4	7.0	6.1	8.4	7.5

SOURCES: Daniel Creamer, *Changing Location of Manufacturing Employment— Part I: Changes by Type of Location, 1947–1961,* Studies in Business Economics No. 83 (New York: National Industrial Conference Board, 1963), Table 18, p. 84, Table 20, p. 88, and Appendix Table D-1, p. 138; and Daniel Creamer, *Manufacturing Employment by Type of Location,* Studies in Business Economics No. 106 (New York: National Industrial Conference Board, 1969), Table 11, p. 42, Table 17, p. 57, and Appendix Table C, p. 112. The location types are the same as those shown in Table 11-1 above.

where in the Maryland-Virginia metropolitan area to the 14 largest federal labs. The highway . . . runs through some wooded areas that are ideal for development as industrial parks, and are shielded by some of the nation's toughest residential zoning laws. Smokeless, tidy R&D is about the only industry that home-conscious residents will tolerate in Maryland's Montgomery and Prince Georges counties, and Virginia's Arlington and Fairfax counties.

More than a dozen companies immediately set up shop near the Beltway, including four in the publicized "new town" of Reston, Va. . . . Local boosters predict a research boom on the Beltway rivaling that on Boston's Route 128.[7]

Fig. 11-2 shows a typical present-day cluster of such facilities in and around a major metropolis.

[7] "Research Labs Swarm to Capital," *Business Week* (April 23, 1966), p. 145.

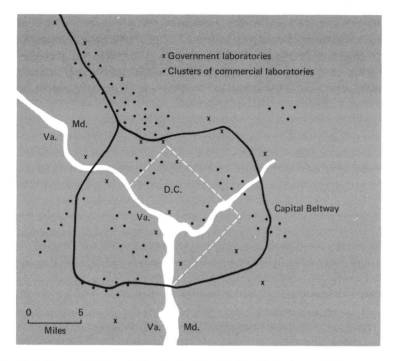

x Government laboratories

• Clusters of commercial laboratories

Md.

Va.

D.C.

Va.

Capital Beltway

Va.

0   5
Miles

Va.   Md.

Fig. 11-2. Research Laboratories in the Washington, D.C., Area, 1966
SOURCE: "Research Labs Swarm to Capital," *Business Week* (April 23, 1966),
p. 144.

RESIDENTIAL LOCATION

Urban populations have become richer, more leisured, and more widely
mobile in terms of their day-to-day journeys within urban areas. These
changes have been associated with more dispersed residential location
patterns. Analysis of the residential density gradients, as noted in the
previous chapter, discloses that such gradients are flatter in cities where
income levels and car ownership are higher, and that the rich characteristically live farther out than the poor, particularly if they have children.

Tables 11-3 and 11-4 provide some relevant evidence of the major
trends. When we simply compare the central cities of metropolitan areas
with the remainders of those areas and with the nonmetropolitan United
States, it is clear that the bulk of our population growth in 1950–1968
took place in metropolitan suburbs, while nonmetropolitan areas grew
more slowly and central cities hardly grew at all after 1960. There is
sharp contrast between the trends for whites and for nonwhites in the
1950s (the latter showing a marked clustering in central cities); but in
1960–1968 the nonwhite population seems to have begun to share in the

TABLE 11-3. Metropolitan and Nonmetropolitan Population Growth and Composition by Color, 1950–1968

	Annual rate of percentage increase						Percentage of population nonwhite		
	Total		White		Nonwhite				
	1950–60	1960–68	1950–60	1960–68	1950–60	1960–68	1950	1960	1968
Total United States	1.7	1.3	1.6	1.2	2.4	2.1	10.7	11.4	12.2
Standard Metropolitan Statistical Areas	2.4	1.5	2.2	1.3	3.9	2.9	10.0	11.7	13.0
Central cities	1.0	0.1	.5	-.5	4.1	2.6	13.1	17.9	21.8
Outside central cities	4.0	2.8	4.0	2.8	3.2	3.8	5.7	5.1	5.5
Nonmetropolitan areas	.7	1.0	.7	1.0	.1	.5	11.6	11.1	10.7

SOURCE: U.S. Department of Commerce, Bureau of the Census, *Current Population Reports; Population Characteristics*, Series P-20, Nos. 157 and 181 (Washington, D.C.: Government Printing Office, December 16, 1966 and April 21, 1969). The SMSAs, for all years shown, are those recognized in the 1960 Census.

TABLE 11-4. Characteristics of Suburban and Satellite Communities in the New York Metropolitan Region in Relation to Median Income of Families and Unrelated Individuals

Places according to rank in 1949 median income	Median income, 1949*	Average number of dwelling units per place, 1954	Dwelling units per acre of residentially developed land, 1954–1955	Percentage of dwelling units in multifamily structures, 1950*	Average access-zone rating†	Percentage increase in dwelling units, 1950–1954
All places	$3,929	8,057	8.06	—	2.85	10
Top fifth	5,128	3,510	3.69	12	2.92	18
2nd fifth	4,288	4,040	4.94	13	3.12	12
3rd fifth	3,925	7,519	7.51	16	2.80	14
4th fifth	3,572	9,016	8.34	23	2.84	8
Bottom fifth	3,235	16,365	14.32	39	2.56	7
Bottom tenth	3,078	24,476	19.10	39	2.23	4

* Unweighted median of urban places in each group.

† The access-zone rating measures commuter travel time to central Manhattan. Each access zone after the first one entailed about 15 minutes of additional travel time.

SOURCE: Edgar M. Hoover and Raymond Vernon, *Anatomy of a Metropolis* (Cambridge, Mass.: Harvard University Press for the Regional Plan Association, 1959), Table 38, p. 168.

337

suburbanization trend. Table 11-3 also shows that some time between 1950 and 1960 the nonwhite population became "more metropolitan" than the white population, and that nonwhites were more than proportionately represented in central-city populations even in 1950, and have become increasingly more so.

Table 11-4 is taken from one of the reports of the New York Metropolitan Region Study of the late 1950s and applies to a "land use survey area" within the New York Metropolitan Region intermediate between New York City itself and the outer ring of suburban territory. In this table, individual communities are classified by income level, and various characteristics are shown for each major income bracket. Higher family income appears strongly associated with smaller communities, lower residential density, prevalence of single-family dwellings, rapid population growth, and distance from Manhattan.

It appears that (1) urban population in the aggregate has been rapidly suburbanizing, (2) the higher income groups have shown the strongest preferences for suburban location, and (3) nonwhites, until some time in the 1960s at least, were concentrating more and more in central cities, though they may subsequently have begun to follow the suburbanization movement. (This last surmise, based on Table 11-3, must be regarded as tentative since the figures in the table are subject to a considerable sampling error.) These, then, are the principal trends to be explained.

Let us first look at the relatively rapid suburban population growth in the aggregate. We should expect such a differential if there were some upper limit to residential densities. As the older and more central areas approached that limit, their growth would slow to a halt, while growth would remain more rapid in the outer zones where densities were farther below the ceiling. This view might be called a "filling-up" or "saturation" model of urban population growth, with each zone from the center outward filling up to its capacity, and subsequent increments of population spilling out into the next zone.

There are indeed economic, social, and administrative (that is, zoning) limits to residential density that lend some validity to this picture. But in the explanation of recent and current trends it is important to note that the ceilings are soft and have become progressively lower.

Lowering of the density ceilings for single-family housing is demonstrated by a comparison of the lot sizes in newer versus older parts of an urban area. The houses being built today, in the fringe zones of new subdivisions, are on larger lots than those in older areas which were on the fringe of new development 20, 30, or 50 years ago.[8] Lower density is

---

[8] Some data on this point, for suburbs of the New York metropolitan region in 1950–1957, are given in Hoover and Vernon, *Anatomy of a Metropolis* (Cambridge, Mass.: Harvard University Press for the Regional Plan Association, 1959), Table 49,

thus being built into new single-family residential areas as they are created. Some single-family areas, of course, are at any given time shifting to multifamily development by conversion of large old houses and erection of new apartment buildings; and densities at that stage jump to a much higher level. But we also observe that the peak densities associated with inner-city slums seem to be generally lower now than in former times. In Manhattan, for example, the highest density area in 1900 had 400,000 people per square mile, compared with a maximum of 165,000 in any area in 1850, but the maximum was down to 260,000 in 1940 and 221,000 in 1957. Density in the 1957 peak density area had fallen to 171,000 by 1968. The situation was similar in Brooklyn, where a peak of 147,000 was passed in 1930, and in Jersey City, with a 1920 peak of 75,500. In Brooklyn, however, the somewhat newer slum areas of Bedford-Stuyvesant and Brownsville both increased slightly in density between 1960 and 1968. During the same period, densities in Central and East Harlem fell about 20 percent.[9]

The general trend toward a flattening of residential density gradients, noted in the previous chapter, can rather easily be explained on the basis of income levels, transportation, and job locations. As people acquire more income and more leisure (shorter work weeks and longer vacations), they have both a greater desire for more spacious sites and a greater ability to pay for them. More space can be acquired only by going farther from the city center or from major radial transport corridors, but increased automobile ownership has lessened or removed the access disadvantages of large stretches of suburban territory that were prohibitively inaccessible when nearly all employment was centrally concentrated and could only be reached quickly by radial transit lines.

There is a degree of circularity, of course, in explaining residential suburbanization on the basis of an increasingly suburban pattern of employment opportunities and at the same time explaining the suburbanization of business activities on the basis of access to an increasingly suburban consumer market and labor force. On each side of the relationship, however, other decentralizing factors have been noted. The market and commuting linkages between residence and jobs merely reinforce the suburbanization incentives to which each is subject.

---

p. 220. These figures are brought down to 1960 in Regional Plan Association of New York, *Spread City* (New York: Regional Plan Association, 1962). Between 1950 and 1960, the average lot sizes in new subdivisions in a group of suburban counties increased at an average rate of roughly 4 percent per annum. The size of this figure is, of course, not to be taken too seriously, since it is based on experience over just one decade in part of a single metropolitan area.

[9] *Ibid.*, Table 50, p. 224, and more recent estimates supplied by the Regional Plan Association of New York. The areas involved are wards, assembly districts, and New York City health areas.

Since part of the explanation of the overall suburbanization of population lies in rising average income levels, and since the wealthier can afford spacious sites and modernity, we are not surprised to see the upper income groups leading the outward trek and continuing to live farther from the center than those with lower incomes. So far, relatively few upper income people, mainly those without children, have moved into close-in areas despite the access advantages and amenities now available.

The aging of housing and neighborhoods plays an important role in shifting residence patterns. According to the "filter-down" theory, housing deteriorates with the sheer passage of time. Thus, if new housing is bought mainly by the well-to-do, housing units will in the course of time be handed down to occupants lower and lower on the income scale. Each stratum of urban society except the top will have access to housing relinquished by the stratum above.

This filter-down process is indeed familiar in the used car market; but it does not fit as well when applied to housing. As Lowry has pointed out, housing deterioration is by no means so closely related to age as is deterioration of automobiles. Instead, condition depends primarily on maintenance, the structure itself being almost indefinitely lasting if adequately maintained.[10]

There is, nevertheless, substantial correlation between the age and the condition of structures. Moreover, housing (and nonresidential structures) can lose some of its attractiveness with time regardless of how much or how little it may physically deteriorate. Preferences change. The design of a house that was well adapted for a typical well-to-do family of 1890 or 1920 may not correspond to what a similar family prefers in the 1970s in the context of newer alternatives. Neighborhood land-use layouts in terms of lot sizes, front and back yards, block sizes, street widths, and the like are likewise vulnerable to obsolescence and loss of favor in the face of changing conditions and tastes. Finally, there is the factor of prestige attached to newness per se, whether it refer to the family car, the family dwelling, or the neighborhood.

Despite the fair number of instances in which old neighborhoods and old housing are judiciously refurbished and cherished (most older cities have such neighborhoods, exemplified by Georgetown in Washington, D. C., and Beacon Hill in Boston), it is generally true that householders and businesses that can pick and choose are especially strong bidders for newly developed sites, and that the oldest neighborhoods and structures fall mainly to those who have little choice.

---

[10] Ira S. Lowry, "Filtering and Housing Standards: A Conceptual Analysis," *Land Economics*, 36, 4 (November 1960), 362–370.

LOCATION OF CONSUMER-SERVING ACTIVITIES

Consumer-serving activities (of which retail trade is the largest category) have been subject to some interesting locational shifts, different from those of any of the other categories of activity so far discussed.

The important locational factors for consumer-serving activities within an urban area are (1) access to population, (2) economies of scale and agglomeration, and (3) space requirements affecting the activity's ability to bid for expensive land.

Market access means somewhat different things for different types of retailing or consumer servicing. Convenience goods like cigarettes, magazines, or candy bars are bought mainly "on the run" by people bound on some other errand to which these purchases are incidental, and the market is really the stream of sidewalk traffic. Similarly, filling stations are located along major streets with moderate to heavy traffic density.[11] Daytime population, rather than simply residential population, is the relevant measure of market for a wide range of goods or services that are bought both by housewives and by employees during lunch hour. Access to residential or "night-time" population is the most relevant for stores and shopping centers to which most journeys are made from homes (such as food supermarkets). Finally, some kinds of specialty shops and services cater mainly to certain groups of the population, who may be concentrated in particular neighborhoods (for example, large bookstores, antique shops, and luxury boutiques).

We have already seen that both residential and daytime population distributions have been suburbanizing as a result of growth per se plus changes in income, transport, and job location. It is no surprise, then, that consumer-serving activity in general has shown a similar outward trend. Downtown department stores, for example, have not flourished. Many have disappeared or merged, and many of the rest have established suburban branches or even shifted outright to a suburban location. Restaurant, theater, and hotel-motel businesses have reacted similarly.

Two factors other than market access, however, have also affected retail and consumer service location trends. One of these is agglomeration economies. The degree to which such economies can be realized is limited (as Adam Smith said long ago) by the extent of the market, or number of customers who can be attracted to any one location. The motorized shopper can not only travel farther but can also buy in larger

---

[11] Retailing location factors have been researched in great detail and rating systems devised to pinpoint especially desirable sites. For example, it has been determined that filling stations along a commuting artery generally do better business if located on the right-hand side of the road for homecoming commuters—partly, perhaps, because commuters are in less of a hurry on the homebound trip than they are in the morning rush hour.

quantities at one time (for example, a whole week's food shopping at the supermarket), which makes a long journey more worthwhile. At the same time, some kinds of stores have been able to realize new scale economies by labor-saving store layouts and mechanized sales, and to exploit still further the advantages of goods variety that depend on the sales volume of a store or a cluster of competing stores. Consequently, the broad pattern of decentralization within the urban areas has been associated with increasing agglomeration in large stores and large shopping centers. A microcosmic central-place hierarchy of different orders of shopping centers, from neighborhood to regional, has evolved within our urban areas.

Finally, the location patterns of consumer-serving activities (except the sidewalk-convenience type) have been significantly affected by the larger space requirements imposed by the need for parking space. This consideration reinforces the trend to the suburbs, and perhaps also reinforces the tendency to cluster in large shopping centers where the pooling of parking space can lead to its more efficient utilization.

Looking at these changes in consumer-serving activity patterns in terms of a system of central places within the urban area, we observe that both extremes of the hierarchy have suffered some decline in relative importance—both the corner store and the central business district, that is to say, have had to give ground in competition with such intermediate-sized central places as the supermarket and the shopping center. Interestingly enough, we observed a parallel tendency with respect to changes in the central-place hierarchy of urban places as units on a national scale: hamlets and the very largest cities have tended to grow more slowly in recent decades than have places of intermediate size.

SELECTED READINGS

Editors of Fortune, *The Exploding Metropolis* (Garden City, N.Y.: Doubleday, 1958).

Jean Gottman, *Megalopolis* (New York: Twentieth Century Fund, 1960).

Edgar M. Hoover and Raymond Vernon, *Anatomy of a Metropolis* (Cambridge, Mass.: Harvard University Press for The Regional Plan Association, 1960).

Raymond Vernon, *Metropolis 1985* (Cambridge, Mass.: Harvard University Press for The Regional Plan Association, 1960).

Homer Hoyt, "Changing Patterns of Land Values," *Land Economics*, 36, 2 (May 1960), 109–117.

Regional Plan Association of New York, *Spread City* (New York: Regional Plan Association, 1962).

Wilbur Thompson, *A Preface to Urban Economics* (Baltimore: Johns Hopkins Press, 1965).

Edward L. Ullman, "The Nature of Cities Reconsidered," in H. W. Eldredge (ed.), *Taming Megalopolis*, Vol. I (Garden City, N.Y.: Doubleday, 1967), 71–92.

James R. Pinkerton, "City-Suburban Residential Patterns by Social Class: A Review of the Literature," *Urban Affairs Quarterly*, 4, 4 (June 1969), 499–519.

Harry W. Richardson, *Regional Economics* (New York: Praeger, 1969), Ch. 7.

Colin Clark, *Population Growth and Land Use* (New York: St. Martin's Press, 1969), Ch. IX.

Edwin S. Mills, "Urban Density Functions," *Urban Studies,* 7, 1 (February 1970), 5–20.

INTRODUCTION

There is no dearth of urban problems; indeed, the consensus is that things are going so badly that references to "the urban crisis" or "the urban mess" have become clichés. In almost every period of history, city life has evoked adverse criticism on cultural, political, economic, moral, and health grounds; but rarely, if ever, has so much dissatisfaction been voiced as in present-day America.

It is possible to view the urban crisis in terms of four major problems. The most pressing of these is the slum. Concentrated poverty, inadequate housing, and denial of opportunity give rise to a festering social conflict and a potentially catastrophic polarization of interests and attitudes, with increasingly geographic aspects as the ghettos crystallize and the contrast between the poor black central city and rich white suburbia heightens. A second conspicuous problem, in all but a few of the larger metropolises, is economic obsolescence and decay in the downtown core (which can have serious cultural and social implications as well). A third crisis involves transport and traffic congestion. The fourth is the fiscal crisis: the increasing inability to finance adequate public services of almost every kind, even with rapidly rising tax burdens. In addition, there are other serious problems, notably spoiling of the natural environment through air and water pollution and trash.

We are aware that these ills are related to one another in a complex syndrome. While most other countries face a similar set of problems in large urban areas, some peculiarly American conditions and institutions aggravate the urban crisis here. These include the heterogeneity of urban populations, and particularly the color line; the free enterprise tradition that inhibits effective planning or control of urban land uses; the fragmentation of government and fiscal responsibility in urban areas into rival and jealously independent jurisdictions; our almost total attachment to a mode of personal transport that is both an inefficient user of space and the major polluter of the atmosphere; and systematic underrepresentation of urban areas in our legislative assemblies.

12
Some Spatial Aspects of Urban Economic Problems

In a single chapter, it would be unrealistic to try to deal with all aspects of these problems, which extend far beyond regional economics and beyond economics as such. Accordingly, we shall be selective, concentrating on those aspects of urban problems and solutions to which an understanding of the economics of space and location seems most directly pertinent.

DOWNTOWN

On the basis of the simple structure and growth models already set forth, we could accept it as normal that the central core of an urban area will tend to show less rapid growth (in terms of employment, business sales, and daytime population) than peripheral areas. No special problem or basis for concern would arise from such a trend. Actually, however, the downtown areas of American cities are in trouble, and their ills constitute part of the whole complex of urban problems.

There are three principal symptoms of distress: declining levels of activity, congestion, and environmental deterioration. The distress is, of course, felt in different ways by such different groups as downtown merchants, property owners, commuters, residents, shoppers, and taxpayers.

Declining Levels of Activity

The acute cause for concern here is, as noted above, *absolute* losses rather than merely a failure to keep up with the suburbs. Although the number of office jobs is increasing in many downtown areas, especially those of the larger metropolises, a great many other activities are shrinking. Fig. 12-1 shows a dramatic example: the Chicago Loop. It appears that total downtown employment in Chicago has been falling since the late 1940s, with a similar but even more marked trend (percentagewise) in the number of other visitors who contribute to the daytime population. During this same period, the population of the city of Chicago remained roughly stable and that of the metropolitan area rose about 20 percent.

Fig. 12-2 illustrates another case—the Manhattan central business district, comprising that part of the island below 61st St.—over a longer period and with some information on the types of vehicles in which people entered the downtown area. It appears that the total traffic peaked some time around the end of World War II and then fell off as in Chicago's case, but that it began to rise again in the 1950s. There was a large increase in the use of individual motor vehicles (automobiles, taxis, and trucks), though the absolute decline in transit use appears to have been checked by the early 1960s. Both Chicago and New York are well provided with rapid transit; in cities lacking such facilities, the decline in the relative importance of the central business district as a trip destination has generally been more marked, as is suggested by Table 12-2 later in this chapter.

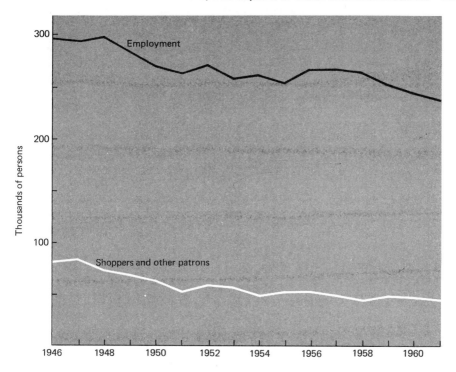

Fig. 12-1. Approximate Daily Employment and Number of Shoppers in the Chicago Central Business District, 1946–1961

SOURCE: J. R. Meyer, J. F. Kain, and M. Wohl, *The Urban Transportation Problem* (Cambridge, Mass.: Harvard University Press, 1965), Table 7, p. 38. These estimates are based on traffic and transportation studies. Approximate employment is based on number of persons accumulated downtown between 7:00 a.m. and 9:30 a.m.; number of shoppers and other patrons is based on excess of peak accumulations of persons over the employment. The same source (pp. 35–38) presents selected data for 13 different cities to demonstrate a general trend toward reduced travel to downtown areas in the 1950s.

Reasons for the reduced locational attractiveness of the downtown areas in recent decades have already been adduced for manufacturing, wholesale and retail trade, residence, routine office work, and some types of information-processing activities like research. Activities historically attached to downtown locations are (1) those that require a great deal of daily face-to-face contact with a variety of activities that are themselves subject to strong cluster economies (such as the financial district, law firms, power-structure luncheon clubs and the like), (2) activities like opera houses, city halls, newspapers, or museums serving the entire metropolitan population at a single location, and (3) activities catering to large numbers of out-of-town visitors (such as hotels, convention halls, and wholesalers' or manufacturers' salesrooms for visiting buyers).

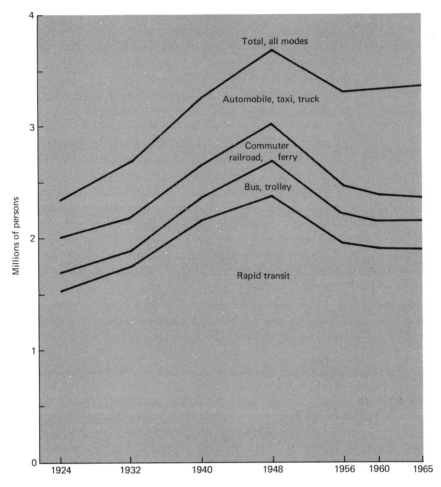

Fig. 12-2. Number of Persons Entering Manhattan Central Business District (South of 61st St.) in Vehicles on a Typical Business Day, 1924–1956
SOURCE: Data supplied by the Regional Plan Association, New York.

The use of airplanes and cars by out-of-town visitors has greatly weakened these central ties for such categories as hotels and convention halls, and an increasing number of business conferences are being held in suburban motels and rented space at airports. Regional sales and service offices that are the home bases for traveling sales or servicing personnel have similarly found access advantage in outlying locations. After these and other defections, the corporate headquarters office has remained as a bulwark of downtown areas. Even in this activity, however, there are evidences of a weakening attachment and intimations that actual declines in downtown employment might be forthcoming. The number of employees in central offices of manufacturing firms in the central cities of major industrial areas rose less than 2 percent (from 276,268 to 280,532) between 1958 and 1963, while those in the suburbs and satellites of such industrial areas increased from 75,488 to 130,948, or more than 57 percent.[1] Although these data cover only a short period, apply only to manufacturing firms, and refer to central cities as a whole rather than to their central business districts, they suggest a loosening of downtown concentration.

Accordingly, it appears that declining downtown employment is either already prevalent or threatened in virtually every category of activity that has historically made up the city core. The mutual interaction between fewer employees and fewer customers is obvious.

Though the actuality or the prospect of absolute decline in central business districts obviously injures property owners and others who have a stake in the level of downtown activity, we need not fall into the Place Prosperity fallacy of assuming that every location as such has a "right" to be shielded against obsolescence. If downtown decay is to be treated as a legitimate public concern justifying preventive action, the case for such concern and action should be made on a broader basis than the interest of the property holders immediately involved. The basic questions for policy judgment are (1) whether an active and viable downtown is a valuable part of the urban economic and social complex, affecting its overall efficiency and quality of life, and (2) whether there are substantial hidden social benefits and externalities not taken into account in the market pricing system. It is hoped that the rest of this chapter will be of some help to the reader in forming his own opinion.

Congestion

Another cause for concern in downtown areas is traffic congestion— which is not only inordinately wasteful of time and street space, but is certainly one of the important reasons for the declining popularity of downtown locations. Concern with congestion may seem paradoxical since total travel to downtown areas is apparently not growing much, and in many cities it is even diminishing. The explanation lies partly in the greater use of automobiles and partly in the increased peaking of the traffic in rush hours.

Congestion affects two types of movement: circulation within the downtown area by vehicles and pedestrians and movement into and out of the area (primarily by vehicles). The former problem has been acute as long

---

[1] Daniel Creamer, *Manufacturing Employment by Type of Location,* Studies in Business Economics No. 106 (New York: National Industrial Conference Board, 1969), Appendix Table C, p. 112. More comprehensive data from the same source appear in Table 11-2 on p. 334 above.

as large cities have existed, and is probably not getting any worse. In ancient Rome, chariots were excluded in daytime hours in an effort to cope with traffic jams. Faded photographs of Fifth Avenue in horse-and-buggy days show it crammed from curb to curb in the rush hour. Mobility within downtown areas is an activity in which it would be difficult to demonstrate any great progress or retrogression, in terms of speed or comfort.

Getting into and out of downtown has however become more of a problem with the decay of public transit, greater distances from residential areas, and vastly increased use of the space-consuming private automobile. For those who do make the trip, evidence from traffic surveys suggests that the time required is at least as much as it was, while the average distance is greater. Such averages, of course, omit the increasing proportion of workers and shoppers who have simply stopped going downtown regularly.

Unfortunately, comparable information on travel patterns and times for more than one survey date is available in very few cities, so that our knowledge of trends such as those suggested is quite sketchy. But it is at least a fair presumption that the time required for downtown circulation and access has not been reduced. In the face of improved access by suburbanites to suburban jobs and shopping facilities, this implies deterioration in the *relative* access advantages of downtowns.

Amenity

There is abundant evidence that the troubles of downtown areas involve in part some unfavorable manifestations of obsolescence. The street utility layouts and the buildings of high-density downtown areas are more expensive to modernize than those of less intensively developed neighborhoods. In situations of rapid locational and technological change, it is especially difficult for districts and buildings to grow old gracefully and to develop the positive attractions associated with maturity and age in downtown areas (such as those of many old European cities) that have grown up under more stable and regulated conditions. American downtown areas are more obsolete than those of most other countries, because in this country the dislocations resulting from transport changes and population shifts have been more drastic and because land use controls and planning to recognize externalities and protect the public interest have been lacking or ineffective. So far at least, it seems clear that our downtown amenities have not merely failed to keep pace with those of outer areas but have suffered absolute deterioration.

Greater use of automobiles is partly responsible. Whether parking at the curb, in open lots, or in multilevel garages, cars occupy large amounts of scarce downtown space and thus reduce convenience of access by increasing the distance from one work or shopping destination to another. In a thoroughly motorized city such as Los Angeles, more than two-thirds of the downtown area can be preempted by streets and parking facilities, and this is all "dead space" as far as any ultimate destinations are concerned. The prime potential advantage of a downtown—quick and convenient access among multifarious activities—is thus dissipated.

Another factor in deterioration of the quality of downtown life reflects the changing distribution of various income groups of the population. As the middle and higher income people have led the way in suburbanization, the populations with closest access to downtown areas are increasingly the poor. The changing composition of downtown consumer demands is apparent in the cheapening of stores, restaurants, amusements, and all other types of consumer-serving facilities; and this, of course, further discourages the more affluent from choosing downtown as a place to work or play or shop.

The Challenge, and Some Responses

We have identified and explained some aspects of a major urban problem variously identified as "strangulation," "the downtown dilemma," "dry rot at the core," and in other equally vivid terms. What can or should be done about it?

It is important to keep reminding ourselves that the *raison d'être* of an urban concentration is provision for close, easy, and multifarious interpersonal contact. From this standpoint, an urban pattern is "efficient" when there is a focal point for concentration of as many as possible of those activities that require access to a high proportion of the firms and households of the area and are best concentrated (because of scale economies or external economies of close agglomeration) in one single location in the area.[2]

Among the activities that are logical candidates for central location on the basis of their access and agglomeration requirements, terminals for interregional passenger transport are certainly included. Yet airports, in the present state of air transport technology, are obviously far too space consuming and noisy to be eligible for anything like a central location, and become increasingly remote as they get larger. If the interurban public transport of the future can be compactly designed and compatible with intensive development in its terminal area, it is reasonable to expect cities to have their main passenger terminals integrated centrally with their in-

---

[2] For a suggested "hierarchy of CBD land uses and land values," identifying a series of specific business activities and the ranges of land values that they can support, see Larry Smith, "Space for the CBD's Functions," *Journal of the American Institute of Planners*, 27, 1 (February 1961), Table 4, 38.

ternal transportation as it was a generation ago.[3] Current and foreseeable developments in fast interurban ground transport (for example, in the Boston-Washington "Northeast Corridor") suggest some hope in this direction. Prospects for relocating air terminals to city centers seem much more conjectural. But it is possible that at some future time urban historians will consider as a curious temporary aberration the mid-twentieth-century period in which interurban transport did not go direct from one city center to another.

Perhaps the most fundamental and abiding urban problem involves the search for ways to exploit the city's unique potential for maximum mass and diversity of contact, choice, and opportunity without unduly sacrificing other values. However, we need to understand a great deal more (and in more specific and quantitative terms) about what urbanism contributes to economic and social progress through its contact opportunities. A recent and valuable multidisciplinary survey[4] has illuminated the question from many angles, some of them new. But it would seem that up to now, urban economists and other "urbanists" have made little headway in developing adequate operational knowledge on the external economies associated with urbanism and more specifically with intraurban concentration. There is room for more empirical analysis as well as for amplification of the theories of location and regional development to cover complex spatial relations involving contact and time as major parameters. A host of suggestive hypotheses still await verification.[5]

The problem of advantages of concentration and how to exploit them comes to a head in the central business district, since there the potential contact opportunities are highest and the conflict with space requirements the most serious. A basic challenge to the ingenuity of urbanists is to devise ways of improving downtown areas in the three relevant aspects: making them *easy to get to, easy to get around in,* and *attractive and effective* as places to work or visit.

As yet, we do not know very much about the effectiveness of various methods of increasing the realized contact potential of central business districts. Efforts in this direction in the United States have been fragmentary and often mutually conflicting, and there has been some reluctance

---

[3] This suggestion is introduced simply as provocative speculation. J. R. Meyer, J. F. Kain, and M. Wohl, *The Urban Transportation Problem* (Cambridge, Mass.: Harvard University Press, 1965), Ch. 2, expect *freight* terminals to move to beltway junction locations, and I should not dispute the reasonableness of that projection.

[4] Philip M. Hauser and Leo F. Schnore (eds.), *The Study of Urbanization* (New York: Wiley, 1965).

[5] See, for example, two sources cited in earlier chapters: Robert M. Lichtenberg, *One-Tenth of a Nation* (Cambridge, Mass.: Harvard University Press for the Regional Plan Association, 1960) and Benjamin Chinitz, "Contrasts in Agglomeration: New York and Pittsburgh," *Papers and Proceedings of the American Economic Association,* 51, 2 (May 1961), 279-289.

to regard experiences in foreign cities (such as Rotterdam or even Toronto) as applicable to American cities. Pedestrian malls have been tiny and tentative. New downtown amenities have mostly been in the form of wider streets, parking garages, convention halls, and shiny skyscrapers. Radical modernization of mass transit, integrated with adequate parking and transfer facilities at outlying stations and adequate intra-downtown facilities (such as mini-buses and moving sidewalks), cannot be said to have been tried. Policies of various public authorities on transport have generally been both conflicting and self-defeating, as will be shown later. Imaginative and consistent transport planning is basic to any improvement or even maintenance of the functional effectiveness of downtown areas, though clearly not the only essential element in a solution. The possible benefits of a more efficient system for bringing large numbers of people into close contact in agreeable surroundings appear large in terms of revitalization of the urban mechanism at its most vital spot.

THE GHETTO

Reasons for Increasing Concern

Blighted areas and slums have always been a feature of large cities in the United States and nearly all other countries, although, as we noted earlier, the slum areas have not always been as typically central as they are in present-day America. Two basic and unfortunate facts go far to explain this condition. First, a sizable fraction of the urban population is too poor to afford socially acceptable housing, and few governments have been willing or able to support adequate housing for all through public subsidy. Second, the explosive pattern of change in American urban areas creates a large supply of obsolete structures and neighborhoods in the oldest residential areas of the central city. The poor have no alternative but to rent this cast-off housing. In similar fashion, aged and obsolete business structures in blighted areas are occupied (often intermittently and with high turnover) by the least desirable types of businesses until some opportunity arises that may make it worthwhile to clear and redevelop the site.

In the Burgess schematic model of urban land uses mentioned in an earlier chapter, the areas of blight and slum were pictured as transition areas: expanding downtown development was casting its shadow over the surrounding commercial and residential areas next in line for conversion to more intensive business use. Today it is increasingly clear that these blighted areas are not going to be renovated or even significantly pushed outward by lateral spread of central business districts in the foreseeable future. Some slums, in fact, are at considerable distances from downtown, though nearly all are within the boundaries of central cities. Black slums, which in the 1950s and 1960s came to be called ghettos, tend to be more centrally located than other poverty areas.[6]

Why is the ghetto of today a matter of more acute concern than the slums of yesterday? A more awakened social consciousness and public responsibility may be part of the answer, but certainly is not all of it. The intensity of crowding in present ghettos (as measured by density of population or floor space per inhabitant) is generally *lower* than it was in the immigrant slums of New York and other large cities around the turn of the century; and most indicia of housing quality, sanitation, and public services are also less abysmal. But there are at least four new factors that make the present situation even less tolerable than the old one.

First, the ghetto of today is essentially a *black* slum.[7] Its people, marked by conspicuous skin color as well as some characteristics stemming from a background of subjection, face more formidable barriers to assimilation in the dominant society than did any of the earlier immigrant groups; some have, in frustration, rejected assimilation and have chosen instead the far more problematical goal of creating a viable separate culture and economic organization. Socially and politically, the present ghettos foster more dangerous disaffection than any poverty pockets of our past.

A second aggravating factor is the sheer size and cohesiveness of the ghettos. Modern American ghettos represent segregation on a grand scale, in contrast to a pattern of small poverty or minority group pockets. And it is all too clear that a given aggregate amount of poverty and deprivation is a far more serious problem if it is solidly massed in one large ghetto than if it were scattered throughout many smaller ghettos. This will be recognized in theoretical terms as a case of adverse "neighborhood effects" or external diseconomies of agglomeration.

In a large ghetto, a much greater proportion of the residents live far from the edges, where there would be at least some exposure to superior opportunity, amenity, evidences of hope, and avenues of gradual escape. Inside the large ghetto, the "outside world" comes to be something remote and alien, identified as an oppressive and hostile "establishment." Polarization of ways of life and attitudes between ghetto dwellers and outsiders is fostered. In more specific terms, access to jobs is harder, and genuine integration of schools and other public facilities becomes impossible without controversial devices such as the long-distance busing of school children

---

[6] Concentration of ghettos within the central city is the rule even in cases like Boston and Pittsburgh where the central city has unusually restricted boundaries relative to the size of its metropolitan area. In the Pittsburgh SMSA, for example, nearly three-fourths of the metropolitan population lives outside the city of Pittsburgh. The term "ghetto" implies ethnic segregation rather than poverty per se, and was originally applied to those parts of medieval Italian cities to which Jews were confined.

[7] A few ghetto areas are predominantly Mexican, Indian, or Puerto Rican. The principal Indian slums are still rural (on the reservations).

and the creation of mammoth "educational parks" to replace the traditional neighborhood schoolhouse. Improvement, rehabilitation, and renewal of housing are more difficult in an extensive slum, since the prevailing character of the neighborhood determines both the incentive to improve an individual property and the benefits thereby achieved. Maintenance of public safety likewise poses greater problems in massive areas of poverty and social stress.[8]

The symptoms of maladjustment and frustration in ghettos are all too apparent, even apart from the occasional outbreaks of wholesale violence and the hardening of militant attitudes. Low levels of health and educational attainment (particularly if measured in some more discerning way than a simple count of school years completed), rapidly rising crime rates, and extremely high unemployment, especially for young adults, are among the distressing indicia of the problem.

Still another aggravating factor is poor access to employment opportunities. Although ghettos are typically rather central, their people are at an increasing disadvantage in job access. This partly reflects the fact that they are the least mobile group in the whole urban area, in terms of either the journey to work or change of residence. Not only are they at the bottom in terms of information, education, and salable skills, but many cannot afford cars and find even transit fares a serious financial burden. Overall home-to-work commuting speeds by most existing modes of transit are lower than by car, which restricts the feasible range of commutation. (Halving one's commuting speed reduces by 75 *percent* the area that is within 1 hour's travel time.)

At the same time, the jobs (particularly those in manufacturing and construction) have gradually moved farther away from the ghetto, to suburban locations which are difficult if not impossible to reach by public transport. Even without any racial discrimination in hiring, the black ghetto dweller would find it more and more difficult to find a job that he can reach.

Some Approaches to Solution:
Spatial Aspects

Were it possible to prescribe a simple, workable solution, the ghetto problem might be solved by now. All that we shall try to do in this brief discussion is to indicate some of the peculiarly locational aspects.

---

[8] For further discussion of the evils of slum "compaction," as he calls it, see Jack Lessinger, "The Case for Scatteration," *Journal of the American Institute of Planners*, 28, 3 (August 1962), 159–169. The author emphasizes that compaction is independent of, and not necessarily correlated with, density.

IMPROVING THE GHETTO. Some policy approaches stress physical improvement of the ghetto areas. The most direct and primitive kind of action—and the least helpful—is the practice of "slum clearance": simply tearing down the obsolete buildings and redeveloping the land in some other way without any particular thought for the displaced inhabitants. Since they must live somewhere and cannot afford any but the worst housing, the effect is to shove the slum into the nearest area of actual or incipient decay. But even this program requires heavy subsidies to make it work, and disenchantment with it was reasonably complete by the early 1960s.[9] The basic idea had one merit—it recognized the strength of neighborhood effects that discourage piecemeal rehabilitation or renewal of neighborhoods—but the major error was in overlooking the social costs and the futility of uprooting slums on one area merely to sow them in another.

A somewhat more sophisticated approach, which does face up to the question of displacement, entails rehousing the inhabitants of a slum in new, subsidized high-rise projects in the same neighborhood. Here, too, the results have been somewhat disappointing, and at best only a dent had been made by 1970 in the shortage of decent housing.

Experience with these attempted solutions showed that more attention needed to be given to such elements of neighborhood viability as community consciousness, organization, and enterprise. These may well be more important than physical improvement of structures, and can enable a neighborhood to achieve gradual economic and physical rehabilitation without massive razing and displacement. This new emphasis—leaning more heavily on the expertise of the sociologist and social worker and less on that of the construction engineer—has gained ground since the late 1960s.

Since the most urgent need of ghetto populations is more jobs, efforts to stimulate new business growth in and near ghetto areas are a logical part of any attempt to improve those areas. This is not easy, since the prevailing trends of location are in the opposite direction, with increased emphasis on just those things that the inner-city areas lack: ample space for expansion, low taxes, and a community environment offering amenity, visibility, prestige, and quick access to circumferential and intercity highways. It can be surmised that a large permanent subsidy would be needed to entice enough private employers to locate near ghettos and employ wholly or mainly ghetto workers; and that such large sums might better be used in other ways to provide improved job access.

A policy akin to "import substitution" has had some strong adherents. This entails assistance to ghetto entrepreneurs to establish small consumer-

---

[9] A good survey of various urban renewal policies in the United States up to the mid-1960s is James Q. Wilson (ed.), *Urban Renewal: The Record and the Controversy* (Cambridge, Mass.: M.I.T. Press, 1966).

serving businesses within the area. The assumption is that such "Black Capitalism" can take advantage not only of an ample low-cost labor supply but also of a somewhat protected home market (that is, the ghetto consumers will prefer to patronize a firm operated and staffed by neighbors). It is also argued that the profits of such enterprises will accrue to ghetto residents and will, to a greater extent, be spent in the neighborhood. Moreover, in the long run, experience in founding and running small businesses will develop black entrepreneurial skills and financial backing so that blacks can win a more adequate foothold on the middle and higher rungs of the business management ladder.

Unquestionably, the nurturing of a much larger cadre of black business managers and entrepreneurs and the accumulation of capital and creditworthiness by black-controlled firms must play an essential part in redressing the wide interracial gap in levels of opportunity that exists today. At the same time, there are obvious limitations on what can be accomplished in the kinds of businesses that can be expected to survive within ghetto areas proper. With respect to actual creation of additional black employment, it is not realistic to expect much more to materialize than the equivalent of replacing whites now working in ghetto areas. Such a number would be small compared to current ghetto unemployment.[10]

IMPROVING ACCESS FROM THE GHETTO. All the measures discussed above share a Place Prosperity approach in that they focus on improving conditions and opportunities within the distressed area itself. This is not to say that such measures are misguided or unnecessary. But a complementary line of endeavor, involving opportunities outside of present ghettos, may have greater promise.

Reference has already been made to the relatively long distances between ghetto areas and the areas of positive employment growth: a handicap compounded by inadequacy of public transit, low car ownership, generally low job qualifications, and discrimination. These component factors of the access problem were being attacked in various cities by the late 1960s or were the subject of serious proposals for government action. Special bus routes were established on a trial basis to take ghetto workers to employment locations previously out of reach; programs were proposed for financing automobile purchase or rental by ghetto workers wanting to extend their commuting range; continuing public programs of education, training, and inducement to cooperating employers nibbled away at the problems of inadequate training and employer discrimination; and some progress was made in attacking the more serious and extensive racial discrimination practiced by unions.

---

[10] For a sobering appraisal of programs to stimulate new business enterprises in ghettos, see Sar Levitan, Garth Mangum, and Robert Taggart III, *Economic Opportunity in the Ghetto: The Partnership of Government and Business* (Baltimore: Johns Hopkins University Press, 1970).

A logical complement to the policy of easing commuter access from ghettos is that of facilitating migration out of the ghettos to neighborhoods where both job access and environment are better. The major barriers are two: inability to afford new housing and the opposition of white suburbanites. These barriers reinforce one another, since housing discrimination drastically narrows the area of choice for blacks and inflates the prices of the housing they can find in the few black or mixed suburbs. Obstacles to migration (according to one of the "laws of migration" cited in Chapter 7) increase selectivity: under present conditions the blacks most likely to escape from city ghettos are those with the highest incomes, education, skills, and economic ambition. Although statistically the average "quality" of ghetto populations will suffer from their departure, migration is clearly a necessary part of any acceptable long-term solution. This is true not simply in terms of the welfare of the individuals involved, but also in terms of the unhealthy social implications of a growing polarization between white suburbia and black city. The balance of conflict and cooperation between city and suburb is delicate enough without any additional aggravation from such polarization.

The bottling up of the bulk of the urban black population in inner-city ghettos has had the further unfortunate result of inflating residential real-estate prices and rents in the cities, since the space demands of growing ghetto populations have confronted an artificially inflexible supply. At the same time, prices in the white suburbs are lower than they would be if blacks were fully admitted to the competition. These price distortions have not only increased the economic squeeze on blacks but have also abetted the white flight to the suburbs.[11]

It is sometimes supposed that poverty is the main reason for black concentration in the inner city. The falsity of this proposition, however, is manifest in Fig. 12-3, where we have a measure of the degree of suburbanization of white and black populations of similar income levels. Though there are substantial differences among cities, and the degree of suburbanization is greater for the well-to-do than for the poor of each race, it is clear that blacks are far more centralized within our major urbanized areas than whites *of the same income level.*

---

[11] This point has been persuasively argued by John F. Kain, "Effect of Housing Market Segregation on Urban Development," in *Savings and Residential Financing* (proceedings of a conference sponsored by the U.S. Savings and Loan League; Chicago, 1969). He concludes, ". . . the first requirement is devising methods for opening suburban housing to blacks. Only when the city loses its monopoly on black poverty will it have a chance. As long as the ghetto continues its rapid growth, prices in central cities will remain at high levels and the expectation that the city will become a lower class slum will persist. If the growth of the ghetto can be arrested, positive programs aimed at making the central city attractive to middle income families, be they white or black, have a chance."

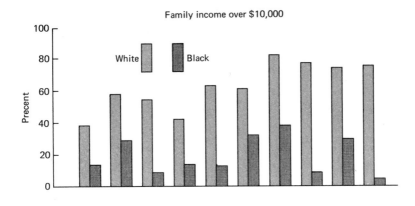

Family income over $10,000

White   Black

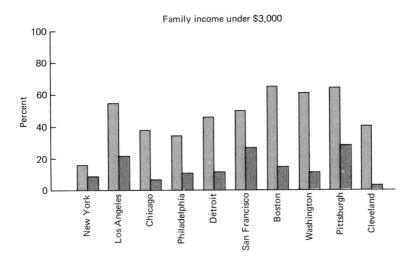

Family income under $3,000

New York
Los Angeles
Chicago
Philadelphia
Detroit
San Francisco
Boston
Washington
Pittsburgh
Cleveland

Fig. 12-3. Percentage of Families Living in Suburban Ring in the 10 Largest U.S. Urban Areas, 1960, by Color for Selected Income Groups

SOURCE: John F. Kain, "Effect of Housing Market Segregation on Urban Development," in *Savings and Residential Financing* (proceedings of a conference sponsored by the U.S. Savings and Loan League, Chicago, 1969), Table I, p. 92; based on data from *United States Census of Population, 1960.* For New York and Chicago, the suburban ring is the difference between the SMSA and the central city. For all other cities, it is the difference between the urban area and the central city. The San Francisco-Oakland, Los Angeles-Long Beach, and Philadelphia-Camden urban areas each have two central cities.

Another myth is that the ghetto concentration of blacks is largely voluntary. Although we have alluded earlier to the beaten-path incentives that initially lead black newcomers to the ghetto, the bulk of the ghetto population does not like it there and would prefer to move to an integrated neighborhood. Kain (*op. cit.*, p. 93) cites evidence from attitude surveys in the 1960s indicating that such a preference prevailed by about 2 to 1 for urban blacks in general, and much more strongly still at higher income levels and in Northern cities.

The seriousness of the ghetto problem was greatly aggravated in the 1950s and 1960s by the rapid growth of ghetto populations through in-migration. Increasing population keeps housing prices and rents high and makes city officials understandably reluctant to enforce health and building codes or condemn decrepit buildings for fear of creating an impossible relocation problem. It also imposes a larger fiscal burden for welfare and other services, since the poor bring larger public costs than revenues.

Accordingly, it is fairly clear that anything that might reduce the influx would at least provide a breathing spell to the hard-pressed cities and would probably hasten an acceptable solution. In other words, it would be desirable to have slower black migration to central cities but faster black migration from those cities to the suburbs. This is one of the arguments that has been advanced for (1) programs to increase employment opportunity in and near areas of black emigration (mainly in the rural South) and (2) programs to equalize levels of welfare assistance in different parts of the country to eliminate the artificial stimulus to migration of the poor into urban areas where such benefits are many times higher. Such equalization would alleviate, though not eliminate, the awkward problem that arises because migration tends to flow particularly to those cities that take the lead in ghetto improvement—thus penalizing and partly thwarting their progressive efforts.

By 1970 the tide of black migration to large cities had at least temporarily abated. There was also some fragmentary statistical evidence (see Table 11-3 on page 336) suggesting that black mobility into suburbs was increasing.

We have indicated the various ways in which a solution of the ghetto problem may be achieved. It is not yet possible to judge just how large a role each of the remedial measures will play; but among the essentials are understanding and patience, without which the best opportunities for progress may fail to be exploited.

TRANSPORTING PEOPLE

Among the four major urban problems covered in this chapter, transportation has a special claim to our attention—not because it is necessarily the most pressing or the most complex, but because it is the most fully identified with the economics of location and space which is the province of this book. Furthermore, we have already seen that transport factors play a large role in the problems of ghettos and downtowns; and transport is also directly relevant to the problems of financing public services, which will be taken up later in this chapter.

Urban transportation in America today involves mainly the uses and requirements of the private automobile, and the serious problems confronting us mainly emerge from difficulties in locational accommodation to the very rapid adoption of this mode of travel. Table 12-1 shows that in

TABLE 12-1. Percentage Distributions of Journeys to Work by Transport Mode, for Residents of Central Cities, SMSAs, and Nonfarm Areas Outside SMSAs, 1963

| | All modes | Private automobile | | | Public transportation | Walking | Other |
		Total	Driver only	Passengers			
Residents of central cities of SMSAs	100	67	47	29	29	3	1
Residents of SMSAs outside central cities	100	90	65	25	9	1	*
Nonfarm residents outside SMSAs	100	92	58	34	2	4	2

* Less than one-half of 1 percent.

SOURCE: U.S. Department of Commerce, Bureau of the Census, 1963 Census of Transportation, Vol. 1, Passenger Transportation Survey (Washington, D.C.: Government Printing Office, 1966), Part 2, Table 3, p. 64.

1963, 90 percent of the journeys to work (both inside and outside urban areas) by metropolitan suburbanites were in private automobiles (including 65 percent in cars carrying only the driver), while 9 percent used some means of public transport and most of the remaining 1 percent used the oldest of all modes of transport, walking. The relative use of public transport was substantially higher for people living and/or working in the central areas of cities, but with the exception of travel to the central business districts of large metropolitan areas served by rapid rail transit systems, it did not account for a majority of trips. The number of passengers carried by local public transit in the United States diminished in the 1950s at an average rate of 5.9 percent per annum, and between 1960 and 1966 at about 2.5 percent per annum. Railroad commuter traffic, however, increased 4.5 percent between 1962 and 1968.[12]

The twentieth-century locational adjustments required by the use of the automobile have been even more drastic and far-reaching than those required in the nineteenth century by the railroad. In the United States at any rate, the speed of introduction of the new means of transport has been somewhat greater in the case of the automobile. The changed conditions of transport apply to a wider range of distances, routes, and types of travel. A higher proportion of the population—approaching 100 percent —is directly affected. More potent and articulate political pressures are generated because of the greater number of parties directly involved. Coming at a later stage of economic development, the locational impact of the automobile was imposed on a larger complex of fixed facilities than was the impact of railroads; for that reason it created more functional and locational obsolescence of capital. Particularly relevant within urban areas is the fact that the automobile is not merely a conqueror of distance but, at the same time, is in its own right a major claimant for scarce space. A substantial part of the difficulty caused by automobile use in urban areas is precisely due to its large space requirements.[13] Moreover, the automobile has worsened access for substantial groups of the population by destroying public transit services and by creating more dispersed location patterns. Finally, the automobile appears to be the chief culprit in the air pollution crisis which is now beginning to threaten the very habitability of our densely urban areas.

Specific Aspects of the Urban Transport Problem

What, then, are the manifestations that justify reference to a "problem" in urban passenger transportation?

One of these shows up in the statistics of travel distances and times, not to mention the complaints of individual commuters. It seems that the search for quicker journeys, to work and to other destinations, has been

---

[12] Based on statistics from *Transit Fact Book* (Washington, D.C.: American Transit Association, annual), and Association of American Railroads, *Statistical Summary No. 53* (Washington: September 1969), p. 7.

[13] One expert judgment runs as follows: "the general rule that transportation is a decreasing cost industry may not hold true within highly industrialized areas. Without much data to go on, one can hazard the guess that for highway transportation this situation [*increasing* cost with higher traffic density] is likely to occur chiefly in metropolitan areas with populations of 1 million or more, and within the central business districts of cities of over 100,000 population; for rail transportation the only likely instances in the United States are the Chicago area and the New York-Philadelphia area." William Vickrey, "Current Issues in Transportation," in Neil W. Chamberlain (ed.), *Contemporary Economic Issues* (Homewood, Ill.: Irwin, 1969), p. 187.

in large part self-defeating. This is particularly true with regard to daily work trips in urban areas, both large and small. By and large, the advantages of speed, flexibility, and better roads have been offset by increased traffic and, most importantly, by a vastly wider separation of residences and work places. The average commuter travels greater distances in an American urban area than he did 10 or 20 years ago, but spends about as much time en route. Relative to the time spent at work, time spent in traveling to and from work has probably even increased.[14] In addition, the trip is more costly. As to whether the strain or disutility of the trip is greater for the automobile driver or for the public transit rider, there appears to be no consensus; this is likely to remain a matter of personal tastes. But up to the present, the direct consumer benefits of automobile ownership seem to involve not reduction of travel times, but somewhat more spacious styles of living and a greater variety and frequency of recreational and other nonwork journeys.

A second aspect of the transport problem, affecting some of the people all the time and all of the people some of the time, is the emasculation of public transport services that has resulted directly from automobile competition and indirectly through dispersed residence and employment patterns fostered by highway transport. Mobility has become increasingly difficult and expensive for anyone unable to drive or unable to afford a car, and for nearly everyone when the family car is preempted, or laid up for repairs or by weather conditions. As it was once succinctly put to me by a Los Angeles cab driver, "Brother, in L.A. without wheels you're dead."

A third aspect of the problem is traffic congestion, already mentioned in connection with downtown areas but actually of much wider incidence. Increased traffic often reaches the saturation point, well known to traffic engineers, where the number of vehicles passing a given point in a given time begins to fall.

Finally, there are some important impacts of transport use upon other problems such as ghetto employment, downtown blight, health and amenity, and the fiscal difficulties of local governments, which will be referred to more specifically later.

Approaches to Solution

In a theoretically perfect "transportation market," the person wanting transport would choose the most efficient mode and would be willing to

---

[14] The statement on trend in average travel times is based on rather fragmentary evidence since systematic travel studies are a relatively new source of data and very few have been repeated in the same area for different dates in such a way as to disclose trends of change.

pay for it up to the point where incremental benefits no longer exceed incremental costs. Each kind of transport service provided by others to the user would be made available in response to demand up to the point where incremental revenues no longer exceed incremental costs of providing the service.

In the present urban setting, however, such an ideally efficient allocation of resources is an unattainable and therefore partially irrelevant goal. The obstacles to any easy attainment of an efficient solution lie partly in the traveler's assessment of his own costs, partly in the externalities involved in transport investment and traffic congestion, partly in the lack of coordination of public policies, and partly in the feedback effect of the supply of transport services and facilities upon subsequent demand.

EVALUATION OF THE TRAVELER'S OWN COSTS. The costs of operating a private automobile have been variously estimated in a range of 8 to 20¢ per mile as of 1969, depending, of course, on the type of car, the roads used, allowances for tolls, and the distance driven per year.[15] These estimates do not include parking fees (or fines!).

The commuter making a decision on whether to drive to work or use public transit, however, is more likely to look just at the immediate out-of-pocket cost associated with the specific trip—that is, gasoline plus any parking fees or tolls involved—which may be something like a quarter of the average costs per mile suggested above, or even less if passengers share expenses.[16] These out-of-pocket costs are often no more than the transit fare, so the added convenience and speed of automobile commuting lead him to prefer it in normal weather conditions, unless he finds driving onerous.

This outcome reflects a degree of consumer irrationality. Possibly it could be argued that the traveler needs a car in any case, so that his license fees and some of the depreciation accrual are fixed costs unaffected by amount of car use. Maintenance, repairs, and insurance premiums, however, are in fact affected by mileage driven; and in a growing proportion of families, the issue of having a second car is relevant. If the need for a second car depends on whether the major breadwinner drives to work, then obviously the whole cost associated with owning that second car ought to be taken into account in the choice of commuting mode.

---

[15] The best-known estimates are those of the U.S. Department of Transportation, the American Automobile Association (AAA), and Runzheimer & Co. of Rochester, Wis., a firm specializing in cost-accounting services for firms operating fleets of cars. The AAA estimates, rather surprisingly, run about 2¢ a mile higher than those of the Department of Transportation.

[16] See Table 12-1 above, on relative numbers of drivers and passengers. The data indicate that metropolitan suburbanite commuters carry an average of less than 0.4 passenger per trip.

PUBLIC POLICIES. Even if the traveler were fully rational in weighing his own costs, a misallocation of resources in urban transport could result from a failure to charge him for the use of highways, parking facilities, or public transit in accordance with how much it costs to provide those facilities.

The building and maintenance of highways (including the necessary traffic control appurtenances) is necessarily a public function. It is financed, in the United States, by the proceeds of state and federal motor fuel taxes and license fees plus further funds from the public treasuries. The U.S. Bureau of Public Roads estimated that by 1970, roughly $20 billion were being spent annually on highways by all levels of government in the United States: close to $100 per head of the population or $200 per motor vehicle. It is often argued that motor travel within cities and elsewhere is heavily subsidized, which would help to explain the growing extent of private automobile commuting and the decay of public transit services.

The existence and magnitude of such subsidy are extremely difficult to establish. A searching study by Meyer, Kain, and Wohl in the early 1960s reached the conclusion that the user charges levied on motorists nearly if not wholly cover the costs of providing urban facilities for motor traffic except on "local streets and roads" and peak-hour travel on high-cost urban expressways.[17]

There is not, however, general agreement that the subsidy element is inconsequential. The authors argue that partial payment for local roads and streets out of general funds is not really subsidy, since such facilities would be needed regardless of whether private automobiles or transit were used for "trunk line" traffic. But since local roads and streets include everything that is not a state or federal highway, it is hard to believe that their widths, construction costs, and maintenance expenditures are in the long run really independent of the number of cars in operation. If such streets (or, say, everything beyond minimal two-lane access roadways) were built and maintained solely from charges on motorists, there would doubtless be fewer motorists, fewer highway commuters, a smaller effective demand for freeways, and better transit.

The exception noted by the same authors in regard to peak-hour travel is a vital one. The size and design of a roadway have to be geared to maximum rather than average traffic load, and in this sense the incremental cost of providing for one more car is many times greater in the rush hour than at off-peak hours. This principle is, of course, equally true for public transit services.

Congestion costs are a prime example of the multifarious externalities of urban economics that pose a challenge to the pricing system and the

---

[17] Meyer, Kain, and Wohl, *op. cit.*, especially Ch. 4.

economic insight of public authorities. The "marginal traveler" in the rush hour is to some extent penalized for his timing by having a slower and less pleasant journey; but he is not charged anything for the discomfort and delay he imposes on the rest of the traffic stream. Nor are the rush-hour travelers as a group made to pay any larger share of the costs of the next added expressway lane than the off-peak drivers have to pay.

Various measures have been tried and suggested for reducing the waste of resources entailed in the peaking of traffic volumes. In the nearly unique situation of Washington, D. C., where the federal government is the principal employer, it has been possible to spread the peak and improve the average utilization of transport capacity by staggering the work hours of different federal agencies. The saving in transport investment is gained, however, at the cost of some loss in the essential advantage of urban concentrations; namely, easy daily contact between agencies and individuals. When some offices do not open until 9:30 and others close at 3:30, there are only six hours of the working day (minus the lunch hour) during which the city as a whole is really "all there." Voluntary staggering plans have not been conspicuously successful in other cities.

A more sophisticated and promising approach is to internalize the cost of peak travel: that is, make the rush-hour traveler pay at least some of the extra costs for which he is responsible. Ingenious suggestions have been formulated that would make it possible to assess and collect "congestion tolls," both for public transit and private automobiles. For example, individualized electronic signals emitted by cars could be recorded at short range by receivers along congested routes, appropriate charges automatically figured by electronic computer, and bills periodically rendered to the car owner.[18]

The role of various levels of government in financing highway and transit improvements also significantly affects the balance between private automobile and public transit. All road investment is public; and since World War II the state and federal governments have shouldered increasingly large shares of the financial responsibility as long-distance intercity and interstate routes assumed more importance and the cost of road building outran the revenue-raising powers of local governments. By the 1960s, up to nine-tenths of the cost of an urban freeway could be covered by federal money and the rest by state money. Even though all, or nearly all, of the total cost is ultimately met from state and federal taxes on vehicles and fuels, the fact that most of the funds come from Washington

---

[18] See William S. Vickrey, "Congestion Theory and Transport Investment," *American Economic Review*, 59, 2 (May 1969), 251–260, and "Current Issues in Transportation," in Chamberlain (ed.), *op. cit.*, 185–240. Professor Vickrey has led the way in developing the theory of congestion tolls and in working out practical ways of assessing and collecting them.

naturally makes such expressways appear to the local and state governments and their citizens as goodies to be won, rather than as investments to be judiciously pondered.

At the same time, state and federal governments have allocated only insignificant amounts, primarily in the form of support for planning studies, to any support of public transit or improvements therein. Consequently, in the few cases where such improvements have been undertaken on any substantial scale (for example, in the San Francisco Bay area), the reluctance of local voters to approve giant bond issues to cover the cost has been a major obstacle. No comparable local financial commitment has been necessary in order to finance much larger sums for expressway projects.

How can this striking bias in public investment be explained? The apparent historical and political reasons for it are interesting. State, and especially federal, aid to highway building has been justified on two quite separate grounds. One is *fiscal:* Local sources of taxation have simply not been adequate to finance all of the public services and investments demanded. The other reason is *geographical:* Intercity and interregional highways serve much more than a local need.

In financing intrametropolitan expressways, the fiscal justification is, of course, applicable. The same justification could be invoked in support of state and federal aid to urban transit, since such transit is recognized as an essential public service in any sizable urban area and private transit firms have long been strictly regulated as public utilities. But there has been a good deal of delay in recognizing that unaided private enterprise can no longer compete effectively with automobiles operated on the public highways, and government has been slow to accept any responsibility. It has been much easier (though harder on the patrons) to let the private transit firms sink into bankruptcy before finally taking over their equipment at junk prices.[19]

The *geographical* justification for state and federal aid is not legitimately applicable to the transport within metropolitan areas with which

---

[19] For the entire U.S. transit industry (including all privately and publicly owned local passenger transport agencies except taxicabs, suburban railroads, and sightseeing and school buses), the net operating income was 10.4 percent of revenue in 1940, 4.6 percent in 1950, and negative (that is, a net operating *deficit*, before any allowance for fixed charges) each year from 1963 on. *Transit Fact Book* (Washington, D.C.: American Transit Association, annual). The Port Authority of New York is a good example of the reluctance of local public authorities to assume responsibility for really supporting local transit. The Port Authority enthusiastically built and operated profitable bridges, tunnels, and a central bus terminal but refused to help salvage any form of rail transit (on the grounds that its overall earnings position would be impaired) until it was finally pressured into taking over the trans-Hudson tubes on a "just this once but never again" basis. For a critique of the prevailing local-government posture toward private transit firms, see E. M. Hoover, "Motor Metropolis," *Journal of Industrial Economics,* 13, 3 (June 1965), 177–192.

we are concerned in this chapter. But in terms of governmental organization and legislative authority, roads are roads. State and federal aid does not stop at the city or metropolitan boundary but carries a predominant share of the burden for major arteries and particularly expressways within urban areas serving local needs. It seems obvious that urban transit facilities and services should be equally eligible for outside financial support, but such support has not been provided. The main reason is that federal and state highway authorities, enjoying their own special revenue sources,[20] are a ready-made and powerful mechanism for channeling money into urban streets and expressways; there is no corresponding administrative organization or source of funds for transit aid since transit is quite different in character from interregional transport modes. By the late 1960s a little progress had been made in setting up departments of transportation at the federal and state levels, which in principle should coordinate public support of all modes of transport. The highway bureaucracy remained dominant, however, and with the help of motorists' associations jealously guarded its exclusive access to motor vehicle and fuel tax revenues, which is in fact written into many state constitutions.

If highway and transit investments were both financed in the same way, it would be feasible and eminently logical to pose the investment decisions to voters as explicit alternatives, spelling out the tradeoffs. For example, the benefits of a projected rapid transit route could be assessed in terms of how much highway investment would be saved as a result. Even more broadly, one might try to include the savings in private automobile ownership and operating costs; and more broadly still, one could evaluate the long-run implications of the decision in terms of the transportation costs involved in a dispersed, road-oriented metropolitan complex compared to those in a partially transit-oriented spatial pattern.[21]

---

[20] In 1967, motor fuel tax collections amounted to $3.1 billion by the federal government and $5.0 billion by state and local governments; federal use taxes on heavy trucks brought in $0.1 billion, and state and local motor vehicle taxes and operators' license fees $2.4 billion. The grand total was $10.7 billion. U.S. Internal Revenue Service, *Annual Reports of the Commissioner* 1967, 1968; U. S. Bureau of the Census, *Quarterly Summary of State and Local Tax Revenues,* October–December 1967 (Washington: March 1968).

[21] Vickrey argues that the usual methods of evaluating costs and benefits of alternative types of urban transport have a built-in bias in favor of modes that require large amounts of space, and against "land-saving" modes (mass rapid transit). Briefly, his argument runs as follows. The differential access advantages of urban sites are not fully reflected in rent bids and land prices, since part of the benefits of proximity accrues to parties other than the occupier of a given site—it is in fact these mutual or external economies of proximity that constitute the main basis of urbanism. Since urban land tends, then, to be valued in the market at less than the true social value created by its access opportunities, cost assessments for alternative transportation projects (for example, transit versus highways) understate the costs of the more land-using type of transport compared to those of the more land-saving type. Vickrey, "Current Issues in Transportation," *op. cit.,* 220–221.

Our previous discussion explains why the issue is almost never posed in such terms. And unless voters are asked the right questions, they can hardly be expected to give the right answers.

A further instance of lack of coordinated public policy, with a probable bias toward private automobile transport, involves the provision of public parking facilities in downtown areas. Some space is provided free at the curb, an additional amount at the curb for quite low fees, and a growing amount in garages built by municipal parking authorities and either operated publicly or leased to private operators. An element of subsidy is implied, of course, by the fact that municipalities are in the parking business at all. The argument advanced for this activity is that there is a demand for the service which could not otherwise be met; but this argument can involve a degree of circularity. The demand for downtown parking depends on how easy it is for people to drive into the downtown area; thus, each new expressway creates fresh evidence in support of the parking authority's desire to expand. At the same time, provision of easier and cheaper parking downtown makes more people want to drive there, producing fresh evidence in support of the highway planners' projects. Since two or more separate agencies and budgets are involved, coordination is, at best, difficult to achieve. It is a little reminiscent of the man who took another piece of bread in order to finish his butter, and then another piece of butter in order to finish his bread . . . .

Perhaps a rational policy would be to determine first the maximum number of private automobiles that can efficiently circulate within the downtown area, given the rather inelastic limits of downtown street space. This could then be translated into needed parking capacity, and parking fees could then be set at such a level as to discourage any additional downtown trips. Such a policy, however, would require a degree of coordination and bureaucratic restraint which apparently does not widely prevail.

The rate schedules for parking are likewise open to criticism on economic grounds. A reasonable schedule of rates would heavily penalize the all-day parker who comes in at the peak hour in the morning and leaves at the peak hour in the evening, and would offer much lower rates to the short-time off-peak parker, who adds little to traffic congestion but much to the sales of downtown merchants. In practice, however, the opposite principles are generally followed. Hourly rates are lowest for the all-day parker who is the real culprit in creating peak-hour congestion; and rates are generally designed to promote the fullest use of the facilities, regardless of the effect upon traffic.

A minor but interesting misallocation of resources can arise from the provision of parking space that is free or below cost by business establishments or institutions for their employees or patrons. Space is *not* a free good, so the cost of a "free" parking lot is in effect shared among all the employees or patrons, including those who do not use it. Transit riders and pedestrians are thus made to subsidize drivers. Urban universities, for example, are always under strong pressure from majorities of the students and staff to furnish subsidized parking space. It may be overlooked that this policy really amounts to a special penalty on the members of the university community who do not use cars to get there; and that these may be less affluent than those who benefit.

Effects of Transport on Central Cities and Slums

A conspicuous deficiency of nearly all urban transport planning studies is that they treat the transport problem in isolation. The urban transport system (highways and transit systems) is simply judged in terms of how well it satisfies current demands for travel between existing origin and destination points, and plans for future transport improvements are only aimed at satisfying some projected future pattern of trip desires. It is quite rare to find in such studies any real evaluation, or even acknowledgment, of the effect of alternative transportation policies upon the developing land use pattern of the urban area.

Some general indications of the way in which transport services and costs shape urban patterns have been given in this and earlier chapters. We can mention here two specific cases, related to the problems of central cities and slums respectively.

RAPID TRANSIT AND CENTRAL-CITY DECLINE. The difficulties of downtown areas are traced in part to the massive switch to private automobile travel and the consequent decay of public transport services. It is argued that the high-density downtown areas of our older cities in particular, laid out long before automobiles were in common use, are simply incompatible with reliance on a new mode of passenger transport that requires so much more space both for circulation and parking. Among the policies suggested for reviving downtown areas, rapid transit on separated right of way is widely advocated as a means of improving access and reducing congestion.

> Adequate rapid transit, it is argued, would halt and reverse this [decentralization] trend. The implied hypothesis is that there should be some correlation between urban areas' levels of transit service and the rates at which they are decentralizing. That is, cities with little or no public transit should be decentralizing much faster than others.[22]

The authors of the above quotation provide a tabulation that can be used to test the hypothesis. Table 12-2 shows rates of employment growth

---

[22] Meyer, Kain, and Wohl, *op. cit.,* p. 44.

or decline in four kinds of activity (manufacturing, wholesaling, retailing, and services) in three groups of large metropolitan areas, not including New York. The classification of SMSAs is based on degree of transit use, as measured by the percentage of central-city workers using public transit; thus, a comparison among the "transit use" groups gives an indication of the relation between transit use and employment growth.

For each activity in each group of SMSAs, growth rates are shown separately for the central city and the "metropolitan ring" (remainder of the SMSA). The growth rates are consistently higher in the low transit use group, essentially reflecting the fact that these are newer metropolitan areas still in a vigorous growth phase, and with less reliance on public transit since they were mainly settled after the dawn of the automobile

TABLE 12-2. Percentage Rates of Change in Employment, 1948–1958, in Manufacturing, Trade, and Services in Central Cities and Rings of 37 Large SMSAs, According to Degree of Transit Use

	Manufacturing (1947–1958)	Wholesaling	Retailing	Services
High transit use				
Metropolitan ring	4.5	28.6	8.9	15.0
Central city	−1.4	−0.2	−0.8	2.4
Difference in favor of ring	5.9	28.8	9.7	12.6
Medium transit use				
Metropolitan ring	13.4	21.1	15.8	24.9
Central city	1.2	0.9	−0.4	2.8
Difference in favor of ring	12.2	20.2	16.2	22.1
Low transit use				
Metropolitan ring	30.5	40.4	26.3	37.4
Central city	2.5	1.1	0.2	3.2
Difference in favor of ring	28.0	39.3	26.1	34.2

SOURCE: J. R. Meyer, J. F. Kain, and M. Wohl, *The Urban Transportation Problem* (Cambridge, Mass.: Harvard University Press, 1965), Table 11, p. 45. Central-city and ring areas have been adjusted for boundary changes resulting from annexations. The 37 SMSAs represented are the largest in the United States except that New York, Newark, and Jersey City have been excluded. The specific SMSAs included in each of the 3 transit use classes (based on percentage of central-city workers using public transit) are listed in the source table. Italicized figures are added.

age. Thus, low transit use areas include Dallas, Denver, Houston, Los Angeles, Phoenix, and San Diego, while such old metropolitan areas as Boston, Baltimore, Chicago, Philadelphia, and St. Louis are in the high transit use group characterized by slower present rates of employment growth.

The hypothesis to be tested is that high transit use is associated with slower *decentralization* of employment. To measure the rate of decentralization, we can take the difference between the suburban and central-city growth rates, as shown by the italicized figures in the table.

The results are remarkably consistent. In each of the four classes of activities, our "index of decentralization" is smallest in the high transit use SMSAs and largest in the low transit use group. These data would appear, then, to support the idea that better transit service can be of substantial assistance in fighting downtown and central-city decline.[23]

TRANSIT AND SLUMS. It was suggested earlier that one of the undesirable features of slums (and particularly racial ghettos) is their continuity— a given total number of deprived people present a more difficult social and economic problem when they are concentrated in one massive clump than they would if separated into a number of smaller concentrations. Lessinger has argued that "compaction" in development is the main source of our slum problem, and that urban land use and transport planning should therefore aim to promote "scatteration." By this he means the encouragement of "leapfrogging" in developing new residential areas, with plenty of intervening land left for later development, and, consequently, a greater ultimate dissimilarity in age of housing among contiguous neighborhoods. He feels that the benefits of scatteration outweigh any additions to transport costs entailed by more gaps in the settlement pattern, and that a development design involving radial corridors with rapid transit is fated to produce nothing but finger-like slums. Accordingly, among the possible policies for discouraging compaction, he suggests indefinite postponement of such transit projects and continued reliance on private automobiles.[24]

This conclusion can be challenged. To the extent that access is a controlling factor on the timing of development of urban areas, the pattern will depend on how travel time is related to airline distance. Transport modes in which time is closely related to distance in any direction (involving a smooth continuous "transport surface" and a fine-grained network of possible routes of travel with free access) should produce a relatively solid, continuous wave of development, of which a prototype might be found in the patterns of cities when nearly all travel was by foot or horse-drawn vehicle. At the opposite extreme, transport modes in

---

[23] The authors did not calculate these differences or any specific measure of the rate of decentralization, but concluded merely that ". . . transit is obviously not a sufficient, or perhaps even a necessary condition for central-city development." *Ibid.*, pp. 44–46.

[24] Lessinger, *op. cit.* For a contrary view, see Mason Gaffney, "Containment Policies for Urban Sprawl," in Richard L. Stauber (ed.), *Approaches to the Study of Urbanization*, Governmental Research Series No. 27 (Lawrence: University of Kansas Publications, 1964), 115–133.

which there are a limited number of relatively fast routes, and in which stops along these routes are also limited in number, should be expected to lead to development patterns highly uneven in density, with separated local clusters around the stops. Possible prototypes of this are the suburbs that developed around fairly widely separated stations on commuter rail lines and also the newer developments that are occurring around airports and at the interchanges of limited-access highways.

Thus, if we are looking for urban transport policies and plans that facilitate scatteration, we should try to make the transport surface *discontinuous*. This can be done by stressing channelized and limited-access modes of transport, including rapid transit with much greater extension and more widely spaced stops than conventional subway systems, rather than relying exclusively on modes in which travel time is closely related to distance in a fine-grained, unlimited-access network of highways and streets.

FINANCING URBAN PUBLIC SERVICES

Another major problem area, closely related to those of slums, central cities, and transport, is urban public finance. Strain upon the fiscal resources of local governments is evidenced by rising local tax rates, growing dissatisfaction with the quality of public services, and rapidly increasing reliance upon state and federal financial support and programs.

It is easy to explain rapidly rising local expenditures in urban areas. The bulk of our population growth is occurring in these areas. Per capita "needs" or demands for most public services, including roads, schools, health and welfare services, water supply, sewerage, and public recreational facilities, are rapidly increasing as we become more urban, more affluent, and more sensitive to social inequities. Radical changes in population distribution and land use within metropolitan areas call for large public capital outlays both to accommodate growth and to redress obsolescence.

Local Government Fragmentation

These increased demands for public outlays would not in themselves create the pressing financial problems that plague the urban public sector today, were it not for the fact that each major urban area is served by a multitude of politically separate governments, each with its own budget. The demands for services and the sources of revenue are differently related to one another in different jurisdictions. The problems that concern us here arise mainly from the spatial (interjurisdictional) disparities in public revenue sources and public expenditure needs within the metropolitan area.

In 1962, according to the U.S. Census of Governments, there were 91,184 units of local government in the United States, of which 18,442 were within Standard Metropolitan Statistical Areas. The average SMSA (population about 550,000) contained 87 units (76 of which could levy property taxes), comprising 1.5 counties, 20 municipalities, 12 townships, 28 school districts, and 26 special districts.[25]

Welfare-Related Expenditures

Table 12-3 shows outlays by each level of government for four categories of expenditure that account for well over half of all local govern-

TABLE 12-3. Selected Categories of Federal, State, and Local Government Expenditure, 1966 (Billions of dollars)

	Federal	State	Local	Gross totals	Duplications*	Net totals
Education	4.6	17.7	25.8	48.1	13.3	34.8
Public welfare	3.8	6.0	3.7	13.5	6.5	7.0
Health and hospitals	2.8	3.2	3.0	9.0	0.6	8.4
Housing and urban renewal	1.6	0.1	1.4	3.1	0.7	2.4

* These figures essentially represent transfers from federal to state, federal to local, and state to local governments.

SOURCE: U.S. Department of Commerce, Bureau of the Census, *1967 Census of Governments,* vol. 6, Topical Studies No. 5, Historical Statistics on Governmental Finances and Employment (Washington, D.C.: Government Printing Office, 1969), Tables 2–6, pp. 33–47.

ment spending (among the excluded categories are highways, police and fire protection, sewerage, utility services, parks and recreation, and interest on debt). For each of the categories shown in the table, it can be persuasively argued that the expenditures in any local government unit should be financed not from taxes collected there but on a broader regional or national basis. Public support of education is clearly a matter of national concern, if only because people move about and an "investment in human resources" made in one local community is likely to pay off somewhere else. Every community has at least as great a stake in the education and training of future in-migrants as it has in the education and training of those who now happen to live in the community. Health and public welfare expenditures also are related to the quality of potential migrants,

---

[25] For his study of local governments in the New York Metropolitan Region in the late 1950s, Robert C. Wood chose the startling but approximately accurate title, *1400 Governments,* A Report of the New York Metropolitan Region Study (Cambridge, Mass.: Harvard University Press for the Regional Plan Association, 1961). The precise count was 1,467.

so that—even apart from any considerations of equity—the appropriate goal is a nationally uniform standard, nationally financed. Housing and urban renewal may be less obviously related to national objectives, but are at least of common concern to the metropolitan area as a unit.

Within the metropolitan area, the expenditure burdens per capita are generally much higher in central cities than in suburban communities for all of the welfare-related functions shown in Table 12-3. Housing is older and more in need of rehabilitation or replacement; public welfare loads are vastly greater because of the concentration of the poor in inner-city slums; the poor have a greater need for health services and are less able to pay for them. Educational cost, too, is (or should be) heavier, despite the fact that many central cities have a smaller proportion of children in their populations than do the suburbs. The deficient educational and cultural backgrounds of the poor, and particularly of ghetto children, require larger expenditures per child (smaller classes, more remedial and other special programs, and the like) to produce an acceptable result than do middle and high income backgrounds. School boards are now aware of this, and in recent years there has been a sharp trend toward allocating more rather than less school funds per pupil in the poor neighborhoods of a district than in the wealthier neighborhoods. Special federal and state grants for disadvantaged children have played a major role in this shift.

As Table 12-3 suggests, a considerable share of the cost of providing these welfare-related services in local communities has been assumed by the state and federal governments. The figures in the "Duplications" column of the table reflect such assistance by these higher levels of government. But this urgently needed redistribution of the fiscal burden is far from complete. According to Netzer, the central cities of the 12 largest metropolitan areas, with an eighth of the nation's population, account for nearly 40 percent of the health and welfare outlays financed from *local* taxes.[26] Meanwhile, the heavier burden of welfare-related public costs in central cities makes the financial positions of most of these cities extremely difficult. Other necessary services are starved and maintenance of public facilities deferred. Local tax rates are raised and new taxes desperately sought. The higher tax burdens and deterioration in quality of services have the unfortunate effect of speeding the exodus of employers and higher-income residents and taxpayers.

The foregoing discussion seems to lead inescapably to the conclusion that the large category of welfare-related public services—at least up to an adequate nationally uniform minimum standard—should be primarily financed with federal funds and considered a responsibility of the tax-

---

[26] Dick Netzer, "Financing Urban Government," in James Q. Wilson (ed.), *The Metropolitan Enigma* (Washington, D.C.: Chamber of Commerce of the United States, 1967), p. 60.

payers of the entire nation. This is not inconsistent with local administration of the programs and services themselves.

Metropolitan Area Needs for Public Services

For some other important types of public services, the metropolitan area seems to be the logical unit for planning, operation, and financing, and no real case can be made for selective state or federal assistance to individual local governments. Water and sewerage systems, intrametropolitan highways and transit, airports, large metropolitan outdoor recreation areas, and programs to control environmental pollution seem to fit this category. Fairly strong arguments could be made for adding to the list such services as police and fire protection, libraries, and museums.

For these activities, the economies of scale and the need for coordination are so strong that independent efforts by individual municipalities produce wasteful duplication, inefficiently small facilities, and much bickering. Metropolitan governments, however, are virtually nonexistent in the United States and do not seem likely to proliferate soon. In default of an appropriate existing unit of government, the most practical recourse seems to be the creation of special-purpose metropolitan authorities or districts, with the constituent cities and towns sharing the costs, benefits, and ultimate control. Such districts are particularly common in cases of water supply, sewerage, and rapid transit services, and there are also a number of metropolitan park districts; more fragmentary jointures of two or three adjacent small municipalities or rural school districts also exist for special purposes.

Another recourse is to bring the state or federal government into the picture, either via direct investment or through aid to individual municipalities. It is important to remember, however, that the public services in question are a metropolitan rather than a national responsibility. The higher (state or federal) level of government should be regarded solely as an expedient substitute for a suitable *metropolitan* fiscal unit with adequate taxing power. Our earlier discussion of the prevailing bias in aid to intraurban highways compared to transit underlines the necessity of a clear understanding of the appropriate role of external financing of those services that benefit a single metropolitan area rather than the whole country.

User Charges for Public Services

The fact that a service is provided by a public agency does not mean that it has to be provided free and thus paid for by the taxpayers as a group. On the contrary, there are cogent arguments (to be found in any elementary economics textbook) for applying the pricing mechanism as far as is feasible as a check upon demand and a guide to supply. The exceptions are cases in which it is technically unfeasible or socially undesirable to charge individual users (such as public safety, parks and other civic amenities, and basic education).

The desirability of applying the user charge principle more widely to transport facilities and services has already been suggested. If users of street space, transit, and curb or off-street parking space were charged according to the incremental costs that they impose upon the public authority, depending on the time and place of use, a more efficient use of scarce space and transport investment could be achieved. Charges for such utility-type public services as sewerage and water supply could also be geared more closely than they are to the incremental cost of providing such service to the individual user or the individual neighborhood.[27]

In the long run, this policy would discourage leapfrogging in suburban development and would promote a land use pattern more compact in character and conducive to lower average cost of all utility-type services including transportation. As we noted earlier, however, Lessinger and others see disadvantages in "compaction."

The price mechanism (in the form of special charges) could also be used to a far greater extent than it is in attacking the growing problem of environmental pollution (see p. 255 above).

"Fiscal Mercantilism"

Although the refusal of suburban municipalities to merge or even cooperate with the metropolitan central city can be most frustrating and exasperating to planners, it is understandable and even to some extent defensible. If the residents of one community prefer a different level and mix of public services, and a different density and land use pattern, from those of another community, they should not be denied their freedom of choice. As we shall argue later, one of the ultimate virtues to be sought in an urban community is wide individual choice among alternative opportunities and ways of life.

To a considerable extent, the differential aspirations of the various communities in a metropolitan region can be satisfied and reconciled with objectives of overall economic efficiency by three lines of policy already recommended; namely, the financing of at least adequate minimum

---

[27] Two excellent treatments of this complicated question are Patrick Mann, "The Application of User Charges for Urban Public Services," *Reviews in Urban Economics*, 1, 2 (Winter 1968), 25–46, and William W. Vickrey, "General and Specific Financing of Urban Services," in Howard G. Schaller (ed.), *Public Expenditure Decisions in the Urban Community* (Washington, D.C.: Resources for the Future, 1963), 62–90.

welfare-type public services through external funds, the wider application of user charges to utility-type services, and the formation of metropolitan districts to obtain the economies of metropolitan-wide planning, operation, and financing of certain services such as water supply and local transportation.

There remain, however, certain undesirable and avoidable aspects of existing systems of local taxation, land use control, and provision of public services. The problem has been aptly characterized by Netzer as the practice of "fiscal mercantilism" by individual municipalities and particularly by the more affluent suburbs.[28]

The real property tax is still the main source of local public revenue, and a municipality simultaneously controls its property tax rates, residential lot sizes and other restrictions upon land use, the level of municipal services, and to some extent the kinds of business activity that are admitted or encouraged to locate within its boundaries. In a small suburban community, the relation between taxes paid and services received is more direct and certainly more obvious to the citizenry than it is in a large central city.

Accordingly, such a community will want to use its powers over land use and activity-mix in such a way as to get the most for the property tax dollar: that is, to keep taxes low and public services high. Alternative policies of land use zoning and industrial promotion will be weighed largely in terms of the fiscal criterion.

From this standpoint, the preferred in-migrant family is a wealthy family without any school-age children, and the preferred in-migrant business is a nice, clean type of industry that employs skilled high-income people, produces no smoke, noise, or dirt, and builds an attractively landscaped "campus-type" facility—for example, a research laboratory. Once a community can establish such a residential and business complexion, it will be better able to maintain it in subsequent development. The per capita costs of welfare-type services, public safety, and environmental protection will be low and the revenues that can be raised from the property tax will be relatively high. Thus, it can offer superior public services at bargain rates as a still further enticement to the right kind of new residents and new employers.

By the same token, communities (including, generally, the central city and the lower income suburbs) that have large numbers of poor people and children, little natural amenity, and either no industry or "nuisance" types of industry, are likely to be in a cumulatively deteriorating fiscal position, with high property tax rates required to support mediocre levels

---

[28] Dick Netzer, *Economics of the Property Tax* (Washington, D.C.: Brookings Institution, 1966), 125–130.

of public service and a consequent inability to attract fiscally profitable types of residents or businesses.

One undesirable feature of this outcome is, of course, the accentuation of inequalities of welfare between rich and poor communities. But in addition, fiscal mercantilism

> . . . encourages economic activity to locate in low-tax jurisdictions, which may or may not be the optimal locations for particular forms of economic activity. Equally important, it encourages communities to plan land use for fiscal advantage, rather than on the basis of broader considerations.[29]

Since fiscal mercantilism depends on close links between (1) land use and local revenue and (2) local revenue and the level of local public services, it could be combatted by weakening either or both of these links. In practice, this can entail a diminished reliance on local real property taxation or the financing of more welfare-related public services on a broader base than the individual municipality. Both trends are in evidence already. We noted earlier the increased participation of state and federal governments in the financing of welfare-related activities, and property taxes seem to be accounting for a gradually diminishing percentage of total locally raised general revenue.[30]

Changes in Real Estate Taxation

The real property tax has increasingly come under attack for a number of reasons, and particularly because as presently administered it tends to discourage the intensive development, improvement, and redevelopment of urban sites.[31]

In principle, however, the real objection is to the taxation of structures and other improvements. A tax on the site value of land per se would not be open to most of these objections; on the contrary, it has some great potential virtues, first proclaimed in the 1880s by Henry George in *Progress and Poverty*. A tax on site value is not a deterrent to productive activity; land does not have to be created as does artificial capital, but already exists as a gift of nature. The rent is appropriated by the owner by virtue of possession, and not as a reward for any productive effort on his part. If some of the rents he collects are taken in taxes, he cannot pass any of the tax to the land user by raising the rents, since the rents already

---

[29] Dick Netzer, *Impact of the Property Tax: Its Economic Implications for Urban Problems,* Joint Economic Committee, 90th Cong. 2 sess. (Washington, D.C.: Government Printing Office, May 1968), p. 27. This report was prepared for the National Commission on Urban Problems.

[30] The percentage in question, for local governments in the 38 largest SMSAs, was 68 in 1962 and 66 in 1965–1966. These and further figures, based on U.S. Census data, appear in Netzer, *Impact of the Property Tax,* Table 2, p. 7.

[31] The major criticisms are forcefully stated in Netzer, *Impact of the Property Tax.*

represent all that users can afford to pay (that is, the entire surplus of receipts over the costs of inputs other than land).

Consequently, land taxes are borne entirely by land owners, cannot be "passed on," and have no effect on rents, advantages of different land uses, or different locations for any given use. All the tax does is reduce land values proportionately. This, of course, means a loss to whomever owns the land at the time the tax is imposed or increased. But it is a one-time impact: once the land values are written down in response to the tax, future investors in land can obtain just as good a net return on their investment (net after taxes) as before. But they must be wary not to be caught owning land at a time when the tax rate is *increased*.

George and his earlier followers reasoned on this basis that public services ought to be financed by a "single tax" on land alone, in preference to other taxes that, in one way or another, discourage productive effort. The argument was based partly on grounds of equity (nature gave the land, so no individual has a right to appropriate it for his private unearned gain) and partly on grounds of economic efficiency (a land tax, as long as it falls short of 100 percent, preserves the incentive to devote each site to the most productive use, whereas any other tax is likely to distort resource allocation).

Socialist governments (see p. 95 above) carried this principle to its logical conclusion: abolishing the private ownership of land. This in itself could have been made consistent with efficient allocation of land, provided that a land pricing system (involving users bidding rents for the use of sites and the awarding of land to high bidders) had been retained. Some socialist economies have taken steps toward a partial reinstatement of a pricing system for land.

A number of discerning economists (notably Mason Gaffney) have persuasively argued the merits of changing the existing tax on land plus improvements to a tax on site values alone—though it has not been established that a pure land tax could be made to yield enough revenue to permit freeing improvements altogether from taxation, as George's single tax proposal assumed. It is not difficult to demonstrate that a shift in this direction would encourage private redevelopment of obsolete properties, discourage the speculative holding of land in unproductive uses or no use at all, and foster a more compact urban development pattern that would yield economies in transport and utility service costs.[32]

---

[32] For a recent, cogent statement of the case, see Mason Gaffney, "Land Planning and the Property Tax," *Journal of the American Institute of Planners*, 35, 3 (May 1969), 178–183. Netzer, *Impact of the Property Tax*, pp. 41, 42, concurs (". . . the case for site value taxation is a good one. . . . In theory, there are few if any legitimate economic arguments against site value taxation"), but adds, "On an operational level, there are grounds for hesitation." Lessinger (see p. 355 above) would presumably not regard the encouragement of more compact settlement patterns as a favorable argument.

Accurate assessment of site values is by no means easy, but perhaps not much more difficult than the assessment of combined land and improvements values under present practices. In a few areas (Pittsburgh, Hawaii, and much of Australia, for example), land is already assessed separately from buildings so that higher tax rates can be levied on land. But the principal obstacle to shifting to site value taxation is the equity of present property owners. They invested their money in good faith in real estate rather than in other forms of income-yielding property, and those whose realty investment is mainly in land would suffer an inequitable capital loss (equivalent to a perpetual loss in income). But on this ground, it could be argued just as logically that property tax rates should never be raised or lowered, since any change inflicts undeserved penalties or awards undeserved windfalls to property owners. If we are really convinced of the basic virtues of land taxation, we could make equitable progress in that direction either by raising rates very gradually or by having public authorities buy up land from private owners and lease or resell it to users.

THE VALUE OF CHOICE

We have covered four important problems of present and foreseeable urban life—with emphasis throughout on the spatial aspects, wherein the special interests and competences of the regional economist are particularly relevant. It should now be clear that judgments about goals and policies have to be made in a broad context that recognizes at least the major interrelationships among slums, downtown areas, transport, and public finance.

Having these insights, however, does not endow even the most learned urban economist with a set of "right answers." What, then, is his useful role? He can contribute to a realistic and objective presentation of the implications of alternative courses of development, especially in terms of spatial patterns, access, neighborhood character, public services, and fiscal burdens, so that voters will know what they are really voting for and decision makers will know what problems they are creating for themselves. He can use the economist's criterion of efficiency to expose hidden costs, externalities, and demonstrably self-defeating or inconsistent combinations of policies. Finally, on the basis of his insights into the nature of the processes of urban change, he can advocate *flexibility and variety* as basic aims on a par with the conventional objectives of high income, low unemployment, equity, and security.[33]

Recognition of the value of flexibility follows from recognition that an urban economy is a live organism. Thus, any formal design for the physical

---

[33] For a good statement of the value of wide choice in this context, see Webb S. Fiser, *Mastery of the Metropolis* (Englewood Cliffs, N.J.: Prentice-Hall, 1962), pp. 160 ff.

layout of an urban area should be challenged with the question of what happens in response to the forces of change discussed earlier in this book: growth, aging, economic improvement, and the unforeseeable variety of changes in technology. No design can be judged until pictured in a state of adjustment. Our most acute distresses, and our most intriguing opportunities, are accompaniments of adjustment.

A fundamental urban value that is partly distinct from flexibility is variety. A recurrent theme in these final chapters has been that the prime function of a city is to provide opportunities for the widest possible variety of contacts. The employer wants to be able to tap a labor market and find, on short notice, the right skills and aptitudes; the job seeker wants to find a job that fits his abilities, interests, and personal preferences; the business firm wants to be able to choose from a wide range of technical, advisory, transport, and marketing services; the shopper wants a large selection of wares from which to choose; the homeseeker wants to find a neighborhood and a house tailored to his needs; and so on. Wide freedom of choice in these and other respects is unquestionably both desirable and conducive to the best utilization of the community's resources, quite aside from any other merits or faults that cities may have.

Sheer size is associated with increased latitude of choice. A larger city contains not merely *more* of each kind of activity and opportunity but *more kinds,* permitting a closer and more efficient fit of supply to demand. But size is not the only determinant of variety—this is a characteristic that can vary rather widely among cities of a given size, and one that can be enhanced or impaired by technical change or other factors. Let us merely note here a few of the many ways in which urban variety of choice relates to the spatial pattern.

A conscious policy of fostering variety of opportunity and choice will entail efforts to increase interoccupational, interindustry, and spatial mobility. Our programs of education, training and retraining, and improved placement organization are directed this way. These developments, in addition to providing greater spatial mobility, more effective communication, and progress in softening racial and other discriminatory barriers, should widen effective job choice—making urban labor markets less imperfect as markets, while at the same time increasing interregional mobility and choice.

Two spatial factors are principally involved in widening job choices: residential segregation and transportation. Both are especially applicable to low-income, low-skilled, and nonwhite members of the labor force; these are the people for whom and from whom the greatest economic benefits will accrue in the widening of urban residential and work choice and the fuller utilization of manpower resources that this makes possible.

The above suggests that intraurban transportation (private, public, or both) has a case for subsidy (though not necessarily an ever-increasing amount of subsidy).[34] On the basis of the general virtues of widened choice, one could argue for preserving and developing a wide range of densities of development and a wide range of *modes* of intraurban transport. High-density, high-speed transit services on special rights of way go with a strong core-and-radial configuration, in contrast to an overall pattern of more even dispersion, replicated subcenters, and a deemphasized central core or stem.

One thing that makes comparative evaluation difficult is that, in terms of return on the transport investment, each of the schemes tends to be somewhat self-justifying. That is, a well-developed rapid transit system fosters the kind of settlement pattern that gives such a system good business, while reliance on highways fosters the kind of settlement pattern that can least economically be served by anything but the private automobile. Obvious though this proposition may seem, it has still not been given real recognition in most planning and transportation studies.

In deciding on the relative merits of contrasting layout alternatives, it is both appropriate and important to note that the "radial corridor" type of layout embraces a full range of development densities, concentrations of access potential, and traffic densities; while the alternative, more uniformly dispersed pattern embraces a much smaller range in each of these respects. The latter excludes the highest range of intensities and densities. Perhaps this throws away a unique economic advantage of urban agglomeration; but we have as yet no way of gauging this effect quantitatively. No one really can say what advantages Los Angeles is missing by not having the kind of compact center that an auto-oriented metropolis must forego, and what it gains in return. But in the absence of adequate knowledge, it would appear good strategy to rely on the principle that a wide choice of types of environment, contact densities, and transport modes is desirable per se, and hence to lean toward the incorporation of at least a basic framework of really fast and really compact public transport as part of any major urban structure.

Another aspect of variety in the urban pattern is variety in levels and "styles" of public services. Reference has already been made to the strong desires of small suburban municipalities to preserve independence in this regard; this is related to but not identical with their desire to preserve homogeneity in such characteristics as race, income, or religion. We cannot consistently condemn their resistance to annexation or metropolitan government while still recognizing the value of keeping the latitude of choice of environments as wide as possible.

---

[34] On the rationale for subsidy to *public* transport in urban areas, see Benjamin Chinitz (ed.), *City and Suburb* (Englewood Cliffs, N.J.: Prentice-Hall, 1964), 35–41 (part of a section written by the editor).

The difficulty, and the challenge to administrative ingenuity, comes in reconciling diversity and local pride with a suitable degree of coordination in basic services of common importance to the whole metropolitan area, such as water management, health services, higher education and transport.[35]

We are still groping for an answer to this problem. Apparently what a large urban area needs, for optimum functional efficiency and satisfaction, is great heterogeneity and diversity on a macrospatial scale; but this is associated in practice with homogeneity on a microspatial scale.

SELECTED READINGS

Raymond Vernon, *Metropolis 1985* (Cambridge, Mass.: Harvard University Press for the Regional Plan Association, 1960).

Robert C. Wood, *1400 Governments* (Cambridge, Mass.: Harvard University Press for the Regional Plan Association, 1961).

Lyle C. Fitch and Associates, *Urban Transportation and Public Policy* (San Francisco: Chandler, 1964).

Bernard J. Frieden, *The Future of Old Neighborhoods* (Cambridge, Mass.: M.I.T. Press, 1964).

Philip M. Hauser and Leo F. Schnore (eds.), *The Study of Urbanization* (New York: Wiley, 1965).

Julius Margolis (ed.), *The Public Economy of Urban Communities* (Baltimore: Johns Hopkins Press, 1965).

John R. Meyer, J. F. Kain, and M. Wohl, *The Urban Transportation Problem* (Cambridge, Mass.: Harvard University Press, 1965).

Wilbur R. Thompson, *A Preface to Urban Economics* (Baltimore: Johns Hopkins Press, 1965).

Dick Netzer, *Economics of the Property Tax* (Washington: Brookings Institution, 1966).

H. Wentworth Eldredge, *Taming Megalopolis,* 2 vols. (New York: Anchor Books, 1967).

James Q. Wilson (ed.), *The Metropolitan Enigma* (Washington: Chamber of Commerce of the United States, 1967).

Harvey S. Perloff and Lowdon Wingo, Jr. (eds.), *Issues in Urban Economics* (Baltimore: Johns Hopkins Press for Resources for the Future, 1968).

John F. Kain, "Housing Segregation, Negro Employment, and Metropolitan Decentralization," *Quarterly Journal of Economics,* 82, 2 (May 1968), 175–197.

Mason Gaffney, "Land Planning and the Property Tax," *Journal of the American Institute of Planners,* 35, 3 (May 1969), 178–183.

Wilbur R. Thompson, "The Economic Base of Urban Problems," in Neil W. Chamberlain (ed.), *Contemporary Economic Issues* (Homewood, Ill.: Irwin, 1969).

William Vickrey, "Current Issues in Transportation," in Neil W. Chamberlain (ed.), *Contemporary Economic Issues* (Homewood, Ill.: Irwin, 1969).

Anthony Downs, "Housing the Urban Poor: The Economics of Various Strategies," *American Economic Review,* 59, 4 (September 1969), 646–651.

Dick Netzer, *Economics and Urban Problems* (New York: Basic Books, 1970).

---

[35] An excellent analysis of the suburban independence question is in Oliver P. Williams and others, *Suburban Differences and Metropolitan Policies: A Philadelphia Story* (Philadelphia: University of Pennsylvania Press, 1965).

Index

About the Author

Edgar M. Hoover is Distinguished
Service Professor of Economics at the
University of Pittsburgh. He received his
A.B., A.M., and Ph.D. from Harvard
University. He has taught at the
University of Michigan and Harvard
University, and has served with the
National Resources Planning Board, the
Office of Price Administration, and the
Council of Economic Advisers. In
1959–63 he was Director of the Economic
Study of the Pittsburgh Region for the
Pittsburgh Regional Planning
Association, and in 1962 was president
of the Regional Science Association. He
has served as economic consultant to
various government agencies,
foundations, research institutes, and
business firms.
Dr. Hoover is the author of *Location
Theory and the Shoe and Leather
Industries* (1937) and *The Location of
Economic Activity* (1948), and is
coauthor of *Population Growth and
Economic Development in Low-Income
Countries* (1958) and *Anatomy of a
Metropolis* (1959). His articles and
reviews have appeared in a number of
professional journals.

A Note on the Type

The text of this book was set on the
Linotype in a face called TIMES
ROMAN, designed by Stanley Morison
for The Times (London), and introduced
by that newspaper in 1932.
Among typographers and designers of
the twentieth century, Stanley Morison
has been a strong forming influence, as
typographical advisor to the English
Monotype Corporation, as a director of
two distinguished English publishing
houses, and as a writer of sensibility,
erudition, and keen practical sense.

*Composed by Cherry Hill Composition,
Pennsauken, N.J.
Printed and bound by H. Wolff Book
Mfg. Co., Inc., New York, N.Y.*

Designed by J. M. Wall